ANDREWS UNIVERSITY SEMINARY
DOCTORAL DISSERTATION SERIES
VOLUME VIII

JUSTIFICATION AND MERIT: LUTHER VS. CATHOLICISM

by
Johann Heinz

WIPF & STOCK · Eugene, Oregon

"Unica Christianorum gloria est in solo Christo."
M. Luther, Praelectiones in prophetas minores,
1524–26 (WA 13, 570, 16–17).

Wipf and Stock Publishers
199 W 8th Ave, Suite 3
Eugene, OR 97401

Justification and Merit
Luther vs. Catholicism
By Heinz, Hans
Copyright©1984 by Heinz, Daniel
ISBN 13: 978-1-62032-435-6
Publication date 11/1/2012
Previously published by Andrews University Press, 1984

TABLE OF CONTENTS

LIST OF ABBREVIATIONS   v

ACKNOWLEDGEMENTS ix

REMARKS xi

INTRODUCTION   1

PART I

LUTHER AND THE PROBLEM OF JUSTIFICATION AND MERIT

Chapter

I. CONTROVERSIAL ASPECTS OF LUTHER'S DOCTRINE
   OF JUSTIFICATION 13

   Justification as the Focal Center
      of the Gospel 13
   Luther's Paulinism in the View of
      Modern Catholic Theology 25
   The Central Position of Justification
      as a Controversial Problem 33
   Declaring Righteous and Making Righteous 37
   Lutheran and Catholic sola fide 45
   The Pauline Message of Justification and
      the Teaching of Merit 81
   Summary 93

II. LUTHER'S STRUGGLE AGAINST THE DOCTRINE OF MERIT 95

   The Development of the Idea of Merit 95
   The Defeat of the Concept of Merit
      in Luther 158
   Luther's Reconstruction of Justification
      "sine meritis" 174
   Luther's Doctrine of Work and Reward 217
   Summary 246

PART II

THE PROBLEM OF JUSTIFICATION AND MERIT IN MODERN CATHOLIC THEOLOGY

Chapter

III. THE DEBATE ON LUTHER'S DOCTRINE OF
JUSTIFICATION AND CRITICISM OF MERIT
IN MODERN CATHOLIC THEOLOGY 251

    The Evaluation of Luther's Doctrine
       of Justification 251
    The Justification of Luther's
       Criticism of Merit 291
    The Place of the Doctrine of Merit
       in Modern Catholic Theology 303
    The Council of Trent in the
       Conflict of Opinions 312
    Summary 326

IV. THE DOCTRINE OF MERIT IN MODERN CATHOLIC
THEOLOGY: ITS THEOLOGICAL FOUNDATIONS 331

    Exegesis and the Doctrine of Merit 331
    Dogmatics and the Doctrine of Merit 342
    The Question: Justification/Merit
       and Vatican II 391
    Summary 405

GENERAL SUMMARY AND CONCLUSION 407

BIBLIOGRAPHY 419

LIST OF ABBREVIATIONS

AAS	--	Acta apostolicae sedis
Ang.	--	Angelicum
AnGr	--	Analecta Gregoriana
Anton.	--	Antonianum
ARG	--	Archiv für Reformationsgeschichte
ASm	--	Schmalkaldische Artikel
Bib.	--	Biblica
BKV	--	Bibliothek der Kirchenväter
BSLK	--	Bekenntnisschriften der evangelisch-lutherischen Kirche
CaC	--	Christianity and Crisis
CathEnc	--	Catholic Encyclopedia
Cath(M)	--	Catholica. Münster
CCath	--	Corpus catholicorum
CDT	--	Catholic Dictionary of Theology
Conc(D)	--	Concilium. Einsiedeln
Dok.	--	Dokumente
DS	--	Enchiridion symbolorum. Ed. Heinrich Denzinger and Adolf Schönmetzer
DSp	--	Dictionnaire de spiritualité, ascétique et mystique
DTC	--	Dictionnaire de théologie catholique
DT(P)	--	Divus Thomas. Piacenza
EKL	--	Evangelisches Kirchenlexikon

EThL	--	Ephemerides theologicae Lovanienses
EvQ	--	Evangelical Quarterly
EvT	--	Evangelische Theologie
EvW	--	Evangelische Welt
GCS	--	Die griechischen christlichen Schriftsteller der ersten drei Jahrhunderte
Gr.	--	Gregorianum
HNT	--	Handbuch zum Neuen Testament
HThG	--	Handbuch theologischer Grundbegriffe
HTR	--	Harvard Theological Review
HWP	--	Historisches Wörterbuch der Philosophie
ICC	--	International Critical Commentary
Irén.	--	Irénikon
Ist.	--	Istina
JTS	--	Journal of Theological Studies
KD	--	Barth, Karl. Die kirchliche Dogmatik
LTK	--	Lexikon für Theologie und Kirche
LuJ	--	Luther-Jahrbuch
LV	--	Lumen vitae
LW	--	American Edition of Luther's Works
MThZ	--	Münchener theologische Zeitschrift
NCE	--	New Catholic Encyclopedia
NIC	--	New International Commentary
NOrd	--	Neue Ordnung
NTA	--	Neutestamentliche Abhandlungen
Oec.	--	Oecumenica
Orien.	--	Orientierung
ÖR	--	Ökumenische Rundschau

PG	--	*Patrologiae cursus completus.* Accurante Jacques-Paul Migne. Series Graeca
PL	--	*Patrologiae cursus completus.* Accurante Jacques-Paul Migne. Series Latina
RB	--	*Revue biblique*
RE	--	*Realencyklopädie für protestantische Theologie und Kirche*
RechSR	--	*Recherches de science religieuse*
Ref.	--	*Reformatio*
RevScRel	--	*Revue des sciences religieuses*
RGG	--	*Religion in Geschichte und Gegenwart*
RHPR	--	*Revue d'histoire et de philosophie religieuses*
RR(StM)	--	*Review for Religious. St. Mary's*
RTP	--	*Revue de théologie et de philosophie*
Sal.	--	*Salesianum*
SC	--	*Sources chrétiennes*
SKZ	--	*Schweizerische Kirchenzeitung*
SM(E)	--	*Sacramentum mundi. New York*
S.Th.	--	Thomas Aquinas. *Summa theologiae*
TBLNT	--	*Theologisches Begriffslexikon zum NT*
ThStKr	--	*Theologische Studien und Kritiken*
ThWNT	--	*Theologisches Wörterbuch zum NT*
TLZ	--	*Theologische Literaturzeitung*
TQ	--	*Theologische Quartalschrift*
TThZ	--	*Trierer theologische Zeitschrift*
TU	--	*Texte und Untersuchungen*
TZ	--	*Theologische Zeitschrift*
US	--	*Una Sancta*

WA	--	Luther, Martin. Werke. Kritische Gesamtausgabe (Weimarer Ausgabe)
BR	--	Luther, Martin. Werke. Briefwechsel
DB	--	Luther, Martin. Werke. Deutsche Bibel
TR	--	Luther, Martin. Werke. Tischreden
WWKL	--	Wetzer und Welte's Kirchenlexikon
ZKT	--	Zeitschrift für katholische Theologie
ZST	--	Zeitschrift für systematische Theologie
ZTK	--	Zeitschrift für Theologie und Kirche
ZZ	--	Zwischen den Zeiten

ACKNOWLEDGEMENTS

The idea for the present investigation evolved in the course of study on the faculty for Catholic theology at the Paris Lodron University in Salzburg. The dissertation was presented in the summer of 1981 to the theological faculty of Andrews University (Field: Historical theology).

I especially wish to thank Dr. Hans LaRondelle, the chairman of the dissertation committee, for accepting the topic and for his careful examination of the manuscript. Similarly, I would thank Dr. Raoul Dederen and Dr. Gerhard Hasel for their assistance in evaluating the text. Because the original draft of this dissertation was written in German, the author is very conscious of the linguistic limitations of the English version and requests the reader's understanding.

Especial thanks also go to Dr. Leona Running, without whose selfless and willing assistance the translation would have been considerably more difficult. With her exemplary dedication, Dr. Running witnessed to that faith which works by love. I would also like to express my appreciation to Mrs. Joyce Jones and Mr. Thomas Baker for their recommendations in formulating the English text. To the librarians of both the University of Notre Dame (Indiana) and of Andrews University I express my indebtedness for their ready assistance.

And finally, I thank my wife Louisette and my son Daniel, who agreed to accompany me from Austria to the United States and who actively supported me in the completion of this work.

$\Delta\delta\xi\alpha\ \theta\epsilon\tilde{\omega}$.

Berrien Springs   1981   Johann (Hans) Heinz

REMARKS

In order to write the present work use had to be made principally of German, but also of Latin, French, and Italian sources. For the English reader, therefore, foreign citations in the text were translated and the original citation--as far as important statements are concerned--was set in parentheses or taken into the footnotes. A similar treatment was given to theological terms which are often difficult to translate. Unless otherwise noted, the translations are by the present writer. When English words are used in this work differently from their daily usage, this is so indicated in the notes.

INTRODUCTION

On October 3, 1567, Pietro Carnesecchi was condemned to death by the Roman Inquisition.

It was charged against him that since 1540 he had believed and taught the "heretical, erroneous, impudent and scandalous propositions" of justification by faith alone, of the certainty of salvation, and of good works as testifying to salvation and not as producing salvation, "according to Luther the arch-heretic."[1]

Carnesecchi can be considered "perhaps the most illustrious of all Italian martyrs,"[2] for as papal protonotary he had been a confidant of Clement VII and a friend of Paul III and Pius IV. But as under Pius V the persecution of the evangelically minded increased, Carnesecchi's fate, as well as that of many of his fellow Italians who held the same beliefs, was sealed. He accepted death with "confidence and joy" and "went to the execution as to a triumph."[3]

Rome has needed four hundred years in order to judge Luther and his followers in a more Christian and just way as to their main concerns. In July 1970 Cardinal Willebrands, the chairman of the

---

[1] Karl Benrath, Bernardino Ochino von Siena, 2nd ed. (Brunswick: Schwetschke & Sohn, 1892), p. 65.

[2] Robert Baird, Sketches of Protestantism in Italy (Boston: B. Perkins, 1845), p. 126.

[3] Ibid., p. 128.

Vatican Secretariat for the Unity of Christians, explained before the gathering of the Lutheran World Council in Evian-les-Bains:

> Qui oserait nier aujourd'hui que Martin Luther était une personnalité profondément religieuse qui a cherché honnêtement et avec abnégation le message de l'Evangile? . . . Dans une session qui a choisi pour thème "Envoyés dans le monde," il est bon de réfléchir à un homme pour qui la doctrine de la justification a constitué l'<u>articulum stantis aut cadentis Ecclesiae. Il peut être notre maître commun dans ce domaine</u> en affirmant que Dieu doit rester constamment le Seigneur et que notre réponse humaine la plus essentielle doit rester la confiance absolue et l'adoration de Dieu.[1]

Perhaps nothing shows more clearly the change in theological opinions than the comparison between the inquisitional judgment of the sixteenth century, cited above, and the statement of the Roman Cardinal, also cited. People have divided themselves and strenuously fought over Luther's teaching of justification; is it possible that the opposition groups will ever arrive at a consensus over this issue?

For hundreds of years this question had to be decidedly and unambiguously denied. Today Lutheran as well as Catholic theologians believe that "an <u>agreement</u> over the doctrine of justification is <u>possible</u>,"[2] even that "material consensus"[3] exists on this point, because "the controversial theological situation has not turned so far to the positive in any other matter of faith as it has in this

---

[1] Daniel Olivier, <u>Le procès Luther 1517-21</u> (Paris: Fayard, 1971), pp. 217-18, italics mine.

[2] Horst Georg Pöhlmann (Ev. Luth.), <u>Rechtfertigung</u> (Gütersloh: G. Mohn, 1971), p. 378. Dass "eine <u>Einigung</u> in der Rechtfertigungslehre <u>möglich</u>" ist.

[3] Otto H. Pesch (Rom. Cath.), "Gottes Gnadenhandeln als Rechtfertigung des Menschen," in <u>Mysterium Salutis</u>, 5 vols. (Einsiedeln: Benziger, 1965-76), 4/2:897.

one."[1] In fact one may speak of "problems that have been thoroughly explored."[2]

Especially, in the years around the Second Vatican Council the dialogue, carried out predominantly in the German-speaking area, reached noteworthy high points. Thus in 1957 H. Küng's book Rechtfertigung appeared, which, while it focused on the narrower problem of a consensus with K. Barth, nevertheless, for the first time, brought the whole dialogue between the confessions really into movement. Already in 1953 Peter Bläser (Rechtfertigungsglaube bei Luther) and in 1954 Yves Congar (Regards et réflexions sur la christologie de Luther) had presented important studies on the question. In 1965 dissertations were presented to several Catholic faculties on single aspects, dealing with the problem from different viewpoints, of which three, appearing in book form, have been very influential: 1967, Otto H. Pesch: Theologie der Rechtfertigung bei Martin Luther und Thomas von Aquin; 1968, August Hasler: Luther in der katholischen Dogmatik; and 1969, Harry McSorley: Luther: Right or Wrong? An Ecumenical-Theological Study of Luther's Major Work, "The Bondage of the Will."

On the Protestant side two works need to be especially mentioned. Both cover the majority of questions systematically in the form of an inventory and try to give a survey of the present

---

[1] Paulus Wacker (Rom. Cath.), Theologie als ökumenischer Dialog (Munich: F. Schöningh, 1965), p. 173. Weil "wohl kaum bei einer anderen Glaubenswahrheit sich die kontroverstheologische Situation so zum Positiven gewandt" hat.

[2] Hans Küng (Rom. Cath.), "Anfragen an die Reformation heute," Ref. 27 (1978):376. Man kann von einem "grundsätzlich aufgearbeiteten Problemfeld" sprechen.

state of the dialogue: Martin Bogdahn's dissertation in 1967, published in 1971 as a book titled <u>Die Rechtfertigungslehre Luthers im Urteil der neueren katholischen Theologie</u>, and Horst Georg Pöhlmann's <u>Habilitationsschrift</u> of 1969, which appeared in 1971 under the title <u>Rechtfertigung, die gegenwärtige kontrovers-theologische Problematik der Rechtfertigungslehre zwischen der evangelisch-lutherischen und der römisch-katholischen Kirche</u>.

That every interconfessional conversation on the doctrine of justification must be conducted in reference to Luther can be shown as <u>opinio communis</u> in polemical theology and comes to expression clearly in the cited literature. Regardless of how manifold the problems and the interpretations of the Reformation may seem to be, they certainly find in the person and teaching of Martin Luther their truest and most lively expression, "for Luther <u>is</u> the Reformation" (denn Luther <u>ist die Reformation</u>).[1]

Luther's doctrine of justification climaxes in the sole agency of God, denying categorically any human cooperation to attain salvation and, thereby, any claim of merit. Catholic dogma, to the contrary--as it was defined at the Council of Trent--requires this cooperation explicitly, both in preparation for justification (<u>DS</u> 1525) and in the justification event itself (<u>DS</u> 1529), which is understood as sanctification-act (<u>DS</u> 1528) and growing sanctification-process, in which faith works together with the good works (<u>DS</u> 1535). From the intertwining of divine grace

---

[1] Joseph Lortz, "Martin Luther, Grundzüge seiner geistigen Struktur," in <u>Reformata Reformanda</u>, ed. Erwin Iserloh and Konrad Repgen, 2 vols. (Münster/W.: Aschendorff, 1965), 1:215. Cf. Karl Adam, <u>Una Sancta in katholischer Sicht</u> (Düsseldorf: Patmos, 1948), p. 39.

and human cooperation, "true" and "personal merits" develop for the believer (DS 1546/1582), through which he can earn increase in grace, eternal life, the attainment of eternal life, and the increase of glory.

Thus, the Catholic doctrine of merit justifies the continued existence of the controversy. For although the doctrine of merit according to the Catholic view does not pertain to justification any more, both still stand in close interrelationship with each other. Justification appears to be the precondition for the merit itself, the merit appearing as the crowning conclusion of justification. From the superstructure of merit, in our view, the fundamental questions of the controversy ultimately develop:

1. Have the works of the believer (works by grace) consecutive or final[1] character? I.e., do they result from salvation (konsekutiver Heilsweg) or do they represent means for salvation (finaler Heilsweg)?

2. What part does man have in his redemption?

3. How, then, can one speak of merits?

We are aware that one can choose other approaches to the problem (e.g., simul peccator et justus, assurance, the sole agency of God, the concept of grace). We think, however, that all these are bracketed within the thought of merit and that therefore this is the real shibboleth of the controversy. This also is apparent

---

[1] The word "final" (finalis) is always viewed teleologically in the sense of an ultimate goal to be reached.

today on both sides of the issue,[1] although the participants in the dialogue often prefer to choose other ways of tackling the problem.

There is of course a further basic question: Can contemporary Catholic theology show clearly that Luther's doctrine of justification is compatible with the Catholic thought on merit, thus eliminating the basis of the controversy and opening the way to an eventual consensus?

In the literature cited above this problem emerges only partially. Bogdahn completely excludes it from the dialogue; Hasler expresses it only within the general doctrine of good works. Pesch handles it in the confrontation between Thomas and Luther and asserts that the "objections raised by Lutherans" as far as they are directed against "the genuine doctrine of Thomas" are to be

---

[1] Walther von Loewenich (Ev. Luth.): "An zwei Punkten scheint mir aber einstweilen doch eine bleibende Gegensätzlichkeit zu bestehen: a) Die katholische Lehre kann sich aufgrund des Tridentinums . . . nicht entschliessen, den Verdienstgedanken radikal preiszugeben. . . . Hier ist der Gegensatz nicht nur theoretisch, sondern greift tief hinein in das Verständnis der christlichen Existenz. b) Es ist ein Unterschied, ob man mit Luther von dem 'Christus in nobis' oder mit der katholischen Lehre von der gratia habitualis spricht." "Evangelische und katholische Lutherdeutung der Gegenwart im Dialog," LuJ 34 (1967):87.
Wilhelm Dantine (Ev. Luth.): "Die Nagelprobe stellt offenkundig das Verhältnis von justificatio sola gratia und dem Verdienstgedanken dar." Die Gerechtmachung des Gottlosen (Munich: Chr. Kaiser, 1959), p. 39.
Gerrit C. Berkouwer (Ev. Ref.): "The relation between sovereign grace and the merits of good works still forms a wall of disagreement between Rome and the Reformation churches." Faith and Justification, trans. Lewis B. Smedes (Grand Rapids, MI: Eerdmans Publishing Co., 1954), p. 13.
Piet Fransen (Rom. Cath.): "Unserer Auffassung nach ist aber die Verdienstlehre der einzige kritische Differenzpunkt zwischen der Reformation und dem katholischen Verständnis der Gnadenlehre . . ." "Dogmengeschichtliche Entfaltung der Gnadenlehre," in Mysterium Salutis, 4/2:721.

explained as "misunderstandings,"[1] indeed that Luther himself has fallen prey to this misunderstanding, owing to the Late Scholastic interpretation of Thomas.[2]

Only Pöhlmann deals with this problem on a broader basis, when in a special chapter ("Die Rechtfertigung aus Gnaden und das Verdienst des Menschen") he examines principally the Lutheran confessional documents--those of Trent and the modern Lutheran and Catholic Dogmatik, with Luther himself involved only marginally. Pöhlmann's starting-point is that at first glance the Catholic doctrine of merits "appears to open an unbridgeable chasm between the churches," that, however, on the basis of a rapprochement of reward and merit in modern Catholic exegesis "an agreement is not excluded."[3] But the vocabulary of dogmatics speaking of a merces ex iure obstructs on "agreement between the confessions."[4]

Since we--as mentioned above--consider Luther the leader in the dialogue, and the thought on merit an important element in the attempt to measure every consensus claimed in the doctrine of justification, it seems appropriate to us to grapple with the theme:

---

[1] Otto H. Pesch, Theologie der Rechtfertigung bei Martin Luther und Thomas von Aquin (Mainz: M. Grünewald, 1967), p. 786. "Von hierher erledigen sich die zahlreichen, immer wieder von lutherischer Seite erhobenen Vorbehalte gegen die Verdienstlehre als Missverständnisse - jedenfalls, soweit sie sich gegen die genuine Thomaslehre wenden."

[2] Ibid., p. 788.

[3] Pöhlmann, Rechtfertigung, pp. 193, 213: "Die römisch-katholische Verdienstlehre scheint einen unüberbrückbaren Graben zwischen den Konfessionen aufzureissen." Aber "eine Verständigung . . . [ist] nicht ausgeschlossen."

[4] Ibid., p. 213.

Justification and merit in the dialogue between Luther and the modern Catholic theology, and to investigate the problem of consensus. Hence, we wish to propose the following outline:

1. Luther's concentration on justification is presented in the framework of his understanding of Paul. We wish to emphasize those aspects in his doctrine which bring into focus the main point of the controversy--the final and meritorious character of Roman Catholic ethics. This is done in dialogue with important Catholic representatives of the pre-Vatican and post-Vatican theology of our century.

2. After a survey of the origin and development of Roman Catholic thought on merit until the Reformation period, Luther's teaching on justification is developed in the light of those features that led to his overcoming the theology of merit in the time of the Reformation.

3. Following this, the modern Catholic reaction to Luther's teaching of justification and criticism of merit is presented. We deal with the change of attitude in judging Luther's doctrine in modern Catholic Luther research and show the extent to which Luther's criticism is acceptable to Catholic thinking.

4. Finally, we investigate the interpretation and evaluation of the doctrine of merit in modern Catholic theology before and after the change in Catholic scholarship on Luther (1900-1940/1940 to the present). We ask whether a different approach to the thought on merit, i.e., new interpretations, new evaluations of rank, and supplements are sufficient to resolve the "polemic

over merit"[1] and the controversy over the doctrine of justification.

---

[1] Otto H. Pesch, "Die Lehre vom 'Verdienst' als Problem für Theologie und Verkündigung," in *Wahrheit und Verkündigung*, ed. L. Scheffczyk, W. Dettloff, and R. Heinzmann, 2 vols. (Munich: F. Schöningh, 1967), 2:1898.

PART I

LUTHER AND THE PROBLEM OF
JUSTIFICATION AND MERIT

CHAPTER I

CONTROVERSIAL ASPECTS OF LUTHER'S DOCTRINE OF
JUSTIFICATION

Justification as the Focal Center of the Gospel

Luther viewed the doctrine of justification as the "principal teaching" of Christianity (heubt artickel, heubtstueck, heubtlere, hoher Heuptartickel),[1] ascribing to faith alone "without any works" (on alle werck)[2] the justifying power before God. Herein lay for him the "sum of Christian doctrine" (summa doctrinae christianae)[3] and the "foundation of the New Testament" (fundamentum Novi Testamenti)[4] from which all sources of divine wisdom flow to us.

This article produces and maintains the Christian Church.[5] By it the Church stands or falls,[6] and without it the whole Christian doctrine,[7] even Christianity itself, would be lost.[8] It

---

[1] WA 30III, 366 24; WA 31I, 255, 35; WA 21, 219, 21; ibid., 36-37.

[2] WA 30III, 366, 27.   [3] WA 40III, 352, 2.

[4] WA 25, 332, 12-13.

[5] "Ex illa enim et in illa sola doctrina fit et consistit Ecclesia." WA 40I, 49, 26-27.

[6] ". . . quia isto articulo stante stat Ecclesia, ruente ruit Ecclesia." WA 40III, 352, 3. "Wer den Artickel hat, wirdt nicht jrren, aber wer des Artickels fhelet, der wirdt nichts ausrichten." WA 33, 165, 42-166, 3.

[7] WA 40I, 48, 28-29.   [8] Ibid., 355, 6.

alone-- and not the doing away with images and ceremonies--is what promises the right of the Reformation to exist and to triumph.[1] With it a clear line of separation can be drawn between true and false religion; for error says: "If I do this or that, I have a God who is favorably disposed toward me,"[2] but truth says: "Our doctrine is not . . . merit, but a gift through Christ."[3] Therefore Satan and the world are aroused to persecute and remove all those who seek grace and salvation from God through Christ and not through works and law-keeping.[4]

However, God has established this truth like a sun that enlightens the holy Church;[5] therefore it must also be the "master and sovereign, lord, ruler and judge of all kinds of doctrines.[6]

This conviction is in Luther's theology a constant, permeating factor. With his gaze upon justification, as "Junker Jörg" in 1521, he translated and interpreted the New Testament, and toward the end of his life, as God's "unworthy evangelist,"[7] he wrote in the "Articles of Smalkald" concerning justification in its relationship to the crucified and resurrected Christ, the word that sounds like his legacy:

---

[1]"Ideo 'victoria nostra' heisst 'fides' et per Jesum, non per abolitionem imaginum et ceremoniarum." Ibid., 10-11.

[2]"Si sic fecero, erit mihi deus clemens." WA 40I, 603, 10.

[3]"Nostra doctrina non est . . . meritum sed donatio per Christum." Ibid., 601, 4-5; WA 25, 330, 8-13.

[4]"Denn das ist auch allein der Artikel, der da allzeit mus verfolgung leiden vom Teuffel und der Welt." WA 46, 19, 36-37.

[5]WA 40III, 352, 2-3. "Ipse sol, dies, lux Ecclesiae et omnis fiduciae iste articulus." Ibid., 335, 9-10.

[6]WA 39I, 205, 102.   [7]WA 30III, 366, 26.

>Von diesem Artikel kan man nichts weichen oder nachgeben, Es
>falle Himel und Erden, oder was nicht bleiben wil . . . Und auff
>diesem Artikel stehet alles, das wir wider den Bapst, Teufel und
>Welt leren und leben. Daruemb muessen wir des gar gewis sein,
>und nicht zweiveln, sonst ist alles verloren, und behelt Bapst
>und Teufel und alles wider uns den Sieg und Recht.[1]

Luther was well aware of what was "new" and "wonderful"[2] in his teaching. Nowhere in Scholasticism is the doctrine of justification made so central as by him. Peter Lombard, for example, handles

---

[1] WA 50, 199, 22-25; 199, 31-200, 6. That the doctrine of justification forms the center of Luther's theology is asserted by many Luther-scholars. So, for example, Rudolf Hermann, Gesammelte Studien zur Theologie Luthers und der Reformation (Göttingen: Vandenhoeck & Ruprecht, 1960), pp. 367, 373; Paul Althaus, Die Theologie Martin Luthers, 4th ed. (Gütersloh: G. Mohn, 1975), p. 195; Ernst Kinder, RGG, 3rd ed., s.v. "Rechtfertigung--Dogmengeschichtlich (Luther)."
  The attempted separation of Christology (main article) and Soteriology (subordinate article) in the ASm by Pöhlmann (Rechtfertigung, pp. 26-27), does not seem convincing. For, when in the second Part of the ASm, Article 1 (BSLK 415, 4-5) Jesus Christ is mentioned, it is done expressly in connection with "Ampt und Werk . . . [so] unser Erlosung betreffen," i.e., under the viewpoint of justification, for "die Rechtfertigung . . . ist nicht ein Zweites, . . . jener Satz . . . bezieht sich auf Christi Werk und die Rechtfertigung in eins. Der Artikel von der Rechtfertigung ist nichts anderes als der recht verstandene Glaube an Christus." Althaus, Theologie Luthers, p. 196. Cf. Pesch, Theologie der Rechtfertigung, p. 157. Pöhlmann's reference, that the Mass (2nd Part, Article 2) and the Papacy (2nd Part, Article 4), which Luther likewise regards as impossible to unite with the main article, break up the justification character of the first article, overlooks the point that one is concerned, in the doctrinal points mentioned, exactly with their soteriological meaning. The Mass as meritorious and satisfactory work (BSLK 416, 8-17) and the necessity of the Papacy for salvation (BSLK 428, 4-20; 431, 5-6) stand for Luther in contradiction to justification by faith alone. Because Christ and justification are indivisible, both form in unity the "main article." A major portion of Lutheran theologians are now as ever ready to follow Luther in attributing to the doctrine of justification the central role in Christian belief. Justification is called "Mitte" (E. Wolf), "Vorzeichen" (W. Dantine), "Kriterium" (W. Trillhaas). See Eilert Herms, "Explikationsprobleme des Rechtfertigungsthemas und die Prinzipien des wissenschaftlichen Dialogs zwischen protestantischer und röm. kath. Theologie," KuD 21 (1975):287-88.

[2] "Mira et nova deffinitio iusticie." WA 57II, 69, 15. "Atque hic unus articulus est nostrae fidei et religionis, quem totus mundus ignorat" WA 25, 282, 32-33.

it in the framework of the doctrine of sacraments[1] and Thomas Aquinas treats it in connection with the teaching about grace.[2] A special article on justification as constituting the valuable position of the center of belief and the norm of determining every type of error, was unknown to the theology of the Middle Ages.[3] Nowhere was the sola fide--as excluding every type of final accomplishment and merit--so precisely and pregnantly defined as in Luther. Ever since the Church Fathers, faith had often been reduced to fides quae creditur[4] and therefore stressed especially as assensus.[5] Consequently, redeeming faith was merely conceived as adding love to faith.[6] In this view faith takes an initial, but not a universal, position.[7] And although faith is grounded on the

---

[1] Sent. Lib. 4, dist. 4 (PL 192:846-850).

[2] S. Th. 1a2ae. 113.

[3] Ernst Wolf, "Die Rechtfertigungslehre als Mitte und Grenze reformatorischer Theologie," EvT 9 (1949/50):299.

[4] "Fides in regula posita est." Tertullian Liber de praescriptionibus 14 (PL 2:32). "Christianus es, crede quod traditum est." Idem De carne Christi 2 (PL 2:801).

[5] With Origen the faith of the average man anticipates by assent what the philosopher finds through rational insight. Contra Celsum 1. 10 (PG 11:674). With Augustine, faith is sometimes an act of assent to facts as is also required for the "historia gentium." Conf. 6. 5. 7 (PL 32:722). Hence faith is "assensio" (Enchirid. de fide, spe et carit. 20. 7 [PL 40:242]) and "cum assensione cogitare." De praed. Sanct. 2. 5 (PL 44:963).

[6] Idem In Epist. Joannis ad Parthos 10. 1 (PL 35:2054). Sermo 168. 2 (PL 38:912). Augustine therefore rejects sola fides as fides mortua, because works are lacking through which one "becomes worthy" of salvation. De fide et operibus 14. 22; 15. 25 (PL 40:212-214).

[7] "Initium bonae vitae . . . recta fides est." Idem Sermo 43. 1. 1 (PL 38:254). "Credamus ergo Deo, fratres. Hoc est primum praeceptum, hoc est initium religionis et vitae nostrae." Ibid., 38. 3. 5 (PL 38:237).

"canonical Scriptures,"[1] it is nevertheless bound to the authority of the Church, without which the gospel also would become unbelievable.[2]

Scholasticism followed essentially these paths: Salvation is based upon faith, the sacraments, and good works.[3] Therefore no one can please God sola fide; faith must be fides sociata[4] or fides formata,[5] that is, it must first as assent-faith[6] be qualified by love so that love is involved as the main substance in the justification and in the eventual redemption,[7] while faith is granted only the function of the initiating spark.[8] What is embodied in works of grace is thus a trend to an increase of grace[9] and a final

---

[1] "Habet ergo et fides ipsa quoddam lumen suum in Scripturis . . ." Ibid., 126. 1. 1 (PL 38:698). "Credit etiam Scripturis sanctis et veteribus et novis, quas Canonicas appellamus, unde fides ipsa concepta est . . ." Idem De civ. Dei 19. 18 (PL 41:646).

[2] "Ego vero Evangelio non crederem, nisi me catholicae Ecclesiae commoveret auctoritas." Idem Contra epist. Manichaei 5. 6 (PL 42:176).

[3] "Quae sunt illa sine quibus salus ab initio haberi non potuit? Tria sunt, id est fides, et sacramenta fidei, et opera bona." Hugh of St.-Victor De Sacram. legis naturalis et scriptae (PL 176:35).

[4] "Sola fide nemo potest placere Deo nisi charitas illi sociata fuerit." Ibid.

[5] ". . . charitas, . . . omnes informat." Peter Lombard Sent. Lib. 3, dist. 23 (PL 192:805). "Motus fidei non est perfectus nisi sit caritate informatus." Thomas Aquinas S. Th. 1a2ae. 113, 4 ad 1.

[6] "Credere ad intellectum pertineat prout est a voluntate motus ad assentiendum." Ibid., 2a2ae. 2, 2.

[7] "Per charitatem autem consequimur veniam peccatorum." Ibid., 3a. 49, 1. "Et ideo meritum vitae aeternae primo pertinet ad caritatem." Ibid., 1a2ae. 114, 4.

[8] "Fides est habitus mentis, qua inchoatur vita aeterna in nobis." Ibid., 2a2ae. 4, 1.

[9] ". . . quolibet actu meritorio meretur homo augmentum gratiae . . ." Ibid., 1a2ae. 114, 8 ad 3.

tendency of winning salvation;[1] the believer can now only hope that God will be gracious to him in the judgment; without special revelation he cannot now be certain of his salvation.[2]

The formula sola fide indeed has its representatives in pre-Scholasticism (Sedulius Scotus, Rabanus Maurus),[3] in Early Scholasticism (Bruno the Carthusian, Peter Lombard),[4] and in High Scholasticism (Thomas Aquinas),[5] but it was used mainly (as in the Ancient Church by Pelagius,[6] Marius Victorinus[7] and Ambrosiaster[8]) as a reduction-formula for the forgiveness of sins up to

---

[1] "Homo sua voluntate facit opera meritoria vitae aeternae . . . ad hoc exigitur quod voluntas hominis praeparetur a Deo per gratiam." Ibid., 109, 5 ad 1.

[2] Thomas knows a threefold way. Only through revelation can a believer know whether he has grace. There is no certain knowledge through stringent conclusions. Only on the basis of signs (aversion to the world, desire for divine things, freedom of conscience from mortal sin) may one "conjecture" whether one belongs to the saved. See S. Th. 1a2ae. 112, 5. Bernard of Clairvaux seems to form an exception. He speaks of a certainty grounded in God's love ("Vides quomodo non solum de amore suo certum te reddat . . ."). Sermones in Cantica 69. 8 (PL 183:1116). See Friedrich Loofs, Leitfaden zum Studium der Dogmengeschichte, 7th ed. pts. 1 & 2 (Tübingen: M. Niemeyer, 1968), p. 560.

[3] See Arthur M. Landgraf, Dogmengeschichte der Frühscholastik, 4 vols. (Regensburg: F. Pustet, 1952-56), 1:204; Enarrationum in Epp. Pauli Lib. 2.--In Epist. ad Rom. (PL 111:1343).

[4] Expositio in Epistolas Pauli.--In Epist. ad Rom. (PL 153:41); Collectanea in Epist. D. Pauli.--In Epist. ad Rom. 4:1-8 (PL 191:1367).

[5] Super Epistolas S. Pauli Lectura. 1 Ad Tim. Lectio 3. 21.

[6] Loofs, Leitfaden, p. 336.

[7] In Epist. ad Eph. 2 (PL 30:827).

[8] Comment. in Epist. ad Rom. 3:24 (PL 17:83).

baptism.[1] Where the dynamic of the biblical faith tries to break through, as for example in the comparison "hope is trust" (spes fiducia est), the proper fides, which "pertains to the intellect" (ad cogitationem pertinet),[2] is excluded, or formulations like the Augustinian: "By faith we love, by faith we cherish, by faith we turn to Him" (Credendo amare, credendo diligere, credendo in eum ire)[3] are repeated, which, however, are unable to burst the framework of "faith by grace" (Gnadenglauben) and "works by grace" (Gnadenwerk).[4]

But because the simple believer was often unable to penetrate the subtle intellectual faith, since 1200 the distinction between

---

[1] Exceptions are found among the mystics. Behind the sola fide of Bernard of Clairvaux ("Quisquis . . . credat in te qui justificas impium, et solam justificatus per fidem, pacem habebit ad Deum." Sermones in Cantica 22. 8 [PL 183:881]) stands a total concept of grace which excludes real merits for eternal life (In festo annuntiat. Beatae Mariae Virg. Sermo 1. 3 [PL 183:383]), because righteousness consists "in absolutione peccatorum." Sermones in Cantica 22. 6 (PL 183:880). "Es liegt hier vielmehr, noch deutlicher als bei Bruno dem Karthäuser, eine wirkliche Parallele zu Luthers Gedanken vor." Loofs, Leitfaden, p. 427. Similar to Bernard's view is that of Catherine of Siena: "Herr, du rufst mich und ich komme, nicht durch meine Verdienste, sondern allein durch deine Barmherzigkeit, die ich anrufe in deinem Blut." Quoted in Christoph E. Luthardt, Kompendium der Dogmatik (Leipzig: Dörffling & Franke, 1933), p. 408. A similar statement is attributed to Staupitz, the Vicar General of Luther's order ("Allein durch den Glauben seines Blutvergiessens"), quoted in Karl von Hase, Evangelisch-Protestantische Dogmatik, 5th ed. (Leipzig: Breitkopf & Härtel, 1860), p. 308. But since for the Thomist Staupitz, grace is what makes works possible, no direct line should be drawn to Luther's sola fide. Cf. Heinrich Fausel, D. Martin Luther, 2 vols. (Munich: Siebenstern, 1966), 1:49.

[2] Hugh of St.-Viktor De sacram. legis naturalis et scriptae (PL 176:36).

[3] Augustine In Joannis Ev. Tract. 29. 6 (PL 35:1631).

[4] ". . . qui habet tempus operandi, merces non imputatur, id est non dabitur, secundum gratiam fidei tantum, sed secundum debitum operationis suae." Peter Lombard Collectanea in Epist. D. Pauli.--In Epist. ad Rom. 4:1-8 (PL 191:1367).

fides implicita and explicita arose. This removed from the believer the personal striving for the truth and discovered a duty,[1] even a merit in the assent to the teaching of the Church.[2]

In Late Scholasticism this development became more condensed and gross. Sola fide was either denied, as with Gabriel Biel,[3] or held to be only for the first justification (baptism) but not for the eschatological justification (judgment); so, for example, with Thomas Bradwardine and with Wendelin Steinbach, the student of Gabriel Biel.[4] The reduction of the concept of faith to notitia and assensus, as well as the assertion of a bonum morale also following the Fall, no longer permit, with Ockham, any separation between Christians and pagans; only on the basis of the potentia ordinata does a person need grace in order, through love, to win salvation.[5] What already in Franciscan theology of High Scholasticism (Summa Halensis, Bonaventure) was favored, "if man does what is within his power, God likewise does what is in His" (si facit homo quod in se est, Deus facit, quod in se est),[6] which indeed still needed the gratia gratis data as "incitement" in order to earn

---

[1] DS 1869, 3011.

[2] Loofs, Leitfaden, p. 465.

[3] Heiko Augustinus Oberman, Werden und Wertung der Reformation (Tübingen: J. C. B. Mohr [P. Siebeck], 1977), p. 127.

[4] Ibid., pp. 84, 126-27.

[5] Loofs, Leitfaden, p. 508; DTC, s.v. "Occam et Duns Scot," by P. Vignaux.

[6] Summa Halensis Lib. 3, p. 3, inqu. 1, tract. 1, qu. 5, m. 3; Bonaventure Sent. Lib. 4, dist. 16, p. 2, a. 2, qu. 2.

the gratia gratum faciens (justification) ex congruo,[1] becomes in Late Scholasticism an appeal to the natural forces of persons to earn justification ex congruo according to the principle: "If man does what is within his power, God necessarily grants His grace" (Facienti quod in se est, Deus necessario dat gratiam).[2] According to Biel, thereby the eschatological justification is also a working together of God and the human being, for Christ is not the "only and total meritorious cause" (sola et totalis causa meritoria), because, indeed, the congruent and condign merits of the human are added to the work of Christ.[3] These views, similar to Semi-Pelagianism,[4] may have convinced Bradwardine that in his time there were practically only Pelagians,[5] although even the "Academic Augustinianism,"[6] as it was represented by him and Gregory of Rimini, arrived at no pure new construction of the Pauline doctrine of justification.

---

[1] "Tenendum est igitur quod liberum arbitrium, si excitetur per aliquod donum gratiae gratis datae, potest ad gratia gratum facientem se de congruo disponere." Ibid. Lib. 2, dist. 28, a. 2, qu. 1.

[2] Biel Collect. in Sent. Lib. 2, dist. 27, qu. 1, a. 3, d. 4. See DTC, s.v. "Mérite," by J. Rivière.

[3] Collect. in Sent. Lib. 3, dist. 19, qu. 1, a. 1, c. 4.

[4] "Scholastischer Neo-Semipelagianismus." Landgraf, Dogmengeschichte, 1:250. "Krassester Neo-Semipelagianismus." Loofs, Leitfaden, p. 508. "Pelagianisierender Voluntarismus." Hans Küng, Rechtfertigung (Einsiedeln: Johannes Verlag, 1957), p. 214. "New form of Semi-Pelagianism." Harry J. McSorley, Luther: Right or Wrong? (New York: Newman Press, 1969), p. 200.

[5] Heiko Augustinus Oberman, Forerunners of the Reformation (New York: Holt, Rinehart & Winston, 1966), p. 135; idem, "Facientibus quod in se est Deus non denegat gratiam," HTR 55 (1962):336 ("Totus etenim paene mundus post Pelagium abiit in errorem").

[6] Idem, Werden und Wertung, p. 83.

It is certain that Luther's protest against the "fools and pig-theologians" (Stulti Sawtheologen)[1] is directed above all against the Late Scholastic doctrine of justification, in which he had been predominantly instructed and which he himself at the beginning had represented.[2] In any case, according to H. A. Oberman, Luther's protest is an attack on the whole of Scholasticism,[3] for he was well aware of the differences among the several schools[4] and found nowhere the identification of iustitia Christi (justification) and iustitia Dei (judgment)[5] and thus also nowhere the renunciation of the thought of merit. With his understanding, Luther had to reach back over Scholasticism, and even beyond Augustine, and join with Paul. For in spite of how much he valued Augustine,[6] with whom he thought he was always in agreement,[7] yet he was conscious

---

[1] WA 56, 274, 14.

[2] WA 4, 262, 4-7; 312, 40-41. McSorley, emphasizing the "Recte ergo prius auxilium gratie poscit . . . Quia nihil est propositum nostrum, nisi gratia dei ipsum disponat" in Luther's Scholion to Ps 118:11 (309, 9-11), seems to make a rapprochement between Luther and some Franciscans, such as Alexander, Bonaventure and Scotus. See Luther: Right or Wrong?, p. 223.

[3] Heiko Augustinus Oberman, "The Reformation: Proclamation of Grace," in God and Man in Contemporary Christian Thought, ed. Charles Malik (Beirut: American University, 1970), p. 60. Cf. Wilfried Joest, Die katholische Lehre von der Rechtfertigung und von der Gnade (Lüneburg: Heliand, 1954), p. 8.

[4] Idem, "'Iustitia Christi' and 'Iustitia Dei'," HTR 59 (1966):6.

[5] Ibid., pp. 19-26.

[6] "Wo S. Augustinus aus der Veter zal geworffen wird, so sind die andern nicht viel werd." WA 50, 526, 2-3. "S. Augustinus, interpres (divi Pauli) fidelissimus." WA 1, 353, 14.

[7] "Auch bin ichs nicht allein, noch der erste, der da sagt, Allein der glaube mach gerecht, Es hat fur mir Ambrosius, Augustinus

that even the doctor gratiae had not fully comprehended the Pauline teaching of justification.[1]

The issue of justification has shifted in Augustine from the judgment seat of God to the heart of the human being.[2] Justification is healing[3] and repair[4] of the person, for justificare means justum facere.[5] Through the infused grace the person is made capable of meritorious works that bring salvation, works that indeed come into being wholly sola gratia,[6] but which do not have consecutive but final character.[7] Luther's view is essentially

---

und vil andere gesagt." WA 30II, 642, 26-27. "Doch zeigt dies Wort Augustini (sola fide) gnugsam an, dass ers mit uns hält." TR 6, 152, 5-6.

[1]"Augustinus proprius accedit ad sententiam Pauli quam omnes scholastici, sed non attingit Paulum." TR 3, 180, 9-10. "Principio Augustinum vorabam, non legebam, sed da mir in Paulo die thur auffgieng, da ich wusste, was iustificatio fidei ward, da ward es aus mit yhm." TR 1, 140, 5-7.

[2]"(Lex) eum forinsecus terrificet . . . (spiritus), ut eum intrinsecus iustificet." De spiritu et littera 17. 30 (PL 44:219), italics mine.

[3]"Per gratiam sanatio animae." Ibid., 30. 52 (PL 44:233).

[4]"Non quod per naturam negata sit gratia, sed potius per gratiam reparata natura." Ibid., 27. 47 (PL 44:229).

[5]"Quid est enim aliud, justificati, quam justi facti . . .?" Ibid., 26. 45 (PL 44:228). "Quid est justificare? Justum facere." Sermo 292. 4. 6 (PL 38:1324).

[6]"Intelligenda est enim gratia Dei per Jesum Christum Dominum nostrum, qua sola homines liberantur a malo, et sine qua nullum prorsus sive cogitando, sive volendo et amando, sive agendo faciunt bonum . . . Hanc quippe inspirationem bonae voluntatis atque operis poscebat Apostolus . . ." De corrept. et gratia 2. 3 (PL 44:917).

[7]Augustine interprets the Pauline formula of Rom 6:23 (death = wages, life = gift) as (death = deserved pay, life = deserved pay). Ep. 194. 5. 20 (PL 33:881). The wages are, however, exclusively ascribed to grace.

different. Faith as trusting faith (<u>fiducia</u>) is totally a gift of God. With this gift alone the person grasps the promised salvation, which is to him like a verdict of righteousness before God, bridging the present (justification) and the future (judgment). As long as the fire of faith is kindled in the person, he stands in the light of salvation, for "faith is a living, audacious reliance upon God's grace . . . it makes one happy, bold and cheerful toward God" (<u>glawb ist eyn lebendige erwegene zuversicht auf Gottis gnade</u>; <u>. . . macht frolich, trotzig und lustig gegen Gott</u>).[1] In this, however, it does not stand idle, for "faith is a divine work in us, which changes us and makes us new from God . . . faith is a lively, diligent, active, powerful thing, which makes it impossible that it shall not unceasingly do good works" (<u>glawb ist eyn gotlich werck ynn uns, das uns wandelt und new gepirt aus Gott . . . es ist eyn lebendig, schefftig, thetig, mechtig ding umb den glawben, das unmuglich ist, das er nicht on unterlas solt gutts wircken</u>).[2] With these good works man thanks God and serves his neighbor. This new life flows constantly to the believer from the personal fellowship with God over the Word. All work witnesses to this relationship.

With this relationship man also stands before God's last judgment, for if he had to present his grace-created works, as a condition of salvation, or even had to include himself meritoriously in it, then he could never be sure of this salvation relationship and would assume, even if in a small part, that he was a coworker in his eventual redemption. In this Luther sees summarized in clear

---

[1] DB 7, 10, 16-18.   [2] Ibid., 6-10.

focus the revelation of salvation in Christ; this is for him <u>the</u> gospel.[1]

The question that arises here, and has often arisen in centuries of polemics, is: Has Luther properly understood Paul?

In the framework of this study we can cite neither the totality of Protestant answers nor the large number of Catholic replies from the past. We wish, however, to ask important representatives of Catholic exegesis and dogmatics from our century about it.

Luther's Paulinism in the View of Modern Catholic Theology

That Luther was a Paulinist is a truism. According to his own confession he had overcome the theology of his time through Paul,[2] and predominantly from Paul he dared to carry on his struggle against the Roman Catholic Church.[3] For him the Pauline gospel was the substance of theology.[4]

Otto Scheel, to be sure, has clearly pointed out that Catholicism also wished to be understood as Paulinism.[5] "Paul was

---

[1] "Evangelium ist eine gute Botschaft . . . ist keine Predigt von unseren Werken. Darüm wer da saget, dass das Evangelium Werk fordert zur Seligkeit nöthig, der ist ein Lügener." TR 6, 136, 31-36.

[2] "Ego Christum amiseram illic [in theologia scholastica], nunc in Paulo reperi." WA 2, 414, 28.

[3] "Nunquam fuissem ausus (papae) angelicum splendorem aggredi, nisi Paulus tantam clarissimis testimoniis et confutationibus futuram caecicatem Papatus ostendisset." TR 3, 598, 17-18.

[4] "Sed haec est fides, quae involvit Christum et apprehendit Christum. Extra Paulum non est illa theologia." Ibid., 211, 1-3.

[5] Otto Scheel, Martin Luther, 2 vols. (Tübingen: J. C. B. Mohr [P. Siebeck], 1930), 2:143.

the great teacher also of the Catholicism of the Middle Ages and the Late Middle Ages . . . nobody was conscious of a turning away from Paul."[1] But just the role of works in relation to salvation and the question of merit separated the traditional interpretation of Paul from that of Luther. Thus in Luther's eyes the traditional explanation of Paul must have seemed "another gospel."[2]

But that is just what Catholic exegesis, dogmatics, and church-history research was never ready to admit. In Catholic research before the great ecumenical turning point caused by Joseph Lortz's explanation of Luther in "Die Reformation in Deutschland" (1939/40), clear witnesses can be found who categorically deny to Luther every genuine understanding of Paul. They are of the opinion that Luther stands not only in contradiction to tradition, but also in contradiction to all sound exegesis of Paul.[3] His teaching is diametrically opposed to that of Paul,[4] it is a falsification of

---

[1] "Paulus war der grosse Lehrer auch des mittelalterlichen und spätmittelalterlichen Katholizismus . . . einer Abkehr von Paulus war man sich nicht bewusst." Ibid.

[2] "Die sittliche Leistung des Christen wurde die Grundlage des göttlichen Urteils. Hatte der Sünder in der Taufe das Christentum als Gnadenreligion kennengelernt, so erlebte es der Getaufte hinfort als Gesetzesreligion. Entscheidend ist nicht die "Werkheiligkeit," sondern, dass die Werke unter den Gesichtspunkt der Vergeltungsordnung treten, darum wie auch im Judentum besondere Anerkennung oder Verdienste begründen . . . Ein anderes Evangelium, dem Paulus aufs äusserste widerstanden hatte, wurde mit seinen eigenen Worten gepredigt." Ibid., 2:145.

[3] "Luther, sous l'influence d'expériences personnelles, en vint à interpréter S. Paul dans un sens tout opposé à celui de la tradition et à celui d'une saine exégèse." Léon Cristiani, Luther et le Luthéranisme (Paris: Librairie Bloud, 1908), p. 63.

[4] Marie-Joseph Lagrange, in discussing Luther's teaching of sinfulness of good works, poses the question: "Comment Luther a-t-il pu aboutir, en se servant de S. Paul, à un résultat dia-

Paul[1] in the form of a reduction and deformation,[2] because Luther was not ready to submit his explanation to the judgment of the Church.[3]

However, this tone meets us also at times in the controversy before Vatican II,[4] until in our days it yields to a many-voiced pluralism, which reaches from rejection[5] to restrictions, mostly in single questions,[6] to open, even enthusiastic, agreement. Exactly that for which Luther was reproached, he is now praised. This can be seen in the opinions expressed, i.e.: Luther's interpretation of Paul was not only justified with regard to the Late Scholastic doctrine of works,[7] but it is also a necessary force

---

métralement opposé?" "Le Commentaire de Luther sur l'épître aux Romains," RB 13 (1916):104.

[1] "Il a faussé le sens de S. Paul." DTC, s.v. "Luther," by J. Paquier. Cf. ibid., s.v. "Justification," by J. Rivière.

[2] Ibid., s.v. "Luther," by J. Paquier.   [3] Ibid.

[4] "Die Kirche [hat] von Anfang an die Paulusbriefe nie anders verstanden und Luther [hat] eine bis dahin unbekannte, neue Lehre aufgebracht. . . . Es spricht aber nicht für die Wahrheit einer angeblich biblischen Lehre, wenn sie von den ersten Tagen des Christentums an 1500 Jahre lang vollkommen unbekannt gewesen ist." Luther simply supported himself "auf falsch gedeutete Paulusbriefe." Hermann J. Schmidt, Brückenschlag zwischen den Konfessionen (Paderborn: F. Schöningh, 1951), pp. 148-149, 205.

[5] "His theology . . . is basically a misinterpretation of both St. Paul and St. Augustine." CDT, s.v. "Grace," by P. de Letter.

[6] These concern mostly the doctrine of sin, a radically held simul peccator et justus, which is viewed as unpauline. See Henri Bouillard, Karl Barth, 2 vols. (Paris: Aubier-Montaigne, 1957), 2/1:105; Jared Wicks, Man Yearning for Grace (Washington, D.C.: Corpus Books, 1968), p. 276; Karl Rahner, Schriften zur Theologie, 12 vols. (Einsiedeln: Benziger, 1954-75), 6:265; Rudolf Schnackenburg, Neutestamentliche Theologie, 2nd ed. (Munich: Kösel, 1963), p. 95.

[7] "Luther ne pouvait que puiser à ses devanciers (Paul et Augustin) contre la justice des oeuvres du catholicisme de la fin

against the constant threat of nomism in Christianity.[1] Luther's teaching is a return to the Scriptures,[2] his new discovery of Paul[3] is biblically justified.[4] Luther has not only Paul behind him,[5] but he is also the one who has best understood him,[6] for, whenever Luther speaks, one hears the Apostle speak.[7]

These judgments are in any case not unanimous; they come mostly from the pen of the ecumenical <u>avant-garde</u> and especially

---

du Moyen Age. C'est de cette difficulté que partait la Réforme et Luther n'avait pas le choix de la réponse et de son interprétation de Paul." Daniel Olivier, <u>La foi de Luther</u> (Paris: Beauchesne, 1978), p. 136.

[1]"En engageant la lutte contre la justice des oeuvres, Luther s'attaque en effet à un problème permanent du Christianisme." Ibid.

[2]"Dabei gründen Luthers Rechtfertigungslehre . . . in der Rückkehr der Kirche und ihrer Theologie zum Evangelium Jesu Christi, wie es in der Hlg. Schrift ursprünglich bezeugt ist." Hans Küng, "Katholische Besinnung auf Luthers Rechtfertigungslehre heute," in <u>Theologie im Wandel</u>, ed. Kath. theol. Fakultät Tübingen (Munich: E. Wewel, 1967), p. 464.

[3]"Wiederentdeckung der ursprünglichen paulinischen Lehre." Ibid., p. 467. "Neuentdeckung der paulinischen Rechtfertigungslehre." Pesch, "Gottes Gnadenhandeln," in <u>Mysterium Salutis</u>, 4/2: 839. The Pauline justification was "doctrine oubliée." Olivier, <u>Foi de Luther</u>, p. 132.

[4]"Niemand kann also insoweit [d.h., was den forensischen Charakter betrifft] dem reformatorischen Rechtfertigungsverständnis mangelnde biblische Fundierung vorwerfen." Pesch, "Gottes Gnadenhandeln," in <u>Mysterium Salutis</u>, 4/2:848.

[5]"Luther hat mit den Grundaussagen über die Rechtfertigungslehre . . . das Neue Testament und insbesondere Paulus . . . hinter sich." Küng, "Katholische Besinnung," in <u>Theologie im Wandel</u>, p. 465.

[6]"Luther hat wie in den 1500 Jahren vor ihm keiner, selbst Augustin nicht, einen unmittelbaren Zugang zu der so bald nicht mehr ursprünglich verstandenen Rechtfertigungslehre des Apostels gefunden." Küng, "Katholische Besinnung," in <u>Theologie im Wandel</u>, p. 467.

[7]"On croit entendre l'Apôtre lui-même." Olivier, <u>Foi de Luther</u>, p. 132.

from the ranks of the "systematicians," to whom a reworking of the "Catholic Luther" is not sufficient, because one should not only understand Luther but also learn from him. The "historians," who strive for an integration of what is Catholic in Luther, express themselves less strongly. Lortz, the Old Master and head of this group, indeed admits that Luther fell back upon the Bible,[1] but subjectively,[2] and in an unbalanced way.[3] In this sense Luther also cannot be valid as a "Vollhörer" ("one who fully hears")[4] of the Holy Scriptures.

The dramatic change within modern Catholic Paul-Luther comparison becomes clearest in the works where Catholic theologians observe Luther the exegete at work. We shall illustrate this by three selections from Luther's Lecture on the Epistle to the Romans.

After the rediscovery of Luther's manuscript of this lecture at the beginning of our century, Marie-Joseph Lagrange wrote two articles in the Revue Biblique on Luther's work on Romans. He acknowledges that in this we are concerned with an exegesis

---

[1] In Luther's striving for God's righteousness "[bringt] das Wort der Bibel endlich den Umschwung." "Das gibt ihm für seinen theologischen Aufbau und in der Polemik jenes staunenswerte Gefühl des Zuhause- und Überlegenseins." Joseph Lortz, Die Reformation in Deutschland, 5th ed., 2 vols. (Freiburg i. Br.: Herder, 1962), 1:180, 190.

[2] Idem, "Grundzüge," in Reformata Reformanda, 1:237.

[3] "Luther kannte, 'wusste' die ganze Heilige Schrift in bewundernswürdiger Fülle. Aber er verkündete sie keineswegs gleichmässig. . . . Luther war Paulinist. Niemand in der Geschichte der christlichen Offenbarung hat die Stimme Pauli so intensiv gehört wie er. Aber das besagt nicht, dass der ganze Paulus gleichmässig in Luther eingegangen wäre." Ibid., 1:242-43.

[4] "Der grosse Hörer des Wortes Martin Luther war nicht Vollhörer des Wortes." Ibid., 1:243.

"which has transformed the religious life of millions of persons" (qui a transformé la vie religieuse de millions d'âmes).[1] Luther's genius consisted of the fact that he understood how to interpret the trend and the interests of his time.[2] But Luther's fate is the German fate: to him everything became a paradoxical dialectic, long before Hegel and Schelling had introduced the dialectic principle into philosophy.[3] Therefore the simul justus et peccator is a "distressing doctrine" (doctrine désolante)[4] and the teaching of Paul is diametrically opposed to it.[5] In that Luther translated faith with trust rather than with acceptance,[6] and in that he understood under righteousness, "declaration of righteousness" instead of "making righteous,"[7] he misrepresented the Pauline thought (il a dénaturé la pensée de l'apôtre).[8]

A somewhat more balanced attempt at judging is made by Georges Bavaud, who in the year 1970 published a short study on the same topic. He states that Luther in the Lecture on the Epistle to the Romans is certainly not yet the Reformer; indeed, if Luther had developed further in the direction of the meaning of the lecture, the Reformation probably would never have led to separation from the Church, for Luther, had, as his lecture hints, landed in "double justification," which indeed also represents an

---

[1] Lagrange, "Commentaire de Luther," RB 12 (1915):456.
[2] Idem, "Commentaire de Luther," RB 13 (1916):91.
[3] Ibid., p. 90. [4] Ibid., p. 103.
[5] Ibid., p. 104. [6] Ibid., p. 117.
[7] Ibid., p. 114. [8] Ibid., p. 120.

"erroneous doctrine" (<u>doctrine erronée</u>)[1] but has no church-separating character.[2]

In addition Bavaud also repeats the standard reproach of Catholic polemical theology: man is, with Luther, too little engaged personally in the question of salvation.[3] Luther's error consisted in the fact that he carried over the question of total human sinfulness from the plane of existential spirituality to the plane of doctrinal teaching,[4] that the exaggeration of the <u>lex accusans</u> had led to the teaching of the remaining <u>peccatum radicale</u>, that Luther overuses the little word <u>solus</u>,[5] that he--influenced by Nominalism--excluded the aspect of <u>ultima finis</u> from the problem of concupiscence.[6]

Bavaud sees the difference between the Lutheran Reformation and Catholicism in sanctification. Here, according to Catholic understanding, the outward accusing law becomes an inward integrated law, or the tension "faith-sin" comes to a harmonious resolution in the removal of sin: "Indeed, what separates Catholicism from Lutheranism is a different interpretation of the prophecies concerning the gift of the Spirit in the New Covenant."[7]

Much more detailed and more frank than Bavaud, or even Lagrange, Lortz deals with Luther's <u>Lecture on the Epistle to the</u>

---

[1] Georges Bavaud, "Luther, commentateur de l'épître aux Romains," <u>RTP</u> 20 (1970):260.

[2] Ibid., p. 240. [3] Ibid., p. 250. [4] Ibid., p. 254.

[5] Ibid., p. 256. [6] Ibid., p. 258.

[7] "En fait, ce qui sépare le catholicisme du luthéranisme, c'est une interprétation différente des propheties concernant le don de l'Esprit dans la Nouvelle Alliance." Ibid., p. 261.

Romans. Lortz is--as we have already seen--in no way of the opinion of the Reformer in everything. He judges much more tentatively than the representatives of the ecumenical avant-garde (Küng, O. H. Pesch, Olivier), but also much more positively than the customary polemical theology, especially in what concerns the catholicity of the early Luther.

Lortz says that Luther worked out the sermon on the Epistle to the Romans in "surprising depth," but as a result of the Reformer's study, the Epistle has become more difficult and complicated,[1] because Luther carried on the development of justification with "a certain onesidedness" (mit gewisser Einseitigkeit).[2]

It is nevertheless sure that in an astonishing way he had newly discovered for himself the peculiarity of the Holy Scriptures.[3] Luther from the beginning, that is, from the First Lecture on the Psalms, thinks outward from the Scriptures[4] and is a radical Paulinist.[5]

Karl Holl's view, that Luther was already a Reformer in the Lecture on Psalms, according to Lortz does not apply even to the Epistle to the Romans.[6] One cannot bring too great a reproach against Luther that he has left the traditional ways of Scholasticism, for he grew up in a world of confused opinions.[7]

Luther did not falsify the message of Paul when he brought

---

[1] Joseph Lortz, "Luthers Römerbriefvorlesung," TThZ 71 (1962):129.

[2] Ibid., p. 137. [3] Ibid., p. 133. [4] Ibid.

[5] Ibid., p. 134. [6] Ibid., p. 139. [7] Ibid., p. 140.

into central position the dual concepts justitia-justificatio. For thereby one comes unambiguously to the theologia crucis,[1] to the struggle, which Paul also carried on, against law-righteousness and for the cross as lifesaving power.

While Lagrange thought he had already discovered, in the exegete of the Epistle to the Romans, the heretic, and Bavaud, the theological but still churchly outsider, Lortz witnesses to the Catholic orthodoxy of Luther in his Epistle to the Romans: "It would be difficult to deny to this original Lutheran, often recondite character the witness that it remains within Catholic teaching" (Es dürfte schwer fallen, dieser original lutherschen, oft gewundenen Prägung das Zeugnis zu verweigern, sie bleibe innerhalb der katholischen Lehre).[2]

In summary it can be said that Catholic polemical theology with reference to Luther's understanding of Paul is definitely prepared today to pronounce more or less differentiated but still positive judgments. Does this also hold true for all aspects of Luther's Paulinism? This question we investigate with reference to the following points: Centrality of the teaching of justification, forensic declaration of righteousness, sola fide in consecutive or final sense, and the thought of merit in Paul.

The Central Position of Justification as a Controversial Problem

Catholic literature before Vatican II shows a rather closed front to this question. For example, works that are especially

---

[1] Ibid., p. 149.   [2] Ibid., p. 247.

written for a broader readership lack altogether a special chapter on justification.[1] And whenever justification is dealt with in dogmatic theology, the topic occurs in the form of a subsection of a chapter within the doctrine of grace. In no way can one here speak of a central position of justification in Paul or anywhere in Christian doctrine, as it is asserted by Luther.

Well-known dogmatic textbooks illustrate this assertion. Whether one takes up Bernhard Bartmann's work written from the biblical and patristic perspectives,[2] the Thomistic Franz Diekamp,[3] Joseph Pohle and Joseph Gummersbach with their Molinistic tendencies,[4] or the ecumenical Michael Schmaus[5] there is never any agreement with Luther in the latter's ranking of justification as the center of the Pauline message. This is true especially for the dogmatic works appearing before the Council of Vatican II and less circulated in German-speaking areas.[6] It extends, however, also to

---

[1] See Bernhard Bartmann, Des Christen Gnadenleben, 3rd ed. (Paderborn: Bonifacius, 1922); Daniel Feuling, Katholische Glaubenslehre, 3rd ed. (Salzburg: O. Müller, 1950).

[2] Bernhard Bartmann, Lehrbuch der Dogmatik, 8th ed., 2 vols. (Freiburg i. Br.: Herder, 1932).

[3] Franz Diekamp, Katholische Dogmatik nach den Grundsätzen des hlg. Thomas, 11th & 12th ed., 3 vols. (Münster/W.: Aschendorff, 1959).

[4] Joseph Pohle and Joseph Gummersbach, Lehrbuch der Dogmatik, 10th ed., 3 vols. (Paderborn: F. Schöningh, 1956).

[5] Michael Schmaus, Katholische Dogmatik, 5th ed., vol. 3/2 (Munich: M. Hueber, 1956).

[6] See Franc. X. de Abárzuza, Manuale theologiae dogmaticae, 2nd ed., vol. 3 (Madrid: Ediciones Studium, 1956); Josepho A. de Aldama, Severino Gonzalez, and Jesu Solano, Sacrae theologiae summa, vol. 3 (Madrid: Biblioteca de autores cristianos, 1953); Conradus Baisi, Institutiones theologiae scholasticae, vol. 3 (Milan: Editrice Ancora, 1949); Jean Berthier and Sidney A. Raemers, A

the majority of dogmatic literature which appeared during or after the council.[1] Their judgment agrees with that of Friedrich Richter who, when he compared the Reformer with Loyola, said of Luther that he has simply overstressed the doctrine of justification.[2]

Only in most recent times is there a noticeable change. In the dogmatic compilation <u>Mysterium Salutis</u> there is a separate chapter, "Gottes Gnadenhandeln als Erwählung und Rechtfertigung des Menschen" ("God's Work of grace in the Election and Justification of man") in which the section on justification (by O. H. Pesch) appears separated from that on sanctification (by Fransen), and

---

Compendium of Theology, trans. Sidney A. Raemers, vol. 1 (St. Louis, MO: Herder, 1931); Louis Billot, De gratia Christi, 4th ed. (Rome: Apud Aedes Universitatis Gregorianae, 1928); Carolo Boyer, Tractatus de gratia divina (Rome: Apud Aedes Universitatis Gregorianae, 1938); Johannes Brinktrine, Die Lehre von der Gnade (Paderborn: F. Schöningh, 1957); Franciscus Dander, Summarium tractatus dogmatici, vol. 2 (Innsbruck: F. Rauch, 1953); Reginaldus Garrigou-Lagrange, De gratia (Turin: Casa Editrice Marietti, 1946); Maurus Heinrichs, Theses dogmaticae, 2nd ed., vol. 2 (Hong Kong: Studium Biblicum O.F.M., 1954); Jean M. Hervé, Manuale theologiae dogmaticae, 18th ed., vol. 3 (Westminster, MD: Newman Bookshop, 1943); Hermanus Lange, De gratia (Freiburg i. Br.: Herder, 1929); Heinrich Lennerz, De gratia Redemptoris, 3rd ed. (Rome: Apud Aedes Universitatis Gregorianae, 1949); Josephus Mors, Institutiones theologiae dogmaticae, vol. 4 (Petropolis: Editora Vozes, 1939); Geraldus van Noort, Tractatus de gratia Christi, 3rd ed. (Bussum: Sumptibus Societatis Editricis Anonymae, 1920); Matthias Premm, Katholische Glaubenskunde, vol. 4 (Vienna: Herder, 1953); George D. Smith, ed., The Teaching of the Catholic Church, 6th ed., vol. 1 (New York: Macmillan, 1952); Richardo Tabarelli, De gratia Christi (Rome: M. Bretschneider, 1908); Adolphe Tanquerey, Synopsis theologiae dogmaticae, 13th ed., vol. 3 (Cincinnati: Benziger, 1911).

[1] See Johann Auer and Joseph Ratzinger, Kleine katholische Dogmatik, vol. 5 (Regensburg: F. Pustet, 1970); Charles Baumgartner, La grâce du Christ (Tournai: Desclée, 1963); Ludwig Ott, Grundriss der Dogmatik, 7th ed. (Freiburg i. Br.: Herder, 1965); Michael Schmaus, Katholische Dogmatik, 6th ed., vol. 3/2 (Munich: M. Hueber, 1965).

[2] "Luther lays far more stress on his doctrine of justification than it deserves in the sum total of Christian revelation." Friedrich Richter, Martin Luther and Ignatius Loyola, trans.

justification is no longer seen from the viewpoint of the <u>gratia habitualis</u>. The priority of justification is, however, mildly denied here also when Pesch says that the article on justification is not necessarily experienced as <u>articulus stantis et cadentis ecclesiae</u>, it is only <u>one</u> interpretation of the grace of God.[1]

Also in a recent work by Schmaus (<u>Der Glaube der Kirche</u>), justification appears as a separate part, while in contrast with his <u>Dogmatik</u>, grace--with a stress on the concept of "actual grace" --is treated in a subordinate chapter.[2]

The fact, however, that in Paul "Christian righteousness," indeed even justification, is conceded as center of theological reflection comes to expression in a few authors.[3] It is even admitted that in certain historical situations the article of justification can function as a critical instance.[4]

But Catholic theologians are skeptical about the

Leonard F. Zwinger (Westminster, MD: Newman Press, 1960), p. 96.

[1] Pesch, "Gottes Gnadenhandeln," in <u>Mysterium Salutis</u>, 4/2:904.

[2] See Michael Schmaus, <u>Der Glaube der Kirche</u>, vol. 2 (Munich: M. Hueber, 1970).

[3] "[Justice chrétienne], c'est sans doute l'essentiel de son Evangile." Ceslaus Spicq, <u>Théologie morale du Nouveau Testament</u>, 2 vols. (Paris: Lecoffre, 1965), 1:167. "Die Rechtfertigungslehre des Paulus [nimmt] mit Recht den Platz im Zentrum seiner theologischen Reflexionen ein." Karl Kertelge, <u>Rechtfertigung bei Paulus</u> (Münster/W.: Aschendorff, 1967), pp. 280, 304. "Paulus . . . [versteht] das ganze Gnadengeschehen zentral als <u>Rechtfertigungsgeschehen</u>." Pesch, "Gottes Gnadenhandeln," in <u>Mysterium Salutis</u>, 4/2:836.

[4] Ibid., p. 902.

identification of the gospel and justification.[1] Even for the most ecumenical among them it is true that justification and revelation of Christ cannot be considered as identical and that the teaching of justification is not the central doctrine of Christianity.[2]

Declaring Righteous and Making Righteous

The recognition that the non-reckoning of sin represents one aspect of justification has long been demanded of the Catholic theologian by the church dogma. In the same breath, however, the dogma forces him to identify this forensic declaration completely with effective sanctification.[3]

Justification thereby cannot occur extrinsically (circa hominem) but always only internally (in homine). Justification is not a declaration which consecutively works itself out in a making righteous (sanctification), but it is "a repair of the soul" (reparatio animae [Bonaventure]),[4] a "kind of transformation from the state of injustice to the state of justice" (transmutatio quaedam de statu injustitiae ad statum justitiae [Thomas Aquinas])[5]

---

[1] "Die Untersuchung des Terminus εὐαγγέλιον im Neuen Testament ergibt, dass er in einem sehr weiten Umfang gebraucht wird und nicht einer bestimmten Sache, etwa der Lehre von der Rechtfertigung sola fide et gratia, vorbehalten ist, gerade auch nicht beim Apostel Paulus." Franz Mussner, Praesentia Salutis (Düsseldorf: Patmos, 1967), p. 171.

[2] "Die Rechtfertigungslehre ist nicht das Zentraldogma des Christentums . . . das Zentraldogma des Christentums ist das Christusgeheimnis." Küng, Rechtfertigung, p. 128. Cf. James F. McCue, "Ecumenical Reflection on Justification," The Ecumenist 18 (1980):49.

[3] DS 1528.   [4] Sent. Lib. 4, dist. 17, p. 1, d. 4.

[5] S. Th. 1a2ae. 113, 1.

and a "passing" from the state of sin "to that of grace" (<u>translatio
. . . in statum gratiae</u> [Council of Trent]).[1] It is basically
therefore, an inner and outer removal of sin, which aims at the
aquirement of merits in order to attain future salvation.

Luther's position that righteousness of life (sanctification)
is a <u>consequence</u> of the present act of declaration (justification)
which grasps in advance the eschatological judgment-sentence
through faith--a concept for which Luther bases himself on Paul[2]--
can only with difficulty be brought into harmony with the Roman
Catholic concept of effective justification, if the final cause
(the eschatological judgment-sentence) depends on the <u>condition</u> of
the formal cause (the inherent righteousness), which is required
as a growing justification and as a salvation-working, meritoriously
effective power.[3]

From this it is understandable that in the pre-Vatican discussions the Lutheran identification of the forensic declaration with justification was represented very poorly in Catholic polemics. It is characterized as a contradiction of Paul,[4] as a cutting contradiction to the whole Bible,[5] as a contradiction to

---

[1] <u>DS</u> 1524.

[2] "Non sic, impii, dicit Paulus. Verum est sine operibus <u>solam fidem iustificare</u>, sed <u>de vera fide</u> loquor, quae, <u>postquam iustificaverit</u>, non stertet ociosa, <u>sed est per Charitatem operosa</u>." WA 40II, 37, 23-25, italics mine.

[3] <u>DS</u> 1529-1531, 1535, 1541, 1545, 1561, 1574, 1576, 1582.

[4] "Doctrine . . . manifestement étrangère et contraire à la pensée de Paul. . . ." <u>DTC</u>, s.v. "Justification, La doctrine dans saint Paul," by J. Rivière.

[5] "Mit der biblischen Auffassung von der Sündenvergebung steht also die protestantische Lehre von blosser 'Nichtanrechnung'

reason,[1] as a perversion of the Pauline thought,[2] as an invention of Luther[3] and, therefore, as a heresy.[4] Paul set forth no forensic justification, but taught the Catholic concept of justification.[5] It is erroneous to conceive of the righteousness of God as a righteousness which counts <u>before God</u>, and not as "an effusion of God's righteousness <u>upon man</u>."[6]

These strong reactions against the forensic justification for which Luther based himself on Paul,[7] still continue in the time

---

oder 'Zudeckung' in schneidendem Widerspruch. . . . Die 'Zudeckungstheorie' [ist] unbiblisch, ja widerbiblisch." Pohle and Gummersbach, <u>Dogmatik</u>, 2:700.

[1]"Die protestantische Rechtfertigung ist also eine Art <u>justificatio mere forensis</u> durch Gott. Liegt nicht darin schon von selbst ein Widerspruch? Wie kann der allwissende Gott jemand, den er mit Sünden behaftet sieht, für heilig erklären, sozusagen gegen sein besseres Wissen?" Premm, <u>Glaubenskunde</u>, 4:207.

[2]Luther has "dénaturé la pensée de l'Apôtre." Lagrange, "Commentaire de Luther sur l'épître aux Romains," <u>RB</u> 13 (1916):120.

[3]See Fernand Prat, <u>The Theology of Saint Paul</u>, trans. John L. Stoddard, 2 vols. (London: Burns, Oates & Washbourne, 1945), 1:170.

[4]"Häretisch ist die Lehre Luthers, die habituelle Gnade bestehe nur in der göttlichen Huld (<u>favor Dei</u>), die sich in der Gerechterklärung des Sünders betätige, ohne dass dieser innerlich umgewandelt werde." Diekamp, <u>Dogmatik</u>, 2:432.

[5]Bartmann, <u>Dogmatik</u>, 2:85.

[6]Max Meinertz, <u>Theologie des Neuen Testamentes</u>, 2 vols. (Bonn: P. Hanstein, 1950), 2:118-19.

[7]". . . iustificari Iustum apud Deum reputari. . . ." WA 56, 39, 9. The word "forensic" is in any case not used by Luther. Melanchthon employs "usus forensis" and "locus forensis" for the first time in the Apology (<u>BSLK</u> 209, 34;219, 43). See Werner Elert, <u>Morphologie des Luthertums</u>, 2 vols. (Munich: C. H. Beck, 1958), 1:92. Nevertheless Luther is acquainted with the matter when he speaks of the tribunal of mercy <u>coram Deo</u> (WA 34II, 140, 6-8) as well as of the judgment seat, which becomes the mercy seat (WA 36, 372, 20-21).

of the dialogue before and after Vatican II. Protestantism became unfaithful to Paul with the separation of forensic and effective righteousness,[1] and therefore Augustine also would have decidedly rejected the Reformation teaching of justification, for his teaching is the Catholic teaching.[2]

A more objective evaluation of the Pauline foundation of Luther's teaching of justification has become increasingly noticeable in recent years, and for the following reasons:

1. Because of a more unprejudiced exegesis of the words δικαιόω and δικαίωσις.

2. Because of the recognition of the results of research by many Protestant Luther specialists, such as Paul Althaus, Gerhard Ebeling, Rudolf Hermann, Wilfried Joest, Regin Prenter, and Edmund Schlink,[3] who have demonstrated that in Luther the divine declaring righteous is a creative judgment, which can be expressed with Walther von Loewenich as "making righteous through declaring righteous" (Gerechtmachung durch Gerechtsprechung).[4] Therefore in Luther the word justificatio is also used for sanctification,[5]

---

[1] Baumgartner, Grâce du Christ, p. 106.

[2] Willem H. van de Pol, Das reformatorische Christentum (Einsiedeln: Benziger, 1956), p. 399.

[3] "Denn Gottes rechtfertigendes Urteil ist niemals 'nur' Urteil, sondern dieses Urteil setzt Wirklichkeit." Edmund Schlink, Theologie der lutherischen Bekenntnisschriften, 3rd ed. (Munich: Chr. Kaiser, 1948), p. 140. Cf. Schmaus, Dogmatik, 3/2:126-27.

[4] Walther von Loewenich, Der moderne Katholizismus vor und nach dem Konzil (Witten: Luther-Verlag, 1970), p. 22.

[5] Luther sometimes uses justificari as a synonym for sanari (WA 2, 495, 2-3) and justificatio in the sense of sanctificatio, which refers to the eschatological justificatio as completion:

which however must always be interpreted as an event that follows.[1]

Pesch, for example, states emphatically that a Catholic exegete no longer has an objection when one translates δικαιοῦν with "to declare righteous," for the biblical origin of justification attests to the judicial nature of the event. Thus no one should reproach the Reformers with a "lack of biblical foundation."[2] Luther did not misunderstand Paul, but Scholasticism, which was burdened with justificare=justum facere, could not free itself from Augustine's concept of internally working grace.[3]

According to Otto Kuss, Paul makes use of a juridical-forensic expression, to which the Apostle, however, gives a completely new sense, because "to declare righteous" before God does not take place as in a human tribunal according to fixed norms, merits, and works. The person is freely awarded salvation. This declaration of righteousness is called transformation.[4]

We find a similar connection of thought also in Schmaus. According to him, justification, as Paul uses the term, means a judicial verdict. This NT meaning comes from the OT where the word "is mostly used in a forensic (juridical) sense." But judgment is not only a declarative but also a creative word. "When God declares

---

"Interim dum hic iustificamur, nondum est completa. . . . Es ist noch jhm bau." WA 39I, 252, 9-12.

[1]Pesch, Theologie der Rechtfertigung, p. 180.

[2]Idem, "Gottes Gnadenhandeln," in Mysterium Salutis, 4/2:848.

[3]Ibid.

[4]Otto Kuss, Der Römerbrief (Regensburg: F. Pustet, 1957), pp. 121-22.

a person righteous, He makes him righteous."[1]

Karl Kertelge also expresses himself in this way: "No one can deny the forensic meaning of δικαιοῦν in the LXX and in the representation of justification in Late Judaism."[2] On this concept Paul is completely dependent. But the justifying verdict possesses an effectual power, if one takes God's word seriously as a creative word.

Küng enumerates eight points which, according to him, speak unambiguously for the forensic character of justification:[3]

1. Paul uses the OT terminology which has a forensic meaning.

2. The forensic aspect of the synagogue teaching on justification remains unaffected by the Pauline-Pharisaic controversy.

3. The linguistic usage of the LXX attests to the forensic meaning. Paul uses this translation.

4. The identification of "to justify" with "to reckon as righteousness" (Rom 4:3; Gal 3:6).

5. The unambiguous forensic tone of δικαιοῦν in the eschatological contexts (Rom 2:13; 8:33).

6. The contrast between δικαιοῦν and κατακρίνειν (Rom 8:33-34) and the use of the characteristic judgment formula "before Him" (Rom 3:20) and "before God" (Rom 2:13; Gal 3:11).

---

[1] Schmaus, Glaube der Kirche, 2:574. "Wenn Gott einen Menschen für gerecht erklärt, dann macht er ihn gerecht."

[2] Kertelge, Rechtfertigung, pp. 115-16. "Niemand kann die forensische Bedeutung von δικαιοῦν in der LXX und in der Rechtfertigungsvorstellung des Spätjudentums leugnen."

[3] Küng, Rechtfertigung, p. 208.

7. The usage of δικαίωσις in contrast to κατάκριμα (Rom 5:18).

8. Finally, in all the remaining places where δικαιοῦν appears, the underlying juridical keynote speaks for the forensic meaning.

Küng even goes so far as to deny justification as a sanctifying process _in_ the person,[1] because then the fundamental character of justification as the verdict of acquittal would be endangered.[2] This is often too little regarded by Catholic exegetes for fear of having to give credit to Luther.[3]

A series of other Catholic voices demonstrates how well taken Küng's criticism is. Not everywhere is one ready to admit that Luther represents a dynamic concept of justification,[4] and that declaring righteous represents the real meaning of justification. For a large number of Catholic interpreters the ontological

---

[1] "'Rechtfertigung' ist nach dem Neuen Testament tatsächlich nicht ein physiologisch verstandener, im menschlichen Subjekt sich abspielender übernatürlicher Prozess, sondern ist das Urteil Gottes, in welchem Gott dem gottlosen Menschen seine Schuld nicht anrechnet, ihn in Christus gerecht erklärt und gerade so wirklich gerecht macht." Küng, "Katholische Besinnung," in Theologie im Wandel, p. 465.

[2] "Der forensische Charakter ist für die Rechtfertigung von fundamentaler Bedeutung, weil es nicht nur um irgendeinen physischen Vorgang im Menschen geht, sondern um ein Rechtsprechen und ein Gerechterklären, um ein Gerichtsurteil, um ein Nichtanrechnen der Sünde und ein Anrechnen der Gerechtigkeit Christi (Imputation)." Hans Küng, "Rechtfertigung und Heiligung nach dem Neuen Testament," in Begegnung der Christen, ed. Maximilian Roesle and Oscar Cullmann (Stuttgart: Evangel. Verlagswerk, 1959), p. 254.

[3] Küng, Rechtfertigung, p. 208.

[4] "Luther refuse à la justice divine l'efficacité intérieure: elle laisse le pécheur tel qu'il était et ne le purifie pas de ses souillures." François Amiot, L'enseignement de saint Paul, 6th ed., 2 vols. (Paris: Lecoffre, 1946), 1:221.

making righteous still stands in the foreground, while, as Küng explains, the making righteous really is only a subsequent event, the result of God's verdict manifesting itself in personal categories.[1]

Claude Tresmontant disputes the forensic meaning in Paul and asserts that the Apostle represented a metaphysical-theological concept of justification, which consists of the "total transformation of man."[2] Lucien Cerfaux sees a change of meaning taking place in the Christian usage of δικαιοῦν. While the word in itself actually means "declare righteous," it was changed by Christian usage into "make righteous" and thus received a new meaning.[3] Thus, in dogmatics justification can be defined as the "arrival of a form" (Ankunft einer Form [Th. A. Deman]).[4]

Hermann Volk follows a middle course, interpreting justification as declaratory judgment (spruchhaft) and as transformation (Verwandlung).[5] Thomas Sartory asks, whether Luther by his juridical concept (Judikatur Gottes) perceived the whole word of God and whether he was not simply uninterested in grace as inherent quality.[6]

---

[1] Küng, "Katholische Besinnung," in Theologie im Wandel, p. 465.

[2] Claude Tresmontant, Saint Paul and the Mystery of Christ, trans. Donald Attwater (New York: Harper Torchbooks, 1957), p. 113.

[3] Lucien Cerfaux, Le chrétien dans la théologie paulinienne (Paris: Les Editions du Cerf, 1962), p. 360.

[4] Thomas A. Deman, Der neue Bund und die Gnade. Dt. Thomasausgabe, vol. 14 (Heidelberg: F. H. Kerle, 1955), p. 411.

[5] Hermann Volk, Gesammelte Schriften, 2nd ed., 3 vols. (Mainz: M. Grünewald, 1967), 1:120.

[6] Thomas Sartory, "Gesetz und Evangelium," in Mysterium Kirche, ed. Ferdinand Holböck and Thomas Sartory, 2 vols. (Sazburg: O. Müller, 1962), 2:958.

It appears as though the conservative representatives, who see the primary aspect in the making righteous and are willing to allow only the character of a subsequent judgment sentence to the declaring righteous, are fighting a retreating battle. Küng has pointed out the weaknesses of their position when he referred to the inadmissible anthropopathism--God states with satisfaction that the one made righteous is righteous--and when he exposed the unbiblical character of such an order, since God declares the "wicked" righteous (Rom 4:5) and not the "righteous one."[1]

Although the ontological making righteous in the act of justification must always be kept in mind as a dogmatic requirement, one can agree with Reinhard Kösters that the tendencies become stronger in modern Catholic theology to consider justification primarily as a forensic event:

> Der <u>forensische Grundcharakter</u> der Rechtfertigung wird auch auf katholischer Seite mehr und mehr anerkannt. Im paulinischen δικαιοῦν ist das Urteil Gottes nicht als nachträgliches Konstatieren, sondern als ursprüngliches Konstituieren der aus Gott stammenden Gerechtigkeit des Menschen zu verstehen.[2]

Lutheran and Catholic sola fide

The well-known <u>sola</u> formulas appear very early in Luther's work: <u>Sola gratia</u>,[3] <u>sola fides</u>,[4] <u>solus Christus</u>,[5] <u>solus Deus</u>.[6]

---

[1] Küng, <u>Rechtfertigung</u>, p. 209. Cf. the contrary opinion in Thomas Aquinas (<u>S. Th.</u> 1a2ae. 113, 6-8).

[2] Reinhard Kösters, "Die Lehre von der Rechtfertigung unter besonderer Berücksichtigung der Formel 'simul justus et peccator.' <u>ZKT</u> 90 (1968):313.

[3] WA 56, 255, 19.   [4] WA 3, 320, 21; 4, 438, 4-5; 56, 172, 1.

[5] WA 56, 247, 1.   [6] Ibid., 305, 28.

They are only partly equivalent to the sola fide known from the Ancient Church and the Middle Ages. Even as early as his Lecture on the Epistle to the Romans, Luther denies any justifying efficiency not only to the works that precede justification but also to the works which follow it.

The difference between this period and later years (1518 or 1520) lies only in the fact that Luther still recognized a preparation by works for justification[1] and did not yet have final certainty about the consecutive character of the works.[2] For the idea that the sola fide is valid not only for the beginning--speaking in the Catholic way, for the first justification--but spans the whole Christian existence into the future-eschatological dimension--thus including the second justification--Luther based himself expressly on Paul.[3] Therefore he was always skeptical when the opposite side --thus, for example, Eck--asserted that it was also Catholic teaching that man is justified through faith.[4] The opponents (Catholics,

---

[1] "Immo nec opera precedentia nec sequentia Iustificant. . . . Precedentia quidem, quia preparant ad iustitiam; Sequentia vero, quia requirunt iam factam Iustificationem. Non enim Iusta operando Iusti efficimur, sed Iusti essendo iusta operamur." WA 56, 255, 15-19.

[2] According to Hans Pohlmann, Hat Luther Paulus entdeckt? ([Berlin: A. Töpelmann, 1959], pp. 25. 52), Luther still taught in 1515/16-1520 the final character of works in the sense of Augustine. Only in the work Von der Freiheit eines Christenmenschen did he arrive at the consecutive character of works. His personal breakthrough came in 1515/16 (Turmerlebnis, tower experience), and in 1520-1525 the Reformation break-away from Rome. According to Ernst Bizer, Fides ex auditu, 3rd ed. ([Neukirchen-Vluyn: Neukirchener Verlag, 1958], pp. 122, 175), both events occurred in the year 1518. Cf. also Kurt Aland, Die Reformatoren (Gütersloh: G. Mohn, 1976), p. 22.

[3] WA 11, 300, 1-10; TR 6, 151, 15-33.

[4] BR 5, 577, 11-12.

fanatics)--so he complained--had indeed learned to imitate the words, but they missed the reality.[1]

Luther found comfort in the fact that major Church Fathers --as he thought--also had taught the sola fide, although he recognized that they nevertheless had not set it forth in a completely correct manner[2] and that the sola fide was really "his dogma."[3]

He wrestled concerning this possession his whole lifetime.[4] Often he stressed that the article of justification is not so quickly learned, that he still felt like a beginner in it,[5] and that he continually learned more about it.[6] After years of study and struggle his thoughts still circled day and night about the one thing: justification of the sinner by faith alone.[7] The correct

---

[1] "Nihil ergo a nobis didicerunt quam verba recitare, rem ipsam non tenent." WA 40I, 252, 18.

[2] "Mihi valde gratum est, postquam scio, quod sola fide iustificamur, (Id enim in scriptura sancta tanquam dialecticam argumentum copiose probatum et explicatum est) quod Augustinus, Hilarius, Cyrillus, Ambrosius idem dicunt, etsi fundamenta non sic urgent, et minus proprie aliquando loquuntur." WA 43, 14, 4-8.

[3] "Hoc dogma meum: Sola fides iustificat." WA 11, 302, 22-23.

[4] Karl Barth says, for example, that probably no theologian has in this question "worked, suffered and above all prayed more" than Luther ("mehr gearbeitet, gelitten und vor allem gebetet hat"). KD 4/1:579.

[5] "Nam et ego in hoc articulo Alphabetarius discipulus sum." WA 31II, 347, 14.

[6] "Ich studir noch ymer dran, denn es ist seer schwer, das ein sunder sol sagen: Ich hab ein stuel ym himel neben S. Peter." WA 32, 93, 14-15. "Illam artem nondum novi, sed lerne noch dran." Ibid., 164, 3-4.

[7] "Nam in corde meo iste unus regnat articulus, scilicet Fides Christi, ex quo, per quem et in quem omnes meae diu noctuque fluunt et refluunt theologicae cogitationes." WA 40I, 33, 7-9.

understanding of faith and works he regarded as the high art of theology,[1] as the teaching that is to be carried to the whole world, and as that which holds the Christian church together.[2]

Relating *fides*, *spes*, and *caritas* (faith, hope, and love) to each other,[3] he created a dynamic concept of faith and restored the religious nature of the biblical πίστις concept (trust-faithfulness). By concentrating on *fiducia* as justifying element,[4] he recovered for faith its personal character.[5] He showed why only trusting faith can justify, for the God of the Covenant is not the God of the philosophers; He does not require agreement with propositions, but unreserved trust in His promises.

Nevertheless this faith is not without a cognitive dimension. It also has a knowledge of God's deeds and words. Luther discovered in the biblical historical facts the character of promise and thereby the requirement to trust and not to rely solely on information.[6]

Nor is this faith without love and works of love. It is

---

[1] "Sic primus lapis ponendus qui Christus est i.e. incipiendum a fide, quae non levis ars, sed ein hoch trefflich ding, daran homo zu lernen hundert tausent, si viveret. Deinde habes rechtschaffene opera quae sequuntur fidem." WA 29, 494, 13-16.

[2] WA 21, 219, 21-34.   [3] WA 42, 565, 29-34.

[4] See Reinhold Seeberg, *Grundriss der Dogmengeschichte*, 4th ed. (Leipzig: A. Deichert, 1919), p. 125.

[5] "Sondern das ist der recht gnadenreych glawb, den gottis wortt und werck foddert, das du festiglich glewbist, Christus sey dyr geporn, und seyne gepurt deyn sey, dyr tzu gutt geschehen." WA 10I, 71, 6-8; cf. WA 39I, 46, 3-10; 40I, 546, 18-23.

[6] See *LTK*, 2nd ed., s.v. "Glaube im protestantischen Glaubensverständnis," by W. Pannenberg.

not the Scholastic concept of "faith, being a crude and unattractive monogram" (fides monogramma rudis et insuavis), which needs the addition of love in order to become alive;[1] but faith itself is this love because it proves itself true as justifying trust in surrendering love. Thus, Luther conceives the interrelationship of faith and works in the unity of a living faith. Faith as trust grasps the promise and experiences justification; faith lived through love fulfills the commandment and demonstrates its genuineness.[2] So it comes to sola fide numquam sola--to faith that alone justifies, but it does not remain alone.[3] Thus good works are necessary to testify to faith, but they are not necessary to effectuate salvation.[4]

Protestant students of Luther believe that Luther thereby had found the correct order of faith and works.[5] Like no one before or after him, he had thought through so deeply this whole issue from

---

[1] WA 42, 565, 5-8.   [2] Ibid., 13-42.

[3] "Etiam sola fides infusa satis est ad iustificationem impii. Imo, nisi sola sit sine ullis operibus, nihil est neque iustificat. Opera sequuntur iustificationem fidei infallibiliter, cum non sit otiosa." WA 6, 85, 21-23. "Vere autem non credit, si opera Charitatis fidem non sequuntur." WA 40II, 37, 16-17.

[4] "Necessaria sunt opera gratiae, ut testentur de fide." WA 39I, 224, 1-2. "Novitas nostra est quidem necessaria, sed non ad salutem, non ad iustificationem nostram. Ad salutem seu iustificationem nostram necessaria est sola misericordia Dei, quae apprehenditur fide." Ibid., 225, 3-9.

[5] See Heinrich Bornkamm, Luthers geistige Welt, 4th ed. (Gütersloh: G. Mohn, 1960), p. 105. This is one of the firm constants from the beginning, in the otherwise very unsystematic proclamation theology of Luther. See Pesch, Theologie der Rechtfertigung, p. 304.

the viewpoint of the Scriptures,[1] that he had the support, not only of Paul, but also of the other witnesses of the NT.[2]

Can modern Catholic exegesis and dogmatics also agree to the sola fide principle? If so, in what sense? Is Luther's sola fide the same as the Catholic? If not, how far can Catholic theologians follow Luther?

In order to answer these questions, we shall consider the sola fide problem under four headings: (1) the controversial sola fide; (2) the conceded-"Catholic" sola fide; (3) the limited-"Lutheran" sola fide; and (4) the conceded-"Lutheran" sola fide.

The controversial sola fide. The representatives of the view that faith alone is not sufficient for either the first or the second justification can find support in the Council of Trent.[3] For the first justification a preparation is expressly required,[4] which indeed must be awakened by actual prevenient grace,[5] and in which the person, through cooperation, takes part.[6] This shows itself first in dogmatic faith (to hold as true), then in hope, trust, love, penitence, and in the purpose of keeping the divine

---

[1] See Albrecht Peters, Glaube und Werk (Berlin: Lutherisches Verlagshaus, 1962), p. 14.

[2] See Althaus, Theologie Luthers, p. 214; Adolf von Harnack, Lehrbuch der Dogmengeschichte, 4th ed., 3 vols. (Darmstadt: Wissenschaftliche Buchgesellschaft, 1964), 3:822; Lennart Pinomaa, Faith Victorious, trans. Walter J. Kukkonen (Philadelphia: Fortress Press, 1963), p. 78.

[3] DS 1531, 1559, 1574, 1582. "Nach Luther rechtfertigt der Glaube allein, nach dem Tridentinum sind ausser dem Glauben . . . auch noch andere übernatürliche Akte beteiligt." Martin Grabmann, "Das Konzil von Trient als Fortschrittsprinzip der katholischen Dogmatik," in Das Weltkonzil von Trient, ed. Georg Schreiber, 2 vols. (Freiburg i. Br.: Herder, 1951), 1:38.

[4] DS 1525.   [5] Ibid.   [6] Ibid.

commandments.[1] The council refused any merit <u>ex congruo</u> in the sense of Late Scholasticism (for deeds <u>ex puris naturalibus</u>)[2]--leaving open the question on congruent merit in the sense of High Scholastic Franciscan theology (for the cooperation of grace and free will).[3]

In this sense the <u>sola fide</u> even today appears very questionable, indeed, even false, to Catholic theologians.[4] This is expressed in the old Dogmatics about the turn of the century[5] as well as in the modern ecumenical dialogue.[6] These still require

---

[1] <u>DS</u> 1526.   [2] <u>DS</u> 1525.

[3] Whether the "promereri" (<u>DS</u> 1546) and "vere mereri" (<u>DS</u> 1582) intend to make clear the difference between <u>meritum de condigno</u> and <u>de congruo</u> is a dispute which pervades the confessions. While the Protestant H. A. Oberman and the Catholics J. Rivière, E. Stakemeier and E. Schillebeeckx maintain the view that the council continued the concept of congruent merit by including it in "promereri" and "vere mereri" as condign merit, the Protestant H. Rückert and the Catholic H. Küng refuse this interpretation. For Rückert "promereri" can be a synonym for "mereri" and thereby designates simply merit in the state of habitual grace with the exclusion of the congruent merit. See Heiko Augustinus Oberman, "Das tridentinische Rechtfertigungsdekret im Lichte der spätmittelalterlichen Theologie," <u>ZTK</u> 61 (1964):251-82; Edward Schillebeeckx, "Das tridentinische Rechtfertigungsdekret in neuer Sicht," <u>Conc(D)</u> 1 (1965):452; Hanns Rückert, <u>Vorträge und Aufsätze zur historischen Theologie</u> (Tübingen: J. C. B. Mohr [P. Siebeck], 1972), pp. 264-92.

[4] Richter, <u>Luther and Ignatius</u>, p. 93.

[5] "Also reicht der Glaube, mag man ihn nun als Glauben an die Offenbarung oder als Fiducialglauben fassen, ganz sicher zur Rechtfertigung nicht hin." Johann B. Heinrich and Constantin Gutberlet, <u>Dogmatische Theologie</u>, 10 vols. (Mainz: F. Kirchheim, 1896-1904), 8:506. "Dass der Glaube <u>allein</u> selig mache . . . ist nirgends, am allerwenigsten klar und <u>deutlich</u> in der hlg. Schrift enthalten." Ibid., pp. 510-11.

[6] "In allgemeiner Form, vom historischen Rahmen abgelöst, kann man unmöglich sagen, die Schrift kenne nur eine Rechtfertigung: die Rechtfertigung allein durch den Glauben." Heinrich Stirnimann, "Zur Rechtfertigung in dialektisch-katholischer Besinnung," <u>SKZ</u> 125 (1957):651.

that acts for the attainment of justification are necessary,[1] and both preparation and justification are depicted as occurrences in which the powers of grace and of the will cooperate.[2]

Since faith is wholly viewed in the Thomistic-Tridentine sense as <u>fides informis</u>[3] and needs in its initiation the cooperation of the will[4] as well as, in its preservation and increase, the cooperation of works[5]--whereby the <u>sola gratia</u> indeed includes the human participation, but through the thought of merit permits a kind of self-value (<u>Selbstgeltung</u>, <u>Selbstand</u>)[6]--naturally Luther's view of faith as <u>fiducia</u>[7] can hardly be admitted. The same is true of the origin of faith through the sinner's struggle as he disputes with God,[8] of the identity of faith and salvation[9] and therefore of the consecutive character of works. According to this theological thrust, faith can always be only <u>one</u> condition but never the <u>sole</u> cause of salvation.[10] Therefore justification occurs more through

---

[1] "Derjenige ist gerechtfertigt, der die zur Rechtfertigung geforderten Akte setzt." Premm, <u>Glaubenskunde</u>, p. 279.

[2] "[Es] besteht ein <u>geheimnisvolles Zusammenwirken</u> von Gnadenkraft und Willenskraft, von göttlichem Angebot und menschlicher Annahme." Bartmann, <u>Gnadenleben</u>, p. 96.

[3] <u>DS</u> 1526; 1562.   [4] <u>DS</u> 1526.

[5] <u>DS</u> 1535; 1541.   [6] <u>DS</u> 1546; 1547; 1582.

[7] "Fiducia in Deum." WA 1, 74, 3. "Glaub, trew, zuvorsicht des hertzen." WA 6, 209, 33-34. "Credulitas." WA 56, 227, 18. "Confidere." WA 3, 651, 17. "Hanc fidem vocamus ein kinderglaube." WA 32, 137, 16-17. "Kecklich gleuben." WA 2, 140, 19.

[8] WA 39I, 104, 22-105, 1.   [9] Ibid., 225, 6-17.

[10] See Heinrich and Gutberlet, <u>Dogmatische Theologie</u>, 8:506-507.

love than through faith.[1] The sola fide can at best be admitted with the idea that the complementary works are excluded only as selfish works, but not as selfless acts,[2] that is to say, that the Jewish works of the law are excluded.[3]

Representatives of this conservative direction therefore especially dispute the idea of fiducial faith; it seems to them "obscure, incoherent and absurd,"[4] like a "contradiction"[5] and an "imagination" (Einbildung).[6] At most, theologians of a more tolerant kind speak of "over-simplification."[7]

The entire weight of criticism falls finally upon Luther

---

[1]"Aber wenn man doch einmal a priori aus der Natur der Sache das wirksamste Mittel zur Rechtfertigung bestimmen will, so ist einleuchtend, dass der Liebe eine hervorragendere Bedeutung in der Erlangung des Heils, in der Sündenvergebung zugeschrieben werden muss, als dem Glauben oder dem Vertrauen." Heinrich and Gutberlet, Dogmatische Theologie, 8:513.

[2]"Es heisst also nicht, dass der Mensch allein durch den Glauben gerechtfertigt wird und nicht durch sein Handeln. Nicht das Tun als solches ist zur Rechtfertigung unbrauchbar, sondern eine bestimmte Art von Tun, die freilich jeder Mensch von seiner Herkunft mitbringt: das selbst-süchtige und eigengerechte Handeln, in dem die Selbsterbauung des 'Rühmens' wirksam ist." Heinrich Schlier, Der Römerbrief (Freiburg i. Br.: Herder, 1977), p. 117.

[3]"Allein auf Grund von Werken des mosaischen Gesetzes . . ." Kuss, Römerbrief, p. 177. Cf. Brinktrine, Lehre von der Gnade, p. 161. Schlier refuses this interpretation, because what is concerned is not only a Jewish-Christian but also a pagan-Christian problem. The formerly "Protestant" Schlier thereby believes he is faithful to the Pauline warning against the constant threat of works, but the "convert" Schlier means that the works cannot wholly be excluded. Römerbrief, p. 117.

[4]Prat, Theology of S. Paul, 2:233-34.

[5]DTC, s.v. "Luther," by Paquier.

[6]Premm, Glaubenskunde, p. 274.

[7]Theological Dictionary, s.v. "Sola Fide," by K. Rahner and H. Vorgrimler.

himself, for with the sola fide he changed and falsified the text of the Epistle to the Romans.[1] Paul does not say: only through faith;[2] Luther's interpretation is simply false[3] and an invention.[4] Paul's teaching is perverted into heresy[5] with the sola fide interpretation, and the Christian ethos is turned into laxity.[6] But this interpretation contradicts not only Paul but also the logical rules of thought, for--so far as a preparation for justification is

---

[1] "On sait que Luther ne s'est pas contenté de traduire πίστει 'par la foi'; il a ajouté 'seule', ce qui était une altération du texte et créait entre la foi seule et la foi avec les oeuvres une opposition qui n'est nullement en situation." Marie-Joseph Lagrange, Saint Paul. Epître aux Romains (Paris: Lecoffre, 1950), p. 79. "Mit der Heiligen Schrift trat Luther in offenen Widerspruch, wenn er Röm. 3, 28 durch Einschwärzung des Wörtchens 'allein' fälschte." Pohle and Gummersbach, Dogmatik, 2:691. "Luther hat . . . das Wort sola fide eingeschoben . . . um seine Lehre, dass der Glaube auch ohne Liebe und gute Werke rechtfertigt und selig macht, zu verteidigen. Er erkannte weder eine Pflicht noch ein Verdienst der Werke an. Er gab nur an manchen Stellen zu, dass die Werke dem Glauben als selbstverständliche Wirkung folgen." Joseph Mausbach, Katholische Moraltheologie, 11th ed., 3 vols. (Münster/W.: Aschendorff, 1960), 2:43. Cf. Joseph Bonsirven, Théologie du Nouveau Testament (Paris: Aubier-Editions Montaigne, 1951), p. 322.

[2] See Schmidt, Brückenschlag, p. 133. "Eine völlig unhaltbare Lehre." Bartmann, Gnadenleben, p. 100.

[3] See Diekamp, Dogmatik, 2:544.

[4] "Der eigentliche Erfinder der sola-fides-Lehre war Luther, der zur Beschwichtigung seiner eigenen Gewissensängste zum Zufluchtsmittel des 'alleinseligmachenden Glaubens' griff und die 'Werkheiligkeit' als pharisäisch und den Verdiensten Christi abträglich verwarf." Pohle and Gummersbach, Dogmatik, 2:688. Cf. DTC, s.v. "Justification, doctrine de la Réforme," by J. Rivière.

[5] "[Luther] verkehrte so den Gedanken des Apostels zur Häresie." Brinktrine, Lehre von der Gnade, p. 162.

[6] See Heinrich and Gutberlet, Dogmatische Theologie, 8:516; E. Towers, "Sanctifying Grace," in Teaching of the Catholic Church, ed. G. D. Smith, p. 566.

accepted--a moral movement toward God is implied which a dogmatic faith simply cannot perform, so that repentance, purpose, hope, and love must be added.[1]

A further logical difficulty in relation to the sola fide interpretation lies in the fact that Luther's material principle (sola fide) and formal principle (sola scriptura) conflict with each other, for the Scriptures know nothing of justification solely by faith, so that the material principle is not covered by the formal principle, while the formal principle already carries this problematic issue in itself, for nowhere does the sufficiency of the Scriptures emerge from the Scriptures. Each attempt to determine correctly the material principle is a repeal of the Protestant formal principle, for the theological a priori of the insufficiency of the Scriptures[2] is necessary for the correct interpretation.

Further citations concerning Luther's teaching show how little many representatives on the Catholic side, even in the most recent past, were ready to listen to Luther and to make an effort to understand his concerns. The accused was simply placed on what was regarded as the absolute Catholic foundation and ground and was therefore condemned. The fact that the sola fide is motivated by a theological concern frequently was not taken into consideration at all. Usually one fell back upon psychological arguments: Luther's teaching of justification represented a construction which served Luther's purpose. In this way the Reformer had absolved

---

[1] Cf. Ott, Dogmatik, p. 306; Dander, Summarium, 2:7.

[2] See Pohle and Gummersbach, Dogmatik, 2:693.

himself and provided peace of soul for himself which he simply could not find, with his scrupulosity, in the traditional teaching of the Church.[1]

Only among more recent Catholic research on Luther is the theological concern recognized. <u>Sola fide</u> and assurance of salvation (<u>pro me</u>!) are prepared by the individualistic tendencies of piety in the late Middle Ages. It is admitted that Luther's application has a biblical origin and that the "by faith alone" should not encourage any morally inferior life.

Luther's interpretation of Rom 3:28 is still the subject of controversy. In his struggle against justification by works Luther over-reacted. His over-reaction was provoked by the optimistic doctrine of works in Nominalism, so that in reality Luther struggled to bring down a Catholicism which was not Catholic.[2]

Therefore, even with the greatest recognition of the religious concern of Luther, a <u>sola fide</u> cannot be conceded. For "Catholic doctrine is very different . . . much more complex . . . it is not a matter of faith alone."[3]

For the conservative, mostly pre-Vatican II stream in

---

[1] "Für jeden aber ist klar, dass das neue theologische Resultat . . . ein ganz und gar auf Luther selbst abgepasstes Ergebnis war, eine Beschwichtigung in seinem eigenen persönlichen traurigen Ringen." Hartmann Grisar, <u>Martin Luthers Leben und sein Werk</u>, 2nd ed. (Freiburg i. Br.: Herder, 1927), p. 99.

[2] Lortz, <u>Reformation</u>, 1:176-88.

[3] Towers, "Sanctifying Grace," in <u>Teaching of the Catholic Church</u>, p. 566. "Luther and his followers denatured the traditional Catholic teaching by basing justification solely on faith, which they falsely defined as mere confidence or trust in the mercy of God." Joseph Pohle and Arthur Preuss, <u>Grace, Actual and Habitual</u>, 11th ed. (St. Louis, MO: Herder, 1945), p. 273.

Catholic theology of our century, Luther and Paul stand directly opposed to one another.[1] The Spanish Jesuit José M. Bover summarized in four points this contradiction and thereby the rejection of the Reformation teaching on justification:

1. Faith is not <u>fiducia</u>.

2. The <u>sola fide</u> is not found in the text of the Bible.

3. Faith is not only an act (<u>fides qua creditur</u>), but stands as a synonym for the whole salvation economy of the New Testament.

4. Justification occurs not only through faith, but also through the sacrament (baptism)--therefore there is no <u>sola fide</u>.

In order to maintain their doctrine, the Protestants must therefore seriously undermine these four points.[2]

<u>The conceded-"Catholic" sola fide</u>. Beside this static "fortress theology" exists a stream of a more open and dynamic "dialogue theology" which sees in the <u>sola fide</u> principle a "good Catholic formula"[3] and which--as we have already noticed at the beginning of this chapter--tries to appeal to Thomas Aquinas and Bernard, and even to Trent. Have the Tridentine Council fathers not also explained that the person becomes righteous through

---

[1] "[Sola fide] doctrina . . . diametralmente opuesta a las enseñanzas de San Pablo." José M. Bover, <u>Teología de San Pablo</u> (Madrid: Biblioteca de autores cristianos, 1946), p. 795.

[2] Ibid., pp. 795-802.

[3] Lortz, "Grundzüge" in <u>Reformata Reformanda</u>, 1:243; <u>Theological Dictionary</u>, s.v. "Sola fide," by K. Rahner and H. Vorgrimler; Heinrich Fries, "Die Grundanliegen der Theologie Luthers in der Sicht der katholischen Theologie der Gegenwart," in <u>Wandlungen des Lutherbildes</u>, ed. Karl Forster (Würzburg: Echter, 1966), p. 174.

faith?[1] Is it not expressly assured that faith in the first justification is beginning, foundation, and root of all righteousness and also always represents the first of all theological virtues in the second justification, through which the believer earns eternal life?[2] Have not the Council fathers in their discussions also used the sola fide formula? Indeed, not only such outsiders as were influenced by the Italian Evangelicalism and strayed dangerously near to Luther[3] but also representatives of the middle line like Cardinal Cervini[4] and defenders of Scholasticism like Domingo de Soto[5] have used this formula.[6]

Of the Council parties, the Augustinian thinkers approached the sola fide with their stress on sola gratia through Seripando,[7] while Scotists and Thomists likewise, in their way, made room for faith to have at least a first-rank position--the Scotists, according to their system, more in the preparation for justification; the

---

[1] DS 1532.   [2] DS 1532; 1535; 1546.

[3] The Englishman Richard Pate is said to have coupled the sola fide with passivity of the will, while Sanfelice La Cava carried the formula forward even to the "enslaved will" reminding of Luther. Giulio Contarini on the other hand stressed the fides caritate formata, but in Reformation framework, in that he denied to works final and meritorious character, because works are only the fruits of faith which witness to faith as the light to the sun. Contarini distinguished himself from Luther only in that he could not attribute fiducial character to the justifying faith. See Hubert Jedin, Geschichte des Konzils von Trient, 4 vols. (Freiburg i. Br.: Herder, 1951-76), 2:158-95; Hanns Rückert, Die Rechtfertigungslehre auf dem Tridentinischen Konzil (Bonn: Marcus & Weber, 1925), p. 162.

[4] See Jedin, Konzil von Trient, 2:38.   [5] Ibid., p. 98.

[6] See Eduard Stakemeier, "Trienter Lehrentscheidungen und reformatorische Anliegen," in Weltkonzil von Trient, 1:100.

[7] Jedin, Konzil von Trient, 2:157.

Thomists by the justifying infusion event itself.[1]

Thus three Catholic meanings of sola fide--which had already found their representatives in Trent--are carved out:

1. A sola fide interpretation in the sense of a strict sola gratia sine meritis at the first justification was proposed. Since all preparatory works[2] have no meritorious character and faith receives the function of the sole access to God, one could and can speak of a Catholic sola fide.

In Trent, Domingo de Soto pointed this out when he said that justification by fides informis only could not be conceded by Catholics, but that one could doubtless agree with Protestants when they exclude good works from justification, for God justifies not on the basis of merits but from pure grace.[3] In a similar way also Salmeron[4] and John of Udine agreed.[5]

Modern Catholic theologians make use of similar formulations. According to Louis Bouyer, grace is "the only origin of our salvation" (la seule origine de notre salut) and faith is "the only possible access to this unique source" (le seul accès possible à cette unique source).[6] When one grasps that everything is grace and all this comes to us via faith, then the formula "solely

---

[1] Ibid., p. 148.   [2] DS 1532.

[3] See Eduard Stakemeier, "Trienter Lehrentscheidungen," in Weltkonzil von Trient, 1:100.

[4] Rückert, Rechtfertigungslehre, p. 157.

[5] Jedin, Konzil von Trient, 2:149.

[6] Louis Bouyer, Du Protestantisme à l'Eglise, 3rd ed. (Paris: Les Editions du Cerf, 1959), p. 14.

through faith" gains a "positive value . . . [which is] perfectly orthodox from the traditional Christian standpoint" (<u>valeur positive . . . parfaitement orthodoxe du point de vue chrétien traditionnel</u>).[1] Max Seckler expresses himself similarly. He refers to the interpretation of Rom 3:28 from the time of the Fathers to the Reformation and states that the "correct understanding" of the text consists in that faith alone without performance and work is the effecting cause of justification. Faith itself, however, is a gift of grace. Only this meaning avoids "constrictions of polemical theology" (<u>kontroverstheologische Verengungen</u>).[2]

2. Since, however, faith is accompanied by hope, initial love, and penitence in preparation and by hope and love in justification, the problem arises how to bring these acts into harmony with the <u>sola fide</u>.

This question has led in the Tridentine discussions to a variant of the above meaning. Since one cannot well exclude <u>in toto</u> the acts performed on the basis of the <u>gratia praeveniens</u>, one referred the exclusion of works to Jewish works of law (Salmeron)[3] or even to only the ceremonial law (Salazar, Pasquali of Motula).[4]

3. The third possibility of meaning which we can distinguish is a <u>sola fide</u> that could have validity not only for the first but also for the second justification. When one thinks of

---

[1] Ibid., p. 15.

[2] Max Seckler, "Glaube," in <u>Handbuch theologischer Grundbegriffe</u>, ed. Heinrich Fries, 2 vols. (Munich: Kösel, 1962-63), 1:540.

[3] Rückert, <u>Rechtfertigungslehre</u>, p. 157.   [4] Ibid.

the priority of faith within the sola gratia--according to Thomas it is indeed "the first conversion to God" (prima autem conversio in Deum)[1] and, according to Trent, "beginning, foundation and root of all justification" (initium, fundamentum et radix omnis iustificationis)[2]--then faith receives in the process of justification a foundational, all-encompassing function. This is further emphasized by the fact that in the second justification, which aims at an increase of righteousness in order to attain eternal life, faith again functions as first in rank with the good works,[3] and hope and love must be added to it.[4]

In this sense Cervini interpreted faith in Trent. Both in the preparation as in the moment of justification, as well as by its outworking and increase, faith has the priority.[5]

Thus it is still interpreted today. Bouyer refers expressly to the fact that also the sola fide can be carried over to the existence of the justified one, if the works as works of grace are not excluded from faith and their worth for salvation is not denied.[6]

Kertelge points out that by his faith a person is delivered from his "self-righteousness" (Eigengerechtigkeit), so that faith represents the "principle and beginning of salvation" (Prinzip und Anfang des Heils). Any other kind of salvation principle is "radically excluded" (radikal ausgeschlossen). Faith must not be confined

---

[1] S. Th. 1a2ae. 113, 4.   [2] DS 1532.

[3] DS 1535.   [4] DS 1530; 1531.

[5] See Stakemeier, "Trienter Lehrentscheidungen," in Weltkonzil von Trient, 1:100.

[6] Bouyer, Du Protestantisme à l'Eglise, p. 149.

only to the fiducial faith; it must include also obedience as an active element with which the person fulfills the "claim of God" (Anspruch Gottes).[1]

Karl Hermann Schelkle questions whether judgment according to works and justification without works form a contradiction, as if Paul had taught a law- and grace-religion at the same time! He attempts to resolve this tension by a reference to the sola fide, which is an active principle. Work remains required; it is grace-work, which encompasses the human work, but in the judgment it is demanded of the person.[2]

In summary it can be said that Catholic theology can thoroughly concede the sola fide under certain conditions. One is aware of the Pauline character of the sentence (paulinischer Ursatz)[3] and of dealing with a formula of "Catholic tradition."[4] Therefore also with Luther there was proposed no "absolute innovation and no substantial falsification" (keine absolute Neuerung und keine sachliche Verfälschung).[5]

Stanislas Lyonnet refers to the pre-Reformation editions of the Bible, which already mention the sola fide: so, for example,

---

[1] Kertelge, Rechtfertigung, p. 225.

[2] Karl Hermann Schelkle, Theologie des Neuen Testamentes, 3 vols. (Düsseldorf: Patmos, 1968-70), 3:73.

[3] Pesch, "Gottes Gnadenhandeln," in Mysterium Salutis, 4/2:837. Cf. Kertelge, Rechtfertigung, p. 225. "Sola fide, . . . is a formulation of a particular evangelical statement." Charles Moeller, "Grace and Justification," LV 19 (1964):729, italics mine.

[4] Küng, Rechtfertigung, p. 244. Cf. Fries, "Grundanliegen der Theologie Luthers," in Wandlungen des Lutherbildes, p. 174.

[5] Schmaus, Glaube der Kirche, 2:557.

the Nuremberg German Bible (1483)--<u>nur durch den Glauben</u>; the
Italian edition (Genoa 1476; Venice 1538 and 1546)--<u>ma solo per la
fede . . . per la sola fede</u>."[1]

Catholic theologians of the present express themselves very
clearly that it is not the formula itself that separates, but rather
the sense with which the formula is accompanied.[2]

<u>The limited-"Lutheran" sola fide</u>. It must therefore be
asked, at which point the "Catholic" and the "Lutheran" <u>sola fide</u>
still begin to separate from each other even today.

According to what has already been stated one could conclude
that the faith concept (<u>fiducia</u> or <u>assensus</u>) represents what really
separates.

But right in the process of thinking through what faith
really means, Catholic theology currently makes a noticeable change
of direction. The rediscovery of the existential nature of biblical faith demanding a decision of the whole person, is being recognized more and more; while often faith as an act of assent is explained as a partial moment of a subordinate function.

In short, one again considers the Augustinian breadth of
faith in which "to believe in God" (<u>credere in Deum</u>) always was

---

[1] Stanislas Lyonnet, <u>Quaestiones in Epistolam ad Romanos</u>
(Rome: Pontificio Istituto Biblico, 1955), p. 145.

[2] "Inde concludere licet non tam formulam esse vitiosam quam sensum quem protestantes postea ei tribuerunt." Ibid. Cf. Schmaus, <u>Glaube der Kirche</u>, 2:557; Lortz, "Grundzüge," in <u>Reformata Reformanda</u>, 1:243. Whether this separation has a church-splitting character is debated in present Catholicism. F. Richter sees positions that cannot be united (<u>Luther and Ignatius</u>, pp. 79, 82). E. Iserloh holds that <u>sola fide</u> is not church-splitting ("Luthers Stellung in der theologischen Tradition," in <u>Wandlungen des Lutherbildes</u>, pp. 46-47).

more than simply "to believe God" (<u>credere Deo</u>).[1] <u>Credere</u> as "to give one's heart" (<u>cor dare</u>) corresponds to the trustful surrender of the whole person[2] and thereby comes close to the active, dynamic fiducial faith of Luther.

Faith is defined as an attitude in which "the whole existential reality of man" (<u>toute la réalité existentielle de l'homme</u>) is involved.[3] The whole person must engage himself in the act of the decision of faith.[4] Faith means a "total human commitment" (<u>eine menschliche Gesamthaltung</u>) in which the whole person turns away from his past and turns to God.[5]

In the OT the element of trust dominates; in the NT that of obedience,[6] but faith is always "the gift of oneself to God" (<u>le don que l'homme fait de lui-même à Dieu</u>).[7]

This existential trait is the deciding one; mental assent

---

[1] Augustinus <u>Enarratio in Ps.</u> 77. 8 (<u>PL</u> 36:988).

[2] "Man believes with his heart and so is justified. . . . The <u>heart</u> is not just a part of man . . . it is the symbol of the center and unity of man . . . <u>the whole man</u> . . . faith signifies an entirely new way of existing in the world." Norbert Brox, <u>Understanding the Message of Paul</u>, transl. Joseph Blenkinsopp (Notre Dame: University of Notre Dame Press, 1968), pp. 86-87. On the other hand, e.g., Feuling: "[Der Glaube] hat die Gestalt menschlicher Vernünftigkeit oder Rationalität." <u>Glaubenslehre</u>, p. 39.

[3] Léopold Malevez, <u>Pour une théologie de la foi</u> (Paris: Desclée de Brouwer, 1969), p. 164.

[4] Seckler, "Glaube," in <u>HThG</u>, 1:540.

[5] Schmaus, <u>Glaube der Kirche</u>, 2:554.

[6] Malevez, <u>Théologie de la foi</u>, p. 165. Cf. <u>DSp</u>, s.v. "Foi," by André de Bovis.

[7] <u>DSp</u>, s.v. "Foi," by André de Bovis.

(Fürwahrhalten) is of subordinate significance.[1] In the Epistle to the Hebrews, for example, trust and belief interpenetrate each other in "indissoluble perichoresis" (unauflösliche Perichorese). With the modern Protestant definition of faith as "commitment" (Hingabe)[2] a difference seems to no longer exist.

That this meaning is already drawing nearer to Luther's is unmistakable. Indeed, for Luther, faith as trust is already justification and not merely its condition.[3] Faith can coexist with

---

[1] H. Fries distinguishes "Du-Glauben" from "Dass-Glauben." The "Du-Glaube" is primary, the "Dass-Glaube" secondary. See Seckler, "Glaube," in HThG, 1:541. "This is no mere intellectual assent to a set of propositions but a commitment of one's entire being." NCE, s.v. "Justification," by D. M. Crossan. "Faith brings with it a challenge and a demand: it is meant to be more than the acceptance of some abstract and remote truths. . . . Man believes with his heart and so is justified." Brox, Understanding Paul, p. 86. "Glauben nach der Bibel heisst, sich Gott mit der ganzen Person unterstellen . . . das feste Fürwahrhalten dessen, was Gott geoffenbart hat, erscheint dann eher wie ein Teilmoment." Rudolf Schnackenburg, Christliche Existenz nach dem Neuen Testament, 2 vols. (Munich: Kösel, 1967), 1:63. "'Glaube' ist nach dem Neuen Testament nicht ein intellektuelles Für-wahr-halten von Wahrheiten, sondern die vertrauende Hingabe des ganzen Menschen an Gott." Küng, "Katholische Besinnung," in Theologie im Wandel, p. 465. (After the withdrawal of the missio canonica and the explanation of Cardinal Ratzinger that Küng "vertrete nicht mehr den katholischen Glauben," the question must be answered: How much validity does Küng still have as a speaker to our considerations? Since he was reproached above all for his attacks on the infallibility of the Church, his contempt for the teaching office, and christological and mariological errors, and because his statements on the doctrine of justification remained unattacked, we believe that we can continue to cite him on this question as a Catholic teacher. Küng was exhibited as a witness to genuine Catholicity by K. Rahner and others after the appearance of his book "Rechtfertigung." See Karl Rahner, "Zur Theologie der Gnade," TQ 138 [1958]:43; Heinrich Fries, "Hans Küng. Rechtfertigung," TQ 136 [1956]:357. On the question of the withdrawal of Küng's missio canonica, see Orien. 44 [1980]: 3-8).

[2] See ThWNT, s.v. "πιστεύω," by R. Bultmann. Differences from many Catholic theologians lie in the Catholic stress, which can still be found, on the fides dogmatica as "caractère principal." See DSp, s.v. "Foi," by André de Bovis.

[3] "At fides iam est gratia iustificans." WA 57III, 191, 24.

sin only if through Christ it achieves penitence and forgiveness, sanctification and victory, for faith and Christ are one;[1] but Luther also can name faith new-birth,[2] obedience[3] and new life.[4] Complete trust works itself out in total surrender, because God has also given Himself totally to the person! So Luther can designate faith as service to God,[5] as all-encompassing life-consummation, through which the Christian who has experienced Christ now is to become himself "Christ" for his neighbour.[6]

It is understandable, therefore, that--so far as the debate in justification over the concept of faith is concerned--contemporary Catholic theologians sometimes designate the whole discussion as "almost purely verbal."[7]

Where, however, does the distinction then lie between the Lutheran and the Catholic sola fide? What permits us really to speak of a reduced sola fide?

---

[1] Luther sets up the comparison: "Christus seu fides Christi" (WA 3, 649, 16). This he can do because faith is "fides apprehensiva" (WA 39I, 45, 21), that is, it grasps Christ and lives with Christ.

[2] "Iustificatio est revera regeneratio quaedam in novitatem." WA 39I, 48, 14. Cf. DB 7, 10, 6-9; WA 47, 14, 7-10; 50, 250, 15-19.

[3] WA 56, 249, 27. Faith is "furnehmist werck . . . heubtwergk." WA 6, 204, 3; 206, 15.

[4] "Hanc fidem comitatur initium creaturae novae, et pugna contra carnis peccatum, quod eadem fide Christi et ignoscitur et vincitur." WA 39I, 83, 39-40.

[5] "Fides est vere latria et primi mandati primum opus." WA 5, 394, 33-34. "Es ist kein ander Gottesdienst denn allein glauben." WA 32, 53, 19-20.

[6] WA 7, 35, 20-35.

[7] Theological Dictionary, s.v. "Fiducial Faith," by K. Rahner and H. Vorgrimler.

The basis lies in that--and this seems to be the reason why the formula found no grace in the eyes of the Tridentine Council majority--that it is not able to cover completely the Catholic justification event; that in the Catholic view it simply seems too narrow.

Why this must be so, we have already indicated. For even if faith receives priority everywhere, it is still not the only cause of salvation; it is just *one* condition.

In Trent this was, e.g., so formulated by Bertano that he said justification occurs not *ex fide*, but only *per fidem*.[1] Hope and love must be added to faith.[2]

However, the question of the tendency of the living, active faith seems to us even more important. For, if contemporary Catholic theologians put love wholly on the side of faith[3] and thereby come close to Luther, still the basic question is not yet answered: consecutive or final?

In Trent, theologians like Bertano have put it this way: Works are not only a sign, but a constitutive element of justification.[4] Therefore, Luther's teaching of the consecutive character of works was condemned and the final, even meritorious character of works was affirmed,[5] whereby good works function not only in fulfillment of the commandments of God but also of the Church.[6]

---

[1] Jedin, *Konzil von Trient*, 2:154.   [2] Ibid., 2:155.

[3] Rahner, "Theologie der Gnade," *TQ* 138 (1958):58; Pesch, "Gottes Gnadenhandeln," in *Mysterium Salutis*, 4/2:862.

[4] Jedin, *Konzil von Trient*, 2:155.

[5] *DS* 1574; 1576; 1581; 1582.   [6] *DS* 1535.

For the majority of modern Catholic theologians, the borderline lies here: practical faith cooperates for salvation and possesses meritorious character, since it includes a person's free will in acceptance and activity.

The convert Willem H. van de Pol focused on this central point of the controversy when he said:

> Katholiken, die zunächst mit Erstaunen von dem Nachdruck hören, mit welchem ein Protestant von Heiligung und guten Werken spricht, werden sich deshalb sehr irren, wenn sie meinen, das bedeute eine Annäherung an die katholische Kirche. Denn es geht nicht um die Frage Werke oder nicht; es geht um folgende zwei Fragen:
> 1. ob die guten Werke aus dem Glaubensakt hervorgehen oder aus der innewohnenden Gnade;
> 2. ob die guten Werke die Frucht oder der Grund der Rechtfertigung sind.[1]

The Catholic majority is concerned, therefore--apparently on the basis of the Tridentine dogma--with finality (the first justification as a precondition for achieving the second, eschatological justification) and with the meritorious nature of works (the possibility that through grace indwelling in man the work can be defined at the same time as meritorious performance of man and of grace).

Although Luther can concede no prepration for justification, Catholic theology is able to assert a kind of consensus for the first justification through the already mentioned comparison of sola fide with the unmeritoriousness of works before and in

---

[1] Van de Pol, *Reformatorisches Christentum*, p. 420, italics mine. Peter Manns: "Die Problematik beginnt da, wo er [Luther] das 'konsekutive' Verhältnis der Liebe und ihrer Werke gegenüber Gnade und Glaube so ausschliesslich zu gestalten scheint, dass jeder finale Bezug der Charitas im Hinblick auf das Heil um der Gnade willen unmöglich wird." "Fides absoluta-Fides incarnata," in *Reformata Reformanda*, 1:292.

justification. This allows it even to use the sola fide formula, although Trent rejected it.[1]

Had Sanfelice La Cava not proposed before the council: "By faith alone we acquire God's grace and justification" (Nos sola fide acquirimus gratiam Dei et iustificationem).[2] In a similar way today H. Schütte speaks:

> Wir werden umsonst gerechtfertigt, gerechtgesprochen ohne unser Verdienst. Den Weg zum Heil erschliesst allein der Glaube; und dieser Glaube kommt nicht zustande ohne die Gnade, ja ohne die Gnade vermögen wir auch nicht das Geringste zum Heile.[3]

The real controversy begins there, where it concerns the works post iustificationem. The definition of La Cava, "Through charity and hope which follow justification, we acquire life eternal" (Sed caritate et spe quae iustificationem subsequentur, acquirimus vitam aeternam), which was enclosed in the above quotation, may seem awkward to many modern Catholic theologians--since they can prove that also in the second justification priority is given to faith--but nevertheless the statement shows clearly that justification in the Catholic view is only an enabling, with the help of

---

[1]DS 1559.   [2]See Lyonnet, Quaestiones, p. 143.

[3]Heinz Schütte, Um die Wiedervereinigung im Glauben (Essen: Fredebeul & Koenen, 1958), p. 68. Cf. Küng, Rechtfertigung, pp. 245-46; Bouyer, Du Protestantisme à l'Eglise, p. 14. These statements, which echo the Reformation, are indeed not so formulated by all Catholic theologians. Schmaus (Glaube der Kirche, p. 551) remarks expressly: "Diese Vorbereitung ist eine Tat Gottes und eine Tat des Menschen zugleich. Gott wirkt nicht allein," (italics mine). "Justification is not solely the action of God, in other words, but a process in which man participates." Gregory Stevens, The Life of Grace (Englewood Cliffs, NJ: Prentice Hall, Inc., 1963), p. 57, italics mine. Jedin sees in the human cooperation in the preparation for justification even the "springenden Punkt" of the discussion. See August Franzen, ed., Um Reform und Reformation (Münster/W.: Aschendorff, 1968), p. 41.

grace and also through other theological virtues, which become concrete in works, to procure eternal life. Works remain--scholastically speaking--<u>actus salutares</u>.

In this final sense the distinction emerges. For these works are, on the basis of the <u>gratia sanctificans</u>, not simply <u>only</u> final like the acts of preparation for attaining justification; they are <u>final-meritorious</u> and express, because they are works of grace <u>and</u> of man, the cooperation of the believer in the attainment of his future salvation.

If it were only a matter of the performing of good works through God's grace in the life of the believer, one could--after the modern Catholic research has acknowledged this for the person[1] and the teaching[2] of Luther--limit the dialogue to the problem of the preparation for justification, or to the justification event. Since the Catholic dogma here does not explicitly mention meritoriousness, often, too hastily, a conclusion is drawn that there is agreement in justification. For Luther, however, it is important that the person also stands in the judgment before God with the <u>sola fide</u>, and <u>sola fide</u> receives eternal life.[3]

Therefore one must always keep in mind the final-meritorious character of obedience when Catholic theologians state that the works of grace <u>post justificationem</u> must be emphasized as an

---

[1] See Lortz, <u>Reformation</u>, 1:191.

[2] See August Hasler, <u>Luther in der katholischen Dogmatik</u> (Munich: M. Hueber, 1968), pp. 195-96; Pesch, <u>Theologie der Rechtfertigung</u>, pp. 308-17.

[3] See Ole Modalsli, <u>Das Gericht nach den Werken</u> (Göttingen: Vandenhoeck & Ruprecht, 1963), p. 34.

unavoidable Pauline demand.[1] The Apostle had only excluded the unchristian, Jewish, or heathen works <u>before</u> grace from the attainment of salvation, but not the Christian works <u>after</u> grace.[2] Without the salvation-attaining works, the eschatological redemption is not obtainable for present Catholic theology,[3] even if today the formula of the <u>fides caritate formata</u> is rarely applied.

We are still facing the same basic question with which the

---

[1] "At certo Apostolus excludere non intendit <u>opera post iustificationem</u>, quae in omnibus suis epistolis a fidelibus exigit." Lyonnet, <u>Quaestiones</u>, p. 148. "One might say that for Paul justification and salvation (life, holiness) are gratuitous gifts of God, but that while the moment of justification is by faith alone, the life that follows in Christ is by a faith that works through Christ's charity." <u>NCE</u>, s.v. "Justification," by D. M. Crossan. Cf. Kuss, Römerbrief, p. 177; Lagrange, <u>Epître aux Romains</u>, p. 45; Amiot, <u>Enseignement de S. Paul</u>, 1:273.

[2] See Schmidt, <u>Brückenschlag</u>, pp. 136-37; Bronx, <u>Understanding Paul</u>, p. 102. <u>LTK</u>, 2nd ed., s.v. "Rechtfertigung. Altes Testament, Judentum, Neues Testament und bibl. theol. Problematik," by R. Schnackenburg.

[3] See Schmidt, <u>Brückenschlag</u>, pp. 142, 146-47, 158, 187; Baumgartner, <u>Grâce du Christ</u>, pp. 115, 214. Many formulations, however, appear to be open fully to the Reformation concept. For example: "Kein Werk, also auch nicht ein Werk der Liebe, rechtfertigt den Menschen." Or: "Es gibt Werke der Liebe; auch sie sind aus der Rechtfertigung ausgeschlossen, obwohl der Glaube des Gerechtfertigten in der Liebe tätig sein muss." Küng, "Rechtfertigung und Heiligung," in <u>Begegnung</u>, p. 261. Here love is separated from works and placed wholly on the side of faith. Cf. Rahner, "Theologie der Gnade," <u>TQ</u> 138 (1958):58; Pesch, "Gottes Gnadenhandeln," in <u>Mysterium Salutis</u>, 4/2:862. Thereby modern Catholic theology--as we have already tried to show--wins a dynamic, Luther-like concept of faith. Do both sides mean the same thing thereby? If Luther thinks of love together with faith, then love follows faith (WA 49, 784, 33-34); the justifying element is the trusting Yes to God's deed of salvation in Christ. <u>Sola misericordia</u>! (TR 6, 149, 13). If also Christian love, as Küng and Rahner say, "von sich wegblickt" and is wholly directed to God, still it has degrees (<u>S. Th</u>. 2a2ae. 24, 5-6)). Where these degrees are the condition for redemption--assurance of salvation is impossible--for <u>fides perfecta, charitas imperfecta</u>! (WA 39II, 214, 1-17). Salvation is then again dependent on the person, even if on the one who has received grace.

Reformation was confronted in the first place, that the sola fide in the Catholic view really has no absolute validity, that it must be limited to the beginning of first grace or, perhaps, have primary position in second grace, and that the works made possible by grace, which follow faith, must be considered as the real foundation of divine acceptance in the judgment.[1]

According to Catholic understanding Luther simply forgot the principle of cooperation[2] and in an unjustified way transferred the Pauline mission situation to the Christian ecclesiological condition of his time.[3] On this basis the sola fide was frequently defined as only a synonym for Christendom.[4]

Thereby, however, as we have already seen, the problem is only deferred from justification to sanctification, if this Protestant ordo salutis may be brought into the discussion. It is

---

[1] Melanchthon notes strikingly on this point in the Apologie: "Sed nonnulli fortassis, cum dicitur, quod fides iustificet, intelligunt de principio, quod fides sit initium iustificationis seu praeparatio ad iustificationem, ita ut non sit ipsa fides illud, quo accepti sumus Deo, sed opera, quae sequuntur et somniant fidem ideo valde laudari, quia est principium." BSLK 174, 21-28.

[2] Lortz, Reformation, 1:187. Luther's doctrine of the sole agency of God is still rejected by the majority of contemporary Catholic theologians. It is called "Überspitzung" (Schmaus), "Fatalismus" (Wacker), "Grundübel Luthers" (Lortz), "Kurzschluss" (H. J. Schmidt), "Häresie" (L. Bouyer), "unchristlich" (J. Lortzing). See Martin Bogdahn, Die Rechtfertigungslehre Luthers im Urteil der neueren katholischen Theologie (Göttingen: Vandenhoeck & Ruprecht, 1971), p. 94.

[3] It is said to be the mistake of the Reformation to interpret the formula "without law" as "without work." "Understanding it as all law-observance and the relevance for salvation of any Christian good work--and concluded that neither is necessary for salvation." Brox, Understanding Paul, p. 103.

[4] See Heinrich and Gutberlet, Dogmatische Theologie, 8:507; Diekamp, Dogmatik, 2:544; Pohle and Gummersbach, Dogmatik, 2:692.

here that Catholic theology has a difficult time bringing the sola
fide together with the fides formata, the works of grace, the merits,
and the eschatological justification to one common denominator.

Nevertheless, some theologians like Küng and Pesch are
able to work out well the sequences faith-works,[1] faith-love,[2]
justification-sanctification,[3] and even to draw conclusions therefrom, completely in the sense of Luther.[4]

An essentially different picture is gained if one reads
Rahner's criticism of this procedure. Although he agreed with the
early Küng, he still made it very clear that justification and
sanctification are not two stages in sequence, but two sides of
one and the same event. Rahner bases his ideas in this matter on
the "Scriptures, the traditional interpretation in Catholic theology
and the Council of Trent."[5] Therefore love also finds room in
justification,[6] and the Lutheran sola fide falls back again into
its limited sense. It is thus more a sola gratia than a sola fide.
Viewed thus, Schnackenburg is correct when he says:

> Die Ausdrucksweise "durch Glauben allein" erkennen auch

---

[1] See Pesch, "Gottes Gnadenhandeln," in Mysterium Salutis, 4/2:862, 875.

[2] See Küng, Rechtfertigung, p. 256.

[3] Idem, "Rechtfertigung und Heiligung," in Begegnung, pp. 269-70.

[4] "Gerechtfertigt wird der Mensch ohne Werke, allein durch den Glauben. Gerichtet aber wird er nach den Werken der Heiligung . . . in ihnen erweist sich die Echtheit des Glaubens." Ibid., p. 267, italics mine.

[5] Rahner, "Theologie der Gnade," TQ 138 (1958):53.

[6] Ibid., p. 59.

Katholiken als paulinisch an; aber damit ist noch kein volles Einverständnis über den Rechtfertigungsvorgang erzielt, und die Mitwirkung des Menschen zum Heil bleibt kontrovers.[1]

The conceded-"Lutheran" sola fide. After reading Schnackenburg's statement, it seems almost superfluous to question any further or to seek for a perhaps conceded-Lutheran sola fide in today's Catholic interpretation. And yet we are forced to do so, because there are statements in the present-day Catholic theology that threaten to destroy everything that has been said so far, and that come so near to Luther's sola fide concept that borderlines are now hardly visible.

The fact that leading contemporary Catholic Luther-researchers must grant the Reformer extensive confirmation on this point is felt by some to be burdensome,[2] but by others to be emancipating.

Daniel Olivier sees in Luther's vindication the necessary purification of the Catholic doctrine from legalism[3] and thus sees in justification by faith the needed support which has preserved the Church in the time of the Apostles in its Orthodoxy and Orthopraxy.[4] At any rate, according to Hermanus Fiolet, Luther's turn from sola gratia to sola fide is of "biblical originality."[5]

With the consistent uncoupling of work and salvation by

---

[1]Schnackenburg, Neutestamentliche Theologie, p. 96, italics mine. Cf. Fries, "Grundanliegen der Theologie Luthers," in Wandlungen des Lutherbildes, p. 175-76.

[2]Pesch, "Gottes Gnadenhandeln," in Mysterium Salutis, 4/2:859.

[3]Olivier, Foi de Luther, pp. 238-41.   [4]Ibid., p. 247.

[5]Hermanus A. M. Fiolet, Die zweite Reformation (Graz: Styria, 1971), p. 108.

Luther, a modern approach to the problem of Christian ethic is now possible, for "if justification means assurance of God's mercy, it relieves man of all radical care for himself . . . [and] makes him free to be ready for service in the world."[1]

The representatives of this ecumenical spearhead are also ready to present their agreement theologically:

1. The biblical trend in today's Catholic theology enables one to accept Luther's way of stating that God accepts the sinner and to avoid the Scholastic-Tridentine manner of speaking of the disposition, produced by grace, for justification.[2] Luther's comparison of creation and redemption (<u>Nihil et omnia sunt unseres Herrgotts materia</u>)[3] is called upon for the justification doctrine.[4] Thereby even the word "sole agency" (<u>Alleinwirksamkeit</u>)[5] can be used, although as a rule it is omitted.[6] The Tridentine talk of "cooperation" is avoided for the whole justification process.[7] The works of the Christian are simply "obedience" (<u>Gehorsam</u>),[8] not any

---

[1] Pesch, "Gottes Gnadenhandeln," in <u>Mysterium Salutis</u>, 4/2: 885. "Wenn Rechtfertigung Gewisswerden des Erbarmens Gottes bedeutet, dann befreit sie den Menschen von aller radikalen Sorge um sich selbst . . . [und] macht ihn frei, sich dem Dienst in der Welt zu stellen."

[2] Ibid., 4:849; Kertelge, <u>Rechtfertigung</u>, p. 225.

[3] WA 39I, 470, 1-2.

[4] Pesch, "Gottes Gnadenhandeln," in <u>Mysterium Salutis</u>, 4/2: 849-50.

[5] Ibid., 4/2:862.

[6] Küng, <u>Rechtfertigung</u>, p. 258; Schmaus, <u>Glaube der Kirche</u>, 2:551.

[7] Kertelge, <u>Rechtfertigung</u>, pp. 254-58.

[8] Ibid., pp. 200-01.

"collaboration" (<u>Mitwerken</u>), but "involvement" (<u>Mitmachen</u>)."[1]

2. Justification and sanctification can therefore be set forth as two successive stages.[2]

3. The <u>sola fide</u> has validity because it is supported by the <u>solo Christo</u>, for faith is wholly from God, Christ and the Holy Spirit. And that means again that every "self-achievement" (<u>Eigenleistung</u>) of the person in preparation for and in carrying out justification is excluded.[3] Thus there is also no work of love which justifies.[4]

4. The <u>sola fide</u> might also be supported by the <u>solo verbo</u>. Here, of course, the ecumenical scholars must speak of a "non settled controversy" (<u>nicht erledigte Kontroverse</u>)[5] for the Catholic thought of sacraments stands opposite the <u>solum verbum</u>. However, scholars refer to the present efforts to overcome the impersonal grace- and sacrament-understanding and assert that through the emphasis on Scripture at Vatican II, Luther really "has found his Council" (<u>Luther hat sein Konzil gefunden</u>).[6]

---

[1] Küng, <u>Rechtfertigung</u>, p. 257. Cf. Fries, "Grundanliegen der Theologie Luthers," in <u>Wandlungen des Lutherbildes</u>, p. 176.

[2] Küng, "Rechtfertigung und Heiligung," in <u>Begegnung</u>, pp. 269-70.

[3] Pesch, "Gottes Gnadenhandeln," in <u>Mysterium Salutis</u>, 4/2:860.

[4] Küng, "Rechtfertigung und Heiligung," in <u>Begegnung</u>, p. 261.

[5] Pesch, "Gottes Gnadenhandeln," in <u>Mysterium Salutis</u>, 4/2:863.

[6] Albert Brandenburg, <u>Martin Luther gegenwärtig</u> (Munich: F. Schöningh, 1969), pp. 137-41, 146.

5. Good works appear in this interpretation wholly in Luther's sense as "fruit" (Frucht),[1] as "accomplishment of the law without law" (gesetzlose Erfüllung des Gesetzes[2] or lex sine lege![3]) and as "proof of faith" (Bewährung des Glaubens).[4] Catholic researchers on Luther, such as Pesch, take a position also in reference to the inner-Protestant controversies in the framework of the discussion with the Reformer. The question whether Luther taught the tertius usus legis, as Althaus and Joest assert[5] and Elert and Ebeling deny,[6] is interpreted in such a way that Luther does not really know the "issue" (Sache) but doubtless the "concern" (Anliegen)[7] of the usus didacticus. In contrast to this, the Scholastic manner of speaking of the gospel as lex nova,[8] through which the person can become righteous,[9] is overcome by such assertions as: "[The] persistence on the principle of law and

---

[1] Pesch, "Gottes Gnadenhandeln," in Mysterium Salutis, 4/2: 849; cf. WA 39I, 106, 24-25.

[2] Küng, "Rechtfertigung und Heiligung," in Begegnung, p. 267.

[3] WA 56, 203, 11; 39I, 433, 1.

[4] Küng, "Katholische Besinnung," in Theologie im Wandel, p. 465; Peter Bläser, "Gesetz und Evangelium," Cath(M) 14 (1960): 19. Cf. WA 10III, 225, 19.

[5] See Althaus, Theologie Luthers, p. 238; Wilfried Joest, Gesetz und Freiheit, 2nd ed. (Göttingen: Vandenhoeck & Ruprecht, 1956), pp. 129, 131-33.

[6] See Werner Elert, Das christliche Ethos, 2nd ed. (Hamburg: Furche, 1961), pp. 386-97; Gerhard Ebeling, "Zur Lehre vom triplex usus legis in der reformatorischen Theologie," TLZ 75 (1950):235-46; RGG, 3rd ed., s.v. "Luther-Theologie," by G. Ebeling.

[7] Pesch, Theologie der Rechtfertigung, p. 73.

[8] S. Th. 1a2ae. 106, 1.   [9] Ibid., 2.

therefore the reiteration of 'self-justice', [is] principally excluded by faith."[1]

Indeed it is stressed again and again that one should not unthinkingly carry over the mission situation of Paul to the ecclesiological situation of any period of Christianity,[2] but that there is an ever-present danger of a Christian work-righteousness. Pesch, for example, asks whether it may not be possible also that the good works of the Christian can "become autonomous" (verselbständigen) and thereby become a "post-condition" (Nachbedingung) of grace. Once they become a post-condition they could finally also again become a pre-condition (Vorbedingung) of grace.[3] This would surely be no "repristination" (Repristinierung) of the historical Pauline proclamation but a breaking-in of legalism and Judaism into the Church. At least the Reformers believed that they were facing this situation.[4]

6. Some Catholic theologians approach the Lutheran sola fide most closely when they, like the Reformer, separate works from salvation, denying them salvific efficacy[5] and ascribing to them merely an altruistic character.[6]

---

[1] Kertelge, Rechtfertigung, p. 224. "[Die] Beharrung auf dem Gesetzesprinzip und damit die Wiederholung der 'Eigengerechtigkeit', [ist] durch den Glauben grundsätzlich ausgeschlossen."

[2] See Brox, Understanding Paul, p. 103; Pesch, "Gottes Gnadenhandeln," in Mysterium Salutis, 4/2:837.

[3] Pesch, "Gottes Gnadenhandeln," in Mysterium Salutis, 4/2:838.

[4] Ibid.   [5] Kertelge, Rechtfertigung, p. 258.

[6] Pesch, "Gottes Gnadenhandeln," in Mysterium Salutis, 4/2:885.

Kertelge points out that the justification indicative--the fact that the believer is righteous--is the basis for the related imperative--the demand to act righteously--and not the reverse. The works of the Christian have no salvation-appropriating significance but rather salvation-preserving significance.[1]

Pesch goes one step further and asserts that in the Catholic tradition there is really no "coupling" (Verkoppelung)[2] of work and salvation. Since for the Catholics also, works mean "necessary consequence of faith" (sachnotwendige Folge des Glaubens)[3] and Luther recognizes a judgment according to works, there can be no contradiction between the two.[4]

If one reviews the various meaning of sola fide in current Catholic theology (major denial of the formula before Vatican II, stress on the Catholic content in more recent times, and finally the approach toward the Lutheran sense), one could say with von Loewenich that the old Catholic reproach--that one cannot differentiate between that which is actually definitive for Protestants and that which is not--now returns to Catholic theology, since evidently the question of "What is Catholic?" can no longer be answered unambiguously.[5]

---

[1] Kertelge, Rechtfertigung, p. 258. Luther would probably say "heilsbezeugend." Cf. WA 39I, 292, 10-12; 39II, 248, 11-15; 10III, 225, 35.

[2] Pesch, "Gottes Gnadenhandeln," in Mysterium Salutis, 4/2: 885.

[3] Ibid., 4/2:860.

[4] Ibid., 4/2:885.

[5] Walther von Loewenich, "Ist Küng noch katholisch?" in Fehlbar, ed., Hans Küng (Zurich: Benziger, 1973), p. 18.

But one should not forget that today--as indicated above--
the Catholic interpretation of Luther moves forward in two main
streams: "<u>Historiker</u>" and "<u>Systematiker</u>." The "systematicians,"
who come so close to Luther's interpretation of Paul that they
appear to separate themselves in speech and content from the
Catholic dogma, are reproached by the "historians" that they were
afraid to measure Luther "unmistakably and clearly by Catholic
truth" (<u>unmissverständlich und klar an der katholischen Wahrheit</u>).[1]

This "Catholic truth" attains, as far as justification is
concerned, its peak in the aspect of merit. The final character of
works attributes to man's activities a salvation-attaining significance, even though the whole process is encompassed by grace.[2]
But the meriting character still makes it plain that in the case
of a <u>meritum de condigno</u>--in the Thomistic view, anyway--there is
"a kind of juridical relationship" (<u>quidam justitiae modus</u>)[3] between performance and reward, since both possess an inner correspondence similar to that of the seed and the tree in nature.[4]
Indeed, the performance comes into being only through grace,[5] but
the person is a participant in it in a double sense: (1) because
he cooperates through the free will[6] and (2) because grace inwardly
is "inherent" in him as "quality."[7]

---

[1] Peter Manns, <u>Lutherforschung heute</u> (Wiesbaden: F. Steiner, 1967), p. 40.

[2] <u>DS</u> 1541; <u>S. Th</u>. 1a2ae. 109, 5 ad 1.

[3] <u>S. Th</u>. 1a2ae. 114, 1.   [4] Ibid., 114, 4 ad 3; 109, 5.

[5] Ibid., 114, 2.   [6] Ibid., 114, 1 ad 1.

[7] The <u>gratia gratum faciens</u> which is received in justification

Luther rejected this as "ruin of the whole theology" (ruina universae theologiae) and as "ignorance of Christ and His cross" (ignorantia Christi et crucis eius).[1] He called the merit-theologians "self-righteous people" (iustitiarii)[2] those who do not wish to allow anything to be given to them, but boast of their own merits. They wish thereby to assure their redemption and so fall right into the greatest uncertainty of salvation.[3] To speak of merits means to insist on one's personal self-value before God.[4]

Here Luther again emphatically called upon Paul--meus Paulus[5]--for it is Paul's teaching that the person receives as a free gift both justification and eternal life.[6]

Did Luther, then, misunderstand Paul or even misrepresent him? It is clear that in Catholicism, where the doctrine of merit in theory and practice played such a great role for hundreds of years, such questions are unavoidable. They lead us to the last point in this chapter.

The Pauline Message of Justification and the Teaching of Merit

The removal of works from the question of salvation, that which Luther considered as genuinely Pauline, is exactly what

---

is "donum habituale nobis inditum" (ibid., 111, 2), "donum creatum" (ibid., 1a. 43, 3 ad 1; 1a2ae. 110, 2 ad 3), "forma et qualitas animae" (ibid., 110, 2), which is inherent in the person (DS 1530; 1547), italics mine.

[1] WA 5, 163, 36-37.   [2] WA 40I, 224, 30.

[3] Ibid., 589, 21; 43I, 178, 34-36.

[4] WA 18, 770, 9-10; 771, 7.

[5] Ibid., 10.   [6] WA 18, 769, 32-35.

Luther is still blamed for by Catholic theologians as being un-pauline.[1] Even though the first justification may be unmerited and by faith, the second needs the cooperation of works, which indeed are carried by grace but are nonetheless the foundation of the <u>true merits</u> of the believer.[2]

The following proofs for the support of a Pauline teaching of merit are brought forward by Catholic dogmatists as well as biblical and historical theologians:

1. As Christ by His sacrifice earned objective redemption and was crowned (Php 2:8-9), so must the person also earn his subjective share of it (Rivière).[3]

2. Paul indeed fought against Pharisaic salvation by works, but equally as often lifted up the thought of reward "in its original jewish form" (Auer).[4]

3. The Apostle's ethical parenesis to fruitfulness of good works (Col 3:23-24) must be understood as a summons to the production of merits (Bartmann, Rivière).[5]

4. The concept of reward ($\mu\iota\sigma\theta\delta\varsigma$) in 1 Cor 3:8, 14; 9:17-18 stands in correlation to the concept of merit. If the Christian receives a reward, this can <u>eo ipso</u> only be earned

---

[1] "On retrouve, pour persévérer dans la justification, la nécessité des oeuvres, vilipendées bien à tort par les Réformateurs du 16e siècle, <u>au rebours de la doctrine constante de l'apôtre</u>." Amiot, <u>L'enseignement de Paul</u>, 1:273, italics mine.

[2] Ibid., 1:275.   [3] <u>DTC</u>, s.v. "Mérite," by J. Rivière.

[4] Auer and Ratzinger, <u>Dogmatik</u>, 5:230. "In seiner jüdischen Urform."

[5] Bartmann, <u>Dogmatik</u>, 2:117; <u>DTC</u>, s.v. "Mérite," by J. Rivière.

(Bartmann, Diekamp, Pohle, Schmaus, Solignac, Tanquerey).[1]

5. Since the works of the believers are different (1 Cor 3:8; 2 Cor 9:6; Eph 6:8), degrees in merits and thereby also in the reward must be assumed. This ranking of rewards is pointed to by 1 Cor 15:41-42 (Rivière, Schmaus).[2]

6. Works of grace establish true merits. The person is a participant through his free will, that is, through his cooperation (Premm, Prat, Molinski, Sullivan, Tanquerey).[3]

7. The concept of "righteousness of God" implies a retribution according to worthiness similar to that of a judge of a race who gives the victorious runners their victory wreaths: 2 Tim 4:7-8 (Diekamp, Rivière).[4]

8. Every racer has a right to the prize. Likewise, the meritorious performances of the believer establish a "legal claim" (Ott, Premm, Rivière, Tanquerey).[5]

9. The Pauline talk of judgment according to works (Rom 2:6-10) is only understandable if it concerns a judging of merits

---

[1] Bartmann, Dogmatik, 2:117; Diekamp, Dogmatik, 2:572; CathEnc, s.v. "Merit," by J. Pohle; Schmaus, Glaube der Kirche, 2:651; DSp, s.v. "Mérite," by A. Solignac; Tanquerey, Synopsis, 3:138.

[2] DTC, s.v. "Mérite," by J. Rivière; Schmaus, Dogmatik, 3/2:515.

[3] Premm, Glaubenskunde, 4:301; Prat, Theology of Paul, 2:84, 250; SM(E), s.v. "Merit," by W. Molinski; NCE, s.v. "Merit," by C. S. Sullivan; Tanquerey, Synopsis, 3:138.

[4] Diekamp, Dogmatik, 2:572; DTC, s.v. "Mérite," by J. Rivière.

[5] Ott, Dogmatik, p. 321; Premm, Glaubenskunde, 4:299; DTC, s.v. "Mérite," by J. Rivière; Tanquerey, Synopsis, 3:138.

(Bartmann, Diekamp, Ott, Rivière, Schmaus, Solignac).[1]

10. Since Paul knows a deserved *demeritum*--righteous and earned judgment of the wicked--so on this basis can an earned *meritum* of the righteous be included (Molinski, Rivière, Schmaus, Tanquerey),[2] even if only "in a lesser, secondary sense."[3]

The Pauline pictures which illustrate the thought of retribution are used frequently in Catholic dogmatics to elucidate the thought of merit.

Auer, for example, points out the following double aspect: At first Paul calls for grasping the divine crown of victory (1 Cor 9:24), which means a challenge to struggle for the reward. Secondly, however, the reward is paid in proportion to the effort (Rom 2:6; 1 Cor 3:8; 2 Cor 9:6; Col 3:24; 2 Tim 4:8).[4]

Premm stresses the dual concepts which are found in Paul:

1. Work--reward: 1 Cor 3:8.
2. Sowing--harvest: 2 Cor 9:6.
3. Righteousness--judgment: 2 Tim 4:7-8.[5]

Baumgartner enumerates the illustrations applied by Paul, which, according to him--Baumgartner--indicate the thought of merit:

---

[1] Bartmann, Dogmatik, 2:117; Diekamp, Dogmatik, 2:572; Ott, Dogmatik, p. 321; DTC, s.v. "Mérite," by J. Rivière; Schmaus, Glaube der Kirche, 2:652; DSp, s.v. "Mérite," by A. Solignac.

[2] SM(E), s.v. "Merit," by W. Molinski; DTC, s.v. "Mérite," by J. Rivière; Schmaus, Glaube der Kirche, 2:652; Tanquerey, Synopsis, 3:138.

[3] NCE, s.v. "Grace (in the Bible)" by W. G. Most.

[4] Auer and Ratzinger, Dogmatik, 5:230.

[5] Premm, Glaubenskunde, 4:299.

1. The illustration of the judgment bar: Rom 14:10; 2 Cor 5:10.

2. The illustration of the race: 1 Cor 9:24-25; 2 Tim 4:7-8.

3. The illustration of weight: 2 Cor 4:17.

4. The illustration of the harvest: Gal 6:7-8.[1]

Lange, on the other hand, attempts to develop the thought of merit out of the vocabulary employed by Paul:

1. ἄξιος (καταξιοῦσθαι): value, worthy (2 Th 1:5).

2. ὁ μισθός: the reward (1 Cor 3:8).

3. τό βραβεῖον: the prize for the race (1 Cor 9:24; Php 3:14).

4. ὁ στέφανος (στεφανοῦν): the distinction of the soldier (2 Tim 2:3-5), the prize for the race (victory wreath) of the runner (2 Tim 4:7-8).[2]

On the basis of this exegetic-dogmatic view of the Pauline statements, it is possible for Catholic theologians to assert that Paul "emphasizes strongly the meritoriousness of works which are produced by faith and love,"[3] and that thereby also the "decisive mistake" (entscheidender Fehler) of the sola fide principle has been discovered, because it leaves no room for the thought of merit.[4]

---

[1] Baumgartner, Grâce du Christ, pp. 214-15.

[2] Lange, De gratia, p. 565.

[3] Brinktrine, Lehre von der Gnade, p. 228. "Auch Paulus, der Apostel der Gnade, betont stark die Verdienstlichkeit der aus dem Glauben und der Liebe hervorwachsenden guten Werke."

[4] Hubert Jedin, Kleine Konziliengeschichte (Freiburg i. Br.: Herder, 1959), p. 90.

Luther has thereby misinterpreted Paul,[1] so that between him and the Apostle there is an unbridgeable contradiction.[2]

The exciting thing in contemporary Catholic theology, however, becomes immediately visible when one remembers that this certainly does not represent the only interpretation of the Pauline statements and that thereby the judgments passed upon Luther can be seen in another light.

O. H. Pesch blames the traditional Catholic interpretation of merit as represented by Rivière and Landgraf--for its "systematic aprioris"[3] which the ecumenically minded theologians would like to overcome in favor of a more unbiased exegetic-historical interpretation. Consequently, clear antitheses often arise with regard to the customary explanations. Some of these are noted here:

1. Paul sharply rejects the concept that the person can attain salvation through his own efforts (Schmaus). Reward with Paul is "reward by grace" (<u>Gnadenlohn</u>), that is, the person has of himself no claim to it (Meinertz).[4]

2. With his soteriology Paul has radically uprooted the doctrine of merit which rests upon the equivalence of performance and reward (Schmid). The Apostle avoids the word $\mu\iota\sigma\theta\delta\varsigma$ when he speaks of justification and judgment. For justification Paul

---

[1] Schmidt, <u>Brückenschlag</u>, p. 205.

[2] Richter, <u>Luther and Ignatius</u>, p. 82.

[3] Pesch, "Die Lehre vom Verdienst," in <u>Wahrheit und Verkündigung</u>, 2:1869.

[4] Schmaus, <u>Glaube der Kirche</u>, 2:652; Meinertz, <u>Theologie des Neuen Testamentes</u>, 2:194.

expressly rejects the teaching of merit-reward (Rom 4:4). He really knows no theological reward doctrine at all; when he speaks of reward (1 Cor 3:8, 14; 9:17-18) he means the "special Apostolic reward," the "aureola doctorum," which is based on the faithfulness of the church congregations and which is revealed in the final judgment as success of mission (W. Pesch). When Paul speaks of believers in the judgment of God, then he speaks of "praise" (Rom 2:29; 1 Cor 4:5), "honour" (Rom 2:7), "glory" (Rom 5:2), "righteousness" (Gal 5:5) and "prize" (1 Cor 9:25; Php 3:14; 2 Tim 4:8). But according to Php 2:12-13, he takes these not as one's own works, but as evidence that a person has not fallen out of God's work (O. H. Pesch). The glory is "pure gift" (W. Pesch). Therefore a biblical and Pauline foundation for the teaching of merit must fall away (Fransen).[1]

3. The Apostolic warning concerning judgment according to works is a reference to God's gifts not to merits (Schelkle). Because God performs everything, "there is no reason to present works before God" (O. H. Pesch).[2]

4. The biblical talk of reward should not be taken literally; it "contains something else" (sie enthält anderes). It is a

---

[1] LTK, 2nd ed., s.v. "Verdienst," by J. Schmid; Wilhelm Pesch, "Der Sonderlohn für den Verkündiger des Evangeliums," in Neutestamentliche Aufsätze, ed. Josef Blinzler, Otto Kuss, and Franz Mussner (Regensburg: F. Pustet, 1963), pp. 201-06; O. H. Pesch, "Die Lehre vom Verdienst," in Wahrheit und Verkündigung, 2:1872-73; Piet Fransen, "Das neue Sein des Menschen in Christus," in Mysterium Salutis, 4/2:977-82.

[2] Schelkle, Theologie des Neuen Testamentes, 3:73; O. H. Pesch, "Die Lehre vom Verdienst," in Wahrheit und Verkündigung, 2:1873. "Weil Gott Wollen und Vollbringen wirkt, gilt es nun nicht, Gott mit Werken aufzuwarten."

cipher for God's gift (Schelkle). With the incalculableness of the gift (God's kingdom) in the Synoptics the meritorious basis for the talk about reward is withdrawn; in Paul and John therefore, we hardly encounter the talk about reward any more (O. H. Pesch). When in the Scripture the writer speaks of merit-morality, it is not the morality of the disciples but that of the Pharisees that is meant (Küng).[1]

5. The distinctions in reward are explained from the "activities of an individual," from the "special reward for the proclaimers of the gospel" (W. Pesch). They have nothing to do with the receiving of salvation, according to 1 Cor 3:14-15 (Didier).[2]

6. The NT "rejects the idea of an equivalence between man's work and God's reward" (O. H. Pesch).[3]

7. The righteousness of God, by which alone the person is able to stand before God, can therefore never be earned but can only be received as a gift (Schelkle, W. Pesch).[4]

8. Thus, man has no claim to the reward (Schmaus, W. Pesch).[5]

---

[1] Schelkle, Theologie des Neuen Testamentes, 3:73; O. H. Pesch, "Die Lehre vom Verdienst," in Wahrheit und Verkündigung, 2:1872; Küng, Rechtfertigung, p. 263.

[2] W. Pesch, "Sonderlohn," in Neutestamentliche Aufsätz, p. 206; LTK, 2nd ed., s.v. "Vergeltung," by W. Pesch; "Spezieller Lohn für die Verkündiger des Evangeliums;" Georges Didier, Désintéressement du chrétien (Paris: Aubier-Montaigne, 1955), p. 48.

[3] O. H. Pesch, "Die Lehre vom Verdienst," in Wahrheit und Verkündigung, 2:1873. "Die vom NT zurückgewiesene Vorstellung von einer Verhältnisgleichheit zwischen des Menschen Werk und Gottes Lohn."

[4] Schelkle, Theologie des Neuen Testamentes, 3:73; LTK, 2nd ed., s.v. "Vergeltung," by W. Pesch.

[5] Schmaus, Dogmatik, 3/2:515; W. Pesch, "Sonderlohn," in Neutestamentliche Aufsätze, p. 206.

9. The Pauline warning of judgment according to works is no "jewish relic" (jüdisches Relikt) or "inconsequence" in reference to justification by faith. The teaching of the Apostle about retribution is directed against "false security" (falsche Sicherheit—1 Cor 10:1-13). The glory of God is a gift (W. Pesch), which, according to 1 Cor 2:9 is beyond any reckoning (Meinertz).[1]

10. Demeritum and gift of God stand in Rom 6:23 in a striking contradiction to each other. Death is really deserved (wages, reward, compensation), life is a gift (gift of grace, donativum). From the demeritum therefore no conclusion can be drawn about the meritum (Schlier, Meinertz, Schelkle). The text is a kind of "mantrap of optimistic theories of merit" (O. H. Pesch).[2]

From these very often expressed reservations against the traditional attempts to make Paul a chief witness of an early Christian merit-theology that contradicts the Reformation, it should not, however, be concluded that the majority of contemporary Catholic theologians find themselves in agreement with Luther.

In the basic concern of the Catholic teaching of merit, that is, in the assertion of the cooperation of the person against the sole agency of God and in the emphasis on a salvation-attaining ethic no basic approach to Luther can be found.

Lortz, Przywara, Congar, Bläser, Moeller, Volk, Van de Pol,

---

[1] LTK, 2nd ed., s.v. "Vergeltung," by W. Pesch; Meinertz, Theologie des Neuen Testamentes, 2:227.

[2] Schlier, Römerbrief, p. 213; Meinertz, Theologie des Neuen Testamentes, 2:194; Schelkle, Theologie des Neuen Testamentes, 3:73; O. H. Pesch, "Die Lehre vom Verdienst," in Wahrheit und Verkündigung, 2:1870. "Fussangel optimistischer Verdiensttheorien."

and Manns here see the "remaining and decisive point of controversy" (den bleibenden und entscheidenden Kontroverspunkt).[1]

According to Thomas McDonough this comes from the teaching of freedom and merit of Thomas Aquinas, which cannot be brought into agreement with Luther's "pessimism."[2] Also O. H. Pesch, for whom the difference between Thomas and Luther seems to be reduced to the distinction between "sapiential" and "existential" theology, must here admit that it is a matter of an "essential difference" (wesentlicher Unterschied).[3] The issue of sole agency versus meritoriousness creates the real tension between Luther and Trent, state Adolf[4] and Eduard Stakemeier.[5] Schmaus[6] and Küng[7] articulate a similar conviction for the present ecumenical Catholic theology: From God's all-encompassing agency does not follow God's sole agency! Within God's agency the cooperation of man must become active. God is the First Cause (causa principalis), the person, the second cause (causa secunda);[8] God is the "main active being" (der Haupttätige),[9] who "produces the activity of the person."[10]

---

[1] Manns, Lutherforschung, p. 10.

[2] Thomas McDonough, The Law and the Gospel in Luther (London: Oxford University Press, 1963), p. 159.

[3] Pesch, Theologie der Rechtfertigung, p. 869.

[4] Adolf Stakemeier, Das Konzil von Trient über die Heilsgewissheit (Heidelberg: F. H. Kerle, 1947), p. 175.

[5] Stakemeier, "Trienter Lehrentscheidungen," in Weltkonzil von Trient, 1:101.

[6] Schmaus, Glaube der Kirche, 2:551.

[7] Küng, Rechtfertigung, p. 258. [8] Schmaus, Dogmatik, 3/2:425.

[9] Idem, Glaube der Kirche, 2:653. [10] Ibid., 2:563.

That is, however, not to be understood as instrumental, but in the framework of the primary-secondary event. That is, within the motivating God the freedom of the person is activated, and also within the realm of grace the human being as "cooperator" comes into action. Thus, divine all-encompassing agency and human cooperation establish the merit.

On this point the controversial aspect par excellence has been reached, as judged on the Lutheran side[1] by Skydsgaard, Peters, and Joest, and on the Reformed side by Berkouwer.[2]

The fact that sometimes in Catholic (Kösters, O. H. Pesch)[3] and Lutheran (Hermann, Kühn)[4] circles a similar culmination in the discussion is granted to the concept of sin is no contradiction of this, but rather a supplement. The teachings of the sole agency or of the meritorious cooperation aim at different pictures of God; the teachings of simul justus et peccator or of the ontological sinlessness aim at different pictures of the believer. With the concept of sin alone, in any case, the whole controversial theological field in justification cannot be covered. What is for the

---

[1] Kristen E. Skydsgaard, "The Council and Evangelical Christians," in The Papal Council and the Gospel, ed. K. E. Skydsgaard (Minneapolis, Minn.: Augsburg Publishing House, 1961), p. 149; Albrecht Peters, "Reformatorische Rechtfertigungsbotschaft zwischen tridentinischer Rechtfergigungslehre und gegenwärtigem evangelischen Verständnis der Rechtfertigung," LuJ 31 (1964):78-80; Wilfried Joest, "Die tridentinische Rechtfergigungslehre," KuD 9 (1963):69.

[2] Berkouwer, Faith and Justification, p. 13.

[3] Reinhard Kösters, "Die Lehre von der Rechtfertigung unter besonderer Berücksichtigung der Formel simul iustus et peccator," ZKT 90 (1968):315, 318; O. H. Pesch, "Gottes Gnadenhandeln," in Mysterium Salutis, 4/2:888-89.

[4] RGG, 3rd ed., s.v. "Rechtfertigung-Dogmatisch," by R. Hermann; Ulrich Kühn, "Die Rechtfertigungslehre in heutiger Sicht," EvW 20 (1966):648.

believer either possible or impossible, hence the question of the final meritorious cooperation in salvation, is shown in full breadth only by the teaching on meritum.

Also the teaching on Law and Gospel, which according to Söhngen, Brandenburg, and McDonough constitute the main aspect of the controversy,[1] flows in at this point; for in final analysis it all depends on whether God's command, fulfilled by His sole agency, becomes the living norm of gratitude, or whether the law through the cooperation of the believer, leads to any merited righteousness.

One could sooner search here for any connection between justification and Church (Maron)[2] as the competitive principle. For it cannot be denied that in the realm of ecclesiology a still broader and deeper front between the confessions becomes visible.[3] But thereby we would be changing to a different theme and would retroject into the time of the Reformation predominantly modern ecclesiological questions.

---

[1] Gottlieb Söhngen, Gesetz und Evangelium (Freiburg i. Br.: K. Alber, 1957), p. 8; Albert Brandenburg, "Die Lutherstudien Rudolf Hermanns," Cath(M) 14 (1960):315; McDonough, Law and Gospel, p. 1.

[2] Gottfried Maron, Kirche und Rechtfertigung (Göttingen: Vandenhoeck & Ruprecht, 1969).

[3] From the many representatives of this view the following are mentioned from the Protestant viewpoint: George A. Lindbeck, The Future of Roman Catholic Theology (Philadelphia: Fortress Press, 1970), p. 78; Ulrich Kühn, "Die Rechtfertigungslehre des Thomas von Aquin in evangelischer Sicht," Oec. 2 (1967):59; Pöhlmann, Rechtfertigung, p. 382; on the Catholic side: Hubert Jedin, Kirche des Glaubens--Kirche der Geschichte, 2 vols. (Freiburg i. Br.: Herder, 1966), 1:365; Wacker, Ökumenischer Dialog, p. 269; Van de Pol, Reformatorisches Christentum, p. 448; Heinrich Fries, "Die Bedeutung der Konfessionen heute," in Neues Glaubensbuch, ed. Johannes Feiner and Lukas Vischer, 8th ed. (Freiburg i. Br.: Herder, 1973), p. 650.

Having attained the soteriological crystallization point of the discussion, however, in God's sole agency versus final meritorious cooperation, we remain with Luther's historical problem and its influence on the present.

Summary

1. The concept that Luther's Paulinism is a total disfigurement and misinterpretation of the teaching of the Apostle (Cristiani, Lagrange, Paquier, Schmidt) seems to have been overcome in Catholic theology today. The views stretch from strong reservations (Bavaud), to an agreement with Luther as Catholic interpreter of Paul (Lortz), and to a positive recognition of the Reformer (Küng, Olivier, O. H. Pesch).

2. The question whether justification occupies the central position in Paul is answered in various ways; whether such a position is also central in Christianity is denied not only by the traditional theology (Schultheologie) but also by ecumenists (Küng, O. H. Pesch).

3. The devaluation of forensic justification by the School dogmatists (Bartmann, Diekamp, Premm, Pohle and Gummersbach) and the pre-Vatican II biblical theology (Meinertz, Prat) gives way presently to a more positive understanding (Kertelge, Kösters, Küng, Schmaus), although not without reservations (Cerfaux, Tresmontant).

4. The sola fide is regarded in part as problematic (Richter, Stirnimann), is rejected (Bartmann, Bover, Dander, Ott, Rivière) or is partly claimed as "good Catholic formula" (Bouyer, Fries, Lortz, Rahner). Not the formula but its meaning and

significance separate the various beliefs (Lyonnet, Schmaus). Although Catholic theologians (Fries, Malevez, Rahner, Schmaus, Schnackenburg) stress increasingly the existential nature of faith, nevertheless the works of faith are conceived as final and are understood as the basis of the eschatological justification (Manns, Van de Pol, Schmidt). When Luther discovered the consecutive character of works in Paul, he forgot the cooperation principle (Lortz). The coupling of works and salvation is rejected, however, in favor of a purely altruistic character of works, by some theologians of the ecumenical outreach (Kertelge, O. H. Pesch).

5. The cooperation principle necessarily leads to merit theology. In opposition to the concept that the teaching of meritum is Pauline (Auer, Baumgartner, Lange, Ott, Premm) the concept is defended that Paul does not connect works and reward in the question of salvation (W. Pesch, O. H. Pesch, Schmid, Schelkle). Paul is said to have known only the "special Apostolic reward" (apostolischer Sonderlohn). Luther's teaching of the divine monergism is, however, aside from O. H. Pesch, categorically rejected (Bouyer, Küng, Lortz, Schmaus, Wacker). Thus any attempt to reach consensus in justification between Luther and Catholic theology must take issue with the decisive controversial point of the final-meritorious cooperation and participation of the believer in his salvation.

CHAPTER II

LUTHER'S STRUGGLE AGAINST THE DOCTRINE OF MERIT

The Development of the
Idea of Merit

The origin and development of the Christian theology of merit frequently have been the subject of historical research and theological evaluation. It is true that a detailed total presentation is lacking in more recent theological literature, but earlier treatments as well as several newer works fill in this gap.

On the Catholic side we know of no more complete investigation than the article "Mérite" in the Dictionnaire de Théologie Catholique by Jean Rivière,[1] which, though it has indeed a definite polemic-apologetic stance, is very well organized. The thought of merit in the Middle Ages is presented in detail by Arthur Michael Landgraf, Johann Auer, Adolar Zumkeller and Werner Dettloff.[2] Otto H. Pesch presents a summary which attempts to "overcome" the

---

[1] DTC, s.v. "Mérite."

[2] Arthur Michael Landgraf, Dogmengeschichte der Frühscholastik, 4 vols. (Regensburg: F. Pustet, 1952-56). Johann Auer, Die Entwicklung der Gnadenlehre in der Hochscholastik, 2 vols. (Freiburg i. Br.: Herder, 1951). Adolar Zumkeller, "Das Ungenügen der menschlichen Werke bei den deutschen Predigern des Spätmittelalters," ZKT 81 (1959):265-305. Werner Dettloff, Die Entwicklung der Akzeptations- und Verdienstlehre von Duns Scotus bis Luther (Münster/W.: Aschendorff, 1963).

"systematic aprioris" of Rivière and Landgraf.[1]

On the Protestant side, both early and recent sketches of the general development are known. Johannes Kunze,[2] one of the earlier writers, and Erdmann Schott,[3] a more recent author must be mentioned. The works of Karl Hermann Wirth[4] and Hermann Schultz,[5] with reference to the origin of the doctrine of merit in the Ancient Church, are still irreplaceable. Among the newer authors who have addressed themselves to this question, Jan Nicolaas Bakhuizen van den Brink[6] may be noted. In the most recent literature Berndt Hamm[7] deals in a very detailed discourse on the problems of the doctrine of merit in the Middle Ages. As for the doctrine of merit in Late Scholasticism and Luther, the opinions of Reinhard Schinzer, Bengt Hägglund, and Vilmos Vajta[8] are valuable.

---

[1] Pesch, "Lehre vom Verdienst," in Wahrheit und Verkündigung, 2:1869.

[2] RE, 3rd ed., s.v. "Verdienst."

[3] RGG, 3rd ed., s.v. "Verdienst-Dogmengeschichtlich."

[4] Karl Hermann Wirth, Der "Verdienst"-Begriff bei Tertullian (Leipzig: Dörffling & Franke, 1892); idem, Der "Verdienst"-Begriff bei Cyprian (Leipzig: Dörffling & Franke, 1901).

[5] Hermann Schultz, "Der sittliche Begriff des Verdienstes und seine Anwendung auf das Verständnis des Werkes Christi," ThStKr 67 (1894):7-50.

[6] Jan Nicolaas Bakhuizen van den Brink, "Mereor and Meritum in some Latin Fathers," TU 78 (1961):333-40.

[7] Berndt Hamm, Promissio, pactum, ordinatio (Tübingen: J. C. B. Mohr [P. Siebeck], 1977).

[8] Reinhard Schinzer, Die doppelte Verdienstlehre des Spätmittelalters und Luthers reformatorische Entdeckung (Munich: Chr. Kaiser, 1971). Bengt Hägglund, The Background of Luther's Doctrine of Justification in Late Medieval Theology (Philadelphia: Fortress Press, 1971). Vilmos Vajta, "Sine meritis--Zur kritischen Funktion der Rechtfertigungslehre," Oec. 3 (1968):146-97.

In view of the relatively plentiful historical material, the renunciation of a historical introduction to Luther would be defensible. However, we believe we cannot renounce making a historical sketch, for Luther's incisive theological breakthrough will be better understood if his thought is compared with the content of the tradition which came to him.

<u>The roots of the concept of merit</u>. The roots of the Christian thought of merit lie in the soil of Late Judaic nomism (זכות-theology, transferal of excess merits), of Hellenistic moralism and juridism (over-valuation of the moral performance-capability through the Stoa, asceticism in Neopythagorism and Neoplatonism, ethical performance-reward scheme in Aristotle, and in the <u>jus Romanum</u>), as well as the ancient cult idea (satisfaction-producing offering, <u>placatio</u>, hope of reward, and fear of punishment as "popular view of antiquity" (<u>Volksanschauung der Antike</u>).[1]

<u>Hebrew thought</u>. Hebrew thought in the OT does not know the זכות-concept at all. Whether the matter of merit can be supported by the concept שכר and its synonyms or in connection with the OT principle of retribution will be dealt with later.

In contrast to the OT, a pluralistic but distinct teaching of merit can be recognized in the Late Judaic (according to the modern designation, Early Jewish) writings (Apocrypha, Pseudepigrapha) and in the sources of Rabbinism (Mekilta, Midrash, Talmud).[2]

---

[1] Wirth, <u>"Verdienst"-Begriff bei Tertullian</u>, p. 73.

[2] As causes can be named: "The rise of apocalypticism." Paul S. Minear, <u>And Great Shall Be Your Reward</u> (New Haven: Yale University Press, 1941), p. 14. Moreover, the fact that the synagogical doctrine of reward became totally dependent on its doctrine

Beside an emphasized theology of grace[1] there is found a synergistic mixture of grace and performance,[2] whereby the performance establishes merits which God counts and weighs,[3] on account of which God established the Covenant with Abraham,[4] on the basis of which He deals with Israel,[5] and for the enabling of which He also established the Torah.[6] There is an exact correspondence[7] between performance and reward. God sometimes appears like a money-lender who lends and to whom payment must be returned.[8] Works also have a sin-cancelling character;[9] they establish a claim before God;[10] they are able,

---

of justification: "Dass ihre [der Synagoge] Lohnlehre in völlige Abhängigkeit von ihrer Rechtfertigungslehre geriet." Hermann Strack and Paul Billerbeck, Kommentar zum Neuen Testament aus Talmud und Midrasch, 4 vols. (Munich: C. H. Beck, 1922-28), 4/1:490. Likewise juridism and the thought of works. See Rudolf Bultmann, Theologie des Neuen Testamentes (Tübingen: J. C. B. Mohr [P. Siebeck], 1953), p. 11; Joachim Jeremias, Neutestamentliche Theologie (Gütersloh: G. Mohn, 1971), p. 208.

[1]A sola gratia is found in the Apocrypha (Baruch 2:19, 27), in Qumran (1QH 13), in Mekilta Shirata 9:69, and in B. Talmud Aboth 1:3.

[2]However, sometimes grace and merit are found in the closest relationship. So, e.g., in 4 Ezra 8:32, 38-40; Genesis Rabbah 60:2; B. Talmud Aboth 3:15.

[3]Deuteronomy Rabbah 7:2; B. Talmud Kiddushin 40a-40b; B. Talmud Shabbath 127b; B. Talmud Aboth 6:6.

[4]Genesis Rabbah 44:5.

[5]Mekilta Pisḥa 16:140; Mekilta Beshallah 4:218.

[6]B. Talmud Aboth 6:1, B. Talmud Berakoth 6b; B. Talmud Makkoth 23b; Numbers Rabbah 15:2.

[7]B. Talmud Aboth 5:23.   [8]Ibid., 3:16.

[9]Sirach 3:3-4; Tobit 12:9; 2 Baruch 14:7; Genesis Rabbah 44:5; 1QS 8.

[10]See Strack and Billerbeck, Kommentar zum Neuen Testament, 4/1:491.

because they are meritorious, to be carried over to other people.[1] Indeed, especially pious persons with their merits could liberate the whole world, from its creation to its end, from the punishing judgment of God.[2]

For Orthodox Jewish thought these views even today form "a major chapter of Jewish theology,"[3] while Christian theology of evangelical origin categorizes them as a "pernicious turning-point" (verderbliche Wendung)[4] of the OT reward-of-grace to the Rabbinic reward-of-merit.

Jewish theologians are conscious of the dangers of their teaching--thought of reward, seeking for reward, pride in reward[5]-- and on the one hand try to justify the concept of striving for reward as honoring God and loving neighbor,[6] and on the other hand to mark a boundary between themselves and Christendom.

The Protestant principle sola fide sine operibus is reproached with the danger of "selfishness and infidelity,"[7] and one attempts to distance oneself from Catholicism through the distinguishing of negative and positive merits. Catholic merits are considered negative, because they consist of avoiding what is permitted,

---

[1] B. Talmud Aboth 2:2; Mekilta Pisḥa 1:5; 16:140.

[2] B. Talmud Sukkah 45b.

[3] See Arthur Marmorstein, The Doctrine of Merits in Old Rabbinical Literature (New York: KTAV Publishing House, 1968), p. x.

[4] Günther Bornkamm, Der Lohngedanke im Neuen Testament (Göttingen: Vandenhoeck & Ruprecht, 1961), p. 12.

[5] Marmorstein, Doctrine of Merits, p. 30.

[6] Ibid., pp. 30-31.   [7] Ibid., pp. 26-27.

thus being of an ascetic nature. Jewish merits are positive, because they result from the keeping of the commandments.[1]

Both could rest upon a misunderstanding. Luther's doctrine of the consecutive way of salvation does not at all exclude--as we have already seen--good works; and Catholic merits result not only from an ascetic conduct of life (renunciation of second marriage, fasting, refusal of luxuries) but from all that is performed in love.

On the contrary, Jewish and Catholic teaching of merit are similar to a great extent, and what seems problematic with one side often, with certain limitations, applies to the other. Both share not only optimism over the moral performance-capability of the person but also the view that God's grace must be taken into account. The free will as power of choice for good or evil is viewed as intact,[2] whereas in Late Judaism's religion a kind of semi-Pelagianism from one's own works, the forefathers' merits, and the kindness of God[3] stands opposite the Scholastic _fides caritate formata_ within the _sola gratia-cooperatio_ scheme. Common to both is also the doctrine of the uncertainty of salvation,[4] the striving for reward,[5] the hierarchy and salvation-function of the perfected

---

[1] Marmorstein, _Doctrine of Merits_, pp. 3, 31.

[2] Life is chosen (4 Ezra 7:130) and attained through good deeds (4 Ezra 7:77); the will is free (Sirach 15:15-17; B. Talmud _Aboth_ 3:15).

[3] Marmorstein, _Doctrine of Merits_, p. 20.

[4] B. Talmud _Berakoth_ 4a; ibid., 28b.

[5] B. Talmud _Sotah_ 22a.

ones,[1] the representative function of substitute works,[2] the works of supererogation,[3] and the <u>extra ecclesiam salus nulla</u>.[4]

Differences lie in the quantitative consideration of the supererogation in Judaism and in the restriction of the thought of election to the nation. In Catholicism, contrary to this, stands a functional valuation of the supererogation, a theological differentiation between <u>meritum</u> and <u>satisfactio</u>, and the supernational, universal thought of salvation.

<u>Jesus' teaching</u>. Jesus' proclamation is a single protest against the Late Judaic teaching of merit. Similarly, the prophets in the OT fought against externalism and formalism, Jesus demands "radical obedience" (<u>radikaler Gehorsam</u>)[5] which goes beyond the formal commandments, in that He emphasizes not only the "what" but also reveals the deepest dimension of the "how," and in that He frees the thought of retribution from the burden of juridism (performance and its merit) and interprets it purely in a religious way (gift and its reception).

Jesus' struggle against the Pharisees is a struggle against the theology of merit. Blessed and to be praised are not those who are rich and in possession of religious works, who believe themselves to have a large spiritual capital at their disposal, but the receptive "beggars" (Mt 5:3, Greek), who long for an "alien

---

[1] Marmorstein, <u>Doctrine of Merits</u>, p. 33.

[2] B. Talmud <u>Aboth</u> 2:2.   [3] B. Talmud <u>Kiddushin</u> 40b.

[4] The world was created for the sake of Israel; the other peoples are nothing and will be annihilated (4 Ezra 6:55-56; 13:49; <u>Numbers Rabbah</u> 3:2).

[5] Bultmann, <u>Theologie des Neuen Testamentes</u>, p. 11.

righteousness," the righteousness of the kingdom (Mt 5:6), which breaks in through Jesus of Nazareth (Mt 12:28) and calls the people to repentance and discipleship. Salvation does not need to be earned, it is already present in the kingdom. Hence the "better righteousness" (Mt 5:20) cannot consist of the external-meritorious work-righteousness of the Pharisees and scribes but of a disposition to be obedient (Gesinnungsgehorsam), of lived salvation (gelebtes Heil), which awaits only the eschatological unveiling.

This ethic, derived and lived from salvation which needs no longer any merit-earning, is Jesus' "Copernican revolution of all other moral systems."[1] The person can live only from what is received in order to retain it in the present and finally to receive it forever. Therefore Jesus speaks of the reward,[2] but it is "grace-reward" (Gnadenlohn), not "debt-reward" (Schuldigkeitslohn),[3] an "illustration" (Gleichnis)[4] for the fact that the works of a person have "irrevocable consequences" (unwiderrufliche Folgen) for eternity.[5]

---

[1] Bo Reicke, "The New Testament Conception of Reward," in Aux sources de la tradition chrétienne (Neuchâtel: Delachaux & Niestlé, 1950), p. 197.

[2] If one excludes material reward, Jesus speaks in the Synoptics (omitting parallels) eight times of reward (Mt 5:12, 46; 6:1, 2, 5, 16; 10:41-42). In the Gospel of John there is only one place (Jn 4:36) which apparently is to be understood of the present joy of the reaper.

[3] Horst Georg Pöhlmann, Abriss der Dogmatik, 2nd ed. (Gütersloh: G. Mohn, 1975), p. 220.

[4] Paul Althaus, Die christliche Wahrheit, 7th ed. (Gütersloh: Bertelsmann, 1966), p. 652.

[5] Bornkamm, Lohngedanke, pp. 8-9.

Therefore to speak of a rightful claim is out of the question. For Jesus the obedience of the disciple is a gladly performed obligation (Lk 17:10). As a "slave" (Lk 17:7, Greek) the disciple is completely dependent on the Lord and has no claim on any reward; as a "publican" (Lk 18:13) he is without any escape and wholly thrown upon the grace of God; as a "child" (Mk 10:15) he is from the beginning an heir--everything belongs to him, how then should he wish to earn anything? As a "steward" (Mt 24:45-47) he can only give account for what has been received. The reward that he receives from the master is paid to him without obligation and is great beyond all measure. As a "friend" (Jn 15:13-15) he finally refuses for himself every do ut des, for he gives himself without reckoning to the one who has given everything for him.

Whoever, on the other hand, boasts of his quality (Lk 18:10-14) is rejected. He has his reward "before men" (Mt 6:1-4) but not before God, for with God only the self-forgetful deed counts. God's eschatological gift is for those who receive the reward with astonishment (Mt 25:37-40), who do not reckon on it at all and thus give up any claim to it.[1] When God gives out "rewards," it is not according to the work performed but out of His sovereign kindness (Mt 20:15). Recognition is not found by those who reckon and claim but by those who simply rely upon God.

With this teaching Jesus stood in direct opposition to the theology of His time on the following points:

1. Jesus denied every claim of the servant on reward (Lk 17:10).

---

[1] Jeremias, Neutestamentliche Theologie, p. 209; ThWNT, s.v. "μισθός," by H. Preisker.

2. Reward is not earned but given. With God all is totaliter aliter and can only be expressed paradoxically. The person is "hired" by God and out of God's goodness is "rewarded" (Mt 20:7, 15).

3. Before God all are alike; differences go back to the one who calls and do not legitimize assertion of a correspondence between performance and reward (Mt 20:1-7, 10, 14-15).

4. The disciple may trust the promise (Jn 10:11), he may wait for it, but may not serve in view of this promise as if it were a due reward. He serves because he has been hired and forgets his service because it is taken for granted (Mt 25:37-39).[1]

5. The motive of the service is not the reward that will be earned, but gratitude and joy over what has already been received (Mt 13:44). The kingdom that has already been given (Lk 17:21) and which was prepared long before any deed was done only awaits its eschatological unveiling. The faithful servant will experience it (Mt 25:34).

6. The reward is not primarily earthly, but in the continuation of the thought of Covenant it is God Himself (Gen 15:1) and fellowship with Him and with those who are His (Lk 13:28-29). Thus, the disciple can rely upon the fact that God is now already a lavish Giver (Mk 10:29-30).

7. Distinctions in the performance ability of the disciples are conditioned by the variety of the spiritual gifts which the Lord has distributed (Mt 25:14-18). A further difference may

---

[1] See Otto Michel, "Der Lohngedanke in der Verkündigung Jesu," ZST 9 (1932):53.

lie in the varied natural capabilities to which they are related or in the conditions under which they are realized (Lk 19:16, 18). The distinguishable "reward in the reward"--a charismatic reward within the general kingdom--transcends however every concept of correspondence and reckoning (Mt 25:21).

Paul's teaching. The Apostle Paul further developed this basic thought in another terminology, for other persons and with the help of a variously structured theological viewpoint. What Jesus expressed with the message of the kingdom, Paul expresses with the concepts εὐαγγέλιον τοῦ χριστοῦ (Rom 15:19; 1 Cor 9:12), χάρις (Rom 3:24; 1 Cor 1:4), ἀπολύτρωσις (Rom 3:24; 1 Cor 1:30), καταλλαγή (Rom 5:12; 2 Cor 5:18-20) and δικαιοσύνη θεοῦ (Rom 1:17; 2 Cor 5:21).

The good news of the gracious God is the proclamation of the redemption and ransom in Christ, which brings the righteousness of God δωρεάν (as a gift) and has the ζωή αἰώνιος (Rom 5:21) as goal. Only the judgment, i.e. divine condemnation, is deserved; everything else is given as a gift (Rom 6:23; 8:32).

With Paul's doctrine of justification, the Jewish thought of merit seems to be totally annulled.[1] According to Rom 4:1-5 the reward by grace excludes every reward by obligation. "Debt-reward" rests upon works, brings fame coram mundo, and raises a claim. "Grace-reward," on the contrary, rests upon faith. But faith is a gift of God (Eph 2:8-9) with which the righteousness of God is awarded to man. And even when this righteousness turns from

---

[1] ThWNT, s.v. "μισθός," by H. Preisker; TBLNT, s.v. "Lohn," by P. C. Böttger.

acquittal to life, from justification to sanctification (Rom 5:16; 6:1-23; 8:1-16), God and God alone still accomplishes everything. Faith is indeed effective through love (Gal 5:6), but Paul nowhere says that love justifies. Indeed, judgment occurs according to works (Rom 2:6), but Paul nowhere says that works justify. All is effective by faith, and is attested in obedience!

But in order to have faith and obedience man must be set free by God (Eph 1:19; Php 2:13). This act stands in a "logically unbalanced dialectic of indicative and imperative" (<u>logisch unausgeglichene Dialektik von Indikativ und Imperativ</u>).[1] That is, the divine imperative, "You shall believe and obey," is only possible on the basis of a divine indicative: God gives faith and obedience! Man experiences this act as personal experience but, nevertheless, can only ascribe its realization to God (Rom 3:27; 1 Cor 1:31). Thereby two things are expressed:

1. The κατεργάζομαι (Php 2:12) is to be understood not of the final but of the consecutive path of salvation. It presupposes the believing, justified Philippian converts. Also in the judgment the person will stand before God with faith (Rom 1:17), the faith that has been effective and by which he has not fallen from salvation.

2. The totally encompassing and sole agency of God indeed includes the psychological experience of faith and obedience, but excludes every theological synergism and thus also every merit (Php 2:13).

---

[1] Edmund Schlink, "Gesetz und Evangelium als kontroverstheologisches Problem," <u>KuD</u> 7 (1961):35.

As we have already seen, Paul otherwise speaks only of the charismatic reward (1 Cor 3:8, 14; 9:17-18). This is conferred to gifts that as a whole come from God (1 Cor 3:10; 4:7; 15:10; 2 Cor 3:5) and thereby draw after them a present (1 Cor 9:18) and a future reward (1 Cor 3:13-14) which rests upon no human co-operation and claim whatsoever. In fact, Paul considers himself as a "fellow workman" of God, but he traces his activity back solely to the grace of God (1 Cor 3:9-10).

In the Gospel of John the concept of salvation-reward is not expressed by the word μισθός. The salvation initiative here also lies wholly with God (Jn 6:44, 65). And here again salvation is present salvation and comes from faith (Jn 3:36; 5:24) until it unveils itself eschatologically (Jn 5:28-29). All the work of the Christian is Christ's work, just as the vitality of the vine works through the branches (Jn 15:4-5). What a person accomplishes and that for which he receives "full reward" (2 Jn 8) must be seen from this angle. That is, it is a given work and thus also a given and received gift in its fullness. Ex analogia also Rev 11:18; 22:12 are to be understood.

The Apostolic unity in the teaching of reward shows itself also in the usage of the word ἄξιος (corresponding, worthy). The later usage in the form of κατ' ἀξίαν τῶν πράξεων[1] (according to the worth of the works) is unknown to the NT. This formulation leading to the thought of merit--which only sounds weaker because the Greek has no exact correspondence to the Latin meritum[2]--"is

---

[1] Justin 1 Apology 12 (PG 6:341); ibid., 44 (PG 6:396).
[2] See DTC, s.v. "Mérite," by J. Rivière; John Burnaby, Amor Dei (London: Hodder & Stoughton, 1938), p. 236.

excluded by the character of the gospel" (<u>ist durch den Charakter des Evangeliums ausgeschlossen</u>).[1] Only God and the Lamb are worthy (Rev 4:11; 5:2). A person may <u>coram mundo</u> be "worthy" (Lk 7:4), but <u>coram Deo</u> he is unworthy (Lk 7:7; 15:19). He also remains unworthy if he refuses God's invitation of salvation (Mt 22:4-5, 8; Acts 13:46), so that there is a genuine <u>demeritum</u> (Lk 12:48; Rom 1:32; Heb 10:29; Rev 16:6). The person becomes "worthy" through God (2 Th 1:11), as the righteousness of Christ is reckoned to and conferred upon him. If he allows this righteousness constantly to be granted to him and safely holds fast in obedient and repentant faith, it will one day reach eternal glory (Rev 3:4). Since everything is received from Christ and belongs to Him, there is no portion of the worthiness that belongs to man.

A dogmatic pluralism in this question does not exist in the NT, but there are doubtless various emphases according to different circumstances and requirements--for example in Paul and James.

However, emphases can very easily be overstressed and lead to distorted views through misunderstood overstretching. This seems to have happened in part already in the Apostolic era, and above all in the post-Apostolic, in a threefold form:

1. Jesus' talk of reward (grace-reward), under the pressure of the contemporary Jewish and pagan moralism, as we know it from Talmud and Stoa, could easily degenerate to reward-arrangement and thereby to the thought of merit.

---

[1] <u>ThWNT</u>, s.v. "ἄξιος," by W. Foerster.

2. The Pauline sola fide--if misunderstood, a dangerous teaching--could easily turn into the quietistic fides informis, that is, the purely dogmatic faith. And indeed in the instant that faith was no longer understood as existential attitude of trust (trust lived in faithfulness), it was reduced to an intellectual knowledge and agreement. Against this James (Jas 2:17-26) seems to struggle.[1] Apostolic Fathers and Church Fathers follow after him.[2]

3. Moreover, the synergism of James (Jas 2:22) could very easily be misrepresented if it is understood not as successive-- from Abraham's pronouncement of righteousness (Gen 15:6; Jas 2:23) to Abraham's obedience (Gen 22; Jas 2:21)--but as supplementary, that is, faith and works form the precondition for man's justification. This temptation has beset almost all of Early Christian theology.[3]

---

[1] "Der Jakobusbrief beweist, dass es . . . Christen gegeben hat, die das sola fide des Paulus missbrauchten, um sich ein bequemes, liebloses und selbstsüchtiges Christentum zurechtzumachen." Adolf Harnack, "Geschichte der Lehre von der Seligkeit allein durch den Glauben in der alten Kirche," ZTK 1 (1891):97.

[2] Cf. Tertullian's refusal of the "fides frivola et frigida." De fuga 3 (PL 2:127). Cf. also Polycarp Phil. 3:3 (SC 10:180); Herm. Mand. 1:2 (GCS 48:23, 8-11); idem Sim. 9:15 (GCS 48:89, 3-8); ibid., 8:9 (GCS 48:74, 16-17). Clement of Alex. Strom. 6. 14 (PG 9:329); Origen Comm. in Joan. 19. 6 (PG 14:569); Gregory of Nyssa In Ecclesiasten Hom. 8 (PG 44:748); Chrysostom In Joannem Hom. 31 (PG 59:176); Augustine De Trinitate 15. 18. 32 (PL 42:1083).

[3] "Soweit uns Quellen für das nachapostolische Zeitalter zur Verfügung stehen, lehren sie einstimmig, dass die Kirche der Überzeugung lebte und sie verkündete, dass der Mensch durch Glaube und Liebesübung gerecht und selig werde." Harnack, "Lehre von der Seligkeit," ZTK 1 (1891):86. Cf. Ignatius Eph. 14:1 (SC 10:70); Herm. Vis. 3:8 (GCS 48:14, 23-15, 3); Clement of Alex. Strom. 2. 6 (PG 8:965); Ambrose Ep. 2. 78. 8 (PL 16:1324-25); Augustine De unico Baptismo 7. 11 (PL 43:601).

The post-Apostolic era. Historical theology can demonstrate how quickly in the post-Apostolic period these indicated possibilities of development entered in. The question of responsibility is naturally answered in different ways. Hans Joachim Schoeps sees the slipping away from the Pauline level, originating in the theology of Paul itself, "for the ethical need of gentile Christianity could not be fulfilled by Paul in the long run" (denn das ethische Bedürfnis der Christen aus dem Heidentum konnte letztlich von Paulus gar nicht erfüllt werden).[1]

The opposite opinion, that religion freed from legalism by Jesus and Paul soon returned to law dominion, that Paulinism in the second century in the Apostolic fathers was no longer understood, or that as by Marcion was misunderstood, meets us in representatives of the Protestant science of religion (F. Heiler), of the history of theology (A. v. Harnack), and of dogmatics (K. Barth) and is shared by progressive Catholic theologians (H. Küng).[2]

Many a clumsy formulation in the post-Apostolic period may account for the so called "innocent legalism" (unschuldige Werksgerechtigkeit),[3] for it was indeed--as Augustine says--the "carefree period" in which the speakers of Christianity could allow themselves to paint with only light strokes the grace-character of the gospel.[4]

---

[1] Hans Joachim Schoeps, Das Judenchristentum (Bern: Francke, 1964), p. 106.

[2] Friedrich Heiler, Der Katholizismus (Munich: E. Reinhardt, 1923), p. 238; Harnack, Dogmengeschichte, 1:192; Barth, KD 4/1:696; Küng, "Katholische Besinnung," in Theologie im Wandel, p. 467.

[3] Barth, KD 4/1:583.

[4] Augustine De Praed. sanct. 14. 27 (PL 44:980).

Nevertheless one must admit that--in respect to Paul--it is possible to ascertain very early in the post-Apostolic church, substantial accent-shifts and the introduction of foreign elements.

Post-Apostolic Christians, to be sure, still knew faith as πεποίθησις (trust)[1] and the formulations: through faith, not through works;[2] or by grace, not by works;[3] but love seems thereby already to have been emancipated from faith; love can precede faith[4]--or the reverse[5]--and it has sin-cancelling power.[6]

The biblical ideas of the "unearned gift,"[7] of faith that "is reckoned as righteousness,"[8] and "justifies a man before God"[9] were not unknown to the second century, but it is doubtful whether they meant the same thing as was meant in Paul.[10] For faith also already appears as fides dogmatica[11] and thereby is assigned to completion through love.[12] Therefore, to the Greek fathers of

---

[1] Clement of Rome Cor. 35:2 (SC 167:156).

[2] Ibid., 32:4 (SC 167:152).   [3] Polycarp Phil. 1:3 (SC 10:178).

[4] Ibid., 3:2-3 (SC 10:180).

[5] Ignatius Eph. 14:1 (SC 10:70).

[6] Clement of Rome Cor. 50:5 (SC 167:182).

[7] Irenaeus Adv. Haer. 4. 36. 6 (PG 7:1096).

[8] Ibid., 4. 5. 3 (PG 7:985).   [9] Ibid., 4. 5. 5 (PG 7:986).

[10] "It cannot, therefore, be maintained that Irenaeus understood the Pauline conception of the righteousness of faith, as he held simply that God regards as righteous everyone who acknowledges Christ and is ready to follow his teaching." Reinhold Seeberg, Textbook of the History of Doctrines, 6th ed. 2 vols., trans. Charles E. Hay (Grand Rapids, MI: Baker Book House, 1966), 1:132.

[11] Herm. Sim. 8:9 (GCS 48:74, 16-17).

[12] Ignatius Eph. 9:1 (SC 10:64).

the third and fourth centuries, faith is only "the first movement toward salvation,"[1] "preceding conjecture and anticipation of the understanding,"[2] and the "teaching understood by reason"[3] which finds its high point in the affirmation of the Trinity.[4] Faith is here merely a synonym for orthodoxy.

Since "they had not made Paulinism inwardly their own," as Harnack says,[5] the sola fide became either a "formula to excuse laxism" (Deckformel des Laxismus)[6] or, as we have already indicated, a reduction formula for the single forgiveness of sin at baptism.[7]

So works had to gain salvation-attaining character because faith was reduced in content as well as in time. Already in the Apostolic fathers alms-giving was valid as expiating sin.[8] In Tertullian and Cyprian this view forms a substantial part of the theology of penitence. Baptism and penitence (fasting, chastisement, prayer, almsgiving) form the "two redeeming planks"[9] through which God is assuaged,[10] sin atoned,[11] and freedom from punishment

---

[1] Clement of Alex. Strom. 2. 6 (PG 8:965).

[2] Ibid. (PG 8:964).

[3] Origen Contra Celsum 1. 13 (PG 11:680).

[4] Basil De Spiritu Sancto 12. 28 (PG 32:117).

[5] Harnack, "Lehre von der Seligkeit," ZTK 1 (1891):88. Sie haben sich den Paulinismus "innerlich nicht zu eigen gemacht."

[6] Ibid., p. 177.   [7] Idem, Dogmengeschichte, 1:190.

[8] Polycarp Phil. 10:2 (SC 10:188); Didache 4:6; Barnabas 19:10 (SC 172:209); 2 Clement 16.

[9] Tertullian De poenitentia 12 (PL 1:1360).

[10] Ibid., 9 (PL 1:1354).

[11] Idem De jejuniis 3 (PL 2:1009); Cyprian De op. et el. 1 (PL 4:626).

won.[1] With this was associated the thought of substitute performance of one for the other[2] and the idea of personal merit performance before God. Thus, one can make God into a debtor.[3]

These performances were regarded as especially meritorious because they went beyond the commandments and were valid as beyond duty (opera supererogatoria).[4] Especially meritorious was the renunciation of the second marriage[5] and the condition of virginity.[6]

As Wirth indicated, the real merit-theology of Tertullian[7] begins here with the opera supererogatoria. Already in the Apostolic fathers the thought of a relationship between work and reward[8] is found--reward as a right[9] and the work of the believer as a return payment to God.[10] The formulation that God will pay in the form of a "worthy reward" (τὰ ἄξια ἐπιτίμια) according to the value of the works is found several times in Justin Martyr,[11] but nevertheless

---

[1] Tertullian De poenitentia 6 (PL 1:1347).

[2] Herm. Sim. 2:5 (GCS 48:48, 23-49, 5).

[3] Tertullian De poenitentia 2 (PL 1:1340); Cyprian De op. et el. 15 (PL 4:637).

[4] Didache 6:2; Herm. Sim. 5:3 (GCS 48:54, 15-16); Tertullian Exh. cast. 10 (PL 2:974).

[5] Herm. Mand. 4:4 (SC 53:163. "Gloire supplémentaire").

[6] Jerome In Ev. Matt. 2. 13 (PL 26:92); Augustine Sermo 354. 9 (PL 39:1568).

[7] Wirth, "Verdienst"-Begriff bei Tertullian, p. 9.

[8] Didache 4:7; Ignatius Ad Polyc. 1:3 (SC 10:146).

[9] Ibid., 6:2 (SC 10:152).   [10] 2 Clement 1; ibid., 15.

[11] Justin 1 Apology 12 (PG 6:341); ibid., 43 (PG 6:393); ibid., 44 (PG 6:396).

the real theology of merit begins with Tertullian.[1]

<u>Tertullian</u>. O. H. Pesch names three possible sources of Tertullian's thought on merit: (1) defense against Marcion's attacks on the God of the OT, (2) ascetic rigorism, and (3) the high valuation of Roman juridism.[2] In any case, it is certain that through his thought and language, he laid the basis for the Catholic doctrine of merit, although later developments partly corrected his teaching.

The whole salvation process is, with Tertullian, an ethical and legal one. From these two sources he draws his theology of merit. Either one performs something extra in the ethical realm or one acquires an excess of performances in the satisfaction process.[3]

Tertullian sees God as the <u>deus offensus</u>[4] who, at the same time, is the injured party as well as the judge. He requires from the accused person <u>satisfactio</u>, <u>commpensatio</u>,[5] and also judges him accordingly. This juridical relationship of God to the person, however, is still more sharpened through the influence of views borrowed from the cultic-religious world-view of the ancients. God, namely as the injured party, is "made angry" and must "avenge"

---

[1] See Schultz, "Der sittliche Begriff des Verdienstes," ThStKr 67 (1894):24; Pesch, "Lehre vom Verdienst," in <u>Wahrheit und Verkündigung</u>, 2:1874.

[2] Ibid. "Juridism" means a view of life based on legal principles.

[3] Wirth, <u>"Verdienst"-Begriff bei Tertullian</u>, p. 35.

[4] Tertullian <u>De poenitentia</u> 11 (<u>PL</u> 1:1358); idem <u>Ad uxorem</u> 2.7 (<u>PL</u> 1:1413).

[5] Idem <u>De poenitentia</u> 7 (<u>PL</u> 1:1352); ibid., 6 (<u>PL</u> 1:1347).

the crime.[1] Ascetic performances of self-humiliation (sackcloth and ashes, uncleanliness, unseasoned foods, prayers, fasting, tears) and martyrdom are "services" which have as their goal the "appeasing of the angry God,"[2] the winning again of His "favor,"[3] and His "softening" (mitigatio).[4] The less man spares himself, the more God spares him.[5] Thus, on the one hand, the performances of penitence become hostia placatoria.[6] On the other hand they also can become, so far as the person has an excess, merits (merita); and in that instance man is no longer a debtor to God; instead, God is a debtor of man, according to the principle: "A good deed has God as its debtor" (Bonum factum Deum habet debitorem).[7]

One can also reach the same goal if the non-sinning Christian does more than is commanded.[8] Everything obeys the law "Like deed involves like merit" (Par factum par habet meritum).[9] This already pertains to this life,[10] but much more so to eternity where God will reward differently "for the variety of merits" (pro varietate meritorum).[11]

---

[1] Idem Adv. Marcionem Lib. 1. 26 (PL 2:303).
[2] Idem De jejuniis 7 (PL 2:1012).
[3] Idem Exh. cast. 3 (PL 2:966).
[4] Idem De poenitentia 9 (PL 1:1354).
[5] Ibid. (PL 1:1355).
[6] Idem De patientia 13 (PL 1:1380).
[7] Idem De poenitentia 2 (PL 1:1340).
[8] Idem Exh. cast. 10 (PL 2:974).
[9] Idem De patientia 10 (PL 1:1376).
[10] Idem De oratione 4 (PL 1:1260).
[11] Idem Scorpiace 6 (PL 2:157).

Asserting that Tertullian knew God only as a judge and reward-giver and forgot the Father of the gospel would certainly be one-sided. It would be just as onesided to ignore Tertullian's concept of grace in the work of the Christian.[1] Tertullian knows God as a kind Father[2] and the works of the Christian as having God as their author.[3]

But the work is nevertheless not consecutively experienced salvation, it is achievement (Werkerei)[4] under the aspect of a lack or excess of merit, and God is only the Father if one effects His favor.[5] Otherwise God is the angry God whose honor consists of fear on the part of man.[6]

Thus, we find that Tertullian was really the founder of the Christian teaching of merit. Nevertheless it remained for Cyprian, his younger compatriot, to become the "father of the doctrine of good works" (Vater der Lehre von den guten Werken).[7]

Cyprian's teaching was wholly dependent on the "Master";[8] and

---

[1] Bakhuizen van den Brink even says that Tertullian really anticipated the Augustinian "promittendo debitorem se deus fecit." "Mereor," TU 78 (1961):334. This seems to us, in view of the ambivalent picture of God in Tertullian, to be a very optimistic judgment.

[2] Tertullian De poenitentia 8 (PL 1:1353).

[3] Ibid., 2 (PL 1:1340).   [4] Ibid., 6 (PL 1:1348).

[5] Ibid., 6 (PL 1:1346).   [6] Ibid., 7 (PL 1:1351).

[7] Harnack, Dogmengeschichte, 1:466.

[8] Also with Cyprian merit is derived from an excess of satisfaction and from supererogation. See Wirth, "Verdienst"-Begriff bei Cyprian, pp. 52, 59. God must be appeased (De op. et el. 5 [PL 4:628]), His mercy must be earned (ibid. [PL 4:628]), Heaven must be earned (ibid., 14 [PL 4:635]). Thus, with God a business is carried on (ibid., 15 [PL 4:637]) by which a person can make himself free from sins (ibid., 1 [PL 4:626]) and beyond this enter capital

when the Montanist Tertullian was no longer heard by the Catholic Church, and his writings were banned by the Decretum Gelasii in 495, the Bishop and Martyr Cyprian reached the ear of his contemporaries and of the following generations. With this legacy the greatest North African Augustine had to come to terms, for there was no way past this tradition.

The era before Augustine. The East, to be sure, had developed similar thoughts also,[1] but they played a subordinate role in view of the different emphases in the East and the West. Practical juridism of the West contributed especially to the success of the doctrine of merit.

Western theology before Augustine shows ambivalences similar to those which later are found in Augustine himself. The most

---

to his heavenly account which will be paid to him on the day of judgment (De orat. dom. 32 [PL 4:558]). God's righteousness consists namely in counting merits (Ep. 58. 10 [BKV 60:214]) and ascertaining who should receive the richer reward (De mortalitate 26 [PL 4:624]).

[1] See Clement of Alex. Strom. 4. 6 (PG 8:1248); ibid., 6. 14 (PG 9:329); ibid., 7. 12 (PG 9:501); Origen De princip. Prol. 5 (PG 11:118); idem Comm. in Epist. ad Rom. 2. 5 (PG 14:880); ibid., 2. 7 (PG 14:887). However, he also emphasizes that the person can not make any demands (ibid., 10. 38 [PG 14:1287]). Only earthly relationships (ibid., 7. 4 [PG 14:1108]) and the sins of the unbelievers can be explained with the concept debitum (ibid., 4. 1 [PG 14:964]). This recognition is, of course, not held consistently, for he knows an earned increase of grace (ibid., 8. 7 [PG 14:1179]), obedience as payment of debt, and the works of supererogation (ibid., 10. 14 [PG 14:1275]). The same discrepant picture is found with the Cappadocians. While Basil stresses grace (Hom. in Ps. 104. 5 [PG 29:492]), Gregory of Nazianzus speaks of eternal life not only as a gift but also as a reward (Oratio 2. 17 [PG 35:425]). Cf. Cyril of Jerusalem (Catech. 18. 1 [PG 33:1017]), Gregory of Nyssa (De pauper. amand. Orat. 1 [PG 46:461]), and Chrysostom (In Epist. ad Rom. Hom. 2. 3 [PG 60:404]). However, a systematical and juridical teaching of merit never developed in the East. See DTC, s.v., "Mérite," by J. Rivière; Stanislaus Tyszkiewicz, "Warum verwerfen die Orthodoxen unsere Verdienstlehre?," ZKT 41 (1917): 400-06.

emphatic stress on grace can not possibly suppress the long accepted thought of merit. Typical of this is Marius Victorinus who, not wrongly, has been called an "Augustine before Augustine" (Augustinus ante Augustinum).[1] With him the grace of God unambiguously has first rank. He is the first to express the formulation sola fide,[2] who sees the person as justified gratia et bonitate,[3] but, is nevertheless, unable to rise above the concept of meritum, which he uses for works after justification. Like Augustine later he can only limit it: "Our merit is grace, for the great gift which is received is beyond merit: it is the glory of the one who has performed it, not of the one who has received it."[4]

This striving concerning the totality of grace with simultaneous respect for the tradition of the Church is found even more clearly in Ambrose, whom Augustine, as we know, called his "praeceptor."[5]

That man has nothing of himself--indeed, that God must even set his will free[6]--and that he therefore only through faith can

---

[1] Loofs, Leitfaden, p. 280; Harnack, Dogmengeschichte, 3:36.

[2] See Walter Koehler, Dogmengeschichte, 2 vols. (Zurich: M. Niehans, 1951), 1:184.

[3] Marius Victorinus In Ep. ad Eph. 1. 2. 7 (PL 8:1255).

[4] Marius Victorinus In Ep. ad Eph. 1. 1. 14 (PL 8:1247). "Et gratia est quae meritum nostrum; ultra enim meritum munus magnum, quod accipitur: gloria ejus est qui praestitit, non ejus qui accepit."

[5] Augustine Op. impf. 6. 21 (PL 45:1549).

[6] Ambrose In Lucam 1. 1. 10 (PL 15:1617).

be justified[1] comes out strongly in several places in Ambrose's writings. In fact, there are some of his tones that ring more clearly than those of his student Augustine and remind us of the most striking confessions of Luther:

> Non habeo igitur unde gloriari in operibus meis possim . . . Non gloriabor quia justus sum, sed gloriabor quia redemptus sum. Gloriabor, non quia vacuus peccatis sum, sed quia mihi sunt remissa peccata.[2]

Harnack called this confession, rightly, "Augustinianism before Augustine, indeed more than Augustinianism" (Augustinismus vor Augustin, ja mehr als Augustinismus).[3]

This, however, is only one avenue of theological thought since the Apostolic Fathers and Tertullian. Beside it there is an uncritical acceptance of popular Catholicism with all its well-known components such as justification through love[4]--which later had a great effect upon Augustine--or components such as the believer, who works like a mercenary for the wages.[5] In the same way, one thinks of God, as a "payer of merits" (remunerator meritorum);[6] of merits, as measured against the performances[7] and counterbalancing sins;[8] of works, which redeem;[9] and of the balance,

---

[1] Idem Enarratio in Ps. 39. 11 (PL 14:1112).
[2] Idem De Jacob et vita beata 1. 6. 21 (PL 14:637).
[3] Harnack, Dogmengeschichte, 3:51.
[4] Ambrose, Ep. 2. 78. 8 (PL 16:1324-25).
[5] Idem Ep. 1. 2. 12 (PL 16:920).
[6] Idem Expos. in Ps. 118. 7 (PL 15:1276).
[7] Idem In Lucam 8. 47 (PL 15:1869).
[8] Ibid., 3. 38 (PL 15:1688).
[9] Idem De Elia 20. 76 (PL 14:759).

which one can tip in his own favor,[1] as well as of God, whom one can make his debtor through good deeds.[2]

A similar tension is found also in Jerome, a contemporary of Augustine. Likewise engaged in the struggle against Pelagius, he cries out in words which remind us of the most beautiful in Ambrose and Augustine: "If we consider our merits, we have no hope."[3] Merits go back to God, for "He crowns and praises in us what He Himself has done."[4] This sentence recalls Augustine's famous formulation: "What else but His gifts does God crown when He crowns our merits?" (Cum Deus coronat merita nostra, nihil aliud coronat quam munera sua).[5]

Yet, he also speaks of praemia[6] and merita,[7] for which we can strive and earn. Supererogatory works gain more honor[8] and salvation is freely given only until baptism; afterward it must be attained through works.[9]

---

[1] Idem Apolog. Proph. David 6. 24 (PL 14:901).

[2] Idem De officiis 1. 11. 39 (PL 16:38).

[3] Jerome In Isaim 17. 64. 8 (PL 24:625). "Si nostra consideremus merita, desperandum est."

[4] Idem Dialog. contra Pelag. 3. 6 (PL 23:601). "Coronat in nobis et laudat quod ipse operatus est."

[5] Augustine Ep. 194. 5. 19 (PL 33:880).

[6] Jerome Dialog. contra Pelag. 3. 5 (PL 23:601).

[7] Idem Adv. Jov. 2. 28 (PL 23:339).

[8] Idem In Ev. Matt. 2. 13 (PL 26:92).

[9] Idem Adv. Jov. 2. 32 (PL 23:344).

Augustine. This theological legacy Augustine had to tackle. No other teacher in the Church since Paul has so strongly emphasized the grace of God. He says, "Our life is nothing else than the grace of God!" (Vita nostra nihil aliud quam Dei gratia).[1] Similar to Luther who through his existential need and resistance of Rome became an ever more convinced Paulinist, Augustine also matured through his life experience and the struggle against Pelagius and the Pelagians to become the doctor gratiae.

But even the most independent and genial thinker cannot withdraw himself from his time and place. The final-meritorious element, from which Augustine was not able to extricate himself, made it impossible for him to construct a complete understanding of the gospel of Paul. The sola fide[2] remained closed to him and the sola gratia was interpreted by acceptance of the traditional doctrine of baptism, by a concept of faith reduced to an intellectual agreement,[3] and by the doctrine of inspiration-grace (diffusio caritatis,[4] inspiratio gratiae,[5] inspiratio caritatis[6]) as "repair[7]-,

---

[1] Augustine De grat. et lib. arb. 8. 20 (PL 44:893).

[2] Augustine understands by sola fide either laxism (Enarr. in Ps. 31. 2. 3 [PL 36:259] or viva fides, i.e. faith working by love in order to earn God's forgiveness (De fide et operibus 22. 40-41 [PL 40:223]).

[3] Idem De praed. sanct. 2. 5 (PL 44:963).

[4] Idem De perf. iust. hom. 5. 11 (PL 44:297).

[5] Idem De div. quaest. ad Simpl. 1. 2. 21 (PL 40:127).

[6] Idem Ep. 188. 2. 7 (PL 33:852).

[7] Idem Enarr. in Ps. 129. 1 (PL 37:1696); idem De spiritu et litt. 27. 47 (PL 44:229).

medicinal[1]- and sanative-process."[2] Thus, justification was transferred into the person[3] and was treated also as final through the process of ever becoming righteous in love.[4] Instead of its being imputative, as with Luther, Augustine thought of it as sanative. Thereby he prepared for the Middle Ages' fides caritate formata; that is, love became again the condition and not the evidence of justification. And although all this--because indeed even love is a gift and the will must first be set free and constantly kept free and activated--in no way justifies one to speak of merits, but rather of the denial of merits, even a man such as Augustine could not escape the demands of the Church, which for hundreds of years felt itself duty-bound to the concept of merit.

Augustine's retention of the meritum-concept appears like a concession to the popular Catholicism of his time.[5] This seems to correspond more with the historical facts than the projection of the Aristotelian-Scholastic principle of the causa prima et secunda back in the doctrine of grace of the Bishop of Hippo.[6]

---

[1] Idem Op. impf. 3. 149 (PL 45:1308); idem Sermo 156. 5. 5 (PL 38:852).

[2] Idem Soliloqu. 1. 6. 12 (PL 32:876); idem Sermo 156. 5. 5 (PL 38:852).

[3] Idem De spiritu et litt. 15 (PL 44:229).

[4] Idem Ep. 167. 3. 13 (PL 33:738).

[5] See Harnack, Dogmengeschichte, 3:231; Norman P. Williams, The Grace of God (London: Longmans, Green & Co., 1930), p. 40. Hence also Augustine's crass manner of speaking in preaching! "Quodam modo Dominus Deus noster mercatores nos vult esse, mutationem nobiscum facit." Sermo 177. 10 (PL 38:959). But he also speaks differently! Cf. ibid., 158. 2 (PL 38:863).

[6] DTC, s.v. "Mérite," by J. Rivière.

Further, it is more true than the assertion of an alleged merit-doctrine in Paul.[1] The latter could be interpreted only--after what has been said about Paul--as a misunderstanding of the Apostle's teaching.

The early Augustine, who speaks like a philosopher and believes like a Semi-Pelagian,[2] still talked very candidly of free will,[3] very hesitantly of grace,[4] and hence, all the more optimistically of merits.[5] The late Augustine--after 396/97[6]--indeed held fast to the concept of merit ("We admit to acquiring merits here but to getting the recompense there"),[7] but annulled its

---

[1] Burnaby, Amor Dei, p. 239.

[2] McSorley, Luther: Right or Wrong?, pp. 65, 73; David E. Roberts, "The Earliest Writings," in A Companion to the Study of St. Augustine, ed. Roy W. Battenhouse (Grand Rapids, MI: Baker Book House, 1979), p. 123.

[3] The early Augustine sees the will as strong in itself and free (De lib. arb. 3. 3. 8 [PL 32:1275]); of course, all is foreseen by God (ibid.), but not determined. A person can overcome sin--a sentence upon which Pelagius based himself(!)--for there is no compulsion to sin (ibid., 3. 18. 50 [PL 32:1295]). Even the late Augustine can say: "Consentire autem vocationi Dei, vel ab ea dissentire . . . propriae voluntatis est." De spiritu et litt. 34. 60 (PL 44:240).

[4] Idem Retract. 1. 9. 2 (PL 32:595).

[5] With "occultissima merita" one can prepare oneself for justification (De div. quaest. 63. 4 [PL 40:72]). The justified one, however, can earn and demand the reward; he is worthy of it (De moribus eccl. cath. 25. 47 [PL 32:1331]). It is an error to believe that the soul has no merits in the eyes of God (Soliloqu. 1. 1. 3 [PL 32:871]).

[6] "The victory of God's grace befell him in the year 396." Burnaby, Amor Dei, p. 235. Cf. Retract. 2. 1. 1: "Vicit Dei gratia" (PL 32:629).

[7] Idem Op. impf. 2. 101 (PL 45:1182). "Hic enim meritum comparari, ibi autem praemia reddi fatemini."

content by referring everything back to grace, everything back to God.[1]

The following considerations clarify this conclusion:

1. The doctrine of praedestinatio gemina is based not as with the early Augustine on a vocatio in consequence of the person's merits, which are foreknown by God, but on the electio ex proposito.[2] God does not will that all people be saved, but of those for whom He does will it, it happens,[3] and indeed, "unchangeably and invincibly" (indeclinabiliter et insuperabiliter).[4] Why God acts thus is a mystery;[5] how He thus proceeds, Augustine explains in different ways: Either everybody is not sufficiently

---

[1] Grace cannot be earned: ". . . et Dei gratiam, quae non secundum merita nostra datur." De dono pers. 20. 51 (PL 45:1025); De div. quaest. ad Simpl. 1. 2. 7 (PL 40:115); De praed. sanct. 3. 7 (PL 44:964); Sermo 169. 2. 3 (PL 38:917); Enarrat. in Ps. 30. 2. 6 (PL 36:234). Merit is itself grace: "Ipsum hominis meritum donum est gratuitum." Ep. 186. 3. 10 (PL 33:820); De praed. sanct. 5. 10 (PL 44:968). Therefore God rewards not the work of the person, but His own gift: "Si ergo Dei dona sunt bona merita tua, non Deus coronat merita tua tanquam merita tua, sed tanquam dona sua." De grat. et lib. arb. 6. 15 (PL 44:891); Ep. 194. 5. 19 (PL 33:880); Sermo 131. 8. 8 (PL 38:733); Conf. 9. 13. 34 (PL 32:778). God does not owe anything to anyone: "Deus autem nulli debet aliquid, quia omnia gratuito praestat." De lib. arb. 3. 16. 45 (PL 32:1293). Does Augustine admit some kind of meritum de congruo? Lange affirms it (De gratia, pp. 569, 579-80), Neveut denies it ("Du mérite de convenance," DT(P) 35 [1932]:9). As a matter of fact, Augustine's statements sound ambiguous. On the one hand, every work before faith is sin (Enarr. in Ps. 31. 2. 4 [PL 36:259]) and no merit precedes justification (De spirit. et litt. 10. 16 [PL 44:210]). Yet, on the other hand, forgiveness is not without merit (Ep. 194. 3. 9 [PL 33:877]) and faith merits justification, i.e., charity which performs good works (Ep. 186. 3. 7 [PL 33:818]).

[2] Idem De div. quaest. ad Simpl. 1. 2. 6 (PL 40:114).

[3] Idem Enchir. 103. 27 (PL 40:280).

[4] Idem De corrept. et gratia 12. 38 (PL 44:940).

[5] Idem De div. quaest. ad Simpl. 1. 2. 16 (PL 40:120).

(congruenter) called[1] or God simply has not called everybody.[2]

In any case, God has predetermined (praedestinavit ad vitam)[3] for life a certain number of those rightly condemned because of their sins,[4] a number which can be neither diminished nor increased;[5] the others are lost (praedestinavit ad poenam).[6] As is the number of angels of God that have fallen away, so is the number of people who are predestined to salvation.[7]

If everything has been determined and worked out by God (electio, initium fidei, perseverantia in finem), then, in reality, every merit of a person is excluded. There are neither merits that precede grace nor real merits in grace, because God alone gives power and success.[8] Indeed, the predestined one can go astray only occasionally, and because of the infallibility of the predestination[9] he cannot be lost (Ex istis nullus perit, quia omnes electi sunt).[10] So although Augustine continues to employ the concept meritum, he

---

[1] Ibid., 1. 2. 13 (PL 40:118).

[2] Ibid., 1. 2. 19 (PL 40:124).

[3] Idem De civ. Dei 22. 24. 5 (PL 41:792).

[4] Sin itself has no root in God. Sermo 176. 5. 5 (PL 38:952).

[5] Idem De corrept. et gratia 13. 39 (PL 44:940).

[6] Idem Enchir. 100. 26 (PL 40:279).

[7] Augustine Enchir. 62. 16 (PL 40:261); cf. Georg Kraus: "Manichäistische Lückentheorie." Vorherbestimmung (Freiburg i. Br.: Herder, 1977), p. 41.

[8] Augustine De grat. et lib. arb. 7. 16 (PL 44:891).

[9] Idem De corrept. et gratia 7. 13 (PL 44:924).

[10] Ibid., 7. 14 (PL 44:924).

has in actuality overcome and dissolved it.

The concept of merit therefore appears like a foreign element in his doctrine of predestination. Obviously, Augustine drew back from the last, logical step, and out of regard for tradition and the Church refused to give up the concept.

2. Augustine's <u>sola gratia</u>--taken to its logical conclusion--likewise leaves no room for any genuine teaching of merit. As in the case of the word "merit," so Augustine behaves in the question of the free will. He applies the concept (<u>liberum arbitrium</u>) formally, but he empties it of meaning.[1] He is conscious that this involves a difficult question.[2] Free will exists[3] and it does not exist.[4] Free will is in the sinner a <u>servum arbitrium</u>,[5] a <u>liberum arbitrium captivatum</u>,[6] that is, it occupies itself continually in choosing sin, for it is incapable of choosing the good. Hence, all deeds of pagans are "vices rather than virtues," too.[7]

The will is not free, it must be set free. A person is by nature an opponent of God and must, like Paul on the way to Damascus

---

[1] Kraus, <u>Vorherbestimmung</u>, p. 35.

[2] Augustine <u>De grat. et lib. arb.</u> 1. 1 (<u>PL</u> 44:881).

[3] Idem <u>Contra duas ep. Pelag.</u> 1. 3. 6 (<u>PL</u> 44:553); idem <u>De grat. et lib. arb.</u> 1. 1 (<u>PL</u> 44:881); ibid., 2. 2 (<u>PL</u> 44:882).

[4] Idem <u>Enchir.</u> 30. 9 (<u>PL</u> 40:246).

[5] Idem <u>Contra Jul.</u> 2. 8. 23 (<u>PL</u> 44:689).

[6] Idem <u>Contra duas ep. Pelag.</u> 3. 8. 24 (<u>PL</u> 44:607).

[7] Idem <u>De civ. Dei</u> 19. 25 (<u>PL</u> 41:656).

be overpowered.[1] The will set free, however, does not act under duress, but along with the caritas God gives a new will which wills what God also wills and is capable also of carrying out what He wills.[2] The free will is thus not power of choice toward good or evil--as the Pelagians asserted--but a person's natural spontaneity toward evil or God-empowered spontaneity toward good.[3] Thus, the natura liberata[4] comes into being.

In all this God effects the beginning as well as the continuation and the completion of will and deed.[5] Thus, God's commandments can be kept because God provides the capability to do so (Da quod iubes, et iube quod vis).[6]

The question raised for us here is whether grace draws the will or whether it forms the will? Does it merely attract it, or does it call it into existence?

One can find either idea in Augustine. However, at the beginning (396/97)[7] and in the middle (411/12)[8] of his late period,

---

[1] Idem De div. quaest. ad Simpl. 1. 2. 22 (PL 40:128); idem De grat. et lib. arb. 14. 29 (PL 44:898).

[2] See Bengt Hägglund, History of Theology (St. Louis, MO: Concordia, 1968), p. 138.

[3] See Burnaby, Amor Dei, p. 227; Paul Lehmann, "The Anti-Pelagian Writings," in Companion to the Study, pp. 217, 219.

[4] Augustine De grat. et lib. arb. 14. 27 (PL 44:897).

[5] Ibid., 17. 33 (PL 44:901).

[6] Idem Conf. 10. 29. 40 (PL 32:796); idem De spirit. et litt. 13. 22 (PL 44:214); idem De grat. et lib. arb. 15. 31 (PL 44:900).

[7] "Ut velimus, et suum esse voluit et nostrum: suum vocando, nostrum sequendo." De div. quaest. ad Simpl. 1. 2. 10 (PL 40:117).

[8] "Consentire autem vocationi Dei, vel ab ea dissentire, sicut dixi, propriae voluntatis est." De spirit. et litt. 34. 60 (PL 44:240).

he makes room for the independent will in a person drawn by grace, while at the end of his life (426) he asserts that the will is being realized "without us."[1] Catholic interpreters find the greatest support in the statements that speak in the direction of a cooperation of "transcendent grace and subordinate will" (J. Saint-Martin),[2] so that the "consensus" of the will is preserved (H. McSorley),[3] and of human concurrence (concours) in the sense of a causa secunda (J. Rivière)[4] as well as of a "self-moving and selfmastery" (Selbstbewegung und Selbstherrschaft) of the will (J. Mausbach).[5] Protestant investigators either see a "shift of gravity" (Verschiebung des Schwerpunktes) between the first and the last statements of the late Augustine (H. Jonas),[6] or generally deny (G. Nygren) that, under the title of Augustinian predestination, room can be made in the will for a "personal authorship" (selbständige Urheberschaft).[7]

If we regard Augustine's late statement that only through

---

[1] "Ut ergo velimus, sine nobis operatur; cum autem volumus, et sic volumus ut faciamus, nobiscum cooperatur." De grat. et lib. arb. 17. 33 (PL 44:901).

[2] DTC, s.v. "Prédestination, Saint Augustin," by J. Saint-Martin.

[3] McSorley, Luther: Right or Wrong?, p. 110.

[4] DTC, s.v. "Mérite," by J. Rivière.

[5] Joseph Mausbach, Die Ethik des hlg. Augustinus, 2 vols. (Freiburg i. Br.: Herder, 1909), 2:27.

[6] Hans Jonas, Augustin und das paulinische Freiheitsproblem (Göttingen: Vandenhoeck & Ruprecht, 1930), p. 53.

[7] Gotthard Nygren, Das Prädestinationsproblem in der Theologie Augustins (Göttingen: Vandenhoeck & Ruprecht, 1956), p. 73.

God, the will becomes capable of good without the participation of the person, as the last word of Augustine on the matter, then, as G. Nygren says, the ground is completely cut from under the thought of merit.[1]

3. Augustine's definition of the reward of merits as the coronation of God by God likewise dissolves the concept of merit completely. For, even if he was of the opinion that the judgment according to works supported the thought of merit,[2] the latter is completely emptied by the view that indeed God works alone[3] and that the working of a person is actually a "being-worked" (Gewirktsein).[4]

But the "being-worked" of the person signifies that <u>God</u> "merits," that He crowns Himself in His gifts. This excludes every human worthiness,[5] every rightful claim,[6] and every morality of

---

[1] "Der Meritumgedanke ist untrennbar mit einer kausalen Betrachtung des menschlichen Willens- und Handlungslebens verbunden. Soll sinnvoll von Schuld bzw. Verdienst gesprochen werden, so muss der Beurteilte immer selber der tatsächliche Urheber der Zustände sein, die für ihn Schuld oder Verdienst mit sich bringen. Nun zeigte es sich aber, dass die Gnade eine Funktion des freien Willens nach der anderen übernimmt: die Bekehrung, die guten Vorsätze, die Kraft sie auszuführen, und den endlichen Sieg. Die Gnade, wie Augustin sie hier darstellt, scheint einfach jeden Gedanken an den freien Willen als selbständigen Faktor auf dem ursächlichen Gebiet auszuschalten und damit auch dem Meritumgedanken den Grund zu entziehen." Ibid., p. 71.

[2] Ibid., p. 70.

[3] "Ea quae dicuntur merita nostra dona sunt eius." <u>De Trinitate</u> 13. 10. 14 (<u>PL</u> 42:1024).

[4] "Agis, si agaris, et bene agis, si a bono agaris." <u>Sermo</u> 128. 7. 9 (<u>PL</u> 38:718).

[5] "Exsultabunt justitia tua, non sua . . . Cui ergo debemus quia sumus, illi debemus quia et justificati sumus." <u>Enarr. in Ps.</u> 144. 10 (<u>PL</u> 37:1875).

[6] "Si ergo gratis, nihil tu attulisti, nihil meruisti: nam

reward.[1] That the working of God occurs in and through a person cannot be denoted as merit, for a person is only receiving and must also be completely prepared for this receiving. God is a "debtor" only through promise;[2] but the promise cannot be earned. Of course, the believer must work toward salvation, but the efficacy consists of "being-worked." Therefore with Augustine works have final but not meritorious character.

Merita nostra thus with the doctor gratiae must be viewed as an inconsequential and dangerous manner of speaking-- inconsequential, because the concept has been emptied of its content; dangerous, because through the retaining of the talk of merits an ambiguous theology arises: a theology which allows that even with the theoretical exclusion of the concept, the Church could in practice leave open the back door, through which worthiness, claim, and reward-morality could slip in again. Since Augustine was not to be ignored, later theology had to "artfully harmonize" (künstlich harmonisieren)[3] grace and performance.

Augustine did not draw the final consequences, despite the "victory of God's grace" (vicit Dei gratia)[4] and the "deliverance

---

si meritis aliquid redditum est, merces est, non gratia." Ibid. (PL 37:1875-76).

[1] "Si gratiam ideo tibi dedit Deus, quia gratis dedit, gratis ama. Noli ad praemium diligere Deum; ipse sit praemium tuum." In Joannis Ev. 3. 21 (PL 35:1405); ibid., 91. 4 (PL 35:1862).

[2] "Debitor enim factus est, non aliquid a nobis accipiendo, sed quod ei placuit promittendo." Sermo 158. 2 (PL 38:863).

[3] Heiler, Katholizismus, p. 103.

[4] Augustine Retract. 2. 1. 1 (PL 32:629).

from merits" (avulsisti merita mea, inseruisti dona tua).[1] This renders to his teaching of grace an ununified, even contradictory, appearance.

Holding fast to the concept of merit exonerated him from having to deny the popular statements used since Tertullian and Cyprian. His teaching of the inspiration of grace, which obliged him to put less emphasis on predestination and caused tension with his view of sola gratia, again enabled the blending of the final with the meritorious element. Works of love then occur not as a result of salvation but take place to achieve salvation, and in this movement receive again the character of an achievement. God does not give (donare) salvation, He pays it out (reddere).[2] Thereby Augustine, as Harnack notes, opened the door again to a kind of "subtile legalism" (feine Werksgerechtigkeit).[3]

Hence many sayings that were customary since the Apostolic Fathers and Tertullian are also expressed by him: God owes and pays, for after He has tested the work He cannot refuse the wages;[4] therefore God and the person have entered into a business relation;[5] God has provided a certificate of indebtedness (chirographum) and a bond for security (cautio);[6] the person is to claim it eagerly

---

[1] Idem Enarr. in Ps. 142. 18 (PL 37:1855).

[2] See Hamm, Promissio, pp. 14-15.

[3] Harnack, Dogmengeschichte, 3:218.

[4] Augustine Sermo 333. 2 (PL 38:1464).

[5] Ibid., 177. 10 (PL 38:959).

[6] Ibid., 110. 4-5 (PL 38:641).

(avarus exactor)[1] when he has done what he should.[2] The picture of scales is suggested, where a plus of good deeds is able to tip the scales against the sins.[3] Thus, the whole arsenal of the ancient Christian manner of penitence and punishment finds its place here again: a threefold forgiveness of sin through baptism (forgiveness of original sin and the deeds of sin before conversion), through fasting and prayer (forgiveness of daily sins), and through confession, the magna poenitentia, for mortal sins. In sentences like "practice alms, fasting, prayers; by these daily sins are purged(!)" (Exercete vos in eleemosynis, in jejuniis, in orationibus. His enim purgantur quotidiana peccata),[4] Augustine is more a pupil of Tertullian and Cyprian than of Paul.

To this penitence of satisfaction, known already from early times, he adds speculation about the effect of works on the future life. Hence he believes that one can also distribute the Eucharist or alms on behalf of the dead: for the righteous ones it will be a thank-offering, for those in the middle an atoning sacrifice, and for the wicked "damnation is made more tolerable (!)."[5]

Augustine vitiated all this through his theology of promise, but his concession to works was a popular trait which only with difficulty could be connected with his teaching of grace and this

---

[1] Idem Enarr. in Ps. 32. 2. 2 (PL 36:286).

[2] Idem Sermo 158. 2 (PL 38:863).

[3] Ibid., 259. 4 (PL 38:1199).

[4] Ibid., 9. 11 (PL 38:88).

[5] Idem Enchir. 110 (PL 40:283-84).

trait was constantly in danger of becoming emancipated.

Instead of building on Paul, Augustine laid the foundation for further construction of the teaching of merit. This construction was slowly prepared in the Late Patristic period and reached its high point in the Scholastic era. Thus the Middle Ages became the real high point of merit-theology. Various factors contributed to this development:

1. The authority of Augustine finally conferred upon the thought of merit the seal of orthodoxy and theological approval. Whoever from then on would oppose it would be suspected of being a Manichaean.

2. However, at the same time one could no longer ignore Augustine's teaching of grace. Whoever still stressed the superiority of the will and devalued grace to a means of helping was branded as a Pelagian.

3. But Augustine's authority was not sufficient to preserve his teaching from reductions. Even where Augustine was followed in the all-encompassing agency of grace and in the final-meritorious way of salvation, the attempt was made to select from the late Augustine the teaching on the realized will and double predestination (Caesarius of Arles, Council of Orange).[1] The rigorous Augustinianism (Lucidus in the 5th century, Gottschalk in the 9th century) therefore could not assert itself.

4. In Semi-Pelagianism (John Cassian, Faustus of Riez) the opposition against Augustine increased with regard to the

---

[1] DS 397.

assertion of a temporal superiority of the will over grace. Since with Faustus of Riez grace reaches man only in the form of preaching and admonition, while human nature in the sense of Pelagius is taken for <u>gratia prima</u>, we find here the first tendencies for the Scholastic division into <u>meritum de congruo</u> and <u>condigno</u>.[1] Efforts of man and grace of God earn merits in order to obtain redemptive grace. Cooperation between human will and redemptive grace finally found real merits. Since the Resolutions of Orange (529) were unknown from the eighth century until 1538[2] and the <u>Indiculus</u>[3] from the fifth century was unnoticed except by Thomas Aquinas,[4] Semi-Pelagian tendencies became the great temptation of the theology of the Middle Ages.

5. Augustinianism ruled theology for eight hundred years[5] until it was absorbed by Aristotelian Thomism. Therefore the thinking of salvation dominated Western theology.[6] But this Augustinianism was one domesticated by the Church and dominated by the popular-Catholic element of Augustine, and thus the thought of merit was cultivated rather than held back. In the sense of Tertullian, God remained <u>arbiter</u> and <u>inspector</u>[7] and the person a

---

[1] Harnack, <u>Dogmengeschichte</u>, 3:250.

[2] Fransen, "Entfaltung der Gnadenlehre," in <u>Mysterium Salutis</u>, 4/2:661.

[3] <u>DS</u> 243, 248.

[4] Pesch, "Lehre vom Verdienst," in <u>Wahrheit und Verkündigung</u>, 2:1879.

[5] Auer, <u>Gnadenlehre</u>, 2:112.   [6] Oberman, <u>Forerunners</u>, p. 123.

[7] Leo the Great <u>Sermo</u> 14. 2 (<u>PL</u> 54:174).

mercenarius who works for his reward.[1] As a result, there arose a middle way between Augustinianism and Pelagianism,[2] which can be designated as Semi-Augustinianism. Merit goes, in the first place, through prevenient grace to the account of God, and in the second place, through the succeeding free will to the account of the person.[3]

6. In ecclesiastical Augustinianism, however, there was so much of Augustine's thought of grace that remained alive that again and again resistance to a too-optimistic teaching of merit could be mobilized from it; for example, in the assertion that there could be no merits before justification, because merits already presuppose grace (Peter Lombard and the later Thomas Aquinas),[4] or in the weakening of the meritum de congruo by the priority of the gratia gratis data (Bonaventure),[5] as well as in general in the struggle of the Augustinians of the Late Middle Ages against the meritum gratiae, in the sense of a meritum de congruo (Thomas Bradwardine, Gregory of Rimini, Hugolin of Orvieto, Dionysius of Montina, John Wycliffe),[6] and against the meritum gloriae in the sense of a meritum de condigno (Gregory of Rimini, Alphonsus Vargas

---

[1] Gregory the Great Moralium 8. 7. 12 (PL 75:808).

[2] Alfred Adam, Lehrbuch der Dogmengeschichte, 2nd ed., 2 vols. (Gütersloh: G. Mohn, 1972), 2:21.

[3] Gregory the Great Moralium 33. 21. 40 (PL 76:699).

[4] Peter Lombard Sent. Lib. 1, dist. 41 (PL 192:633); idem Collectanea in Epist. D. Pauli--In Epist. ad Rom. 3:27 (PL 191: 1365); Thomas Aquinas S. Th. 1a2ae. 114, 5.

[5] Sent. Lib. 2, dist. 28, a. 2, qu. 1.

[6] See Hamm, Promissio, p. 453.

of Toledo and the late Wycliffe).[1]

7. The high point of the thought of grace and, at the same time, victory over the teaching of merit was attained by the Augustinian Luther, who overcame Augustinianism by Augustine, and Augustine by Paul.[2] Thereby total war was declared against the teaching of merit.

Early Scholasticism. In order to understand this war one must keep in mind the most important steps of development in the

---

[1] Ibid., p. 461.

[2] For the young Luther, Augustine is "numquam satis laudatus" (WA 9, 29, 5-6) and "interpres fidelissimus Pauli" (WA 1, 353, 11-13). But the occupation with Paul showed him the limits of the teachers of the Church, even of Augustine. "Da ward es aus mit yhm." TR 1, 140, 7.
How far Augustinianism influenced Luther is still unclarified in the research. Cf. RGG, 3rd ed., s.v. "Augustin-Theologie," by R. Lorenz; Bernhard Lohse, "Die Bedeutung Augustins für den jungen Luther," KuD 11 (1965):116. The viewpoint, represented foremost by Catholic researchers (Denifle, Lortz), that Luther had become, according to his self-witness (TR 2, 516, 6), exclusively an Ockhamist, has been rebutted by Protestant investigators. Cf. Reinhold Seeberg, Die religiösen Grundgedanken des jungen Luther und ihr Verhältnis zu dem Ockhamismus und der deutschen Mystik (Berlin: W. de Gruyter, 1931), pp. 3, 15-36; Leif Grane, Contra Gabrielem (Copenhagen: Gyldendal, 1962), pp. 377-79. The more recent Protestant research assumes a strong influence of Augustine upon Luther. Cf. Lohse, "Die Bedeutung Augustins," KuD 11 (1965):133; RGG, 3rd ed., s.v. "Luther-Theologie," by G. Ebeling; Walter von Loewenich, Von Augustin zu Luther (Witten: Luther-Verlag, 1959), pp. 75-76. Grane even sees in Luther's early theology (1517) a reaction of the "classical" theology of Augustine against Ockhamism. Contra Gabrielem, pp. 375-79. In the current Catholic research Luther seems like an "antithetical Ockhamist," who pulled down Nominalism through Augustinianism. Iserloh, "Luthers Stellung," in Wandlungen des Lutherbildes, pp. 16-46; idem, Luther und die Reformation (Aschaffenburg: P. Pattloch, 1974), pp. 39-43. Luther's thought, however, is also called "nachscholastischer Neuaugustinismus." Daniel Olivier, "Warum hat man Luther nicht verstanden? Katholische Antwort," Conc(D) 12 (1976):480. Luther grew up in a milieu aware of Augustinianism and German mysticism, "dem der Gedanke an die Mängel der guten Werke und aller menschlichen Gerechtigkeit offensichtlich nicht so fern lag." Zumkeller, "Ungenügen der menschlichen Werke," ZKT 81 (1959):305.

teaching of merit of the Middle Ages. The Early Scholasticism (Peter Lombard) brings to maturity the first systematic exposition of the teaching of merit.[1] The idea of merit serves as the explanation of the work of Christ (Anselm of Canterbury)[2] and of the believers. The Porretan School, which then allowed the work of Christ as the sole genuine merit and interpreted the work of the believers from the auctoritas principle, distinguished between proprie mereri (Christ's own true merit) and improprie mereri (the believer's improper merit). Of the convert a merit only in the further, improper and figurative sense ex consortio--from participation in Christ--is recognized.

Although Peter Lombard knew only a merit in the state of grace, his adherents and opponents[3] changed the meaning of the Porretan proprie mereri and improprie mereri into the meritum de congruo (merit on grounds of benevolence) and meritum de condigno (merit on grounds of worthiness).[4] What the Porretans asserted of Christ (proprie mereri) and the believer (improprie mereri) was subsequently transferred merely to the believing person. The time of preparation for justification was viewed as an improprie mereri (de congruo), the time of the state of grace as a proprie mereri (de condigno).

According to Hamm, the term ex condigno was used for the

---

[1] DTC, s.v. "Mérite," by J. Rivière.   [2] Ibid.

[3] According to Landgraf (Dogmengeschichte, 1:268), Robert of Melun, the contemporary and opponent of Peter Lombard, is the first who speaks of a meritoriousness of works before grace.

[4] Hamm, Promissio, p. 40.

first time by Peter the Chanter "with negative designation" (mit negativem Vorzeichen),[1] meaning not for the believer, because the proprie mereri can refer only to Christ.

High Scholasticism. In High Scholasticism, however, the concept is naturalized as meritum condigni (William of Auvergne) and as de condigno (Odo Rigaldi).[2] The expression meritum de congruo, on the other hand, is used in Early Scholasticism (Simon of Tournai, Alan of Lille) for the merit of Mary.[3] For the preparation for justification, one employed the term meritum interpretativum (Stephen Langton).[4]

This important process[5] by which works are granted a certain worth also outside justification[6] developed in High Scholasticism into a new terminology in which the term de congruo is used for the merit of preparation (William of Auvergne, Roland of Cremona).[7] The formula which arose in Early Scholasticism from a variant of Augustine[8] (Facienti quod in se est) also contributed to

---

[1] Ibid., pp. 73, 455.   [2] Ibid., pp. 143, 177.

[3] Ibid., p. 449. According to Auer (Gnadenlehre, 2:78), Peter the Chanter was the first to use the term meritum de congruo.

[4] Hamm, Promissio, p. 451; Auer, Gnadenlehre, 2:78.

[5] Pesch, "Lehre vom Verdienst," in Wahrheit und Verkündigung, 2:1881. "Folgenreichstes Ergebnis."

[6] In the extreme case even a merited salvation of good pagans (e.g., Socrates) was accepted. See Abelard, Theologia Christiana 2 (PL 178:1186).

[7] Hamm, Promissio, p. 451.

[8] Cf. Augustine: "Non enim deseret opus suum, si ab opere suo non deseratur." Enarr. in Ps. 145. 9 (PL 37:1890). Cf. Bartmann, Dogmatik, 2:47. According to Auer and Ratzinger (Dogmatik, 5:87) the expression itself stems from the school of Abelard. Loofs

this development. This saying, criticized as "scholastical Neosemipelagianism" (<u>scholastischer Neosemipelagianismus</u>),[1] rose from humble beginnings to become an important theologoumenon.

While in the Early Scholasticism the incidental character was still stressed, i.e. the formula was not recognized to have any efficient cause--<u>Wirkursache</u>, but only conditional cause--<u>Bedingungsursache</u> (Alan of Lille, William of Auxerre)[2]--and any obligation of God was denied (Stephen Langton, Gaufrid of Poitiers, Roland of Cremona),[3] High Scholasticism (Bonaventure, Duns Scotus) carried through the merit-character of the formula in the sense of a merit <u>de congruo</u>.[4]

With the early Thomas Aquinas it appeared in the form of a preparation in purely natural strength in which grace played only the role of an <u>auxilium</u>, which leads to the favorable opportunity, so that "grace is bestowed on him who does his very best."[5]

In Franciscan theology (<u>Summa Halensis</u>, Bonaventure) it was limited to a "declaration of divine goodness and generosity" (<u>declaratio divinae bonitatis et liberalitatis</u>)[6] and to the

---

(<u>Leitfaden</u>, p. 448) traces the thought back to Jerome, Rivière to Origen, Oberman to Ambrosiaster. See Jean Rivière, "Quelques antécédents patristiques de la formule: 'Facienti quod in se est'," <u>RevScRel</u> 7 (1927):93-97. Heiko Augustinus Oberman, <u>The Harvest of Medieval Theology</u> (Cambridge, Mass.: Harvard Univ. Press, 1963), p. 132.

[1] Landgraf, <u>Dogmengeschichte</u>, 1:250.   [2] Ibid., 1:257-58.

[3] Ibid., 1:261-62.   [4] Hamm, <u>Promissio</u>, p. 453.

[5] <u>2 Sent.</u>, dist. 28, qu. 1, a. 4. Cf. Kraus, <u>Vorherbestimmung</u>, p. 63.

[6] <u>Summa Hal</u>. Lib. 3, p. 3, inqu. 1, tract. 1, qu. 5, m. 2, c. 1, a. 4.

concession of <u>gratia gratis data</u> as initial event,[1] but, nevertheless, with the assurance that grace is bestowed on him who does his best and thus is bestowed "by necessity, i.e. immutability" (<u>necessario, id est immutabiliter</u>).[2]

The late Thomas Aquinas tries to rescue himself from the danger of Semi-Pelagianism through the Aristotelian distinction between God as the Mover and the free will as what is moved. Thus the preparation for grace (<u>facienti quod in se est</u>) has a double aspect. Seen from the human viewpoint, there exists in no way a necessity for the obtaining of grace, because the gift of grace surpasses every preparation by human strength. Viewed from God, the Mover, there does exist a necessity, not in the form of compulsion, but doubtless of infallibility (<u>infallibilitas</u>), because the purpose of God cannot be denied.[3] The late Thomas denies a <u>meritum de congruo</u>, because every merit presupposes justification.[4] But in the state of grace the double consideration of God as Mover and the person as the one moved allows merit as <u>de condigno</u> to be ascribed to grace and as <u>de congruo</u> to be ascribed to the person.[5]

Duns Scotus expresses himself much more optimistically as to the possibilities of the natural person before justification.

---

[1] Ibid., Lib. 3, p. 3, inqu. 1, tract. 2, qu. 1, c. 2; Bonaventure <u>Sent</u>. Lib. 2, dist. 28, a. 2, qu. 1.

[2] <u>Summa Hal</u>. Lib. 3, p. 3, inqu. 1, tract. 1, qu. 5, m. 3.

[3] <u>S. Th</u>. 1a2ae. 112, 3.

[4] Ibid., 114, 5; 114, 5 ad 3.

[5] Ibid., 114, 6. Cf. Henri Bouillard, <u>Conversion et grâce chez S. Thomas d'Aquin</u> (Paris: Aubier-Montaigne, 1944), pp. 35, 154.

On the one hand we find in his works statements that agree with the principles of traditional Franciscan theology,[1] and on the other hand, we find that through his teaching of the natural <u>dispositio de congruo</u>,[2] he prepares the way for the later merit-teaching of Late Scholasticism so vehemently combatted by Luther.

"Before grace we merit <u>ex congruo</u>" (<u>Ante gratiam meremur ex congruo</u>)[3] became thus a winged word in Nominalism.[4] People theologized optimistically over one's possibilities in relation to grace, as if a Pelagian battle had never occurred. Since these theologizers thought they had preserved the supernatural reference in the teaching of the <u>potentia absoluta</u> and <u>ordinata</u>, they considered themselves far removed from Pelagius.

The full-fledged development of this thought occurred in Gabriel Biel, the "last Scholastic." What was still in tension with Duns Scotus is systematized by Biel: A person is able in his own

---

[1] "Prima gratia datur homini, si vult se disponere per liberum arbitrium, quod potest quilibet per adiutorem gratiae datum, quae omnibus viatoribus datur." Parthenius Minges, <u>Ioannis Duns Scoti doctrina philosophica et theologica</u>, 2 vols. (Ad claras Aquas: Typographia Collegii S. Bonaventurae, 1930), 2:403.

[2] The person can <u>ex naturalibus</u> merit grace: "Anima non habens actuale peccatum est summe disposita ad suscipiendum gratiam." Ibid., 2:401. "Non requiritur nisi voluntaria susceptio Baptismi et sine fictione." Ibid. Indeed, the natural person can even earn the actual grace <u>de congruo</u>, and if he uses it well, also habitual grace: "Ex congruo meretur gratiam gratis datam. Et si bene utitur ipsa, cito dabitur sibi gratia gratum faciens." <u>DTC</u>, s.v. "Mérite," by J. Rivière.

[3] Durandus of Saint-Pourçain <u>Sent</u>. Lib. 2, dist. 27, qu. 2.

[4] The idea is found in Ockham, Holkot, Adam Wodham, James Almain. Among the opponents is Bradwardine, who in the introduction of the <u>meritum de congruo</u> saw a return to Pelagianism, and Gregory of Rimini, who fought against every kind of <u>meritum gratiae</u> as modernism. See <u>DTC</u>, s.v. "Mérite," by J. Rivière.

strength to love God supremely,[1] to avoid sin,[2] and, out of the force of the free will, to merit the grace de congruo,[3] which God must grant necessarily according to the principle facienti quod in se est[4] because on the basis of the potentia ordinata He cannot do anything else.[5]

In the light of Thomism and the Council of Trent, such a view may appear "uncatholic."[6] But if we consider that on the eve of the Reformation Thomism embodied only one theological school--one which was not modern--and that Trent was the result only of the Reformation, then we cannot escape the conclusion of designating the Nominalistic teaching of justification as that which at that time was the Catholic one.[7] That this teaching has Pelagian

---

[1] "Viatoris voluntas humana ex suis naturalibus potest diligere Deum super omnia." Collect. in Sent. Lib. 3, dist. 27, qu. 1, a. 3, d. 2, p. 1, italics mine.

[2] "Potest cessare a consensu et actu peccandi, immo odire peccatum et velle non peccare." Ibid., Lib. 2, dist. 27, qu. 1, a. 3, d. 4, italics mine.

[3] "Anima obicis remotione ac bono motu in Deum ex arbitrii libertate elicito primam gratiam mereri potest de congruo." Ibid., Lib. 2, dist. 27, qu. 1, a. 2, c. 4.

[4] "Tunc dicitur quod Deus dat gratiam facienti quod in se est necessitate immutabilitatis." Ibid., Lib. 2, dist. 27, qu. 1, a. 3, d. 4.

[5] "Actus amoris Dei amicitie super omnia non potest stare in viatore de potentia Dei ordinata sine gratia et caritate infusa." Ibid., Lib. 3, dist. 27, qu. 1, a. 3, d. 2, p. 2.

[6] Lortz, Reformation, 1:176.

[7] See Oberman, Werden und Wertung, p. 135.

traits[1] makes the protest of the Reformation only more understandable.

Of no less importance, in the light of the turning-point of the Reformation, was the development of the meritum de condigno in connection with the teaching of grace. Here High-Scholastic solutions--and with them in part also Thomistic ones--met with Luther's Paulinism and caused a struggle no smaller than the problem of the preparation for and the attainment of grace.

The question before which the post-Augustinian theology saw itself placed with reference to the meritum gloriae resulted from the bringing together of grace and performance in the idea of merit. How, really, can one speak of a human participation in the free gift of eternal life? As long as grace was identified by Augustine with caritas[2] and in Early Scholasticism (Peter Lombard) with the Holy Spirit,[3] a distinction between gratia actualis and habitualis was not possible. But as soon as grace was defined as aliquid elevans (Philip the Chancellor),[4] as gratia creata (Summa Halensis),[5] as aliquid creatum (Albertus Magnus),[6] as forma creata,[7]

---

[1] "It is . . . evident that Biel's doctrine of justification is essentially Pelagian." Idem, Harvest, p. 177.

[2] "Charitas gratia est Testamenti Novi." Quaest. in Heptateuchum 5. 15 (PL 34:755). "Charitas autem usque adeo donum est, ut Deus dicatur." Ep. 186. 3. 7 (PL 33:818).

[3] "Spiritus Sanctus, cum sit Deus, vocatur etiam donum Dei." Sent. Lib. 1, dist. 17 (PL 192:566). "Gratia Dei liberat, scilicet per Spiritum Sanctum." Collectanea in Epist. D. Pauli.--In Epist. ad Rom. 8:1-2 (PL 191:1432).

[4] See Auer, Gnadenlehre, 2:146.

[5] Lib. 3, p. 3, inqu. 1, tract. 1, qu. 2, c. 1, a. 2.

[6] Sent. Lib. 2, dist. 26, a. 1.   [7] De Veritate 27. 1.

donum creatum,[1] habituale donum,[2] qualitas supernaturalis (Thomas),[3] and thereby as "soul of the soul," it was possible to speak of a habitual grace, of a possession of grace,[4] and thereby of merit as a divine gift and a human work. This "Copernican revolution"[5] was possible through the taking over of Aristotelian ontology (Habitus acquisitus), which in High Scholasticism was reinterpreted in a Christian way (Habitus infusus). Thus the thought of merit became the driving force[6] of High Scholasticism's metaphysics of the soul and thereby of what was termed the Verdinglichung--"reification" of grace.

This "reification" however, was interpreted in different ways. With Albertus Magnus, for example, it was interpreted very materialistically, so that grace became something in the middle between God and the person, delivered over to be possessed by the human being.[7] In Franciscan theology on the other hand, it was interpreted more theocentrically, that is, as a light from God which constantly streams into the soul so that the possession of grace represents rather being-possessed by God.[8]

---

[1] S. Th. 1a, 43, 3 ad 1; 1a2ae. 110, 2 ad 3.

[2] Ibid., 110, 2.   [3] Ibid.

[4] "Similiter illud solum habere dicimur quo libere possumus uti vel frui." Ibid., 1a. 43, 3.

[5] Bernard J. F. Lonergan, Grace and Freedom (London: Darton, Longman & Todd, 1971), p. 16.

[6] See Pesch, "Lehre vom Verdienst," in Wahrheit und Verkündigung, 2:1880; Auer and Ratzinger, Dogmatik, 5:150.

[7] See Charles Moeller, "Grace and Justification," LV 19 (1964):725.

[8] Bonaventure Breviloquium 5. 1. 5 ("Habere Deum est haberi a Deo").

Thomas Aquinas took an intermediate position. In his interpretation, the gratia creata is a habitus (condition) poured into the soul--a poured-in quality (nature).[1] In this way he avoids the way of crass materializing. But since the soul and its quality are conceived according to the Aristotelian form-matter concept,[2] the personalistic trait so stressed by the Franciscans is lost and is replaced by a physical-ontic concept. The form principle permits grace to be placed in the possession of the human, and thus to preserve man's independence in relation to God. This interpretation is of great significance for the doctrine of the meritum de condigno, especially when we realize that at Trent Thomas was basically affirmed and that the theology of Thomas is considered as the "normative theology" by the Roman-Catholic Church.[3]

For Thomas the whole life of the believer is an "advance in merit" (profectus meriti).[4] Therefore he is interested above all in the merit of the one who has received grace, the meritum de condigno. According to Thomas, meritum (merit) and merces (reward) stand in relationship to each other, whereby the reward is similar to a prize (pretium) which is gained by achieving (work).[5] Hence from the view of the one who has been served, the reward is an

---

[1] S. Th. 1a2ae. 110, 2.   [2] Ibid.

[3] Since 1567 Thomas has been considered a teacher of the Church, since 1879 as normative theologian, since 1923 as doctor communis. See LTK, 2nd ed., s.v. "Thomas von Aquin," by O. H. Pesch; RGG, 3rd ed., s.v. "Thomas von Aquino," by W. Pannenberg. The Second Vatican Council designated him as master (magister) in the speculative penetrating of the mysteries of salvation. Optatam totius 16.

[4] S. Th. 1a. 94, 3 ad 3.   [5] S. Th. 1a2ae. 114, 1.

obligation (<u>debitum</u>)[1] which, according to justice, is to be paid,[2] but from the view of the one who has earned it, it is a right which belongs to him.[3] But since there is a great inequality between God and man this concept applies only in a limited sense, for between Creator and creation there can be no equal relationship (<u>secundum rigorem iustitiae</u>). Nevertheless, the relationship of justice and right is not annulled. According to God's arrangement, His grace, which is the beginning of glory,[4] should receive the corresponding reward on the road of merit and right.

Righteousness is <u>justitia distributiva</u>; that is, between work and reward there exists an unequal proportion[5]--similar to the unequal proportion between seed and tree.[6] Of a <u>justitia commutativa</u> (relationship of equality) we can only speak according to the force of grace not according to man's act, since grace and glory are on the same level of perfection, while an act proceeding from grace is only proportioned to glory. This interpretation makes it possible for Thomas to say that God is debtor only toward Himself[7] and that man through his own merits, cannot add anything to God but can only work for His honor.[8] Whoever takes this position can assert that "all juridical representations fall,"[9] that "the complete emptying" of all juridical representations which are

---

[1] Ibid., 21, 3.   [2] Ibid., 114, 1.

[3] Ibid., 114, 3; 114, 8.   [4] Ibid., 2a2ae. 24, 3 ad 2.

[5] Ibid., 1a2ae. 109, 5.   [6] Ibid., 114, 3 ad 3.

[7] Ibid., 1 ad 3.   [8] Ibid., 1 ad 2.

[9] Pesch, "Lehre vom Verdienst," in <u>Wahrheit und Verkündigung</u>, 2:1884. "Alle juridischen Vorstellungen fallen."

connected with the concept of merit is difficult to exceed[1] and that Thomas teaches a "reward without claim."[2]

It is striking to observe that other scholars in Scholasticism, such as Auer, read out of Thomas the exact opposite--that man has "a genuine claim, a demand upon God on the basis of grace," and that "the thought of work is foundational for the view of grace."[3] What is the foundation for this variation of interpretation? For Thomas, the share of a person in merit and reward is not excluded if he is in the state of grace. In his thought, the Augustinian teaching of grace is fused with Aristotelian metaphysics and ethics.[4] Thus his thought of merit is at the same time a triumph of God and a co-triumph of man.

In soteriology Thomas is thinking in the framework of the Aristotelian causa prima or movens (God)[5] and the causa secunda or motum (man).[6] The believer is included as a secondary element in the activity of the work-cause (God) and the work-basis (habitual grace) and can in this inclusion also merit the goal (salvation). Man's share can thereby be understood on two bases:[7]

1. On the basis of free will; that is, that the nature of

---

[1] Idem, Theologie der Rechtfertigung, p. 775.

[2] Ibid., p. 786. "Lohn ohne Anspruch."

[3] Auer, Gnadenlehre, 2:153-54.

[4] Harnack, Dogmengeschichte, 3:498.

[5] S. Th. 1a2ae. 114, 3 ad 2; 109, 6.

[6] Ibid. 114, 3 ad 2. Cf. Bouillard, Conversion et grâce, p. 24.

[7] De Veritate 29. 6; see William D. Lynn, "Christ's Redemptive Merit," AnGr 115 (1962):27-28.

the person is only wounded[1] and weakened[2] but, in a limited way, remains capable of performance.[3] And this remaining capability of man suffices to ascribe power of merit-earning to the free will.[4] The worth of this merit-aspect is in any case only that of a merit of congruity and not of condignity.[5]

2. On the basis of God's working; that is, again in two ways:

    a. Through the moving of the Holy Spirit upon the free will, a qualitatively corresponding relationship between the latter and the reward arises in the meritorious act. The Holy Spirit as *causa prima* bestows on the work a supernatural worth which God <u>must</u> reward in a supernatural way if He is to be just toward Himself.[6] As *causa secunda*, the believer has a share in it. As he cooperates with the Holy Spirit he together with God becomes worthy (*con-dignus*)

---

[1] <u>S. Th.</u> 1a2ae. 85, 3.   [2] Ibid., 85, 2.   [3] Ibid.

[4] <u>S. Th.</u> 1a2ae. 109, 5 ad 1; 114, 1; 114, 1 ad 1.

[5] Ibid., 114, 6. A further weakening of the efficacy of the free will can be obtained from the doctrine of predestination of Thomas, if indeed the free will is not set by grace into a relationship of disposition but of consequence. That is, the movement of the free will does not occur in the frame of divine disposition and human self-reaction (Ermöglichungsverhältnis), but in the form of a necessity to correspond (Folgeverhältnis). See Hans Vorster, <u>Das Freiheitsverständnis bei Thomas von Aquin und Martin Luther</u> (Göttingen: Vandenhoeck & Ruprecht, 1965), pp. 219, 318. By the Tridentine interpretation ("libere assentiendo et cooperando," <u>DS</u> 1525) it becomes possible, however, to speak of a "movement from above downward," also of a "movement from below upward," and to conceive the whole process again as disposition and reaction. See Matthias J. Scheeben, <u>Die Mysterien des Christentums</u>, 3rd ed. (Freiburg i. Br.: Herder, 1958), p. 524.

[6] <u>S. Th.</u> 1a 2ae, 114, 3.

of the reward. As to whom the merit really belongs, the Holy Spirit or the person, it is important to grasp that the work would be impossible without the Spirit, but it is the person, not the Spirit, who earns it.[1]

b. Through the participation of habitual grace in the act of merit, man likewise gains a character worthy of eternal life.[2] Since here also cooperation is involved,[3] the work can be ascribed to the person. The cooperation does not ensue additively but is an act of the whole, which belongs wholly to grace but also wholly to man. For the activity of the <u>causa prima et secunda</u> is not separable.[4] Since every good work is initiated by grace, the person possesses the merit only in a subordinate way, but he possesses it because he is a cooperating cause.[5] Such a possession won by merit thus becomes more valuable than one given as a gift.[6]

We may judge this as an "insufficient description" and interpret the whole personalistically as "answer of fidelity to

---

[1] "The principal cause of merit, however, is man cooperating with the Holy Spirit. In a word, it is man, and not the Holy Spirit that merits, although man could not merit without the special movement of the Holy Spirit in the very act of meriting." Lynn, "Redemptive Merit," <u>AnGr</u> 115 (1962):28.

[2] <u>S. Th</u>. 1a2ae. 114, 3.

[3] Ibid., 113, 1 prooem.; 114, 1 prooem.   [4] Ibid., 1a. 23, 5.

[5] "Potest tamen secundario aliquis esse causa sibi alicujus boni habendi, inquantum scilicet in hoc ipso Deo cooperatur. Et sic ille qui habet aliquid per meritum proprium habet quodammodo illud per seipsum." Ibid., 3a. 19, 3.

[6] "Unde nobilius habetur id quod habetur per meritum quam id quod habetur sine merito." Ibid.

fidelity," as an act of the meeting of God and person.[1] But aside from the fact that the manner of speaking of causes (causae), condition (habitus), form (forma), quality (qualitas), and created grace (gratia creata) points to a materialistic rather than to a personalistic relationship,[2] the fact remains uncontested also in the personal framework that the person included in God's activity becomes alive with his own activity. He can earn, demand, and possess because he genuinely earns (ex condigno--by proper worthiness), because he thereby has a right to the reward, and because in the framework of the secondary occurrence he is possessor of what has been earned.[3] It is not, as with Luther, a relationship of giver and receiver. Instead it is a relationship of two who in their own ways are working together, where the one, who is subordinate but nevertheless a genuine participant through free will and a new quality of being suited to him, is also an earner of true merit.

From this it appears problematical when O. H. Pesch says that "the whole doctrine of merit in Thomas is beyond the area that Luther attacks,"[4] that Luther would show no interest in the merit

---

[1] Pesch, "Lehre vom Verdienst," in Wahrheit und Verkündigung, 2:1886. "Unzureichende Beschreibung." "Antwort der Treue auf Treue."

[2] Cf. Auer, Gnadenlehre, 2:154.

[3] Cf. Karl Barth's judgment about Thomas Aquinas' soteriology: "Er hat alles, alles auch gewusst, wenn man das Eine abzieht, dass er nicht gewusst hat, dass der Mensch ein Schächer ist." Karl Barth-Eduard Thurneysen: Briefwechsel, 2 vols. (Zurich: Theologischer Verlag Zürich, 1974), 2:638.

[4] Pesch, Theologie der Rechtfertigung, p. 785. "Die gesamte Verdienstlehre steht beim hlg. Thomas ausserhalb des Feldes, auf dem sie Luther angreift."

of grace (meritum de condigno),[1] that it should be easy to make Luther equivalent to Thomas,[2] and, since both are the same in all important respects, it is all only a "quarrel over terminology."[3]

We agree with Fransen, who on the meritum de condigno knows how to articulate convincingly the reservations of the Protestant conversation partners:

> Darum ist der eigentliche kritische Punkt zwischen der Reformation und dem Katholizismus die Lehre vom Verdienst, denn in den Augen der Reformation besagt diese Lehre, dass das Geschehen auf der horizontalen Ebene gegenüber der erhabensten Initiative in Christus einen gewissen Eigenwert haben könne.[4]

The carrying over of the Aristotelian nature philosophy to soteriology constitutes the "flexibility" (Beweglichkeit)[5] and "peril" (Gefährlichkeit)[6] of the Thomistic doctrine and its interpretation. It facilitates a double interpretation, as it then in Trent actually became dogma[7] and allowed Catholic theology until today to see the problem of merit from either side, according to necessity. Nevertheless, the Thomistic doctrine of merit was in no way so dominant in High and Late Scholasticism as it is today.

---

[1] Ibid., p. 786.   [2] Ibid., p. 784.   [3] Ibid., p. 785.

[4] Fransen, "Entfaltung der Gnadenlehre," in Mysterium Salutis, 4/2:696-97, italics mine.

[5] Wilhelm Link, Das Ringen Luthers um die Freiheit der Theologie von der Philosophie (Berlin: Evangelische Verlagsanstalt, 1954), p. 177.

[6] Ibid., p. 176.

[7] "Sine qua [i.e. virtus Christi] nullo pacto Deo grata et meritoria [i.e. opera bona] esse possent." / "Operibus . . . vitam aeternam . . . consequendam vere promeruisse censeantur." DS 1546, italics mine. "Iustitia Dei . . ." / "iustitia nostra . . . nobis inhaerens." DS 1547, italics mine.   "Dona Dei . . ." / "bona ipsius iustificati merita." DS 1582, italics mine.

For the epoch of Nominalism, which immediately preceded the Reformation, the doctrine of merit of Duns Scotus was of greater significance. While Thomas defined the worth of merit objectively through the ontic quality of the work, Duns Scotus sees the worth subjectively in the acceptation of God.[1] This applies to Christ as well as to the believer. Duns also, indeed, demands the work as <u>actus caritate formatus</u>, because God has bound Himself on the basis of the <u>potentia ordinata</u> to accept such a person, but the work in itself is thereby not yet meritorious; its worth lies in that God makes it valid as meritorious.[2] On the basis of the <u>potentia absoluta</u> it could be completely otherwise. God could, out of His freedom and sovereignty, also accept completely as meritorious any acts <u>ex puris naturalibus</u>.[3]

This view has been called "salvation-historical and personal" (<u>heilsgeschichtlich-personal</u>)[4] and "theocentric" (<u>theozentrisch</u>).[5] One could also designate it as a relativizing of the Thomistic thought of merit. Because Duns denies a distributive correspondence of work and reward, there is no genuine <u>meritum de condigno</u>. The <u>meritum gloriae</u> also is reduced to a <u>meritum de</u>

---

[1] "Meritum est actus potentiae liberae et secundum inclinationem gratiae elicitus, acceptus Deo ut praemiabilis beatitudine." Minges, <u>Duns Scoti doctrina</u>, 2:493.

[2] Bonitas meritoria "est bonitas, qua Deus ex mera liberalitate voluntatis suae acceptat actum elicitum . . . de potentia ordinata . . . tamquam meritorium vitae aeternae." Ibid., 2:494.

[3] See <u>DTC</u>, s.v. "Mérite," by J. Rivière.

[4] Hamm, <u>Promissio</u>, pp. 441-43.

[5] Pesch, "Lehre vom Verdienst," in <u>Wahrheit und Verkündigung</u>, 2:1892.

congruo, because the inequality between work and reward must always be evened out by a special divine act of will.[1]

Late Scholasticism and "Pre-Reformers." With his teaching of the acceptatio and the potentia Dei ordinata and absoluta, Duns prepared the way for the doctrine of merit of the Late Scholastic Nominalism. But while Duns still attempted to hold together work of grace and acceptance, in Nominalism everything went to the extreme. The teaching of acceptance led to the view that God could also, on the basis of the potentia absoluta, condemn man in the state of grace (William of Rubio, Peter de Palude, John Bassolis),[2] and the emancipation of the bonitas moralis from the bonitas meritoria in the moral act bestowed upon the works of the natural person such worth in the eyes of the Nominalists (Ockham, Biel) that they looked upon grace as able to be earned by natural powers.[3] The work of salvation was divided up partim-partim. If the person goes half the distance, God comes to meet him with the gift of grace.[4]

However, it would be mistaken to assume that before Luther there was no kind of resistance against the thought of merit. Early Scholasticism knows of a double reaction:

1. A theoretical reaction from the theology of the school of Gilbert Porreta.

---

[1] See Dettloff, Entwicklung der Akzeptationslehre, p. 235.

[2] See Auer and Ratzinger, Dogmatik, 5:32.

[3] See DTC, s.v. "Nominalisme-Justification," by P. Vignaux.

[4] See Oberman, "Tridentinisches Rechtfertigungsdekret," ZTK 61 (1964):259.

2. A practical reaction from the mystical contemplation of Bernard of Clairvaux.

Theologians of the Porretan school (Alan of Lille, Peter the Chanter) limited the concept meritum so greatly that a proprie mereri or meritum de condigno could be assumed only for Christ. Since the person has no auctoritas operandi, he relates toward God as a tool. But tools do not merit, they are only used (Cardinal Laborans).[1] A correspondence between work and reward does not exist. Good works bring no merits for eternity, but they are the path to eternity (Peter the Chanter).[2] While the thought of merit was thus excluded, nevertheless one held fast to the final way of salvation (finaler Heilszug).

Bernard of Clairvaux came to a similar conviction through mystical contemplation. Man has only a "twisted soul" (curva anima),[3] he is completely impure,[4] there is no meritum ex iure because God does not owe a debt to the person but the person owes a debt to God.[5] It is sufficient to know that merits are not enough,[6] and that to rest one's hope on them is "dangerous because it is going to ruin" (periculosa quia ruinosa).[7] Merit therefore

---

[1] See Hamm, Promissio, pp. 30-31.

[2] See Landgraf, Dogmengeschichte, 1:191.

[3] Bernard of Clairvaux Sermones in Cantica 24. 7 (PL 183:897).

[4] Idem Pro dominica 1. nov. Sermo 5. 9 (PL 183:358).

[5] Idem In festo annuntiat. Beatae Mariae Virg. Sermo 1. 2 (PL 183:383).

[6] Idem Sermones in Cantica 68. 6 (PL 183:1111).

[7] Idem In Ps. Qui habitat Sermo 1. 3 (PL 183:188).

means to hope on God[1] and His mercy (<u>Meum proinde meritum miseratio Domini</u>).[2]

Since Bernard is no systematician, these statements should not be pressed. He holds fast theoretically to the concept of merit, but reduces it so much that it appears almost annulled.[3]

Similar reactions are found among the German preachers of the fourteenth century (Conrad of Brundelsheim, John Tauler, Jordan of Quedlinburg) with contemporary Italian preachers (Albert of Padova, Simon Fidati of Cascia, Angelus Clarenus of Cingoli) and with German preachers of the fifteenth century (John of Retz, Oswald Reindel, Nicholas of Dinkelsbühl, Thomas Ebendorfer of Haselbach, John of Schwäbisch-Gmünd, Ulrich Krafft, Gottschalk Hollen of Körbecke, James of Jüterbog, John Staupitz).[4]

Perhaps the devaluation of the thought of merit with Thomas à Kempis,[5] and maybe also with Savonarola,[6] had a greater influence. In the <u>Theologia deutsch</u> which was so prized by Luther (". . . ist myr nehst der Biblien und S. Augustino nit verkummen eyn buch, dar auss ich mehr erlernet hab . . .")[7] even the

---

[1] Ibid. 15. 5 (<u>PL</u> 183:246).

[2] Idem <u>Serm. in Cant.</u> 61. 5 (<u>PL</u> 183:1073).

[3] "Autant sa théologie de la grâce laisse place au mérite, autant il est certain qu'elle la réduit à son minimum." <u>DTC</u>, s.v. "Mérite," by J. Rivière.

[4] See Zumkeller, "Ungenügen der menschlichen Werke," <u>ZKT</u> 81 (1959):268-301.

[5] Thomas à Kempis <u>De imitatione Christi</u> 2. 9; 3. 14.

[6] See Girolamo Savonarola, <u>Meditations on Psalm 51 and part of Psalm 31 in Latin</u>, ed. E. H. Perowne (London: C. J. Clay & Sons, 1900), pp. 6, 66, 75, 91.

[7] WA 1, 378, 21-23.

consecutive way of salvation of good works is intimated.[1]

The Early Scholastic denial of the <u>meritum gratiae</u> with Peter Lombard[2] revived again in the epoch of Late Scholasticism, apparently as a reaction to the Nominalistic theology, and is found with Thomas Bradwardine, Gregory of Rimini, John Wycliffe, John Hus, Hugolin of Orvieto, John Ruchrath of Wesel, and John Staupitz.[3]

But not only the <u>meritum gratiae</u> was attacked. The majority of its opponents were also skeptical toward the <u>meritum gloriae</u> in the sense of condign merit. The teaching of acceptance of Duns Scotus and the Augustinians of the late Middle Ages provided the weapons for the battle. Since a correspondence between work and reward was contested, what occurred was a dissolution of the <u>meritum de condigno</u> and a reduction to a <u>meritum de congruo</u>.

Beginnings of this view which developed both against Thomas and against Bonaventure are already found in High Scholasticism with Duns Scotus, Henry of Gent, Peter Olivi and Peter of Trabibus.[4] The Augustinians of the late Middle Ages (Thomas Bradwardine, Gregory of Rimini and Hugolin of Orvieto)[5] thought similarly: if

---

[1] See Hermann Büttner, ed., <u>Das Büchlein vom vollkommenen Leben, Eine deutsche Theologie</u> (Jena: E. Diederichs, 1920), pp. 54, 56.

[2] "Nam si debitam ante gratiam mercedem vellet reddere, poenam redderet peccatoribus debitam." P. Lombard <u>Collectanea in Epist. D. Pauli--In Ep. ad Rom. 4:1-8</u> (<u>PL</u> 191:1367).

[3] See Hamm, <u>Promissio</u>, p. 38; Oberman, "Tridentinisches Rechtfertigungsdekret," <u>ZTK</u> 61 (1964):258; idem, <u>Forerunners</u>, p. 184; Gustav Adolf Benrath, ed., <u>Reformtheologen des 15. Jahrhunderts</u> (Gütersloh: G. Mohn, 1968), p. 45.

[4] See Auer, <u>Gnadentheologie</u>, 2:109-10.

[5] See Oberman, <u>Werden und Wertung</u>, p. 85; Hamm, <u>Promissio</u>, p. 38.

any merits count for eternal life, then only congruous merits.

The so-called Pre-Reformers and reform theologians can also be included here. John Wycliffe still held fast to the *fides caritate formata*[1] and to the attainment of salvation *ex gracia et meritis*.[2] Thus, with him there can be no talk of justification *sola fide sine meritis*.[3] However, all merits were insufficient, if God out of His mercy did not accept them *de congruo*.[4]

These thoughts formed the setting for the teaching of John Hus. He also represented the *fides caritate formata*[5] and defined the *meritum de congruo* and *condigno* in a way similar to Thomas. The one is *de pura gratia*, the other *de pura iustitia*; the one rests upon free giving, the other upon a correspondence of performance and reward. This correspondence is, however, not quantitative but proportional.[6] Thus, this correspondence permits no rightful claim on the basis of Rom 8:18, for--as Augustine says--the

---

[1] See Gustav Adolf Benrath, *Wyclifs Bibelkommentar* (Berlin: W. de Gruyter, 1966), p. 262.

[2] Ibid., p. 263.

[3] S. Harrison Thomson, "Unnoticed MSS and Works of Wyclif," *JTS* 38 (1937):35.

[4] ". . . numerus talium meritorum . . . non sufficerent ad aliquem gradum beatitudinis promerentis, nisi quod Deus ex infinitate gracie sue acceptat merita illa de congruo." John Wyclif *De Ecclesia* 23 (Johann Loserth, ed., *Wyclif's Latin Works*, vol. 4 [London: Trübner & Co., 1886], p. 565).

[5] See Gerhard von Zezschwitz, *Die Katechismen der Waldenser und Böhmischen Brüder* (Amsterdam: Editions Rodopi, 1967), p. 98.

[6] Joannis Hus, *Opera omnia*, ed. Wenzel Flajšhans and Marie Kominkova, 3 vols. (Osnabrück: Biblio, 1966), 2:307.

person is only a tool of God,[1] so that the worth of a deed goes entirely on God's account. Hence the believer can merit eternal life only de congruo, not de condigno.[2]

A correspondence of work and reward was contested also by Nicholas of Lyra,[3] John Pupper of Goch[4] and John Staupitz.[5]

Nevertheless, before Luther we cannot speak of an overcoming of the concept of merit, for the limitations mentioned by the mystics were not able to change the doctrine, and those who were attacking the teaching did not eliminate the final way of salvation. But while there where even some who questioned the final way of salvation, this questioning was not done with great clarity and consistency. Only with Luther was the more than thousand-year-old thought of merit radically uprooted from Christendom.

The Defeat of the Concept of Merit in Luther

The "Sententiarius" Luther, who from 1509-11 gave lectures in the University of Erfurt, already shows by his anti-Aristotelian,[6] pro-Augustinian[7] attitude a certain distance from High and Late

---

[1] Hus, Opera, 2:308.

[2] "Ex quo patet, quod inpossibile est creaturam mereri a Deo vel a creatura premium quodcunque, nisi a Deo mereatur illud premium de congruo, non de condigno." Ibid., 2:309.

[3] See DTC, s.v. "Mérite," by J. Rivière.

[4] See Benrath, Reformtheologen, pp. 29, 32.

[5] See Oberman, Forerunners, p. 184.

[6] WA 9, 43, 5.   [7] Ibid., 29, 4-5.

Scholasticism.[1] Indeed, his thought in general follows the traditional line (fides caritate formata,[2] faith=assensus,[3] original sin and concupiscence are different[4]), but he does not shy away from deviating from this in favor of older traditions (Augustine in the interpretation of Peter Lombard). This is shown in the denial of the habitus caritatis in favor of a direct working of the Holy Spirit upon the believer[5] and an Augustinian view of merit in the High Scholastic interpretation. God anticipates all merits by His grace and crowns His gifts in our works.[6] Only if the will is moved by faith can one speak of a meritum de congruo.[7]

In the 1. Psalmenvorlesung (1513-15) an "individual style of thought" (eigener Denkstil)[8] is expressed in spite of reliance on many authorities (Augustine, Nicholas of Lyra, Ockham, Peter of Ailly, Biel, Bernard of Clairvaux, Gerson). While Carl Stange still was of the opinion that Luther's concern was with "pure Scholasticism" (reine Scholastik), more modern interpreters appreciate the reformational change.[9]

---

[1] Cf. RGG, 3rd ed., s.v. "Luther-Theologie," by G. Ebeling.

[2] WA 9, 72, 11-12. [3] Ibid., 92, 28-30.

[4] Ibid., 75, 11-12. [5] Ibid., 43, 1-8.

[6] Ibid., 72, 27-28; 99, 27-28. [7] Ibid., 72, 15-19.

[8] RGG, 3rd ed., s.v. "Luther-Theologie," by G. Ebeling.

[9] "'Katholisches' und 'Evangelisches' liegen verwirrend ineinander." RGG, 3rd ed. s.v. "Luther-Theologie," by G. Ebeling. "Erster Schritt zur reformatorischen Erkenntnis." Pohlmann, Hat Luther Paulus entdeckt?, p. 7. "Nahezu volle Rechtfertigungserkenntnis." Adam, Dogmengeschichte, 2:201.

Through the tropological explanation[1] everything is given a christocentric character. The biblical separation between God and man is opened; God is infinitely good, man wholly corrupt, for concupiscence is the abiding original sin.[2] Indeed, Luther still concedes a free will,[3] but everything depends on faith, which is equated with Christ,[4] humility,[5] trust,[6] grace,[7] and the foundation of merit.[8] Faith as humilitas still appears as a disposition for justification, but it already appears alone (sola fides),[9] and the iustitia passiva already emerges in an implicit sense, even though it is still tinged by Augustinianism.[10]

This has important consequences for the doctrine of merit. Luther distinguishes three comings of Christ: in carnem, spiritualis . . . per gratiam, and futurus per gloriam.[11] For the first coming people no doubt had to prepare themselves, but it could neither be earned by a meritum nor hindered by a demeritum. With the gift of His Son, God deals out of pure goodness; He is debtor from promise,

---

[1] WA 3, 335, 21-22.   [2] WA 4, 207, 25-35; 364, 9-14.

[3] Ibid., 295, 34-35. E. Hirsch interprets the free will in the 1. Psalmenvorlesung still as a self-opening by the person, while A. Gyllenkrok establishes the possibility of the opening by predestination. For both views see Axel Gyllenkrok, Rechtfertigung und Heiligung in der frühen evangelischen Theologie Luthers (Uppsala: A.-B. Lundequistka Bokhandeln, 1952), pp. 20, 22, 31.

[4] WA 3, 649, 16.   [5] WA 4, 127, 10; 231, 7.

[6] WA 3, 651, 16-18.   [7] WA 4, 127, 18.

[8] WA 3, 649, 18-20.   [9] WA 3, 320, 21; 4, 438, 4-5.

[10] WA 4, 19, 27-30, 37-39. The verbatim formulation from De servo arbitrio (1525) on: WA 18, 768, 37-769, 4.

[11] WA 4, 261, 25-262, 2.

not through meritorious works of humans. The situation is exactly the same with justification and the return of Christ.

From this Luther drew a conclusion that had already been suggested in a 1512 sermon: There is no merit of worthiness (ex condigno) for justification.[1] In the sense of tradition and of the present-day Catholic dogma, he still holds, however, to the preparation for justification and ascribes to it the value of a meritum de congruo.[2] He confirms as correct the formula facienti quod in se est:

> Omnis enim qui petit, accipit etc. Hinc recte dicunt Doctores, quod homini facienti quod in se est, deus infallibiliter dat gratiam, et licet non de condigno sese possit ad gratiam praeparare, quia est incomparabilis, taman bene de congruo propter promissionem istam dei et pactum misericordie.[3]

Here two conclusions are forced upon us:

1. Since Luther does not allow validity to any disposition ex puris naturalibus,[4] he is here already in a conflict with Nominalism.

2. Just as the law prepares for Christ's incarnation and prayer prepares for justification, so faith leads to the return of Christ. That is, both the meritum gratiae and the meritum gloriae have only the value of a meritum de congruo; the meritum de condigno has fallen away! Thereby, in 1513-15, Luther is already in conflict with Early and High Scholasticism.

---

[1] WA 1, 10, 24-29.   [2] WA 4, 262, 5-7; 312, 38-41.

[3] Ibid., 262, 3-7.

[4] "Quia nihil est propositum nostrum, nisi gratia dei ipsum disponat." WA 4, 309, 10-11.

The next step in the dismantling of the thought of merit is the Römerbriefvorlesung (1515-16). According to Ebeling it indeed brings forth only an unfolding of what was already to be found in the Psalmenvorlesung,[1] but according to Prenter it is already "new content in old formulas" (neuer Inhalt in alten Formeln),[2] a breakthrough of Augustinianism (K. Meissinger),[3] not quite the Reformation, but "a step towards the Reformation" (ein Schritt zur Reformation--H. Pohlmann).[4] Earlier Catholic scholars (Denifle, Grisar) already saw apostasy here; contemporary interpreters (Lortz, McSorley) state: "Luther's concern here is clearly Catholic."[5]

Judged by the doctrine of merit, Loewenich's interpretation --Luther is no longer Catholic in the sense of the Middle Ages[6]-- seems the most convincing. Thereby we naturally think of the champions of the theology of the meritum de congruo as meritum gratiae in High and Late Scholasticism, for the Lecture on Romans shows that Luther finally breaks with the meritum gratiae. He is also surely in battle with Thomas, for Luther allows validity to the meritum gloriae--as we already know from the Lecture on Psalms--

---

[1] RGG, 3rd ed., s.v. "Luther-Theologie," by G. Ebeling.

[2] Regin Prenter, Spiritus Creator (Munich: Chr. Kaiser, 1954), p. 21.

[3] Karl A. Meissinger, Der katholische Luther (Munich: L. Lehnen, 1952), p. 101.

[4] Pohlmann, Hat Luther Paulus entdeckt?, p. 12.

[5] McSorley, Luther: Right or Wrong?, p. 227.

[6] Loewenich, Von Augustin zu Luther, p. 241.

only as merit of congruity. Luther's understanding in the <u>Lecture on Romans</u> corresponds to that of the Augustinians of the late Middle Ages (Gregory of Rimini, Hugolin of Orvieto), though there is no evidence that he depended on them.

According to his own statement, Luther in the <u>Lecture on Romans</u> won "some knowledge of Christ" (<u>einige Erkenntnis Christi</u>).[1] The <u>solus Deus</u>[2] stands above all. Not only is the human a sinner (<u>curvitas, iniquitas, perversitas, naturale vitium et malum</u>)[3] but also the Christian is a sinner (<u>simul peccator et iustus</u>).[4] Indeed, being a Christian consists of the knowledge of sin,[5] and, although it is for Christ's sake no longer reckoned against him (<u>non-imputatio peccati, reputatio iustitiae per fidem</u>)[6] and the Christian is able to struggle against and prevail over concupiscence[7] (<u>pronitas ad malum, difficultas ad bonum</u>),[8] sin is nevertheless an "abiding sin" (<u>peccatum manens</u>).[9] Healing has already begun, but it will not be completed in this life.[10] The Christian constantly needs the righteousness of Christ[11] and the Christian's best works establish no claim.[12] Therefore there is no "own righteousness" (<u>iustitia domestica</u>) which leaves room for merits; righteousness

---

[1] See Peter Kawerau, <u>Luther--Leben, Schriften, Denken</u> (Marburg: N. G. Elwert, 1969), p. 68.

[2] WA 56, 419, 17.

[3] Ibid., 325, 9; 356, 7.

[4] Ibid., 268, 27-28; 269, 21-24; 272, 17.

[5] Ibid., 230, 20-21.

[6] Ibid., 271, 20-30.

[7] Ibid., 314, 4-6; 346, 9-15.

[8] Ibid., 271, 8.

[9] Ibid., 314, 4.

[10] Ibid., 347, 8-14.

[11] Ibid., 264, 16-21.

[12] Ibid., 268, 11.

comes "from outside" (<u>iustitia extranea</u>).[1] Man, unconverted or Christian, can do nothing of himself; God must bestow the will and the accomplishment,[2] and every good work presupposes grace.[3] Therefore the <u>fides formata</u> is a "damned word" (<u>maledictum vocabulum</u>)[4] and the <u>habitus</u>-teaching is to be denied,[5] because instead of stressing the deep-rooted, constant sin, it reckons with natural forces and the infused quality as cooperation-factors. There is cooperation only--as is already evident in the <u>Lecture on Psalms</u>--through faith.[6] Faith, then, is not the <u>fides informis</u>,[7] but the <u>credulitas</u>[8] (the nonadherence to oneself and the lack of distrust toward God) whereby one looks wholly away from self to God.

Beside this aspiration for a genuine Pauline theology, however, there are still some retarding elements received from theological tradition. In some places Luther still speaks of a preparation for justification.[9] Grace is still <u>gratia infusa</u>.[10] Justification is not yet "by faith alone without works" (<u>sola fide sine operibus</u>), but "inclination towards good" (<u>inclinatio ad</u>

---

[1] Ibid., 158, 10-12. [2] Ibid., 398, 11-14.
[3] Ibid., 172, 10-11.
[4] Ibid., 337, 18. Cf. 40 I, 422, 13.
[5] Ibid., 287, 17-24. [6] WA 4, 601, 8-9.
[7] WA 56, 172, 21. [8] Ibid., 227, 18.

[9] Ibid., 254, 19-255, 19; 287, 21. Sometimes, however, conversion appears as the winning over of the godless to the faith. Cf. ibid., 295, 1-3; 422, 5-9.

[10] Ibid., 200, 9.

bonum,[1] pronouncing just and making just,[2] fulfilling of the law as prerequisite to pronouncing just.[3] The consecutive way of salvation is not yet clear; Augustinian finality still dominates. Therefore Luther still speaks of a "progress of justification" (profectus iustificationis,[4] of a justification "more and more" (magis ac magis),[5] and of a beginning in view of a future perfection (incepit, ut perficiat).[6] Whether he at this time already had the assurance of salvation is contested.[7]

Obviously Luther still lived in peace with the ecclesiastical tradition. He still felt the Church's commands are to be kept,[8] asceticism is good for sanctification, if it comes from faith,[9] and the monk is still a disciple of Christ, if in this way he seeks not salvation but imitation.[10]

---

[1] Ibid., 271, 12. [2] Ibid., 221, 18-19.
[3] Ibid., 22, 24-29. [4] Ibid., 259, 15.
[5] Ibid., 254, 29. [6] Ibid., 258, 20.

[7] An assurance of perfection or of election Luther always denied, as is also seen here (WA 56, 290, 25-31). The assurance of forgiveness, on the other hand, is already breaking through (ibid., 410, 22). On account of the finality-character of works, a whole assurance of salvation cannot be given. Holl, on the other hand, sees here the beginning concept of assurance of salvation as consciousness of an indissoluble partnership of will in justification. Gesammelte Aufsätze zur Kirchengeschichte, 6th ed. 3 vols. (Tübingen: J. C. B. Mohr [P. Siebeck], 1932), 1:151-52. Ebeling senses its presence, though it is unclearly formulated. RGG, 3rd ed., s.v. "Luther-Theologie." Gyllenkrok sees the breakthrough to the assurance of salvation first in the Lecture on Hebrews (1517/18). Rechtfertigung und Heiligung, p. 72. Lortz holds a similar opinion. "Römerbriefvorlesung," TThZ 71 (1962):273. Mau denies the complete breakthrough of assurance in the Lecture on Romans but speaks of an "entscheidende Einsicht zur Begründung." Rudolf Mau, "Zur Frage der Begründung von Heilsgewissheit beim jungen Luther," TLZ 92 (1967):747.

[8] WA 56, 496, 29-32. [9] Ibid., 333, 15-18.
[10] Ibid., 497, 18-32.

These limitations, however, do not change the fact that the discovery of human passivity in the work of salvation is of great significance for a further reduction of the thought of merit. Luther says more clearly than before that there can be no real merit (de condigno).[1] Merits are worked out through Christ and are accepted for His sake. Sin on the human side (peccatum manens) and the promise of mercy in the acceptatio on the divine side make it clear that there is no inherent "ontological dignity" (ontologische Dignität) in the works.[2] But here Luther goes a step further. While even in his Lecture on Psalms we have seen the preparation for justification from the viewpoint of a merit of congruity, now we note his categorical denial of the meritum gratiae.

The battle breaks out over the formula facienti quod in se est. Luther becomes indignant over the Nominalistic optimism that man is able to love God out of his own strength and thereby earn grace. This teaching he regards as pure Pelagianism.

> Quocirca mera deliria sunt, que dicuntur, quod homo ex viribus suis possit Deum diligere super omnia et facere opera precepti secundum substantiam facti, sed non ad intentionem precipientis, quia non in gratia. O stulti, O Sawtheologen![3]

> Huius autem erroris tota substantia est Pelagiana opinio. Nam etsi nunc nulli sunt Pelagiani professione e titulo, plurimi tamen sunt re vera et opinione, licet ignoranter, ut sunt, qui nisi libertati arbitrii tribuant facere, quod in se est, ante gratiam, putant sese cogi a Deo ad peccatum et necessario peccare. Quod cum sit impiissimum sentire, putant secure et audacter, quod cum bonam intentionem forment, infallibiliter Dei gratiam obtinuerint infusam.[4]

---

[1] Ibid., 290, 15-17.

[2] Schinzer, Die doppelte Verdienstlehre, p. 38.

[3] WA 56, 274, 11-14.   [4] Ibid., 502, 14-20.

The conclusion that Luther draws from this is that of himself man is not able de congruo to prepare for justification[1] and that one--so he said somewhat later--must flee, as from the devil, from those who teach that there is a meritum gratiae.[2] Did Luther thereby deny only the Nominalistic meritum de congruo and retain that of High Scholasticism?

In this case--in comparison to the Lecture on Psalms--we would be concerned with a polemic more vigorous in form than in content.

However, the following considerations make clear that Luther is now rejecting the meritum gratiae in general:

1. Everything that man does before justification is sin.[3]

2. Of himself man is incapable of anything; the will is "in bondage" (servum arbitrium).[4]

3. Everything is accomplished through the power of the Word.[5]

4. The person remains purely passive in receiving both grace and glory. This passivity is to be understood theologically; that is, on the plane of human experience there is an asking for grace and a working out from grace. All this is received and accomplished through the Spirit.[6]

5. The Spirit is effective only with those predestined. The redemption does not depend on will and work, but on the election

---

[1] WA 1, 147, 10-12.   [2] WA 4, 612, 4-6.
[3] WA 56, 386, 1, 16-18.   [4] Ibid., 398, 11-12; 385, 17-18.
[5] Ibid., 387, 15.   [6] Ibid., 379, 2-6.

which is carried through as though by necessity. Therefore, merits are excluded.[1]

6. There is no secondary position of free will, and the Scholastic distinction between <u>necessitas consequentiae</u> and <u>consequentis</u>[2] is likewise rejected.

7. Conversion seems, in some places, like an overwhelming of the person.[3]

Since only those predestined are redeemed, God with His Word and Spirit overpowers man, for man of himself is fixated only on sin, cannot do anything good <u>coram Deo</u>, and, therefore, can only be passive in the salvation event--thereby not doing anything to earn grace, not even in the sense of a <u>meritum de congruo</u>.[4]

However, Luther has not yet wholly broken with the thought of merit. The works of the one who has received grace he still designates as <u>merita</u>. What comes forth from love,[5] what is fruit of faith,[6] and what occurs from self-forgetfulness[7] can be designated as merit. These merits, however, need the acceptance of God,[8] that is, they are really only merits of congruity. The <u>meritum</u>

---

[1] Ibid., 381, 24-29; 382, 3-4.

[2] Ibid., 382, 21-383, 10. According to McSorley (<u>Luther: Right or Wrong</u>?, p. 318), because Luther did not understand it; according to Martin Seils, because the Thomistic solution was unknown to him and he knew it only in its changed, Ockhamistic form. <u>Der Gedanke vom Zusammenwirken Gottes und des Menschen in Luthers Theologie</u> (Gütersloh: G. Mohn, 1962), p. 97.

[3] WA 56, 295, 1-3; 422, 7-9.   [4] Ibid., 387, 4-6.

[5] Ibid., 135, 1.   [6] Ibid., 63, 7; 291, 16-17.

[7] Ibid., 370, 14-20.   [8] Ibid., 290, 15-17.

gloriae is thus valued by Luther still in the sense of the Lecture on Psalms.

The same state of knowledge is mirrored in the Galaterbriefvorlesung (1516/17) and the Disputatio contra scholasticam theologiam.[1] The Resolutionen zu den Ablassthesen (1518) again lead a step further, for it is then that Luther breaks with the opera supererogatoria.[2] The Heidelberger Disputation (beginning of 1518) does not signify any important progress compared with the Resolutionen. Luther diminishes the merit of the believer through the peccatum manens. As far as sin resists the good will, so far every work is sin. As far as the will activated by the Holy Spirit carries through, the work is meritorious.[3]

According to Schinzer, the final breakthrough to a merit-free theology ensued in the course of the year 1518.[4] Luther now explains that God does not grant anything at all from merit.[5] Schinzer was able to show that thereby the meritum gloriae is meant,

---

[1] See Schinzer, Die doppelte Verdienstlehre, pp. 40-48.

[2] "Nullus sanctorum in hac vita sufficienter implevit mandata dei, ergo nihil prorsus foecerunt superabundans." WA 1, 606, 12-13. "Sancti per opus eorum omnium perfectissimum . . . non faciunt ultra quam debent." Ibid., 27-28. "Concludo, merita sanctorum nulla esse superflua sibi, quae nobis ociosis succurrant. . . ." Ibid., 607, 17-18.

[3] WA 1, 367, 21-24. See Schinzer, Die doppelte Verdienstlehre, p. 52.

[4] Ibid., pp. 53-54.

[5] "Dis Evangelium drucket nichts aus denn Christi suessigkeit aus dem gehorsam des Vaters, und das er nichts gibt aus verdienst." WA 1, 277, 4-5.

because Luther in a letter to Staupitz expressly refers to the final judgment.[1]

In the Sermo de triplici justitia from the same year Luther denies the thought of merit for two reasons:

1. If one already speaks of "merit," then it is faith (Fides est meritum totum).[2] And since faith and its righteousness are given as gifts (Christus meruit nobis et donavit, donatque quottidie),[3] the thought of merit is dissolved. Luther also speaks here of the meritum gloriae (vannissimum est, ut unus actus subitaneus dicatur dignus vita eterna).[4]

2. Merits are impossible for another reason, because even the best works of the Christian--imbued with concupiscence--are really sins (Quomodo possit esse meritum, cum tamen omnes sancti peccent . . .).[5]

The equation fides = meritum appears again in the Galaterkommentar (1519).[6] That is, Luther still uses the word, but he has already given up its content.

This is shown also by the 2. Psalmenvorlesung of the same year. In it Luther explains in detail his standpoint concerning the theology of merit. Here again he uses the word, but it is parabolic for the works produced only by God[7] and subsequently

---

[1] BR 1, 160, 10-12. See Schinzer, Die doppelte Verdienstlehre, p. 54.

[2] WA 2, 46, 6.   [3] Ibid., 8.

[4] Ibid., 6-7.   [5] Ibid., 9-10.

[6] Ibid., 511, 27-28; 537, 2-3.

[7] WA 5, 162, 20; 169, 19-20.

lived out.[1] Therefore, according to him, hope does not spring from merit, but merit (obedience) from hope.[2] Salvation lies only in the mercy of God (sola misericordia),[3] therefore, man should let go of merits as self-accomplishment and claim,[4] for he does not need them.[5] The theologians of merit are "justiciaries" (iustitiarii)[6] and their teaching, says Luther, is the ruination of all theology,[7] because the proponents of merit betray a lack of knowledge of Christ and His cross.[8]

The famous writings of 1520 finally offer the "pure and new doctrine" (reine neue Lehre):[9] in the Freiheit eines Christenmenschen by the unmistakably expressed sola fide,[10] by consecutive obedience (eyn gutt frum man macht gutte frum werck),[11] and in De Captivitate Babylonica by the promise of forgiveness and salvation from mercy without merit.[12]

These conclusions have been attacked from the Catholic side

---

[1]"Haec enim mortificatio et purgatio (quae fit infusione fidei et spei et charitatis) facit, ut homo operibus suis exutus discat in solum deum fidere et opera bona facere, iam non sibi tanquam merita, quibus praemium quaerat, sed gratuito et libero spontaneo que affectu placendi deo, nihil in ea fidens, sed per ea in gloriam dei serviens." Ibid., 169, 1-5.

[2]Ibid., 164, 1-2. [3]Ibid., 161, 32.
[4]Ibid., 166, 1-3. [5]Ibid., 175, 15.
[6]Ibid., 166, 39. [7]Ibid., 163, 36.
[8]Ibid., 36-37.
[9]Schinzer, Die doppelte Verdienstlehre, p. 63.
[10]WA 7, 23, 20-22; 24, 13-17; 24, 35-25, 4.
[11]Ibid., 30, 31-31, 8; 31, 17-32; 32, 5, 26-34.
[12]WA 6, 515, 18-21.

by Theobald Beer, who states that Luther's distinction between
gratia (justification) and donum (sanctification)[1] permits the Reformer to speak even further of cooperation and merit;[2] indeed, that Luther not only permits it but also that he himself, in the middle and late periods of his activity, "held in high esteem" (hoch gewertet) both cooperation and merit.[3] The distinction between gratia and donum justified Luther in speaking of a double justification,[4] and the key to Luther's teaching was not sola gratia but gratia and donum, not sola fide but sola fides and fides incarnata, not solus Christus but aliud Christus redimens, aliud Christus operans.[5]

From the period after 1517, Beer cites a few statements which he considers proof that Luther held fast to the thought of merit. They can be grouped as follows:

1. Texts in which Luther speaks of reward and payment (WA 32, 541, 19-23; 543, 30-38; 39I, 274, 4-11; 30II, 670, 21-23, 27-30).

2. Sayings about works as merits and salvation as reward (WA 18, 696, 6-7; 18, 785, 16-18; 2, 562, 19-22, 31-34; 6, 26, 14-16; 40II, 504, 33-36).

3. The witness of works in the judgment (WA 27, 303, 20-24; 39I, 247, 26-29; 36, 451, 5, 33-35).

---

[1] WA 8, 106, 10-22.

[2] Theobald Beer, "Die Ausgangspositionen der lutherischen und der katholischen Lehre von der Rechtfertigung," Cath (M) 21 (1967): 72.

[3] Idem, "Lohn und Verdienst bei Luther," MThZ 28 (1977):284.

[4] Idem, "Ausgangspositionen," Cath (M) 21 (1967):69.

[5] Idem, "Lohn und Verdienst," MThZ 28 (1977):284.

He admits, however, that this does not justify speaking of a Catholic teaching of merit[1] and that one cannot make Luther's systematics intelligible from a few places but rather from his whole theology.[2]

If this method is followed, it can be shown that after 1518 we no longer can speak of a merit-doctrine with Luther. For, when the Reformer speaks of forgiveness and sanctification, any meritorious work is excluded, even though he still speaks of "merits and reward" (Verdienste und Lohn).[3] This reward is the "charismatic reward," through which Paul will have more honor than the ordinary Christian.[4]

Man can earn neither de congruo nor de condigno. Such distinctions are "Satanic tricks" (ludibriae Satanae);[5] everything has been freely given by Christ.[6] Salvation is thereby given along with faith in Christ so that a double justification is excluded, for the believer already in salvation goes only toward its unveiling.[7] The Christian does not earn the kingdom, the kingdom earns him.[8] What comes to him reaches him through word and faith, not work.[9] Works are only fruit; when this is well understood,

---

[1] Theobald Beer, "Ausgangspositionen," Cath (M) 21 (1967):73.

[2] Idem, "Lohn und Verdienst," MThZ 28 (1977):261.

[3] WA 32, 543, 1-4, 8-12; 538, 11-14.

[4] Ibid., 543, 7-8; 538, 4-10.

[5] WA 40I, 223, 14-20.   [6] Ibid., 224, 25-28; 32, 538, 15-17.

[7] WA 18, 694, 34-40.   [8] Ibid., 22-24.

[9] WA 32, 540, 14-15.

the word "merit" does no damage.[1] Thus for Luther all merits as such are "cut off" (abgeschnitten)[2] and "thrown away" (weggeworfen).[3]

Luther's Reconstruction of Justification "sine meritis"

With the defeat of the final-meritorious salvation-doctrine of Catholicism--according to Luther's own avowal[4]--the decisive reformational breakthrough had been made. The word "merit" was unmasked as a dangerous word, for it characterizes the theology of the Antichrist,[5] it is lack of knowledge of Christ,[6] and means to crucify Christ again, because man intrudes on the work of salvation.[7] Therefore the teaching of merit is blasphemy[8] and the ruin of theology.[9]

This, according to Luther, is clearly unpauline,[10] stems from tradition, and rests on bad exegesis of Scripture.[11] Whoever subscribes to it has not yet grasped Christ and is simply blind.[12] All great Scholastics, such as Scotus, Bonaventure, Biel, and Thomas Aquinas have therefore only phantasized, for Biel disregarded

---

[1] Ibid., 541, 23-25. [2] Ibid., 538, 14.

[3] Ibid., 540, 12.

[4] "Denn am ersten ist mein Kampf gewest wider das Vertrauen auf die Werk, darauf doch die Welt so hoch pocht und trotzt, als sollten gute Werk auch mit nöthig sein zur Seligkeit." TR 2, 281, 24-25. Cf. Pohlmann, Hat Luther Paulus entdeckt?, p. 34; RE, 3rd ed., s.v. "Verdienst," by J. Kunze.

[5] WA 40I, 220, 4-30. [6] WA 5, 163, 36.

[7] WA 47, 579, 1-7. [8] WA 40I, 236, 33-237, 11.

[9] WA 5, 163, 36. [10] WA 18, 769, 32-35; 771, 10-13.

[11] WA 2, 562, 19-21. [12] Ibid., 25-26.

the Scripture and Thomas let himself be led astray by Aristotle.[1]

Therefore one should avoid using the expression of the necessity of works for salvation, because the final way of salvation leads unhesitatingly to the concepts meritum and debitum.[2]

The definitions of the opponent must be considered carefully, for he is striving to wash himself clean,[3] even to using similar formulations, but with completely different meanings, to those of the evangelical side.[4] The merit-thought of the opponent is extenuated by words but is held high in his mind and in the content.[5]

One can speak of merit only in a negative way (Rom 3:24-- "und werden on [ohne] verdienst gerecht"),[6] else the word must be neutralized by the added explanation. For example:

1. Merit is really promise.[7]

---

[1] TR 3, 564, 3-11. "Thomas est loquacissimus, quia metaphysica est seductus." Cf. WA 8, 127, 19; TR 1, 118, 1-3; TR 2, 193, 5-6. Modern Catholic research denies this judgment, since Luther is thought not to have known Thomas. Cf. Lortz, Reformation, 1:170; Georges Tavard, Protestantism, trans. Rachel Attwater (New York: Hawthorn Books, 1959), p. 24; Wacker, Ökumenischer Dialog, p. 22. Pesch therefore states (Theologie der Rechtfertigung, p. 322) that Luther's polemic against merit with reference to Thomas is like "Luftstreiche." We have explained in discussing the meritum de condigno in Thomas that we cannot completely agree to this opinion. As far as a more exact knowledge of Thomistic theology is concerned, Meissinger (Der katholische Luther, p. 109) is of the opinion that Luther could not have had it (knowledge of Thomas) by the preference of the via moderna in Erfurt and therefore is to be excused. A cursory knowledge of Thomas Luther must probably have possessed, since Staupitz was a disciple of Aquinas. See Fausel, Luther, 1:49.

[2] WA 39I, 25, 1-5.   [3] TR 3, 192, 27-34.

[4] WA 40I, 252, 18.   [5] WA 18, 770, 21-31.

[6] DB 7, 39, 18-19.   [7] WA 18, 693, 19-20.

2. Merit is faith.[1]
3. Merit is fruit.[2]
4. Merit is Christ.[3]

It is important to acknowledge the consecutive way of salvation, for then it becomes possible to give up the teaching of merit.[4] Otherwise there remains only the final-meritorious way, by which, however, salvation can not be attained.[5] On this road one can only find renown from the world.[6] But one moves this way to a dangerous security which is the greatest insecurity in regard to God, because one never knows whether his merits are sufficient to attain salvation.[7]

While the consecutive way is a path of altruistic love serving the neighbor, because he who has been freely given salvation by Christ gladly shares the mercies of Christ with his neighbor without hope for a reward,[8] the merit way is the path of salvation-creating egoism.[9] This seeks human assurance of salvation and thereby leads to human self-assertion[10] and to the struggle against the freely giving grace of God.[11] The path of merit is finally, in spite of all stress on grace, just righteousness by works.[12]

---

[1] WA 2, 46, 6.
[2] WA 32, 541, 25.
[3] WA 1, 428, 36-37.
[4] WA 39I, 256, 15-257, 5.
[5] WA 28, 746, 27-32.
[6] WA 6, 219, 37-220, 2.
[7] WA 40I, 589, 19-28; 43, 178, 34-38.
[8] WA 7, 35, 25-36, 2.
[9] WA 2, 98, 29-33.
[10] WA 18, 770, 10-11.
[11] WA 7, 33, 30-36.
[12] WA 16, 88, 35-37.

Therefore one must struggle against the thought of merit with all one's strength, for to unmask it means to deal a deadly blow to the papacy.[1] That is, with the thought of merit, Luther exposed the <u>shibboleth</u> of Roman theology[2] and recognized where the lever is to be placed in the work of reformation. Thus it is not to be wondered at that on the Catholic side this has been regarded as "one of the most disastrous of Luther's errors."[3] Such a viewpoint, indeed, overlooks the evangelical reconstruction of the Reformation ethic. Just because man himself cannot contribute anything toward his justification and redemption, and everything occurs "without merits by pure grace" (<u>sine meritis pura gratia</u>),[4] ethics can be placed upon a new foundation. It no longer rests upon man, not even upon the one who has received grace, and, thereby, it rests not upon performance, cooperation, satisfaction, merit, or uncertainty of salvation. On the contrary, it rests upon God and, thereby, upon mercy, sole agency, Christ, gratitude, and assurance of salvation. It contains no moralistic and eudaemonistic pull toward salvation; rather, it has a spontaneous and grateful pull

---

[1] WA 40I, 231, 32-232, 13.

[2] Rudolf Hermann, <u>Luthers Theologie</u> (Göttingen: Vandenhoeck & Ruprecht, 1967), p. 151.

[3] "If we are told that our labours have no value, not one man in ten thousand will make the sacrifices which anything like high virtue entails. Assuredly this must be reckoned as being one of the most disastrous of Luther's errors." George H. Joyce, <u>The Catholic Doctrine of Grace</u> (Westminster, MD: Newman Press, 1950), p. 172.

[4] WA 1, 427, 16.

by salvation. How should one who is acting from gratitude[1] be inferior in the moral life to the one who is acting from moralistic and eudaemonistic compulsion? As far as Luther is concerned, the philosophical criticism of the Christian ethic is irrelevant,[2] for in the Reformation view the person who is living in the close relationship of a creature with his Creator will only do good, because it corresponds to God's will, even--in the impossible case--if there were no heaven and no judgment![3] How much more is this true of the redeemed one who has been freely given not only his creation by God but also his status of a child of God!

Luther made this clear long before Kant, R. Hermann asserts.[4] But Luther's ethical reconstruction surpasses not only the Catholic achievement of salvation but also the philosophical moralism of conscience. For in the gospel man is not primarily referred to his conscience, and thereby thrown back upon himself, but to the Father of mercy! The obedience of the Christian--and

---

[1] WA 10I 2, 61, 2-5; 16, 444, 18-27; 31I, 76, 8-9; 40I, 241, 20-21.

[2] Cf. Immanuel Kant: "Der 'Eudämonist', der, bloss im Nutzen und der eigenen Glückseligkeit . . . den obersten Bestimmungsgrund seines Willens setzt, ist 'moralischer Egoist'." Quoted in HWP, s.v. "Ethik," by R. Romberg. Friedrich Nietzsche: "[Mit der] Lohn- und Straflehre ist [im Christentum] alles verdorben." Werke, 3 vols. (Munich: C. Hanser, 1966), 3:642. Ernst Bloch: "Der Himmel als garantierte Belohnungskasse für gute Taten . . . muss leer sein, wenn der Mensch moralisch handeln soll." Atheismus im Christentum (Frankfort M.: Suhrkamp, 1968), p. 317.

[3] "Filii autem Dei gratuita voluntate faciunt bonum, nullum praemium quaerentes sed solam gloriam et voluntatem Dei, parati bonum facere, si, per impossibile, neque regnum neque infernus esset." WA 18, 694, 17-20.

[4] Hermann, Luthers Theologie, p. 151.

Luther leaves no doubt that there must exist such[1]--is no Stoical-
fatalistic compulsion (<u>kein Muss</u>) but a childlike-joyful per-
mission (<u>ein Darf</u>). The only moral motivation of the created
and born-again Christian can be, therefore, solely gratitude.

A whole group of biblical elements Luther stressed anew,
and some, like predestination and temptation as sin, he even
over-stressed to help him define anew righteousness as wholeness
(justification, sanctification and glorification) and to separate
totally from the thought of merit.

First we must mention the <u>theocentricity</u> of his teaching
of justification. A whole army of Catholic interpreters has endeavored to prove that Luther's teaching is anthropocentric[2] and
that he is therefore concerned only with the stilling of his own
conscience at any cost, at the expense of God, the Church, the
world, and of morality.

As a matter of fact, however, Luther's teaching on justification is primarily concerned with God's Deity, with the restitution of the biblical idea of God, and with the divine way of
salvation, which is the recognized divine presupposition for the

---

[1] Without growing out beyond oneself, everything would be "umsonst" (WA 8, 26, 12-13). Daily one must struggle and win (WA 39I, 353, 35-36); the norm of the divine will is the law of God (ibid., 485, 22-24), but just as "lex sine lege!" (ibid., 433, 1). God's commandments must be kept: "Dann on die gebot gottes kan kein mensch selig werden." WA 2, 60, 29.

[2] See Bartmann, <u>Dogmatik</u>, 2:110; Stakemeier, "Trienter Lehrentscheidungen," in <u>Weltkonzil von Trient</u>, p. 103; Van de Pol, <u>Reformatorisches Christentum</u>, p. 392; Jacques Maritain, <u>Trois Réformateurs</u> (Paris: Librairie Plon, 1925), p. 15; Paul Hacker, <u>The Ego in Faith</u> (Chicago: Franciscan Herald Press, 1970), pp. 5-8, 17-19, 33, 133.

peace of the soul, and not a manipulated human excuse. This is conceded today also by Catholic scholars.[1]

For Luther, God is the sole working Creator and ever-giving, loving Father. Both exclude human works as being able to make any contribution. It is exactly the sign for God's Deity that He gives freely[2] and for the person's creatureliness and child state, that he can only receive. Therefore faith is "the only attitude of man corresponding to the essence of God, His divinity (die einzige Haltung des Menschen, die dem Wesen Gottes, seiner Gottheit entspricht).[3] The way of salvation can thus be named only sola misericordia[4] and can be walked only sola fide.

Luther thereby reformed and restored the biblical idea of God. The Jewish thought of God who lends and is owed, and the pagan thought of God who is offended and must be appeased, are withdrawn. What remains is the God of the Covenant, who makes promises and keeps them.

The personality of man is thereby not annulled. It is

---

[1] Lortz states that Luther's leitmotif is the sentence: Not man, but God! On this he points to WA 56, 419, 15-18. "Römerbriefvorlesung," TThZ 71 (1962):141. Cf. Pesch, Theologie der Rechtfertigung, p. 396. It is interesting that the "theocentric orientation" of Luther is even made into a reproach, when it is a matter of the Catholic anthropocentricity (Habitus-teaching, inherent quality). See Thomas Sartory, "Erbsünde," in Mysterium Kirche, 2:958.
But the theocentricity of Luther's teaching has been most clearly brought out on the Protestant side by Paul Althaus. "Gottes Gottheit als Sinn der Rechtfertigungslehre Luthers," LuJ 13 (1931): 1-28; idem, Theologie Luthers, pp. 109-118.

[2] WA 40I, 224, 28-32.

[3] Althaus, "Gottes Gottheit," LuJ 13 (1931):20.

[4] WA 39I, 225, 8.

indeed not the Greek προαίρεσις,[1] the autonomous will, the αὐτεξούσιον,[2] selfsufficiency and the συναίτιον,[3] the co-cause. The biblical picture of man knows neither an absolute nor a relative autonomy of the person. Man is wholly dependent on God, but in contrast to the other creatures he is God's counterpart. He is able to hear and obey God, but he can only do so because God makes him capable of doing so. Man is no automaton; he experiences God's call and command and is capable of carrying them out. But since they are God's thoughts, God must create the will and the strength for carrying them out. To presume that one has a part in this, even if only a very small part, is unbelief, "moralistic hybris."[4] But that is exactly what comes to expression in the thought of merit.

Luther also sees here an unbearable limitation of God's sovereignty. To make salvation dependent on works is an insult to God.[5] For even if such works were possible, God has chosen another way.[6] He wishes to redeem the person by means of grace. Whoever speaks of works and merits as necessary for salvation rebels against the will of God.

But apart from God's chosen way, the fulfilling of the law coram Deo is impossible: with the unconverted, because he either openly transgresses or seeks his honor in outward obedience and

---

[1] Aristotle Nic. Eth. 3. 3. 19 20; Epiktetus Diatr. 1. 1. 23.

[2] Ibid., 4. 1. 62.   [3] Jamblichos De Myster. 2. 11.

[4] Althaus, "Gottes Gottheit," LuJ 13 (1931):19.

[5] WA 40II, 452, 21-23.   [6] TR 1, 32, 18-27.

rests on his autonomy; and with the converted, because all his victories are spoiled by the "remaining sin" (peccatum manens).

Therefore man lives in a double unreality: In the ethical illusion that he is able to meet God's requirements, and in the religious fiction that the biblical God deals like a man according to performances and merits.[1]

God's sovereignty is preserved by the totaliter aliter of the divine method of dealing: God does not let the kingdom be striven for and bought; He has prepared it from eternity for His children and wishes to give it to them.[2] But because God does not blot out sin like a chalk mark, but, on the contrary, takes His righteousness seriously,[3] He, the infinitely rich and powerful One from whom the sinners have shut themselves out, has won them back to Himself. That is, Christ, the personified kingdom, merits us--we do not merit the kingdom.[4] The totaliter aliter reaches its peak in predestination. Merits would limit God's election; God is free like the potter who can make one vessel one way and another differently.[5] In that God accepts whom He will and rejects whom He will, He is unjust according to human philosophy of merit, but according to His sovereignty He remains just.[6]

Thus, with Luther, the idea of predestination appears as a

---

[1] See Althaus, "Gottes Gottheit," LuJ 13 (1931):18.

[2] WA 18, 694, 11-14, 22-23.   [3] WA 10I 1, 470, 18-22.

[4] WA 18, 694, 23-24, 26-27.   [5] Ibid., 730, 10-12.

[6] Ibid., 731, 5-9.

further weapon against the principle of merit.[1] The Reformer, in contrast to Calvin, never worked out the concept of predestination in the form of a proper doctrine[2] and never pushed it into the foreground;[3] he even refused, from pastoral-theological considerations, to make a thorough investigation of the Why of double predestination,[4] but to the end of his life he held fast to it.[5]

Naturally we can go into this comprehensive topic only so far as it is necessary for Luther's struggle against the doctrine of merit.

Since the Lecture on Romans[6] Luther built the double predestination into his soteriology as a helping thought. In De servo arbitrio he expressed himself the most clearly about it.

Since eternity, without reference to later merits, God has elected or rejected.[7] The idea of election therefore excludes any

---

[1] "Election has to a great extent become a weapon against . . . the doctrine of merit." Fredrik Brosché, Luther on Predestination (Stockholm: Almquist & Wirksell, 1978), p. 152.

[2] See Loewenich, Von Augustin zu Luther, p. 179.

[3] See Holl, Gesammelte Aufsätze, 1:148.

[4] WA 18, 686, 10-11; 689, 18-22; 43, 460, 25-26; 461, 33-34.

[5] Cf. Gerhard Rost, Der Prädestinationsgedanke in der Theologie Martin Luthers (Berlin: Evangelische Verlagsanstalt, 1966), p. 71; Erdmann Schott, "Luthers Lehre vom servum arbitrium in ihrer theologischen Bedeutung," ZST 7 (1929):422; Sigurd Normann, "De servo arbitrio als Ausdruck lutherischen Christentums," ZST 14 (1937):307. In contrast to these views, Wolfhart Pannenberg believes the later Luther had overcome the idea of predestination. "Der Einfluss der Anfechtungserfahrung auf den Prädestinationsbegriff Luthers," KuD 3 (1957):109-39.

[6] See Holl, Gesammelte Aufsätze, 1:148; Pannenberg, "Einfluss der Anfechtungserfahrung," KuD 3 (1957):116; Kraus, Vorherbestimmung, p. 104.

[7] WA 18, 724, 35-725, 3.

salvation-achieving work and merit. This pertains not only to merits through which justification is to be earned[1] but also such as have salvation as goal.[2] "These are all yours for nothing and out of pure mercy" (<u>umbsonst und aus lauter barmhertzigkeit</u>).[3]

Of course He does not give equally to all persons. The double predestination forces Luther to thoughts (<u>Deus absconditus --Deus praedicatus</u>,[4] <u>gratia irresistibilis</u>,[5] particular will of salvation[6]), which later Lutheranism has given up[7] and which, in part, are strongly rejected by contemporary evangelical Luther-researchers.[8]

Nevertheless in Luther's doctrine of predestination are found considerations which, because they are connected with his teaching of justification, are of general and timeless significance.

Thus, for example, the thought that God's salvation work is "suffered" (<u>erlitten</u>).[9] Luther speaks of an <u>aptitudo passiva</u>,[10] of the possibility of the person to receive salvation but not to contribute to salvation. Predestination teaches--just as well as

---

[1] WA 45, 697, 22-26.   [2] Ibid., 698, 28-30.

[3] Ibid., 2-3.   [4] WA 18, 685, 1-24.

[5] Ibid., 635, 17-22.   [6] WA 56, 381, 29; 18, 633, 17.

[7] <u>BSLK</u> 818, 34-819, 21; 1065, 23-31; 1073, 36-43; 1076, 4-17; 1086, 26-35.

[8] "Eine dem Glauben fremde theoretische Folgerung." Althaus, <u>Theologie Luthers</u>, p. 243. "Dem reformatorischen Glauben gegenüber ein Fremdkörper." Normann, "De servo arbitrio," <u>ZST</u> 14 (1937):334. "Eine Gefährdung des Glaubenscharakters." Martin Doerne, "Gottes Ehre am gebundenen Willen," <u>LuJ</u> 20 (1938):75. "Diskrepanz zwischen dem Heilswillen Gottes . . . und der <u>omnipotentia</u> Gottes." Loewenich, <u>Von Augustin zu Luther</u>, p. 176.

[9] WA 18, 753, 33-754, 17.   [10] Ibid., 636, 19-20.

does the doctrine of justification--that man can do nothing of himself but has everything only through God.[1] Thereby man's self-assurance is destroyed before God, and the sola gratia and Deo soli gloria are established.[2] On the other side, the doctrine of predestination, like the doctrine of justification, leads to assurance of salvation, because man no longer depends on any kind of merits on his own part. God-given faith is, in each case, the guarantee of salvation. Thereby Luther succeeded in overcoming the anxiety of predestination.[3] For both predestination and justification first bring the desperatio salutaris, and then the assurance that the elected one, or the one sustained by God in faith, will come to the goal.[4]

Both predestination and justification teach that the way of salvation is not supported by any kind of human reckoning according to worth and work. The double predestination--as contested as it may be--with Luther helps to preserve the biblical thought of the holiness (Unverfügbarkeit) of God and the idea "that faith may not be understood rationalistically."[5] Likewise both set aside the striving for reward, for if salvation stands at the beginning, it can only be fully unveiled in the

---

[1] "Das reformatorische servum arbitrium aber war nicht primär Aussage theologischer Reflexion, sondern das Bekenntnis des Sünders, dass er den Bann der Schuld und Verlorenheit durch keinerlei eigenes Tun durchbrechen kann." Schlink, "Gesetz und Evangelium," KuD 7 (1961):27.

[2] WA 18, 632, 33-633, 3.   [3] WA 43, 460, 2-13.

[4] DB 7, 23, 26-34.

[5] Lennart Pinomaa, "Unfreier Wille und Prädestination bei Luther," TZ 13 (1957):348.

eschatological reward. This is result (sequela), not merit.[1] Without work and without merit, believers are set upon a path at the end of which they will find by sight, the life that they already possess by faith.[2] Luther retains the biblical teaching of reward and punishment, but he takes away from it the "eudaemonistic influence" that had been added to it by tradition.[3]

Man must say Yes to God's will, and No to himself; then he is saved. This is Luther's first answer to the question of how one can overcome the burden of predestination.[4] Later he grasps it more christocentrically and speaks of looking in faith to Christ, through whom the burden of being redeemed or not is taken away.[5] That Luther did not mean any lazy, self-assured faith--a temptation that can grow out of the doctrine of predestination as well as from a misunderstood doctrine of justification--is evidenced by the stress on works as the sign of election.[6]

But all this is far from the thought of merit. For just as reason rejects the idea of election, it also rejects God's will and in opposition to it sets up its own will. That is, he who seeks merits wishes to set himself against God's sovereign salvation-will and refuses to surrender completely to God.[7]

---

[1] WA 18, 694, 35.   [2] Ibid., 35-38.

[3] Schott, "Luthers Lehre vom servum arbitrium," ZST 7 (1929):420-21.

[4] WA 56, 391, 9-16.

[5] TR 2, 582, 15-24; WA 2, 690, 17-25; 43, 460, 33-35.

[6] WA 39I, 131, 41-42.   [7] WA 18, 731, 3-5.

Instead of this man should bow under God's hand; then one day it will become apparent that God's unfathomable ways nevertheless were just and good.[1]

Secondary questions--i.e., is Luther's doctrine of the <u>Deus absconditus</u> a Nominalistic relic in his theology?[2] Does Luther teach infralapsarianism or supralapsarianism,[3] or was Luther a determinist or not?[4]--do not contribute anything further to our investigation. We can surely refrain from a discussion of these problems in the framework of the problem of merit. But we cannot refrain from investigating the question of the performance capability of human nature and of free will which, indeed, Luther coupled with the teaching of predestination.

In what condition does <u>human nature</u> find itself? Can it,

---

[1] Ibid., 785, 35-38.

[2] Lortz (<u>Reformation</u>, 1:173); Hasler (<u>Luther in der katholischen Dogmatik</u>, p. 311); McSorley (<u>Luther: Right or Wrong?</u>, p. 348); and Kraus (<u>Vorherbestimmung</u>, p. 113) reflect the Catholic understanding, spread since Denifle, Grisar, and Paquier, when they unambiguously affirm the question. On the Protestant side the question is denied by Holl (<u>Gesammelte Aufsätze</u>, 1:49-52) with the reference to the hidden righteousness in the sovereignty of God. R. Seeberg (<u>Religiöse Grundgedanken des jungen Luther</u>, p. 17) gives assent to a similarity in the doctrine of God between Ockham and Luther but believes it to be relativized by Luther's christocentricity. Althaus (<u>Theologie Luthers</u>, p. 245) denies the question in a way similar to that of Holl.

[3] Since Luther attributes the fall to the human being (WA 18, 709, 22-24; 710, 31-711, 7), God is not <u>causa peccati</u> but only <u>causa acti peccati</u>, that is, He does not take away from the person the power to sin. This leaves room for an infralapsarian interpretation. See Doerne, "Gottes Ehre," LuJ 20 (1938):72; Hermann, <u>Luthers Theologie</u>, p. 166. But since there are passages that sound otherwise (e.g., WA 18, 724, 27-725, 3), there are also supralapsarian interpretations. Cf. Rost, <u>Prädestinationsgedanke</u>, p. 178.

[4] McSorley (<u>Luther: Right or Wrong?</u>, pp. 256-60) offers a good survey of this question.

disposed by grace, become meritoriously effective and thereby attain a part in its own salvation? These questions are of great importance for our object.

Luther clearly designated concupiscence as sin ever since the Lecture on Romans.[1] For him it is the root[2]—the chief sin.[3] He views it as both original sin[4] (Erbschuld) and original corruption[5] (Erbverderben). This corruption he sees as the total fall of all powers of the inner and outer man, so that no one is capable of any kind of good work coram Deo.[6] This applies to the state before grace and in grace. For the root-sin remains in man as long as he lives.[7] Therefore even his good works are sin because they are infected by the root-sin.[8]

Of himself each man is a devil; only by Christ is he holy.[9] Man is of himself flesh; only by faith is he spirit.[10] He is not flesh because he is sensual but because with his whole being he

---

[1] WA 56, 348, 24-27. In this question Luther could call upon Augustine, who designated concupiscence as "peccatum" (Op. impf. 1. 47 [PL 45:1068]), "peccatum originale" (De pecc. merit. 1. 23. 33 [PL 44:128]), and as "peccatum generale" (De div. quaest. 68. 4 [PL 40:72]). This view, represented in Scholasticism by Peter Lombard (Sent. Lib. 2, dist. 30 [PL 192:722]), Luther rejected at first, and he viewed original sin as the lack of original righteousness, in the sense of Anselm of Canterbury, Thomas Aquinas, and G. Biel (WA 9, 73, 23). Still in the First Lecture on Psalms, concupiscence appears as remnant of original sin and is identified with the unsubordinated will (WA 3, 453, 8-9); but it is also equated with sin itself (WA 4, 364, 9-14).

[2] WA 39I, 84, 10.   [3] WA 50, 221, 10.
[4] WA 26, 502, 27.   [5] WA 39I, 85, 3-4.
[6] WA 56, 355, 1-26; 40II, 323, 8-324, 3.
[7] WA 56, 275, 11.   [8] Ibid., 289, 27-29.
[9] WA 1, 277, 1.   [10] WA 2, 509, 27.

opposes God. He is <u>incurvatus in se</u>;[1] he relies on himself and loves only himself. On account of this he is rejected, not only because he does evil deeds but because even in his good works he thinks only of himself, not of God.[2] Only God's grace can help him.[3]

Luther is anxious to show sin in its power and strength (<u>magnificare peccatum</u>),[4] so that man will no longer seek help in himself but will take refuge in God's mercy only and glorify it (<u>magnificare dei misericordiam</u>).[5] This is a "decisive concern of his theology" (<u>ein entscheidendes Anliegen seiner Theologie</u>).[6]

Therefore, he strives to unveil man's wretchedness in all its dimensions before God. The human being once represented as being the image of God has lost that image through sin.[7] As long as man was the image, he trusted God, lived without anxiety, and was satisfied with the grace of God.[8] Now he trusts only himself, lives in constant anxiety, which he tries to ward off by work and merit. Thus, he becomes the image of the devil, "for he is like the one he conforms to" (<u>denn nach wilchem er sich richtet, dem ist er ehnlich</u>).[9] Under Satan's influence, the glory of God's grace

---

[1] WA 56, 304, 26; 356, 5; 40II, 325, 7.

[2] WA 56, 237, 12-15.

[3] Ibid., 325, 2-9. The great, charitable, heroic deeds of humanity are for Luther only deeds of self-glorification. WA 18, 742, 31-36.

[4] WA 56, 157, 6.   [5] WA 3, 429, 1-3.

[6] Althaus, <u>Theologie Luthers</u>, p. 129.

[7] WA 42, 47, 17; 24, 51, 23.   [8] Ibid., 9-11.

[9] WA 24, 51, 13.

is denigrated to a glory of works.[1]

In the Lecture on Romans Luther worked out four levels of man's fall (WA 56, 178, 24-179, 10);[2] Unthankfulness (ingratitudo), vanity in self-love (vanitas), delusion (excaecatio), and rebellion and hatred against God (error erga Deum). From other sources, three levels can be recognized:[3] ingratitude and forgetfulness toward the Giver; self-love (amor sui), which does not give God the place He demands in the first commandment; and pride (superbia), where the person sets faith in his own performance capability in opposition with faith in God's grace. These levels are not in sequential order; they designate the total reality of man's separation from God.

Now the question arises how can man find his way out of this spiritual alienation back to fellowship with God. Luther answers in a threefold manner:

1. With reference to the nature of sin itself: Sin does not belong to the natural reality of the human being, for "nature is good" (natura bona est).[4] Thereby Luther avoids the reproach of Manichaeism. He expressly refuses the thesis that being human is identical with being a sinner as a Manichaean invention.[5] Sin was not in man originally, he fell into it inwardly and outwardly when he let himself be led astray to question the will and the word of God (Das schändliche Quare).[6]

---

[1] WA 42, 112, 27.

[2] Cf. David Löfgren, Die Theologie der Schöpfung bei Luther (Göttingen: Vandenhoeck & Ruprecht, 1960), p. 103.

[3] See Pesch, Theologie der Rechtfertigung, pp. 85-88.

[4] WA 56, 325, 3.   [5] WA 18, 707, 29-31.   [6] WA 47, 43, 9.

2. With reference to God's forgiveness: Through Christ's act of salvation there occurs the "wonderful exchange" (<u>wunderbarlicher wechsel</u>).[1] Through faith, Christ gives everything that belongs to Him (innocence, holiness, salvation) to man and He takes away from the heart of man everything that destroys it (guilt, spoiled life, judgment). Thus what happens is <u>remissio</u> and <u>non imputatio</u> of the guilt, but not <u>ablatio</u> of the sin.[2] Sin as a state and impulse ceases only when this life ceases.[3] Thus, sin as forgiven sin is "dead sin" (<u>peccatum mortuum</u>),[4] and, as for further existing strength it is "sin which is ruled" (<u>peccatum regnatum</u>),[5] for it is indeed held down by the ruling power of the Holy Spirit so that it cannot become a sinful act.[6] The believer, made capable by the power of the Spirit, can struggle victoriously with sin (<u>non consentire peccato</u>).[7] If he loses in this battle, it is because he has previously withdrawn from the Spirit and fallen back on his own powerlessness.[8] Luther sees sin as a bound robber, sentenced to death but not yet killed.[9] Analogously we might add that sin is like a robber who wants to free himself and can become free by the fault of the watchman, until he is again overpowered by one stronger than he. This is the total aspect of the famous <u>simul justus et peccator</u>. Thus, the believer, as a human being inside himself and outside of Christ, is a sinner.

---

[1] WA 10III, 356, 21-30.
[2] WA 56, 274, 8-11; 289, 19-20.
[3] WA 39I, 95, 23-25.
[4] WA 8, 107, 25.
[5] Ibid., 94, 10.
[6] WA 50, 240, 11-15.
[7] WA 8, 114, 16.
[8] WA 50, 240, 16-17.
[9] WA 8, 91, 31-40.

But the person as a believer, in Christ and outside of himself, is righteous.[1] This is a dialectic-static tension that is characteristic of the Christian life: righteous "by reputation" (ex reputatione) and "by hope" (in spe), but a sinner in "reality" (in re).

3. With reference to the renewing by God: With faith man attains not only forgiveness but also "renewal" (renovatio),[2] "regeneration" (regeneratio),[3] "newness" (novitas).[4] That is, the Christian is given the "new obedience" (nova obedientia)[5] so that he no longer has to follow after sin but can keep God's commands. Thus the new creation begins (initium novae creaturae) now,[6] but it will not be completed until in eternity.[7] Now it is only "under construction" (jhm bau).[8] Luther illustrates the possibility of the new life with the thought of the unio. Faith unites the soul with Christ as a bride is united with the bridegroom. Both become "one body" (eyn leyb). Thus, the power of Christ becomes the possession of the soul and, thereby, its "holiness" (frumkeyt).[9] Another image is that of the merciful physician (medicus) who promises full healing for the future, but in the present has already begun the procedure which the patient does not dare to disturb

---

[1] WA 38, 205, 27-29.   [2] WA 39I, 48, 17.
[3] Ibid., 14.   [4] Ibid.
[5] Ibid., 228, 10-11.   [6] Ibid., 83, 39.
[7] Ibid., 252, 5-16; 56, 260, 24-25; 40II, 24, 19-22; 2, 495, 1-5.
[8] WA 39I, 252, 9-12.   [9] WA 7, 25, 35.

through willful behavior.[1] As little as love and mercy can be earned, so little does this new life also stand under the token of any kind of merit. Instead of <u>meritum</u> (earned increase of grace and earned salvation) Luther preaches <u>donum</u> (imparted sanctification and bestowed salvation). With the <u>gratia</u> God forgives and accepts (justification), with the <u>donum</u> He heals (sanctification).[2] But healing is, first of all, keeping away the destroying power of sin (<u>expugnatio</u>),[3] then killing it (<u>mortificatio</u>),[4] and, at last, sweeping it away (<u>expurgatio</u>).[5] Thus, there is a healing process (<u>sanatio</u>) which frees immediately from guilt and gradually from evil.[6] The Christian grows in good works from day to day[7] and the "old man" is driven out more and more.[8] This is the partial aspect of the <u>simul justus et peccator</u>. The Christian is only in part righteous, because he must let himself be given righteousness ever anew; and he is only in part sinner, because he has taken up the battle with sin and is continually challenged to overcome sin within and outside of himself. Here we can speak of a successive-dynamic development, if it is firmly held in mind that in this life it consists always of a progressive becoming but never of a completed state of being righteous.[9] Therefore, Luther also

---

[1] WA 56, 272, 3-11; 347, 11-14.   [2] WA 8, 107, 13-16.
[3] Ibid., 33; 39I, 83, 39.
[4] WA 8, 107, 36; 39II, 236, 3-4.   [5] WA 39I, 432, 7-11.
[6] WA 56, 70, 22-23.   [7] WA 39I, 112, 3-4.
[8] WA 7, 146, 32-33.   [9] WA 7, 337, 30-35.

describes sanctification not as climbing or running toward a goal but as running in a circle,[1] where one again and again must return to the starting point in order to be able to begin again, or in order to take on strength again so that one can run better.

In considering the idea of merit, however, it is above all important to grasp that the righteousness of life does not grow on the basis of an infused quality, but by fixing one's gaze on Christ. The Christian is not holy, "intrinsically and essentially" (<u>intrinsece et formaliter</u>), for holiness is not "in the predicament of substance, but of relation" (<u>in praedicamento substantiae, sed relationis</u>).[2] That is, the whole work of sanctification is the work of Christ through the "reign of the Spirit" (<u>regnum spiritus</u>) over the person.[3] While in faith the believer seizes Christ, His forgiveness and His power, (<u>fides apprehensiva</u>),[4] he is at the same time pulled into Christ (<u>nos rapi de die in diem magis voluit</u>);[5] and his faith and fellowship with Christ grow[6] and, therewith, grows the rulership of the Spirit over his life.

If one finds it necessary to speak of form--but Luther would rather avoid this[7]--then it is not a habitus, an inhering quality, the so-called created grace, but it is Christ Himself,[8] who gives the faith, sustains, enables, and crowns.

---

[1] WA 40III, 366, 19-20.
[2] WA 40II, 354, 2-4; 8, 106, 10-11.
[3] WA 50, 240, 11-15.   [4] WA 39I, 45, 21-22.
[5] WA 8, 111, 33-34.   [6] WA 2, 146, 33-34.
[7] WA 39I, 228, 14-16.   [8] WA 40I, 283, 7, 26.

Regarding the equation of temptation and sin, however, Luther left not only Scholasticism[1] but also Augustine behind him,[2] and--according to the belief of recognized, contemporary Protestant Luther-researchers--Paul as well.[3] In Holl's opinion, Luther's extreme position can be attributed to the fact that between him and Paul stand Augustine and monasticism, both of which have contributed to a "refinement of the sense of personality" (Verfeinerung des Persönlichkeitsgefühls).[4] According to Joest it is a reaction against the Scholastic fomes teaching, in which sinful lust is reduced to a remnant of sin that slumbers in man, instead of being understood as a motivating principle that affects the whole existence. With the teaching of the remaining sin, however, Luther especially reacted, against the Nominalistic theory of a possible fulfilling of the law by natural man and, thereby, against the danger of losing Christ.[5] But with the teaching of total original corruption, Luther, according to Hermann, met the "reality of life" (Wirklichkeit des Lebens) and discovered the true condition of the heart.[6] With it he could appeal to the Pauline

---

[1] See Lortz, "Römerbriefvorlesung," TThZ 71 (1962):145.

[2] See Rudolf Hermann, Luthers These Gerecht und Sünder zugleich, 2nd ed. (Gütersloh: G. Mohn, 1960), p. 48.

[3] See Paul Althaus, Paulus und Luther über den Menschen, 2nd ed. (Gütersloh: Bertelsmann, 1951), pp. 70, 78, 90; Wilfried Joest, "Paulus und das Luthersche simul justus et peccator," KuD 1 (1955): 272, 290, 293, 303, 309.

[4] Holl, Gesammelte Aufsätze, 3:534.

[5] Joest, "Paulus und das Luthersche simul justus et peccator," KuD 1 (1955):310-11.

[6] Hermann, Gesammelte Studien, p. 387.

dialectic of spirit and flesh and the Augustinian doctrine of "evil quality" (mala qualitas).[1]

In any case a wide chasm was thereby opened in relation to Scholasticism:

1. Early Scholasticism often saw the fall of man described in the parable of the Good Samaritan. Man is "half-dead" (semivivo relicto), like the one who had fallen among robbers.[2] Indeed, all of Early Scholasticism, along with Augustine, knew the saying, "good nature in man is corrupted" (naturalia bona in homine corrupta sunt); but this was not a total corruption.[3] The fall brought, according to John of Treviso, only a diminishing of the moral powers (diminutio habilitatis virtutum)[4] and, according to Peter Comestor, man is wounded but not wholly robbed (lesus, non omnino privatus).[5] Peter Lombard sums up the problem with the well-known saying: "Fallen from grace, wounded in nature" (Spoliatus gratuitis, vulneratus in naturalibus). Here man forfeited the state of grace; his nature was thereby wounded.[6] Grace, therefore, became gratia sanans, understood as healing the diseased nature.[7]

2. High Scholasticism went beyond this in that since Philip the Chancellor it viewed grace as "elevating grace" (gratia

---

[1] Augustine De nupt. et concup. 1. 25. 28 (PL 44:430).
[2] See Landgraf, Dogmengeschichte, 1:100.
[3] Ibid., 1:99-100.   [4] Ibid., 1:100.   [5] Ibid.
[6] Sent. Lib. 2, dist. 25 (PL 192:707).
[7] See Auer, Gnadenlehre, 2:146.

elevans),[1] as an "additional gift" (<u>donum superadditum</u>),[2] which, in order to work supernatural good,[3] was added to one already in the state of the uninjured nature. The loss of this supernatural quality could therefore be only of a secondary nature for the natural moral powers. Indeed, Thomas also speaks of the "corrupted nature" (<u>natura currupta</u>),[4] but not precisely as being "totally corrupted" (<u>totaliter corrupta</u>).[5] The moral powers are only diminished,[6] the inclination toward good is still present.[7] Only disorder has come in whereby the will is no longer surrendered to God.[8] Otherwise human nature is similar to a transparent body that can receive light (grace). Supervening clouds (sin) can hinder this without involving the structure of the body.[9] Thus at most we may speak of a partial disobedience of the person outside grace.[10] Man cannot work meritoriously without grace, but he doubtless can perform good works, for which nature is sufficient. He does not sin in everything he does,[11] but he is, indeed, incapable of qualifying himself before God; for this he unreservedly needs God's grace. He can bring his natural powers into grace and, depending on how one views it, he can then of himself or out of the

---

[1] Ibid.

[2] Thomas Aquinas <u>S. Th.</u> la2ae. 109, 1 ad 1.

[3] Ibid., 109, 2.   [4] Ibid., 109, 3; 4; 7; 8; 114, 2.

[5] Thomas Aquinas <u>S. Th.</u> la2ae. 109, 2; 2a2ae. 10, 4.

[6] Ibid., la2ae. 85, 1.   [7] Ibid., 2 ad 3.

[8] Ibid., 109, 7; 82, 1.   [9] Ibid., 85, 2.

[10] Ibid., 109, 4.   [11] Ibid., 2a2ae. 10, 4.

received and possessed quality of grace, de congruo or de condigno, earn merit, for "grace does not destroy nature, but perfects it" (gratia naturam non tollit, sed perficit).[1]

3. In Late Scholasticism, then, this limited nature-optimism began to grow exuberantly. Already Duns Scotus no longer wished to recognize any corruptio naturae and saw sin only as disturbed relationship to God.[2] That the person from natural powers is able to love God, in the eyes of Luther, stamped Duns as the "greatest sophist."[3] The natural abilities of man, then, are a firm part of the theology of the genuine Nominalists (Ockham, Biel). The human will is able of its own strength to love God supremely (ex suis naturalibus potest diligere Deum super omnia),[4] to hate sin and to leave it (immo odire peccatum et velle non peccare),[5] and only on the basis of the potentia ordinata is infused grace and love necessary to enjoy the enduring love of God.[6]

Thus all of Scholasticism could build up its theology of grace upon a more or less unspoiled natural basis. It is otherwise with Luther. Since he rejected as unbiblical the teaching of the donum superadditum[7] and saw nature as wholly fallen, he believed

---

[1] Ibid., la. 1, 8 ad 2.

[2] See Adam, Dogmengeschichte, 2:120.   [3] TR 4, 527, 25-36.

[4] Biel, Collect. in Sent. Lib. 3, d. 27, qu. 1, a. 3, d. 2, p. 1.

[5] Ibid., Lib. 2, d. 27, qu. 1, a. 3, d. 4.

[6] Ibid., Lib. 3, d. 27, qu. 1, a. 3, d. 2, p. 2. Cf. Loofs, Leitfaden, p. 508.

[7] Luther sees the structures of the supernatural (virtues,

every kind of work must be banned from the way of salvation. That is, not the works as such, but any claims before God (Präsentierbarkeit), as they appear in the idea of merit, had to be dropped.[1]

If man is not capable of any good work coram Deo, and every work, even that of the Christian, is marked by sin, then the doctrine of merit is abolished. Man is, on the basis of his nature, always an unprofitable servant; everything must be given to him, so his obedience appears without claim; and he stains everything with sin, so that always--even in his best works--he needs forgiveness.[2] Holding this view, Luther could hardly avoid the issue of free will,[3] especially since the free will was regarded by the

---

such as faith, hope, and love which flow from the supernatural) as having been created in the first human being. Therefore the fall not only wounded the nature but corrupted it (WA 42, 124, 18-21). Therefore to him the supernatural as an added adornment of the nature is to be rejected (WA 42, 123, 28-124, 3), because it hinders one's grasping the total corruption of the nature by sin. Cf. WA 39I, 84, 16-17; 85, 1-4; 176, 20-21. For him the teaching of an integer nature is "mendax doctrina Papae" (WA 40II, 323, 29).

[1] Hermann, Gesammelte Studien, p. 68.

[2] WA 32, 539, 32-39; 1, 353, 25-26.

[3] For the "Sententiarius" in Erfurt the will was still free (WA 9, 31, 9). Wholly in the sense of Scholasticism he considered grace as enabling power which makes the will inclined (WA 9, 62, 28-29). In the First Lecture on Psalms he still recognizes--as we have shown--a meritorious preparation for justification. According to McSorley (Luther: Right or Wrong?, p. 224) the break with the "neo-semipelagian" concept of Nominalism followed in the notes to Biel's Collectorium in quattuor libros sententiarum (1515), where Luther names the free will a haughty principle and denies the theological freedom of choice, since the will is fixed upon evil. In the Lecture on Romans he already speaks of the servum arbitrium (WA 56, 385, 17-18), but since he does not yet see the nature as wholly corrupt and is polemicizing against a preparation for justification without grace, contemporary Catholic investigators judge his position as "clearly Catholic." See McSorley, Luther: Right

Scholastics as entrance to the doctrine of merit.[1] Because either an earning of grace (Nominalism) or an earning in grace (Thomas) was bound up with it, the refutation of this concept must appear to Luther as the "question on which everything hinges" (cardo rerum).[2] Luther thereby rejects the Nominalistic high evaluation of the free will[3] as well as the Erasmian minimization of freedom.[4] For Luther, nothing is earned, neither grace nor salvation, for according to Paul everything is freely given.[5]

---

or Wrong?, pp. 227-28; Lortz, "Römerbriefvorlesung," TThZ 71 (1962): 247. In the Disputatio contra scholasticam theologiam (1517) Luther sees the nature of the person as corrupt (WA 1, 224, 13-14, 22; 225, 9, 29-30; 226, 5; 228, 17-18) and the will as fixed upon evil (ibid., 224, 19). In the Heidelberg Disputation (1518) there appear the famous words: "Liberum arbitrium post peccatum res est de solo titulo, et dum facit quod in se est, peccat mortaliter" (WA 1, 354, 5-6). In explanation Luther says this does not mean that the free will does not exist, but that it is wholly fixed upon evil (ibid., 359, 33-360, 2). Although the thesis was condemned in Exsurge Domine (DS 1486), McSorley finds it "solidly biblical . . . definitely not heretical." McSorley asks whether Rome had spoken at that time "relevantly and with real understanding." Luther: Right or Wrong?, pp. 244, 246, 253. McSorley sees Luther's falling away from the Catholic tradition in the assertion, "omnia . . . de necessitate absoluta eveniunt." In Assertio omnium articulorum (WA 7, 146, 7-8) and De servo arbitrio (WA 18, 617, 19). See Harry J. McSorley, "Erasmus versus Luther--Compounding the Reformation Tragedy," in Catholic Scholars Dialogue with Luther, ed. Jared Wicks (Chicago: Loyola University Press, 1970), pp. 109, 115.

[1] According to Peter Lombard the "libertas arbitrii . . . [is only] ex parte perdita." From this there follows: "Nullum meritum est in homine quod non sit per liberum arbitrium." Sent. Lib. 2, dist. 25; dist. 27 (PL 192:707, 715). Cf. Thomas Aquinas, S. Th. 1a2ae. 114, 1; ibid., 1 ad 1; 3; 6.

[2] WA 18, 786, 30.   [3] WA 56, 385, 15-16.

[4] WA 18, 769, 27-28. According to R. Gerest, Erasmus speaks in De libero arbitrio as a Nominalist and also as a High Scholastic. "Du serf arbitre à la liberté du chrétien. Les cheminements de Martin Luther," LV 12 (1963):110-11. From this can be concluded that Luther fought against all Scholasticism.

[5] WA 18, 769, 34-35.

But even if this were not so, the free will does not come into question for establishing a merit. Luther thereby does not deny the psychological freedom of will,[1] that is, the freedom of choice in the secular realm, which is indeed subordinate to the freedom of God's governing will.[2] In the realm of salvation, however, there is no free will. Thus, Luther speaks of the "things above it" (supra se),[3] of the "kingdom of God" (regnum Dei),[4] and of the "divine things" (res divinae);[5] where it is a matter of "salvation or damnation" (salus et damnatio).[6] Here the will is bound and fixed upon sin. Indeed, the person does not act out of compulsion; he gladly sins, he always makes his own choices and is actively heading towards death. Here, his freedom is not freedom, for through perverted existence come perverted deeds. Man cannot be neutral toward God; the fact is that due to the perversion of

---

[1] See Erdmann Schott, Rechtfertigung und Zehn Gebote nach Luther (Stuttgart: Calwer Verlag, 1971), p. 20; Hermann, Luthers Theologie, p. 153; Friedrich Gogarten, Luthers Theologie (Tübingen: J. C. B. Mohr [P. Siebeck], 1967), p. 130.

[2] WA 56, 385, 19-20; 18, 638, 6-8; 672, 10-13; 752, 7-8; 781, 8-10. That Luther is no fatalist and concedes the psychological freedom of the will is admitted also by modern Catholic Luther-scholars. Cf. Otto H. Pesch, "Freiheitsbegriff und Freiheitslehre bei Thomas von Aquin und Luther," Cath (M) 17 (1963):218; Hasler, Luther in der katholischen Dogmatik, p. 135; McSorley, Luther: Right or Wrong?, pp. 327-28; Kraus, Vorherbestimmung, p. 107; Gerest, "Du serf arbitre," LV 12 (1963):80-81.

[3] WA 56, 385, 21. [4] WA 18, 672, 19. [5] Ibid., 662, 6-7.

[6] Ibid., 638, 10. O. H. Pesch distinguishes "Wahlfreiheit" from "Wesensfreiheit." "Freiheitsbegriff," Cath (M) 17 (1963):218. Kraus speaks of a "psycholgischen" and "theologischen Freiheit." Vorherbestimmung, p. 107. Hans J. Iwand says one can distinguish between "philosophischer" and "religiöser Betrachtungsweise." "Studien zum Problem des unfreien Willens," ZST 8 (1930):242. But he prefers "Handlungs-" and "Seinsfreiheit." Ibid., p. 249. Likewise Vorster, Freiheitsverständnis, p. 289.

sin man happily draws away from God, and even in his best deeds falls back upon himself. The enslaved will is spontaneous toward evil. Luther speaks of a "necessity of immutability" (<u>necessitas immutabilitatis</u>). Man cannot and will not flee from sin; but this does not mean he acts from compulsion (<u>necessitas coactionis</u>).[1]

Viewed this way, it becomes understandable that the free will in relationship to God exists "in name only" (<u>res de solo titulo</u>),[2] and is an "empty term" (<u>inane vocabulum</u>),[3] an "empty phrase" (<u>inanis vocula</u>),[4] and a "mere dialectical fiction" (<u>merum figmentum</u>).[5] The will has lost its freedom to choose God; it will not and cannot of itself turn to God, it is a "selfwill" (<u>eygen wille</u>),[6] bent, and in a battle with God. It can neither seek grace (contrary to Nominalism)[7] nor consent to grace (contrary to Thomism),[8] it can only yield to one who is stronger.[9] God must set the will free, not the good will which needs only to be made capable of

---

[1] WA 18, 634, 21-29. [2] WA 1, 354, 5.
[3] WA 18, 637, 19. [4] Ibid., 670, 35-36.
[5] Ibid., 1. [6] WA 7, 448, 26.

[7] Ibid., 446, 30-33. Cf. Biel, <u>Collect. in Sent</u>. Lib. 2, d. 27, qu. 1, a. 2, c. 4.

[8] Cf. Thomas Aquinas, <u>S. Th</u>. 1a2ae. 55, 4 ad 6. According to Vorster (Freiheitsverständnis, p. 318) this is in any case the interpretation of Trent (<u>DS</u> 1525: "libere assentiendo et cooperando"). The council interpreted the sayings of Thomas in the sense of an "Ermöglichungsverhältnis." According to Vorster however, Thomas stands much nearer to Luther, for grace and will stand in a "Folgeverhältnis." That is, the will is bound to affirmation without having the possibility of a denial (ibid., p. 319). Thus, according to O. H. Pesch, Thomas also teaches a "gebundenen Willen" and thereby stands "der Lehre Luthers gar nicht fern." "Freiheitsbegriff," <u>Cath (M)</u> 17 (1963):198.

[9] WA 18, 634, 34-35.

action, but the evil will which God must recreate and redirect. The free will that has been trampled to the ground by sin[1] must be made alive again by God, and only God can keep it alive and motivate it to the good contrary to its own "aversion to God" (<u>aversio a Deo</u>).[2] So we are indebted to God alone for the <u>regia libertas</u>,[3] the "royal and new freedom" created and constantly sustained in us by Him to love Him and to serve Him.

Thus, hope comes not from merits but from the destruction of merits.[4] The teaching of the unfree will gives the death blow to righteousness of works. For now no one can say that works indeed merit nothing, but free will establishes merit.[5] And even if the free will is made very small,[6] it still distorts the perspective of salvation, for God alone works the will and the work,[7] and He gives grace and salvation together.[8] Speaking of merits thereby knocks down the whole plan of the salvation of God; it means wishing to earn something that cannot be earned, that has long since been given.

The teaching of the unfree will of man is intimately connected with the teaching of the <u>sole agency of God</u>. If the becoming and being efficacious in the kingdom of God must be wholly credited to God, then the sole agency would be a clear and unmistakable

---

[1] Ibid., 615, 14-15; 722, 5.

[2] Here, however, breaks forth an unbridgeable contradiction to Thomas. See O. H. Pesch, "Freiheitsbegriff," <u>Cath (M)</u> 17 (1963):224.

[3] WA 18, 635, 16.   [4] WA 1, 225, 15.

[5] WA 10III, 357, 13-14.   [6] WA 18, 769, 27-38.

[7] Ibid., 634, 20-21.   [8] Ibid., 769, 32-35.

refutation of the doctrine of merit. At the same time an unchristian concept of human personality would thereby be rejected which founds human partnership with God--not on undesired but gladly experienced conversion through God alone--but on man's own cooperation with God; man thereby claims a share, even though minimal, of attaining his salvation.

For Luther the experience of the divine omnipotence and human lack of power is the guarantee of salvation, for human cooperation always involves uncertainty of salvation (or despair) and pride of merit (or presumption).[1] Faith is rich in works, but these works come into existence only through Christ: "Christ Himself in us does all" (Christus ipse in nobis facit omnia).[2] While the person depends on Christ, he is able to do more than by his own strength and merits.[3]

Here we reach what is for Protestant[4] as well as for Catholic[5] interpreters of Luther the decisive point (springender Punkt), for God's sole agency automatically excludes any meritorious share of man in salvation and shuts out every kind of independence (Selbstand) from the idea of human personality. How does Luther establish this?

---

[1] WA 18, 783, 17-39; 17II, 140, 4-141, 16.

[2] WA 39I, 46, 18-19.   [3] WA 21, 401, 31-34.

[4] Holl, Gesammelte Aufsätze, 1:85; Pinomaa, Faith Victorious, pp. 25-26; EKL, s.v. "Luther," by E. Wolf.

[5] Stakemeier, Trient über Heilsgewissheit, pp. 57, 63; Peter Bläser, Rechtfertigungsglaube bei Luther (Münster/W.: Verlag der Hiltruper Missionare, 1953), pp. 15, 17.

In <u>TR</u> 5, No. 5189[1] are found the following considerations:

1. The human will does nothing toward conversion and justification. "[Will] is not the efficient cause of justification, but the material cause" (<u>Non est efficiens causa iustificationis, sed materialis tantum</u>). The Holy Spirit works like a potter with brittle material.

2. Man acts in the process of conversion like Paul acted before the Damascus experience; he struggles against God.

3. The Holy Spirit, however, draws the sinner through the Word to Himself and changes the will of the struggling one.

4. This will, changed by God, is now so constituted that it agrees with God and gladly wills what God requires of it. The will can now cooperate and man can now act righteously.

5. The recognition of the sole agency of God should not terrify man, but call him to prayer, whereby he should rely wholly on God.

Thus, Luther sees man in his original state or in the process of salvation foremost as a creature who is completely dependent on the Creator's gift of life.[2] Man is a work wrought by God (<u>opus dei factum</u>).[3]

---

[1] TR 5, 2, 4-38; cf. WA 18, 753, 33-35.

[2] "Facit solus spiritus in nobis, nos sine nobis recreans et conservans recreatos." WA 18, 754, 11-12. "Non nos operemur, sed deus nos operetur." WA 5, 544, 20-21. "Alles guttes, gedancken, hertz, sinne, krefft, worth und wercke wircket Christus allein, wir thuen nichts darzcw." WA 9, 631, 31-33. "Preterea schlaffen und nigst wircken seyn der Christen werck." Ibid., 407, 35. "Ich byn nur die werckstat, darynnen ehr wirckt." WA 7, 575, 8-9.

[3] Cf. Seils, <u>Zusammenwirken</u>, p. 88.

In contrast to the creation, however, man can expose himself to God in the work of salvation;[1] he can hear the Word and has a passive aptitude (aptitudo passiva) that can be grasped by the Spirit to experience God's working. This distinguishes him from plants and animals, for heaven is not made for geese.[2] This possibility of preparedness to enter into dialogue with God and experience Him as the Worker of salvation makes the human being into a person.[3] Thus, the order develops: hearing, believing, doing, being saved.[4] In this sense, the believer can truly be designated a cooperator with God,[5] if one only holds firmly to the thought that cooperation does not represent independent contribution by the person but, instead, means being grasped and used by a God who works upon His people as a craftsman uses his tools.[6] In this way man can perform the work of God (opus dei actum).[7]

Holl names this cooperation concept of Luther "Werkzeug-

---

[1] "Goth gibt uns von ersten das worth, damit er uns erleuchtet, darnach den H. Geyst, der in uns wircket unnd den glawben anzcundt. Nun alspald man am worth still helth und lesset es eingehn, folgt so bald, das wir erleuchtet werden, und kummeth der heyllige geyst, der durch das worth wircket." WA 9, 632, 32-633, 2.

[2] WA 18, 636, 16-22.

[3] Cf. Gogarten, Luthers Theologie, pp. 167-68.

[4] "Tzum ersten fur allen dingen das wortt gottis höre. Darnach glewbe, darnach wircke, und alszo selig werde." WA 10I, 329, 7-8.

[5] WA 2, 146, 36-37; 4, 61, 18-19; 6, 227, 30; 18, 695, 29; 40III, 210, 14.

[6] WA 57III, 143, 3-5.

[7] Cf. Seils, Zusammenwirken, p. 88.

bewusstsein,"[1] tool-consciousness. Modern Luther scholars speak of "tool *and* fruit principle" (Werkzeug- *und* Fruchtgedanken)[2] as well as of "partnership" (Partnerschaft).[3] They wish thereby to take account of the dynamic of the human way of acting. For, even if man is activated and led by God, he experiences himself as actor and doer.

The Catholic reproach that with Luther it is a matter of a "stone and block theory" (Stein- und Klotztheorie)[4] is thus already proved wrong, because Luther expressly guards against such a static view of man.[5] As man spontaneously experienced sin, so he spontaneously is active and experiences the freedom that is granted to him. In that man believes, he works together with God.[6] Thereby all is really stated. Faith is given, received, and lived. God alone works here, but He works in such a way that man experiences himself as doer though he cannot ascribe anything to himself.

Within the sole agency Luther can even employ the Scholastic terms of God as causa principalis[7] and the human as causa

---

[1] Holl, Gesammelte Aufsätze, p. 419.

[2] Seils, Zusammenwirken, pp. 77, 81.

[3] Hasler, Luther in der katholischen Dogmatik, p. 210.

[4] Pohle and Gummersbach, Dogmatik, 2:694.

[5] "Id quod diligenter discendum est, ne ex Christiano faciamus truncum aliquem, qui peccatum non sentiat. Habet enim adhuc carnem et sanguinem, ideo necessario sentit peccatum et infirmitatem fidei." WA 25, 332, 8-11.

[6] "Credere igitur sufficit: hoc est nostrum cooperari." WA 4, 601, 8-9.

[7] WA 40III, 211, 4; 215, 6.

instrumentalis.¹ But to the secondary causes there pertains within the first cause no independent contribution. They are only "hand, channel, and means" (<u>hand, rohre und mittel</u>)² through which God works. Therefore, Luther's cooperation-thought is sharply distinct from the thought of merit. No human deed, not even that of the person given grace, establishes a merit. With the believers everything occurs <u>solo Christo</u>, <u>solo verbo</u>, <u>sola fide</u>. That is, God works through His Spirit "merit and reward" (<u>Verdienst und Lohn</u>)³ through which His power and man's powerlessness are demonstrated.

To the final cooperation, the correspondence of merit and reward and the legal claim on reward, Luther opposes quite the reverse; i.e.:

1. Salvation is not future, it is already present. The believer has already been taken into the kingdom of God; now he moves only further toward its unveiling in revealed majesty.⁴ The final way of salvation means constraint; the consecutive way, freedom.⁵

2. Thereby everything in work that corresponds to merit and reward falls away. Reward always stands under the token of promise and gift, but work stands under that of witness. This witness does not serve to attain salvation; it serves in love in behalf of man's neighbor.⁶ Moreover, there can be no correspondence

---

¹Ibid., 210, 14. ²WA 30I, 136, 9.
³WA 18, 696, 7.
⁴WA 18, 694, 24, 35-38; cf. WA 2, 98, 34-99, 10.
⁵DB 7, 4, 17-19, 32-34. ⁶WA 39I, 224, 1-4.

between the work of the Christian, affected by sin, and God Himself as reward (Gen 15:1).[1]

3. Since every good work has God as its active sole cause and man as the passive receiver, we have here proof of man's nothingness not of his rights regarding eternal life.[2]

Luther is conscious of the possible objections to the doctrine of the sole agency; for if God works everything and does it alone, why does the Scripture require man to keep God's commandments? He answers that the imperatives--You shall keep the commandments; you shall love; you shall become active; you shall give alms--are all included in faith in Christ and stand under the motto of the Epistle to the Hebrews: Fide (by faith).[3] However, by faith means through Christ, for by the faith that is kindled by God, Christ becomes the Lord of our life. Thus, "by faith" stands for receiving faith and letting Christ become effective through us.

Does God thereby overpower us so He can coerce us into doing good? Luther answers that the drawing of God is not to be depicted as like the executioner's drawing of a thief; instead, God's power of attraction is like that of lovable person to whom we willingly respond.[4] His power transforms our hearts so thoroughly that we are infused with both desire and love for His commandments.

---

[1] DB 8, 73, 17-19.

[2] WA 18, 696, 6-10; 13, 570, 16-17 ("Unica Christianorum gloria est in solo Christo, cui credunt et fidunt").

[3] WA 39I, 47, 5-14.   [4] WA 33, 130, 39-131, 4.

If, however, faith is wholly a gift from God, how can we then speak of "our" faith? Should we not express it rather as "It believes in us?" Luther tries to solve this problem with the concept of creation. For him <u>creatio ex nihilo</u> (creation) and <u>recreatio ex nihilo</u> (conversion) are similar. God gives life, we, his creatures experience this life as our life; likewise, God gives faith, it is solely His gift to us and thereby it becomes "our" faith. But always this faith in us (<u>in nobis</u>) is established through God's working outside us (<u>extra nos</u>). If this exclusive way of working is to be sought <u>extra nos</u>, then all meritoriousness rightly falls away.

We reach a similar result when we investigate Luther's main concept: <u>the righteousness of God</u>. Holl has demonstrated that, whereas even before the time of Luther the "righteousness of God" was understood in the sense of a genitive of author (<u>genitivus auctoris</u>) as God's giving righteousness, this righteousness was always conceived as a righteousness worked out <u>in the person</u>.[1] Such a righteousness possessed by an individual furnished the theological foundation for the doctrine of merit from Augustine to the Scholastics.[2]

But for Luther the righteousness of God means basically a looking from the person to Christ.[3] That is, righteousness is never a possession of the person (<u>iustitia domestica</u>), it is a

---

[1] Holl, <u>Gesammelte Aufsätze</u>, 3:174.

[2] Ibid., 3:175; Heinrich Bornkamm, <u>Luther, Gestalt und Wirkungen</u> (Gütersloh: G. Mohn, 1975), p. 115.

[3] WA 31I, 439, 19-20.

possession of Christ (iustitia aliena).[1] As such it is extraneous and external (extranea and externa)[2] and always "outside of us" (extra nos).[3] It consists of God's mercy[4] and not of some quality possessed by man,[5] as Scholasticism asserted.[6] Therefore it is beyond the human (ultra hominem)[7] and can be attained only as a gift because of Christ (propter Christum).[8] In the marvelous exchange (mirabilis mutatio),[9] in the admirable trade (admirabile commercium),[10] and in the happy exchange (froelicher wechszel),[11] Christ exchanges with the believer. He puts Himself in the deserved judgment and puts man under the given salvation. This has a twofold meaning:

1. For Christ's sake righteousness before God (coram Deo) is placed in the account of the one who has been given faith (imputatio,[12] reputatio[13]).

2. At the same time Christ takes over by faith the lordship

---

[1] WA 56, 158, 10-14.   [2] Ibid.

[3] Ibid., 9.

[4] WA 3, 179, 2-3; 39I, 48, 13; 40II, 353, 3.

[5] WA 8, 92, 39.   [6] S. Th. 1a2ae. 110, 2.

[7] WA 56, 99, 24.

[8] WA 39I, 83, 35-36; 40I, 229, 28-30; 40II, 527, 8-9.

[9] WA 31II, 435, 11.   [10] WA 5, 608, 7.

[11] WA 7, 25, 34.   [12] WA 2, 490, 26.

[13] WA 1, 140, 11; 39I, 83, 35; 40I, 229, 30; 40II, 527, 8; 56, 259, 20. Until the Sermo de duplici iustitia (1519?) Luther still speaks of a iustitia infusa (WA 2, 145, 9; 146, 29-30). From the Galaterkommentar (1519) on he uses imputatio instead of infusio (WA 2, 490, 26).

of the person's life. Christ is constantly active in the believer (<u>Christus actuosissimus</u>)[1] and struggles in him against flesh, world, death, and devil.[2]

Thus, doubtless righteousness is given to man, but it never becomes a part of man. It is found only in Christ, through whom man stands before God and through whom he lives in the world. Therefore, righteousness always comes only from outside as judgment and lordship over the believer. Righteousness is imputed as justification and means lordship as sanctification. Thus <u>justitia passiva</u> is the suitable definition of Christian righteousness.[3]

However, it is thereby also clear that the meritorious aspect is not a constitutive factor in righteousness. The <u>extra nos</u> and the <u>justitia passiva</u> allow no merits. Man has not even earned a right to hear of this righteousness.[4] He who seeks merits through his works has a "servile, mercenary, fictitious, specious, external, temporary, mundane, human righteousness" (<u>iusticia servilis, mercennaria, ficta, speciosa, externa, temporalis, mundana, humana</u>)[5] which is absolutely useless for eternal life; rather it is harmful, for work-righteousness is sin.[6] Not that the works should be annulled! Each work from faith is more valuable than heaven and earth.[7] But none of these works has justifying character.[8] Justifying and redeeming are only the

---

[1] WA 1, 140, 21.   [2] WA 30II, 621, 16-19.
[3] "Ista autem excellentissima iustitia." WA 40I, 41, 15.
[4] WA 2, 490, 27.   [5] Ibid., 489, 30-32.
[6] WA 40I, 516, 30-35.   [7] Ibid., 21.
[8] WA 2, 491, 36-37.

iusticia ex fide, ex gratia,[1] which is a "righteous, liberal, free, solid, internal, eternal, true, heavenly, divine righteousness" (iusticia liberalis, gratuita, solida, interna, aeterna, vera, coelestis, divina).[2] This righteousness seeks nothing more and earns nothing,[3] for thereby it would deny itself. It is opposed to every human way of thinking and is therefore a "contrary" righteousness (iusticia contraria).[4] It must be comprehended from the creating and re-creating activity of God. Just as God creates and resurrects man without his cooperation, so also the righteousness of God comes into being in him.[5] Nowhere is man made a coworker; nowhere therefore is merit to be found. Man does not put himself into heaven, he is placed there only by God.[6]

What can be said of the righteousness of God can also be expressed concerning the grace of God. Grace for Luther is not a quality in the person;[7] it is God Himself,[8] as well as Christ[9] and the Holy Spirit.[10] Luther denies the philosophical teaching of "form." An impersonal quality, which enables one's own accomplishments and merits, is not infused into the person; rather Christ Himself dwells and acts in the believer. He forms the faith[11] and

---

[1] Ibid., 490, 9. [2] Ibid., 491, 12.
[3] Ibid., 13. [4] WA 40I, 41, 3.
[5] Ibid., 64, 25. [6] WA 2, 98, 34.
[7] WA 8, 106, 10-11; 40II, 363, 1, 15; 421, 24; 422, 23-24.
[8] WA 10III, 301, 6; 28, 139, 19.
[9] WA 3, 269, 17.
[10] WA 1, 227, 1-2; 40II, 422, 27-29.
[11] WA 40I, 229, 9, 28.

thereby the person.[1] If, therefore, one speaks of merit, they are the merits of Christ.[2] Grace is not inherent in the soul; rather, the soul hangs on Christ[3] and His righteousness.[4]

Grace is not something inherent and elevating (aliquid elevans), it is something extrinsic (quoddam extrinsecum),[5] namely, God's mercy (misericordia)[6] and favor.[7] Where mercy enters into man (donum),[8] it is faith coming from outside and received from outside. Neither justification (gratia as favor Dei) nor sanctification (fides as donum) can be earned, since they are always something alien (alienum) and never, as in Catholic theology, something that is one's own (proprium).[9] The new life is not quality of being but relation of being. Man is not intrinsically changed but is directed toward God. With a minimum of being is bound up a maximum of power.[10] This personalistic relationship between God and man does not concur with the teaching of ontic inherence[11] and it destroys the basis for a system of merit. Only when man has been denied every independence (Selbstand) and is constantly activated by God is there a genuine soli Deo gloria.[12] In every good work it is a matter of the holy, merciful God, not

---

[1] Ibid., 283, 7. [2] WA 40II, 353, 17-18.
[3] WA 25, 332, 7. [4] WA 8, 111, 32.
[5] WA 40II, 353, 4. [6] Ibid., 5.
[7] WA 8, 106, 22; 40II, 421, 21. [8] WA 8, 106, 20.
[9] See Helmut Thielicke, Theologische Ethik, 4th ed. 3 vols. (Tübingen: J. C. B. Mohr [P. Siebeck], 1972-74), 1:374.
[10] WA 40II, 421, 22-24. [11] BR 9, 407, 51-54.
[12] WA 8, 108, 4-6.

of the holy, meriting human! Therefore, Luther is not interested in such tractates as "De gratia and De meritis," for now man is not yet called to the ontic transformation but to the kingdom of faith (regnum fidei).[1] In this rulership, however, salvation is already given and from now on it must only be witnessed through the new life. Thereby every egotistical striving for merit is excluded,[2] for man does not come to the kingdom, the kingdom comes to him.[3] But when the kingdom is established in man, then the eschatological unveiling is a consequence which the faithful one will experience and needs not earn.[4] Because of this, it seemed senseless to Luther to speak of an increase of grace and merits, for God and His salvation cannot be intensified,[5] although the rulership of Christ over man's life can become stronger day by day.[6]

The comprehension of grace as favor Dei establishes for Luther the assurance of salvation (Heilsgewissheit). For, if salvation is bestowed upon man as a gift from God's kindness, it would be an offense to God to doubt it. Faith, which should be an unreserved trust in God's promise of salvation, would itself become revealed as disbelief, as skeptical mistrust. If, on the other hand, salvation were not bestowed but only made possible, then everything would depend on accomplishments and merits. In this case, however, the believer could never be certain of his

---

[1] WA 8, 89, 6.   [2] WA 2, 98, 29-33.

[3] Ibid., 23-28.   [4] Ibid., 98, 38-99, 10.

[5] See Erdmann Schott, "Christus und die Rechtfertigung allein durch den Glauben in Luthers Schmalkaldischen Artikeln," ZST 22 (1953):204.

[6] WA 8, 111, 33-35.

salvation.[1] Such an attitude cannot be attributed to the true God and true faith,[2] for God is no liar[3] and genuine trust is not deceived.[4]

Thus, we see the doctrine of merit as a part of the monstrous uncertainty (monstrum incertitudinis)[5] that Luther combatted in the name of genuine faith. That he thereby meant no pillow for ethical laxity is recognized by contemporary Catholic Luther-scholars.[6] Luther could not be shaken in his concept of the assurance of salvation though it was denied by all his opponents.[7] His concept of faith,[8] the testimonium spiritus,[9] and the witness of the works[10] confirmed for him the assurance of salvation. That he includes works in the assurance of salvation is explained from the consecutive way of salvation. If works had a final and meritorious character, they would be an unambiguous denial of the teaching of the assurance of salvation. On the consecutive way of salvation, however, they are a witness (sign, seal)[11] of the

---

[1] "Si enim ex meritis res pendet, nunquam possumus esse certi, quando satis meritorum habeamus." WA 43, 178, 34-36.

[2] WA 40I, 579, 17-24. [3] WA 43, 462, 11-15.

[4] Ibid., 460, 20-22. [5] WA 40I, 588, 8.

[6] See Pesch, Theologie der Rechtfertigung, pp. 265-67; Hasler, Luther in der katholischen Dogmatik, pp. 199-201; A. Stakemeier, Trient über Heilsgewissheit, p. 175; Kraus, Vorherbestimmung, p. 126. Although Luther often used the two terms certitudo and securitas as synonyms, still it is unanimously thought that the Reformer draws a real distinction between assurance of salvation and carnal security. Certitudo (WA 2, 458, 31) points in the direction of assurance of salvation, securitas (WA 3, 417, 11-12) in that of carnal security.

[7] WA 1, 373, 29; 48, 223, 29-39. [8] WA 2, 458, 20-22.

[9] Ibid., 25-26. [10] WA 39I, 114, 28-30.

[11] WA 10III, 225, 35-226, 1.

bestowed and experienced salvation. This witness has three values:

1. For the believer himself (in corde nostro).[1]

2. For the believer's environment (coram hominibus et fratribus).[2]

3. In the judgment (darnach wirt dich Gott richten).[3]

Luther can speak of this work-witness wholly without embarrassment because over and over he makes it unmistakably clear that it represents consequence (sequela) and not worthiness (dignitas).[4] Since, however, the doctrine of merit stresses only the worthiness--even in the sense of condignity--Luther must reject it from the viewpoint of his theological thesis as a "Satanic trick" (ludibria Satanae).[5]

Luther's Doctrine of Work and Reward

Luther's unambiguous rejection of the doctrine of merit must not deceive us into thinking that the Reformer does not hold

---

[1] WA 39I, 46, 20-21; 10III, 225, 35-226, 5.

[2] WA 39I, 292, 11.   [3] WA 12, 289, 33-34.

[4] WA 18, 693, 38-694, 14. As far as the works of the pagans are concerned, Luther's sayings sound contradictory. In the Lecture on Romans he affirms the possibility of a redemption of pagans, since they indeed in part fulfill the law (WA 56, 198, 33). This happens by the fact that God gives grace also to those like Job, Naaman, and Jethro (ibid., 25-28), whereby He forgives and enables them (ibid., 198, 33-199, 4). So he can hope that, e.g., Cicero will be saved (TR 3, 698, 10-17; 4, 14, 1-9), or he gives expression to his certainty that it will be so (TR 5, 413, 26-31). In this case he also can call the works merita (TR 4, 14, 9). But in other places he can, with Augustine, designate the works of pagans as fallaciae (WA 2, 458, 17). Seen philosophically, there is a difference between single pagans; judged theologically, they are all alike. They are not under the lordship of Christ but of the devil. Even Cicero did not please God (WA 43, 614, 39-615, 20).

[5] WA 40, 223, 15.

fast to the biblical sayings about reward. In the modern research on Luther in both camps, this firm stance of his is without question.[1]

Respect for the biblical teaching of reward compelled him to hold fast to the concept of reward. This seemed to him all the easier because he saw in the stressing of the "high doctrine of Christ" (hoher artikel von Christo) of Paul and John,[2] the soteriological priority that gave the Synoptics the right to emphasize work and reward.[3] For him Paul and Matthew stand in the unity of the faith which announces itself in works, although he also conceded that the emphasis of his opponents on works "Behold works, works," (Ecce opera, opera) should not be taken lightly on account of his followers.[4]

For Luther it is important that from praemium (reward) we should not conclude a meritum (earning, merit),[5] for anyone who wishes to earn will be lost.[6] He who serves for the sake of earning

---

[1] Walther von Loewenich, Luther als Ausleger der Synoptiker (Munich: Chr. Kaiser, 1954), p. 193; Hermann, Luthers Theologie, pp. 151-52; Peters, Glaube und Werk, pp. 186-207; Pesch, Theologie der Rechtfertigung, p. 321; Hasler, Luther in der katholischen Dogmatik, p. 232. Peters asserts that Luther carries the biblical sayings beyond themselves (pp. 183, 206), because doubtless in the Scripture the solus Deus is present as the direction of assault (fear of God for God's sake), but the opposite position (fear of God for the sake of another thing, namely, punishment and reward) is not denied (p. 200). Luther himself apparently saw no problem in these facts, for he could also refer to the promised reward, from pastoral-theological grounds, as encouragement and, at the same time, relativize it as unmerited (WA 18, 695, 6-17). Looking toward the reward was, for him, looking toward God. This unity he saw also in the Scripture.

[2] WA 32, 352, 37.   [3] Ibid., 352, 33-353, 6.

[4] WA 38, 645, 24-27.   [5] WA 39I, 306, 14-16.

[6] WA 7, 801, 2-13; 18, 694, 15-17.

a reward has not surrendered himself completely to God; he who receives the reward of grace places everything on God. He serves God spontaneously and all the rest comes about as a result.[1] He who serves from fear arrives right where he does not wish to be--in the judgment of God.[2] Merit implies a morality of reward (der genieszsuchtige unreyne geyst)[3] and a spiritual thinking in class structures ("should not a Carthusian earn more . . . than . . . a housewife?").[4] But the biblical reward implies the work for God's sake and is an illustration of the promise of God,[5] which the believer now possesses by faith and will later possess by sight.[6] From this general reward of grace, which consists of the gift of eternal life and is distributed to all in a similar way, Luther distinguishes a charismatic reward which will distinguish Paul, Peter, and the martyrs from the mass of other believers.[7] This greater reward is derived from the greater gifts which were given to the Apostles and the martyrs,[8] gifts which "without any cooperation and thought" (on alle zuthun und gedancken)[9] come from God and therefore do not provide a basis for any merit.

In the framework of these fundamental theological thoughts, Luther's exegesis is concerned with all the texts that his opponents

---

[1] WA 10III, 280, 8-14.   [2] WA 1, 42, 7; 4, 664, 12.

[3] WA 7, 559, 24.

[4] WA 32, 522, 26-27. "Solt ein Cartheuser nicht mehr verdienen . . . den . . . eine ehefraw?"

[5] WA 7, 559, 18-23.   [6] WA 2, 98, 34-40.

[7] WA 36, 652, 15-18; 653, 24-27.   [8] Ibid., 513, 35.

[9] Ibid., 516, 32.

from then until now offer for the establishing of the thought of merit.

Those are, in the first place, texts which seem to show a final relationship of work and reward. Since the idea of one's own goal-directed accomplishment for the attainment of an appropriate reward lies at the root of the final ethical principle, could one not read the concept of merit into such texts as Mt 5:11-12; 6:1-4, 14-15; 19:27; 1 Cor 9:24; 15:58?

Luther is not of this opinion. He knows that the Sermon on the Mount is addressed to Christ's disciples[1] and therefore pertains to the lived faith. But the lived faith presupposes the received salvation. The believer does not need to earn anything more, but he probably needs encouragement and comfort[2] that God rewards--even undeservedly.[3]

The Beatitudes (Mt 5) doubtless emphasize doing. But from where and how this doing comes into being the Evangelist Matthew says in another place.[4] Nevertheless, the first Beatitude already indicates that all works presuppose the right, believing mind.[5] But this--the work in faith--is God's working, therefore does not belong to man but to God.[6] Again and again Luther emphasizes that work is a witness to faith, that faith makes one religious and works demonstrate it.[7] Faith is the commander in the process,

---

[1] WA 32, 543, 34.

[2] Ibid., 339, 34-35; 340, 17-19; 10III, 401, 17-18.

[3] WA 32, 543, 1-4.   [4] WA 38, 459, 9-11.

[5] Ibid., 16-19.   [6] WA 10III, 286, 9-10.

[7] Ibid., 286, 20-287, 6.

work the witness.[1] The work does not really need to be commanded, as such, at all; it occurs by itself with the Christian.[2] Exactly thus, reward is simply the consequence of the work.[3]

If reward is proclaimed in the gospel, it is not that it may be sought and earned, but that it might be recognized.[4] It is not in order to build salvation, but to enjoy the promise.[5] Therefore one should not confuse promise and merit.[6] Even if heaven were to be earned by lifting up a straw, Luther, nevertheless, would not do it for that would revile the honor of God.[7] Even with complete obedience of grace, God's mercy must be called upon, because God so wishes it.[8] Therefore, Luther rejects not only the doctrine of merit of Scholasticism but also the teaching of the final way of salvation by Augustine.[9]

Apparently only the Synoptics speak of works-righteousness, but in reality they--especially Luke--speak of the sola fide which is a sola fide numquam sola. John and James agree with this also. The emphasis on works then, as well as now, must be given because even the faithful are always in danger of neglecting obedience.[10] In this there can be no talk of merits in any case. The thought

---

[1] Ibid., 297, 9-11. [2] Ibid., 289, 15-16.

[3] Ibid., 289, 14-32; 401, 19-20.

[4] Ibid., 289, 28. [5] WA 32, 543, 28-30.

[6] "Da mustu mir nicht ein gemenge machen und die zwey unter einander brewen." Ibid., 30-32.

[7] WA 10III, 280, 10-14. [8] TR 1, 32, 19-30.

[9] Ibid. [10] WA 10III, 293, 3-16.

of merit is cut off in the Scriptures.[1] There is neither a <u>meritum de congruo</u> for justification nor a <u>meritum de condigno</u> for salvation.[2]

Jesus' polemic against the Pharisees (Mt 6:1-4) gives Luther occasion to emphasize the difference between human-merit morality and divine-reward morality. Both have works as the goal,[3] but merit morality (<u>der schendliche Tück</u>) seeks its own honor,[4] while the biblical reward-ethic does all for God's sake--not to attain merit[5] but just as God also gives His gifts daily whether one thanks Him for them or not.[6] This the world cannot learn;[7] only as one becomes a Christian can it be learned.[8] Just to him who seeks no reward and only wishes to please God will the reward freely come,[9] for God has thus promised and He does not lie.[10]

Where the forgiveness of man seems to be a precondition for God's forgiveness (Mt 6:14-15), Luther emphasizes that this is only apparently so,[11] for one must distinguish between inner and outer forgiveness.[12] Through the gospel and word of God man receives forgiveness first in his heart through faith. This is God's work alone and can be compared with the trunk or roots of a tree. Only then is the person capable of forgiving. This is the

---

[1] WA 32, 538, 11-14. [2] Ibid., 539, 33-39.
[3] Ibid., 408, 30. [4] Ibid., 12-15.
[5] WA 32, 409, 8-10, 16. [6] Ibid., 411, 1-8.
[7] Ibid., 408, 40-409, 1. [8] Ibid., 410, 30-31.
[9] Ibid., 410, 20. [10] Ibid., 413, 6-8.
[11] Ibid., 422, 30-32. [12] Ibid., 423, 15-424, 1.

fruit, or as 2 Pet 1:10 says: Works are to confirm the call and election that has already occurred. This is the proper assurance (<u>certificatio</u>) of faith. The one who experiences it in himself knows that this does not spring from his own nature but from the grace of God.[1] Sophists are those who believe that one may earn merits through works. The Christian looks, however, to words such as in Mt 6:14-15, to God's word and promise with the eye of faith. Hence the works that follow become a "sign" (<u>warzeichen</u>) that God is gracious.[2] Thus, forgiveness of one's neighbor doubtless becomes a condition; however, it is not a final but rather consecutively set-up condition which does not strive for salvation, rather it witnesses to salvation, or else faith would not be genuine.[3]

The Petrine question: "What then shall we have?" (Mt 19:27) gives Luther the occasion to go into the problem of the general and the charismatic reward. The person is redeemed only through faith, but he receives the charismatic reward according to works. As now one stands before a congregation through the gift lent to him (<u>suo dono</u>), so also will there be differences in the resurrection of the dead.[4]

At first that seems to contradict another statement about the text where Luther asserts that <u>coram Deo</u> Paul would not stand higher than the rest of the saved.[5] But apparently by this he means

---

[1] Ibid., 424, 1-4. [2] Ibid., 424, 17-25.
[3] WA 15, 484, 14-18. [4] WA 30II, 668, 11-15.
[5] WA 15, 425, 8.

concerning the kingdom of God, which is alike for all because Christ is alike for all.¹

This general reward is totally a reward of grace, for the first will be last and the last first. This is the main point (heubstuck) of the whole matter. It terrifies the saints and comforts the humble. Many misunderstand the Petrine question and aim at work-righteousness. But God takes a "Cinderella" (aschenbrodel) and casts off a monk.² How then is God able to answer for Himself? The answer is: The last will be first! And this rests upon God's sovereignty and grace.³

Peter's assertion that the disciples had left everything already shows that it is only a matter of the work of the Holy Spirit, for nobody of himself is capable of it.⁴ "Widderteuffer" and "Parfuser Munche" (Anabaptists and discalced friars) do this from their own initiative.⁵ Thereby they act as proudly as Diogenes, the saint of the devil, who paraded his poverty.⁶ Paul did not preach that one should leave his family, but that the heart should not be dependent on it.⁷

Theologians divide grace and merit,⁸ acting according to the principle: "When you have accomplished this I will be your debtor" (Si feceris, tum tibi debitor ero). God rewards according to grace. One who recognizes Him as King of mercy is spontaneously given gifts a hundredfold.⁹

---

¹Ibid., 3-4.   ²Ibid., 424, 8-12.   ³Ibid., 13-16.
⁴WA 47, 358, 12-16.   ⁵Ibid., 359, 9.   ⁶Ibid., 360, 9-27.
⁷Ibid., 38-39.   ⁸WA 15, 424, 24.   ⁹Ibid., 17-19.

Pauline texts likewise indicated as final-meritorious Luther answers in a similar way. The challenge to run and to obtain the prize (1 Cor 9:24) does not say anything about how it is to happen. Can one then conclude from the sentence, "If the Emperor defeats the Turks he will be lord of Syria," that he consequently both can do it and does so?[1] Only through faith in Christ is it possible to attain the crown; everything else is in vain, even if the person sweats blood.[2] The works of faith, however, please God and this in itself would be a comfort even if nothing more followed. But this, of course, is impossible, more does follow because God promised the reward of grace which the believer can expect. Thus Luther interprets 1 Cor 15:58.[3]

However, Luther must have been challenged even more by the texts that are seen by some in the sense of a correspondence of work and reward than he was by those which are interpreted in the sense of the final way of salvation; e.g., Mt 5:7 ("Blessed are the merciful, for they shall obtain mercy"), Mt 7:1-2; Lk 6:38 ("For the measure you give will be the measure you get back"), and Mt 10:41 ("He who receives a prophet . . . shall receive a prophet's reward"). He did not allow himself to be irritated by these texts; but he cannot find in them the thought of merit.[4] From his theological viewpoint this is understandable, for there cannot be any correspondence if reward is promise, consequence,

---

[1] WA 18, 693, 21-26.   [2] WA 34I, 158, 12-13; 159, 4-5.

[3] WA 18, 695, 12-17.

[4] "Ego non lego neque invenio in hoc Euangelio, quod aliquid mereamur operibus." WA 27, 245, 9-10.

and result and does not rest upon worthiness.[1] Promise also can never be coupled with claim and correspondence, for it goes far beyond all human thought of right and measure.[2] God Himself is indeed the promise!

Then what do the gospel sayings about work and reward mean? First, the promise should operate similar to law. The law commands and at the same time proves one's incapability, for nobody can fulfill it. Thus, also the promise encourages and, at the same time, shows that the person can do nothing to attain it.[3] Second, one must distinguish between command (praeceptum) and promise (promissio). In the case of a command, the person only produces his indebtedness. Like the servant in Lk 17:10, he has no claim on the reward. He must simply do as he is commanded. It is different with the promise. God out of mercy adds it to the account of what the person owes.[4] Out of this, therefore, no accounting can arise.[5] Third, one could, because of the gift character[6] of the "reward," speak at most of a paradoxical correspondence. He who stands before God like a beggar at the same time stands there like

---

[1] WA 18, 693, 38-39; 694, 37-38.

[2] "Wohl euch die jr barmhertzig seid, denn jr werdet widder eitel barmhertzigkeit finden beide hie und dort, und solche barmhertzigkeit, die all menschliche wohltat und barmhertzigkeit unausprechlich weit ubertrifft." WA 32, 323, 10-12.

[3] WA 18, 695, 2-11.

[4] "Uber das quod debemus, addit promissionem quae non fit ex merito, sed ex misericordia." WA 27, 246, 6-7.

[5] "Si illa [merita] respiceret, wurde er yn ein rechnung tretten." Ibid., 14-15.

[6] WA 32, 479, 8.

a rich man. For the one who boasts of his possessions loses all, but the one who comes with empty hands receives an unspeakably rich gift. Again and again, as Luther emphasizes, the person stands before God with faith, while works apply to the neighbor.[1] Thus, from the beginning there can be no correspondence between work and reward. Works stand, as Luther stressed again and again to his hearers,[2] in consecutive relationship. They are proof of faith (<u>preysung, bewerung, zaychen, sigel, volgen, fruecht, beweysung</u>).[3]

Fourth, Luther sees in Mt 5:7 and Lk 6:31-38 what are simply examples of the "golden Rule" in relationship between persons.[4] There are "spiritual sayings" (<u>etliche sprüch füren den gaist</u>), which deal with faith and the freely given salvation, and there are "bodily sayings" (<u>die den leib füren</u>) which deal with works and the responsibility toward the neighbor. The words of Jesus, "Forgive, and so you will be forgiven;" "Give, and thus it will be given to you;" and "With the measure with which you measure, it will be measured to you" belong in the second group and have reference within the world.[5]

The word about "a prophet's reward" (Mt 10:41) Luther calls a Hebraism. It really has reference only to a received gift. As the preacher can be considered to be Christ because he preaches

---

[1] WA 10I2, 314, 11-13; 10III, 222, 24-223, 8.

[2] "Secht den auslauff muss ich thun, das ich nit sterck der Papisten verstandt." Ibid., 226, 22-23.

[3] Ibid., 225, 18-226, 8; 10I, 2, 318, 15-23.

[4] WA 10I2, 323, 12-28.   [5] Ibid., 319, 1-19; 323, 18-23.

the word of Christ--without there really being a correspondence between Christ and preacher--so it is with the reward, since it is reward only in a symbolic sense.[1] The content of the reward is for the time being the wisdom of the prophet, which is given by the Spirit, and in eternity the everlasting life that God gives. The charismatic reward will be different, for the prophet is a teacher and we are his pupils.[2]

Since Luther's way of interpreting the Scriptures can be called "Biblicism," certain texts must have been especially challenging to him which at first glance seem to be like erratic blocks in his doctrine of reward. Among them is Dan 4:24, a text with which the young and the old Reformer strove again and again, and to which he devoted a disputation of his own in 1535.

Luther expresses the idea that either unbelief or faith precedes all words about sin and good works.[3] Therefore if the person is to be able to give alms, first his heart must become pure[4] and this occurs through Christ and faith.[5] The giving of alms, through which Nebuchadnezzar is to produce righteousness, means the same as the fides incarnata,[6] that is, the faith that makes righteous because it stands the test by good works coram hominibus.[7]

---

[1] WA 38, 515, 8-10.   [2] WA 48, 113, 4-7, 11-16.
[3] WA 30II, 663, 3-6; 39I, 64, 7; 65, 5.
[4] WA 12, 647, 3-7.   [5] WA 39I, 47, 11-12.
[6] Ibid., 65, 6-7.
[7] WA 12, 647, 2-3; 10I, 2, 44, 21-23; 30II, 662, 24-26.

The imperative to the deed is not moral but theological. That is, it does not automatically apply to the powers of the person but to faith.[1] But how could Nebuchadnezzar have faith? Luther says that he had had Daniel as preacher of the true God[2] and could take for himself, like all people in the time of the OT, proleptically the salvation in Christ.[3]

But since the king did not believe and, therefore, did not act accordingly, he was punished for his unbelief.[4] Most important of all for the Reformer is the fact that the <u>fides incarnata</u> (life-righteousness as consequence) is not to be played out against the <u>sola fide</u> (faith-righteousness as ground).[5]

These considerations of the question of the theological imperative lead up to the answer of similar texts in the NT: Mt 6:20 ("Lay up for yourselves treasures in heaven"), Mt 19:17 ("If you would enter life, keep the commandments"), and Lk 16:9 ("Make friends for yourselves by means of unrighteous mammon, so that . . . they may receive you into the eternal habitations").

As to Mt 6:20, Luther thinks that the imperative really would not be necessary because genuine faith always fulfills the will of God.[6] Jesus here is not emphasizing the search for merit and reward; He is warning against greed. It is a call to trust in God alone, for no one can serve two masters.[7] The reference to the

---

[1] WA 40I, 457, 19-23. [2] WA 39I, 65, 18-19.
[3] Ibid., 64, 3-4. [4] WA 30II, 663, 1-3.
[5] WA 39I, 65, 26-28. [6] WA 10III, 289, 15-16.
[7] WA 32, 437, 12-13; 38, 462, 39-463, 18.

"invisible treasure" (<u>der unsichtige Schatz</u>)[1] does not mean final-meritorious accomplishments, but total surrender to God.[2] Therefore Jesus wishes to warn against temptations that could destroy faith.[3]

In any case it would be a grave misunderstanding if one wished to speak of works and reward <u>coram Deo</u> in "human terms" (<u>menschlicher weysse</u>),[4] for with God faith and reward do not follow work; in fact, it is just the opposite--the works follow faith, and living faith has the reward as consequence "without any seeking for it" (<u>on alles suchen</u>).[5]

The passage in Mt 19:17 often occupied Luther, for the Pope boasted on the basis of that text and asserted that not faith but works count before God.[6] Reason also, in this instance, without further consideration, concludes from work to merit.[7] But this "dark saying" (<u>finsterer Spruch</u>) can be illuminated by many lucid sayings,[8] all of which emphasize the keeping of the commandments as a consequence of salvation and not the cause of salvation. For "must" (You must keep the commandments) does not mean "can" (You are able to keep the commandments).[9] The Scripture always is to be understood from Christ (<u>pro Christo intelligenda</u>).[10] From Christ, however, means from faith in Christ (<u>in fide Christi</u>).[11] That

---

[1] WA 32, 443, 8.
[2] Ibid., 443, 9-12.
[3] Ibid., 437, 7-8.
[4] WA 10III, 289, 7-10.
[5] Ibid., 18-22.
[6] WA 47, 341, 39-342, 3.
[7] TR 2, 450, 15.
[8] WA 47, 342, 26-32.
[9] Ibid., 343, 15-35.
[10] WA 39I, 47, 3.
[11] Ibid., 6; 40I, 415, 18-24.

also means that merits have to be diminished, even annihilated.[1] In grace all people are alike; only in merits=gifts are they different.[2]

Luther attempted to grasp Lk 16:9 in the most systematic way. "On geyst mit blosser vernunfft" (without Spirit, with nothing but reason), it seemed to him like a "priestly and monkish gospel" (pfeffisch und munchs Evangelion).[3] According to Luther we must in this text deal with three questions: (1) Does it depend with God on works? (2) Should we perform works for our salvation? (3) Are the friends who receive us the Catholic saints?[4]

The first question he answers thus: It is not our works but our faith that makes us friends of God.[5] Only because the Scholastics always understand faith as the fides informis are we even tempted to mingle works in with the question of salvation.[6] If man had held fast to fiducial faith, the work question would not have come up at all, for works follow the true faith as fruits are brought forth on a tree.[7] We are only made aware of works in the gospel so that we may know what correct faith is.[8] That is, only faith makes pious (religious); works only demonstrate the piety.[9] Faith first makes righteous "inside the spirit" (inwendig im geyst), but works, "outwardly" (eusserlich und offentlich).[10]

---

[1] TR 2, 450, 16.
[2] Ibid., 17-18.
[3] WA 10III, 283, 12-13.
[4] Ibid., 22-29.
[5] Ibid., 283, 30-284, 8.
[6] WA 10III, 285, 3-30.
[7] Ibid., 285, 31-286, 4.
[8] Ibid., 286, 20-29.
[9] Ibid., 31-32.
[10] Ibid., 26-28.

From this the second question also is solved for Luther: It is self-understood that works must happen selflessly and freely. Concerning this he points to Mt 10:8 ("You received without pay, give without pay").[1] Beside the usual argument, that works serve one's neighbor, here stands the thought that works must happen to honor God (Gott tzu ehren).[2]

This Deo soli gloria then solves the third question: The saints cannot do anything for us. As sinners they themselves need God.[3] The friends in the parable Luther sees, not in heaven but on earth. It is the poor who must be helped.[4] The "receiving" is a portrayal of the way that someday they will bear witness before God to our faith, but basically it is not they but God who receives.[5]

Luther, of course, puzzled over the relation between work and reward while interpreting passages in the NT which refer to a "judgment according to works" (Mt 16:27; 25:31-40; Rom 2:6; 1 Pet 1:17; Heb 6:10). He devoted himself especially to the problem in the explanation of Mt 16, but he also took positions concerning it with reference to other passages. He did not intend thereby to battle against works and reward, but against the theology of a humanly earned justification.[6] On the other hand, there must be a judgment according to works, simply because there is no righteousness in the world.[7] For if there were righteousness, then John Hus would not have been executed.[8]

---

[1] Ibid., 288, 16-17.
[2] Ibid., 23.
[3] Ibid., 290, 10-12.
[4] Ibid., 288, 19-27.
[5] Ibid., 290, 28-31.
[6] WA 30II, 670, 29-30.
[7] WA 38, 644, 30-35.
[8] Ibid., 645, 8-16.

Every worldly judgment is, accordingly, concerned with violations of the commandments from the Second Table of the Law and, therefore, a priori only an impoverished judgment (Es ist ein bettlerisch gericht und nicht das a, b, c vom gericht Gottes).[1]

But to conclude something from the text concerning justification is false. It does not concern justification but judgment. It does not ask how a person becomes righteous, but whether he is righteous.[2] The Scripture contains a double aspect: promise and law. Gift corresponds to the first, and work to the second.[3] But the work must not be isolated from the person. Before works occur they are decided in the heart, spirit, will, and understanding. That is, the right person is to be set ahead of the right act.[4] Concerning this there is agreement among philosophers and theologians. The difference lies only in that the philosopher thinks in the category of reason-work, while the theologian thinks in the category of faith-work.[5]

The being righteous occurs sola fide. The being found righteous occurs through the work of faith.[6] Faith and work belong together and should not be separated;[7] both form the inseparable sum of being a Christian (summa des gantzen Christlichen lebens).[8]

---

[1] Ibid., 1-7.
[2] Ibid., 17-22.
[3] Ibid., 32-35.
[4] Ibid., 646, 8-22.
[5] Ibid., 646, 23-39.
[6] Ibid., 647, 9-10; 648, 21-22, 22-28.
[7] Ibid., 647, 24-32; 12, 289, 23-290, 11.
[8] Ibid., 32-33.

Once again the work of faith must not be separated from the person, for not the works but the person is judged according to the works. The works receive no reward, but man who performs the works does (<u>Quare non opera, sed operans recipiet mercedem</u>).[1] Therefore, in the judgment it is a question of the root of the right action, that is, of the person changed by faith, not simply the action itself (<u>credulitas</u> not <u>operatio</u>).[2] Luther wishes thereby to secure the consecutive against the final way of salvation, for one can only be thankful for faith, but he always stands in danger of asserting himself with works. Thus, it is clear that Paul, like every other Christian, will be saved only by grace, but that independent from the question of salvation a greater charismatic reward awaits him.[3]

When we question the relationship between faith and works, we must at least briefly engage Luther's exegesis of Jas 2:14-26. For this mirrors the strained relationship between the Reformer and the Epistle of James ("a strawy epistle," "a papist epistle").[4]

Three different sayings are found in Luther's writings which in an interesting way run parallel in time. In his preface to James and Jude (in 1522) he indeed affirms that James' letter is to be praised for its stress on the law,[5] but that it stands in contradiction to Paul because it ascribes justification to works.[6] In the sermons from the same year, however, he harmonizes Paul and

---

[1] Ibid., 647, 32-35.   [2] WA 57I, 23, 12-13.

[3] WA 30II, 670, 27-29.

[4] DB 6, 10, 33-34; TR 5, 414, 7. "Strohern Epistel," "Papisten Epistel."

[5] DB 7, 384, 3-6.   [6] Ibid., 9-10.

James in that he has the latter speak of dead and living faith by which the living faith is shown in works. Only of these works <u>post justificationem</u> does James speak.[1]

However, in TR 3, No. 3292a (1533) he explains decidedly that Paul and James cannot be harmonized even if many, including Melanchthon, have endeavored to do so with "perspiration."[2] Luther held fast to this view to the end of his life. In TR 5, No. 5443 (1542), he repeats the assertion made in 1522: The Epistle is not Apostolic, nor does it speak of Christ. It comes from a Jew who held the teaching of the law in contrast to the Christian teaching of faith.[3]

In contrast to this stands TR 3, No. 2864b (1533), where he explains that James is right if one takes his word as referring to the external behavior according to the ten commandments. Apparently here Luther means the <u>iustitia civilis</u>, for just prior to this he praises the external discipline and training of the Waldenses. He reproaches them only because they know no <u>sola fide</u> in justification. For only if the position of James is drawn into the question of justification does it contradict God and the Holy Scripture.[4]

From the <u>sola fide</u> principle it was also unavoidable that Luther had to face the NT passages which ascribe to love, along

---

[1] WA 10III, 288, 3-6; 293, 10-11.

[2] "Wer die zusamen reymen kan, dem wil ich mein pirreth auffsetzen und wil mich yhn einen narren lassen schelten." TR 3, 253, 25-29; cf. TR 5, 414, 4.

[3] TR 5, 157, 17-23.   [4] TR 3, 38, 9-18.

with faith and even above faith, justifying or even meritorious value (Lk 7:47; 1 Cor 13:1-2, 13; Gal 5:6; 1 Pet 4:8; 1 Jn 4:17). Luther was all the more unable to avoid this question because his opponents again and again boasted of these texts, especially 1 Cor 13.[1]

In the year 1535 Luther devoted a special disputation to Lk 7:47. For him the exegetical key to the whole section is Lk 7:50: Not love but faith helped the woman before God. Christ does not say to her: Faith and love (fides caritate formata) have saved you.[2]

Luther refers to the fact that where Jesus speaks to the woman, He speaks of her faith and is silent concerning works. But where He speaks to the Pharisees, He speaks of the woman's works and is silent about her faith.[3] He did this because the Pharisees looked on the woman as a public sinner and Jesus could thus rehabilitate her.[4] She saw herself, however, as a sinner before God and was justified by her faith.[5]

Thus, the whole pericope is a commentary on the sola fide numquam sola, that is, on the faith that alone redeems, but that faith does not remain alone, it reveals itself in love.[6] Every

---

[1] "Bei dem gemeinen Man ists ein abenteurlich Epistel, weyls seltzam wort sind, preiset auch die lieb ubern glauben und hofnung, setzt auch, es sey alles nichts, was nicht lieb ist, sind scharffe word, Papisten schliessen hiraus, Der glaub mache nicht selig." WA 49, 351, 23-26.

[2] WA 39I, 128, 5-129, 4.   [3] Ibid., 129, 5-8.

[4] Ibid., 130, 33-35.   [5] Ibid., 131, 5-6.

[6] Ibid., 129, 9-11, 19-20; 131, 41-42.

merit is thereby excluded,[1] for in Romans 4 Paul distinguishes between imputed gift (<u>donum imputatum</u>) and merited reward (<u>merces merita</u>).[2]

The famous Corinthian passage (1 Cor 13:1-13), in Luther's view, has been commented upon in detail by Althaus,[3] so that it suffices to summarize his comments briefly. Luther struggled with these passages throughout his lifetime. Until the thirties he interpreted the pericope in different ways, and only toward the end of his life did he break through to a single interpretation.[4] According to Althaus, the fluctuations are a sign of the difficulties that the Reformer found here.[5]

It is possible to distinguish four explanations in Luther: (1) The faith of which Paul speaks is not the special faith in Christ but the general faith in God--which even the pagans possess.[6] Such a faith can also work miracles. Luther finds proof for this in Judas. Paul cannot have meant the Christian faith because that always draws love after it. (2) But if one wishes to understand by faith the Christian faith, then it is a decadent faith which, out of pride in its own power to work miracles, lets love be absent.[7] (3) However, one could also understand that Paul is in a way speaking of unreality (<u>unmögliches Exempel</u>). That is, in order to emphasize the indispensability of love, Paul sets forth an

---

[1] Ibid., 130, 5-6.   [2] Ibid., 7-8.

[3] Althaus, <u>Theologie Luthers</u>, pp. 357-71.

[4] Ibid., pp. 357-58.   [5] Ibid., p. 372.

[6] WA 17II, 164, 27.   [7] Ibid., 34-36.

impossible example. The impossibility consists of the fact that faith cannot really exist without love. The possibility is, however, only theoretical and has a purely didactic character.[1] (4) At a later time, Luther allowed room for the thought that, in this instance, the faith to be understood is the charismatic gift mentioned in the context (1 Cor 12) and not the salvation-faith at all.[2]

While in 1525 Luther recommended the third interpretation,[3] at the end of his life he had swung around to the first interpretation.[4] According to Althaus, Luther would have come closest to Paul with the second interpretation.[5] Modern exegesis, on the other hand, opts for the fourth interpretation in general.[6]

Luther's interpretation of Gal 5:6 is completely different. Between the young and the old Reformer there is here a permanent concensus. Luther is completely sure that his opponents are falsely interpreting the passage, for it does not speak of becoming righteous (justification), but of the life of the righteous person (sanctification).[7] When it is a question of becoming righteous,

---

[1] Ibid., 165, 6-20. [2] WA 39I, 77, 3; 39II, 236, 8-9.

[3] WA 17II, 165, 14. [4] WA 39II, 310, 13-20.

[5] Althaus, Theologie Luthers, p. 371.

[6] Hans Lietzmann, An die Korinther I-II, in HNT, ed. Günther Bornkamm, 5th ed. (Tübingen: J. C. B. Mohr [P. Siebeck], 1969), p. 61; Archibald Robertson and Alfred Plummer, First Epistle of St. Paul to the Corinthians, in ICC, ed. Samuel R. Driver, Alfred Plummer, and Charles A. Briggs, 2nd ed. (Edinburgh: T. & T. Clark, 1958), p. 266; Frederik W. Grosheide, Commentary on the First Epistle to the Corinthians, in NIC, ed. Ned B. Stonehouse (Grand Rapids, MI: Eerdmans, 1953), p. 286.

[7] BR 9, 407, 40-41.

Paul speaks in Rom 3:11 of a verdict without works and merit.[1] The faith that is effective through love is not the theoretical faith (<u>fides ficta</u>),[2] which for its practical completion needs love as an enlivening element and so becomes <u>fides formata</u>.[3] The faith of which Paul speaks here is the living faith, the <u>fides efficax</u>--as Erasmus also refers to it in the original.[4] This faith must be called the genuine faith (<u>fides vera et vivax</u>).[5] It already has salvation, hence its activity through love has neither a final nor meritorious character. Indeed Paul defines this faith not as one that is justifying through love (<u>iustificat, gratum facit</u>) but as one that works through love (<u>operatur</u>).[6] As a gift of love from God it has come into being, and as a love-gift to fellowmen it extends itself further.

Luther is also concerned with the reference to fellowmen in 1 Pet 4:8. The love that covers sins is no satisfaction activity in the subjective process of salvation, but the reconciliation which ends the quarrel with fellowmen. For before God only faith covers.[7] Inasmuch, however, as one forgives his neighbor, he bears witness that he stands in God's forgiveness.[8] Faith blots out the sin from God's consciousness; love blots it out from man's consciousness.[9]

---

[1] Ibid., 35-37.   [2] WA 40II, 37, 13.
[3] Ibid., 34, 17-20.   [4] WA 2, 567, 19-23.
[5] WA 40II, 37, 14.   [6] Ibid., 35, 21-24.
[7] WA 12, 377, 27-378, 10.   [8] WA 10I2, 44, 18-28.
[9] Ibid., 45, 15-16.

According to 1 Jn 4:17 the Christian can find peace because his love will be remembered in the day of judgment. Luther struggled for some time with this text, as he had with the passage in Corinthians, because he foresaw difficulties for his belief in the assurance of salvation. Since Althaus[1] thoroughly occupied himself with this problem, we need only to mention the most important part of his study.

At first Luther advocated the interpretation that the love used here is not at all a matter of love of the person but of love of God.[2] In other words, because God loves, we need have no anxiety before God's judgment. However, later he gave up this explanation and--according to the context (v. 18) and with the majority of interpreters--he referred this love to the love of the Christian which is revealed through the keeping of the ten commandments. Here he naturally had to ask the question: How is such an activity to be united with the assurance of salvation of the sola fide?

Working out from his theological basic view, he handles this matter in a way similar to that in which he dealt with the judgment according to works. The love of which John speaks is the fruit of faith.[3] Through it faith is made firm[4] and exercised.[5] Thereby love manifests the genuineness of faith itself, the assurance of its genuineness.[6] The "perfect love" is thus for

---

[1] Althaus, Theologie Luthers, pp. 372-85.
[2] WA 20, 757, 26-27.
[3] WA 49, 784, 33-34.
[4] WA 32, 423, 7-8, 18-19.
[5] WA 20, 716, 3-7.
[6] WA 39II, 248, 11-15.

Luther not the complete love--for it always stands in tension with concupiscence--but the genuine love.[1]

Luther also analyzed in great detail 1 Cor 4:4, because his opponents wished to read from Paul's word--"I am not thereby acquitted"--a refutation of the sola fide and the assurance of salvation. Luther points out that Paul simply wishes to say that when a person has a good conscience before other people, he is not necessarily thereby justified before God.[2] The good conscience comes from good works and would mean work-righteousness.[3] But Paul denies just that with "I am not thereby acquitted," for he indeed knows only justification by faith.[4] The one who is thus justified can peacefully stand in God's judgment,[5] for he knows that God accepts not according to works but according to faith. What he does not know is how God will judge his works.[6] Here Paul is not at all speaking about his justification. He is speaking as a Christian who is already justified, for only such a person does works that give a good conscience. As a Jew Paul was a blasphemer of Christianity.[7] But the true good conscience does not come from the works at all, it comes from grace (2 Cor 1:12).[8] Without grace, even the person with a good conscience would be lost.[9] Before men the Christian can stress his innocence and have

---

[1] WA 36, 444, 10-11.
[2] WA 10I2, 139, 31-33.
[3] Ibid., 140, 1 8.
[4] Ibid., 4 11.
[5] Ibid., 11-14.
[6] Ibid., 13-14.
[7] WA 10I2, 140, 15-18.
[8] Ibid., 19-26.
[9] WA 39I, 221, 20-222, 6.

a good reputation, for indeed he keeps the ten commandments, but before God he always stands with guilt and without glory.[1]

What then is the relationship of this interpretation with texts like 2 Tim 4:8, where it speaks about just such a glory (crown) which God (the righteous Judge) gives according to worthiness? Luther allows no doubt to arise that this glory comes to the person not from worthiness (non dignitate) but from mercy (per misericordiam et gratiam).[2] Man, of himself, is in a comfortless state (greulich beschissen [sic]).[3] No kind of justification is alluded to in this text but a comfort is expressed; for God fulfills His promises now only in part, but the Christian can be sure that the complete fulfillment is to come.[4] The works of the one who is received by God are pleasing to God (sub ala graciae sunt placita et meritoria).[5] For the first and second justification (iustificatio, vita aeterna) works do not accomplish anything, for these are gifts.[6] Works occur--as Luther again and again emphasizes--to the honor of God and for the good of the neighbor (pro gloria Dei, pro commodo proximi).[7]

The obedience mentioned in 1 Cor 3:8-9 doubtless makes the person a coworker with God (cooperator), but this cooperation is no contribution of his own, it is the experience which by the Spirit is given inwardly and exercised in order that the gospel

---

[1] WA 10I2, 140, 28-141, 3; 36, 449, 29-450, 27.

[2] WA 39I, 235, 32-36.   [3] Ibid., 37.

[4] WA 30II, 667, 27-31.   [5] Ibid., 32.

[6] Ibid., 667, 35-37.   [7] Ibid., 668, 4.

<u>outwardly</u> may reach other people. Why God makes use of this method is not to be questioned.[1]

This survey of Luther's doctrine of work and reward would be incomplete if we left unnoticed Luther's numerous positions in reference to the parable of the workers in the vineyard (Mt 20:1-16). In this challenging pericope (<u>scharff Evangelium</u>)[2] he finds the basic traits of his work-and-reward doctrine confirmed. Therefore he regards this very parable as an important teaching (<u>notige und nutzliche lehr</u>).[3]

Luther knows that many have already attempted the interpretation of this text;[4] he himself, in the course of his reformational activity, as we will see, has put forth various interpretations of the details of the parable. Nevertheless one thing is irrefutably clear to him from the early (1514-17) to the later (1544) explanations--the parable annuls the thought of merit.[5]

He interprets the vineyard as the Jews,[6] the Christian church,[7] and the Holy Scripture.[8] The workers are not only the preachers[9] but also simply the believers of all times: the former under the office of the letter, the latter under that of the Spirit.[10] In general he distinguishes five groups from among the

---

[1] WA 18, 695, 28-34.   [2] WA 37, 275, 16; 52, 136, 1.
[3] WA 47, 370, 8-9.   [4] WA 9, 563, 11-13.
[5] WA 17II, 140, 33.   [6] WA 47, 371, 2.
[7] WA 9, 562, 30; 47, 371, 17-18.
[8] WA 9, 563, 1.   [9] Ibid., 562, 32.
[10] Ibid., 565, 8.

workers (<u>funfferley erbeiter</u>).¹ (1) There are those who have concluded a contract with the owner and are hungry for reward. Those are the work-righteous Jews, in general (<u>populus Synagogae rudissimus</u>),² or the Jews at the time of Moses, in particular. The contract is the Covenant.³ (2) Another group has not made any contract, but they are still hired hands (<u>mercenarii</u>),⁴ and they, also, are motivated by hunger for reward (<u>non libero corde sed cupiditate</u>).⁵ They are the Jews at the time of the prophets in the OT.⁶ (3, 4) Two other groups are similar to the second for they also serve not freely but by command.⁷ Luther believes he can distinguish yet another (5) group who freely (<u>aus freyem geyst</u>)⁸ and without reckoning serve. It is this group which thus serves that is set in the first place. It consists of the people of the NT.⁹

So in reality there are only two groups: that which serves for reward and the selfless one. The first can be the Jews with their work orientation,¹⁰ proud Christians (<u>Schwermeri</u>),¹¹ monks, and common people¹²--people seeking temporal goods,¹³ yes, even

---

[1] WA 29, 38, 10.

[2] WA 1, 133, 16-18, 23; 21, 87, 38; 27, 39, 34.

[3] WA 9, 563, 14-15.   [4] WA 1, 133, 27.

[5] Ibid., 21.   [6] WA 9, 563, 24-25.

[7] WA 1, 133, 27-29.   [8] WA 9, 564, 38.

[9] Ibid., 563, 28-35.   [10] WA 21, 87, 38.

[11] WA 27, 39, 5-17, 28.   [12] Ibid., 40, 25; 37, 277, 1-2.

[13] WA 17II, 138, 34-37.

Luther himself, if he boasts about his works![1] The second group includes the pagans without works,[2] the people who seek what is eternal,[3] the modest Christians who stand in danger of despair,[4] in short, all who serve in the right disposition--without wish for reward.[5] The first group believes it is a matter of correspondence between work and reward. But with God everything goes against human righteousness.[6] Luther cites the examples of Cain and Abel, Esau and Jacob, Judas and Peter.[7] Before God they are all equal.[8] Men give according to merit; God gives out of kindness (<u>umbsonst, sola bonitate, kein recht, blos auff sein barmherzickeit</u>).[9] Collectors of merit, therefore, are deceiving themselves,[10] those who claim merit are rejected.[11] They want to make God a merchant,[12] but God has radically rejected the idea of merit.[13]

One naturally asks, with good grounds, whether all of the details that the Reformer indicated can be read out of the parable. But this is indeed not the decisive thing! That which counts in the parable, Luther has worked out well. (1) Before God nothing is earned by works. (2) What matters is the disposition (<u>Gesinnung</u>).

---

[1] WA 47, 372, 2-14.
[2] WA 21, 87, 37.
[3] WA 17II, 138, 34-37.
[4] WA 27, 39, 18-25.
[5] WA 9, 563, 34.
[6] WA 11, 12, 10; 27, 41, 4-5; 47, 370, 19-20; 52, 136, 12.
[7] WA 11, 13, 2-6.
[8] WA 37, 276, 1-36.
[9] WA 27, 41, 7; 1, 134, 21; 27, 41, 15; 38, 27.
[10] WA 11, 14, 1-2.
[11] WA 21, 87, 39-40.
[12] WA 27, 40, 22.
[13] WA 17II, 140, 33.

(3) Man has no claims in his relation to God. (4) There is no correspondence between work and reward. (5) God deals with man solely from His kindness (<u>sola bonitate</u>!). Hence it does not seem so important to us whether Luther refined[1] and harmonized[2] the sayings of the NT. Much more important is the question of whether in his work- and reward-teaching Luther has done justice to the intentions of the proclamation of Jesus and the early Christians. In spite of some questions (eisegesis in details, harmonizing tendencies, in general), we think the answer is, "Yes."

Summary

1. The OT knows the concept of retribution but not of merit. The Jewish teaching of merit comes forth only from late Jewish sources (Apocrypha, Pseudepigrapha, Talmud).

2. Jesus' proclamation is a protest against the Late Judaic teaching of merit. He frees the idea of retribution from speculation about reward, schemes, and claims of reward. As to the rejection of the idea of merit, there is unity of teaching in the NT Scriptures.

3. In works as early as those of the Apostolic Fathers are already found the beginnings of a Christian teaching of merit (separation of faith [<u>fides dogmatica</u>] from love, final way of salvation, substitute accomplishments, and supererogatory works).

4. The Christian doctrine of merit itself, however, begins only with Tertullian. Merit (<u>meritum</u>) is what is beyond duty

---

[1] Peters, <u>Glaube und Werk</u>, p. 183.

[2] Loewenich, <u>Luther als Ausleger der Synoptiker</u>, p. 199.

in obedience or is excessive in compensation for sin. The Eastern Church also developed similar ideas, but without systematizing them. The juristic thinking of the Latin West aided the idea of merit to its breakthrough.

    5. Augustine's theology of grace (<u>sola gratia</u>) vitiates the merit idea. But his misunderstanding of the <u>sola fide</u> (justification out of love, final way of salvation) and his concessions to tradition and popular belief finally make room for the thought of merit in Western theology.

    6. Semi-Pelagianism and Semi-Augustinianism of the Early Middle Ages further the idea of merit; Early Scholasticism systematizes (Peter Lombard) or combats it (Porretan school). Followers (Lombard school) and opponents (Robert of Melun) of Peter Lombard separate <u>meritum gratiae</u> (justification) and <u>meritum gloriae</u> (salvation). High Scholasticism calls justification-merit <u>meritum de congruo</u>--merit on grounds of benevolence--and the salvation-merit <u>meritum de condigno</u>--merit on grounds of worthiness (William of Auvergne). There are various views concerning the <u>meritum de congruo</u>. In order to come into existence it needs the impulse of the <u>gratia gratis data</u> (<u>Summa Halensis</u>, Bonaventure); it does not exist at all for justification (the late Thomas Aquinas); man can even earn through merit <u>de congruo</u>, the <u>gratia gratis data</u>. Salvation is earned in the same way, for every merit counts only on the basis of God's acceptance (Duns Scotus). Against this, Thomas teaches a genuine <u>meritum de condigno</u> for savlation; that is, a distributive relationship of the work of grace to the merited reward. Late Scholasticism (Gabriel Biel) draws both together:

justification earned by one's own strengths (<u>Facienti quod in se est</u>) and salvation earned with the help of grace (<u>partim-partim</u>).

7. Luther's real struggle is the fight against the doctrine of merit. By his radical theo- and christocentricity (sovereignty of God, predestination, sole agency of God, concept of extrinsic grace and righteousness, total depravity of the human being) he overcomes the doctrine of merit. Since the <u>First Lecture on Psalms</u> (1513-15) he allows the <u>meritum gratiae</u> and <u>gloriae</u> to be valid only as merit of congruity. In the <u>Lecture on Romans</u> (1515-16) he breaks with the <u>meritum gratiae</u>, and from 1518 on also with the <u>meritum gloriae</u>. However, Luther holds fast to the biblical thought of reward. In the consecutive way of salvation, reward is defined as a consequence, granted as a gift and not as a personally achieved goal. Consequently, every passion for reward, every correspondence of work and reward, and every claim to reward are abolished. Reward is purely a reward of grace, a synonym for God's promise.

PART II

THE PROBLEM OF JUSTIFICATION AND MERIT

IN MODERN CATHOLIC THEOLOGY

CHAPTER III

THE DEBATE ON LUTHER'S DOCTRINE OF JUSTIFICATION AND
CRITICISM OF MERIT IN MODERN CATHOLIC THEOLOGY

The Evaluation of Luther's Doctrine of Justification

For Protestantism Luther's doctrine of justification to this day means the "heart of the Reformation" (das Heiligtum der Reformation).[1] Although the teaching did not stand in the center from the very beginning of the struggle, its central position in the controversy was soon discovered.[2]

As soon as this position had crystallized, Catholic theology set its doctrine of merit against it like a dam. None of the recognized Catholic polemicists of that time (Eck, Cochlaeus, Dietenberger, Mensing, Cajetan, Vehe) failed to set the doctrine of merit against Luther's "Manichaeism."[3] To deny it was considered "antichristian."[4] In Trent, where they prided themselves that the

---

[1] Dantine, Gerechtmachung des Gottlosen, p. 11.

[2] With the Enchiridion of the Franciscan Nikolaus Herborn (1529) the struggle about justification stepped up to first position. Before that, indulgence, sacrament of penance, power of the keys, and purgatory dominated the discussion. See Hubert Jedin, "Wo sah die vortridentinische Kirche die Lehrdifferenzen mit Luther?," Cath(M) 21 (1967):85-91.

[3] See Vinzenz Pfnür, Einig in der Rechtfertigungslehre? (Wiesbaden: F. Steiner, 1970), p. 233. Luther clearly had guarded himself against such an interpretation (WA 1, 224, 20-21).

[4] Nikolaus Herborn, "Locorum communium adversus huius temporis haereses enchiridion," in CCath 12, 32, 32-33.

doctrine of justification could not have been handled better even if all universities and the Lutherans had been present,[1] the doctrine of merit was defined as a fruit of justification,[2] and the Reformers, who denied it, were condemned with an anathema.[3] The council thereby sketched the framework in which the later polemical theology was to move. Thus, Bellarmine could speak of the question of merit as a main controversy (<u>controversia principalis</u>),[4] which had only arisen because the Reformers represented the absurd teaching that no justifying power resides in works[5] and had, therefore, simply dismissed works.[6] From this false freedom (<u>falsa libertas christiana</u>)[7] Calvin, for example, had with boldness denied the concept of merit in the Holy Scriptures,[8] although it is set forth so clearly in passages like Sir 16:14; Heb 13:16; 2 Th 1:5; and Rev 3:4; 16:6.[9]

Bossuet indeed said that neither Luther nor his early followers had anything to criticize in the doctrine of merit (<u>on</u>

---

[1] See Jedin, <u>Konzil von Trient</u>, 2:207.

[2] <u>DS</u> 1545; <u>Catech. Rom.</u> 2, 5, qu. 67.

[3] <u>DS</u> 1582; 1583.

[4] Robert Bellarmine, <u>Opera omnia</u>, 12 vols. (Paris: L. Vivès, 1870-74), 6:343.

[5] "Sententia absurdissima, ab ignoratione Scripturae profecta." Ibid., 6:193.

[6] Ibid., 6:294-95, 314.   [7] Ibid., 6:306.

[8] "Qua incredibili arrogantia non solum totam antiquitatem temere et impudenter accusat, sed ipsum etiam Spiritum sanctum corrigit, qui in factis litteris haec ipsa nomina . . . extare voluit." Ibid., 6:343.

[9] Ibid., 6:344.

n'y trouvait rien encore à reprendre dans le mérite),[1] but in the Formula of Concord all this was destroyed by the later Lutherans.[2] Of course, for Bossuet Luther's assurance of salvation was unbearable (l'Eglise ne peut pas souffrir un tel scandale).[3] He sees three reasons in the doctrine of merit for a separation between the churches: (1) because the Lutherans deny a complete fulfillment of the law; (2) because they deny the concept of condign merit, which is so dear to Catholics (dont tous nos livres sont pleins); and (3) because they assert that all works of the Christian need the acceptance of God.[4] Therefore the Catholic Church and the Augsburg Confession will always be separate (sera éternellement séparée de la nôtre).[5]

In spite of this, toward the end of the seventeenth century, models of reunion which have had an effect to the present day[6] were designed at scholarly levels, especially in correspondence between Bossuet and Leibniz. The exposition-model, e.g., explained the conflict about justification and merit as a word-battle on the basis of misunderstandings. If the Protestants had better understood the Catholic teaching, they would have been able to agree with it. Beside this there was proposed the deference-model, which foresaw the Catholics giving in in customs (celibacy and the lay chalice)

---

[1] Jacques B. Bossuet, Oeuvres, 4 vols. (Paris: F. Didot Frères, 1870), 4:41.

[2] Ibid., 4:42.   [3] Ibid., 4:11.

[4] Ibid., 4:42.   [5] Ibid.

[6] See Manfred P. Fleischer, Katholische und lutherische Ireniker (Göttingen: Musterschmidt, 1968), p. 55.

and the Protestants giving in in doctrine. Leibniz himself viewed the controversy about justification and merit as an inappropriate struggle (<u>importunae quaedam lites</u>).[1] Finally a third idea was proposed, the <u>suspension-model</u> in which insoluble questions (papal primacy and the immaculate conception of Mary) should for the time being be laid aside until a future union council could meet to solve them.

At ecclesiastical levels these irenics did not penetrate; the general polemical theology, on the one hand, took no notice of it, for Luther's rejection of merits appeared to be a contradiction to the Bible and to sound human understanding, a teaching "which opens the door to all kinds of abomination and disorder" (<u>die allem Greuel und allen Unordnungen Tür und Tor öffnet</u>).[2] Catholic polemicists argued, on the other hand, that the sinner, in order to draw the grace of God upon himself, is to practice good works; and the righteous one is to perform good works in order to persevere in grace as well as to earn a "beautiful reward" (<u>schöner Lohn</u>) for himself.[3] Without this cooperation heaven is not to be attained,[4] for the Catholic faith does not teach that the human becomes righteous <u>only</u> through faith, but "through faith together with good works."[5]

---

[1] Fleischer, <u>Ireniker</u>, pp. 60-61.

[2] Johann J. Scheffmacher, <u>Kontroverskatechismus</u> (Strassburg: Le Roux, n.d.), p. 100.

[3] Ibid., p. 98.

[4] Ibid., p. 99.

[5] Ibid., p. 176.

Under the moralizing influence of the Enlightenment in the eighteenth century, Catholic theologians moved up into a veritable merit-eudaemonism. The best example of this is Benedikt Stattler.[1] For him, merits are an increase of happiness. The law thereby serves as a "practical motivator to the good" (praktischer Antrieb zum Guten) allowing an increase in human self-merits. Thus, with the amount of self-participation in redemption, the happiness of the person is also increased. God cannot overlook these accomplishments; He **must** give the reward. Such salvation, worked out and earned, is a higher good than the reward of grace! In this highest happiness the punishment of the evildoers is included. In order to convert them, God employs the fear of hell, which belongs to the basic motivation of human virtue.

The struggle between the denominations, newly kindled by the conservative tendencies of the Restoration period (the first half of the nineteenth century), brought to maturity a new Catholic self-consciousness into the camp of polemical controversy. With Möhler's Symbolik began a Catholic offensive against the foundations of the Reformation which did not shy away from demonstrating its triumphalism exactly with reference to the doctrine of merit:

> Es kann also der Himmel von den Gläubigen verdient werden? Nicht anders: sie müssen ihn sogar verdienen . . . Befördert aber diese Lehre die Werkheiligkeit nicht? Gerade darin geht ihre Bestimmung auf, heilige Werke zu Tage zu fördern. Ruft sie nicht Selbstgerechtigkeit hervor? Das soll sie eben; bewirken nämlich, dass wir selbst gerecht werden.[2]

---

[1] See F. Scholz, "Benedikt Stattler," in Katholische Theologen Deutschlands im 19. Jh., ed. Heinrich Fries and Georg Schwaiger, 3 vols. (Munich: Kösel, 1975), 1:22-23.

[2] Johann A. Möhler, Symbolik, 5th ed. (Mainz: F. Kupferberg, 1838), pp. 201, 205.

The Catholic doctrine assures the "value of the moral law" (Würde des Sittengesetzes); the Protestant doctrine gives it up in the realm of religion.[1] The Catholic teaching is "removal of sin, the uprooting of sin" (Entsündigung . . . Entwurzelung von der Sünde);[2] while the Protestant teaching stands in danger of "turning the redemption in Christ into foolishness" (die Erlösung in Christo in eine Torheit zu verwandeln).[3] Only the religious side is light in the Reformation, the moral side is "dark."[4] In Luther's ethics, humanity would regress to a primordial time when divinity and humanity could not be distinguished and the deeds of both were assimilated.[5] Fortunately, Möhler adds that the Reformers were not conscious of this ethical lack. If they had understood what they taught, they would have rejected their ideas as unchristian.[6] In any case, Luther's doctrine of the unfree will is "a proof of his unscientific spirit" (ein Beweis seines unwissenschaftlichen Geistes).[7] While the Reformer conceded to morality only a temporal value,[8] the Catholic teaching derives salvation from the "undivided inner life of the born again" (ungeteilt inneres Leben des Wiedergeborenen), "from faith and love, from fulfilling of the law" (aus dem Glauben und der Liebe, der Gesetzeserfüllung) or "from the united religious and moral factor" (aus dem vereinten religiösen und sittlichen Moment).[9] Justification is to salvation as cause is

---

[1] Ibid., p. 243.
[2] Ibid., pp. 139-40.
[3] Ibid., p. 243.
[4] Ibid.
[5] Ibid., p. 245.
[6] Ibid., p. 243.
[7] Ibid., p. 252.
[8] Ibid., p. 235.
[9] Ibid., pp. 241-42.

to effect,[1] for salvation develops from the removal of sin,[2] and removal of sin, on the other hand, makes merit possible.[3] The Protestants should first of all learn the difference between self- and grace-work before they simply identify one with the other and reject both.[4]

Rougher tones were adopted by Giovanni Perrone, one of the leading lights of New Scholasticism, which took responsibility for the restorative tendencies of Catholic theology in the second half of the nineteenth century.

The heretics of the sixteenth century--so he writes-- recognize no merit in the justified one; indeed, they even shy back away from the word merit.[5] They have thereby invented a comfortable way of redemption which is unknown even to Gentiles and Muslims.[6] The consequences that grow from this are catastrophic for morality (absurda . . . et impia corollaria).[7] Nevertheless these filthy heretics (hi sordidi haeretici) have dared to rise up as reformers of the Church![8]

Matthias Scheeben, the best-known German dogmatician in the nineteenth century, also described Luther's teaching as "confusion of the most elementary moral concepts" (Konfusion der

---

[1] Ibid., p. 202.   [2] Ibid.
[3] Ibid., p. 200.   [4] Ibid., p. 205.

[5] Giovanni Perrone, Praelectiones theologicae in compendium redactae, 49th ed., 2 vols. (Rome: H. Marietti, 1901), 2:219.

[6] Ibid.   [7] Ibid., 2:217.

[8] Ibid.

elementarsten sittlichen Begriffe)[1] and accused it together with theological and anthropological heresies as "a heap of the worst moral errors" (eine Menge schwerster sittlicher Irrtümer).[2] In contrast to that, he reminded the people that, according to Catholic doctrine, it was through good works that one had to increase his "capital of grace" and multiple it,[3] and, thereby, one could "in a real sense earn and buy [heaven]" (im eigentlichen Sinne [den Himmel] verdienen und erkaufen).[4] God must give the "appropriate reward" for the works.[5] Scheeben thereby sketched a hierarchy of merits: i.e., two persons who do the same thing are not necessarily equal if one, on the basis of earlier merits, has collected more grace and thus stands in higher regard with God (just as indeed in public life one who is at a higher level always earns more). Through more "capital of grace" the Christian becomes ever "more worthy and more loved by [God]" (würdiger und mehr von [Gott] geliebt).[6] Through this higher position of grace the worth of each act "increases."[7] Therefore Christians should pay attention "to earning as much as possible with Him [God]" (soviel als möglich bei ihm [Gott] zu verdienen),[8] and to avoid

---

[1] Matthias J. Scheeben, Handbuch der katholischen Dogmatik, 2nd and 3rd ed., 6 vols. (Freiburg i. Br.: Herder, 1943-61), 6:176.

[2] Ibid.

[3] Scheeben, Die Herrlichkeiten der göttlichen Gnade, 17th ed. (Freiburg i. Br.: Herder, 1949), p. 43.

[4] Ibid., p. 179.   [5] Ibid.

[6] Ibid., p. 182.   [7] Ibid.

[8] Ibid., pp. 183, 187.

sin, in order to not lose the "precious treasures of merits" (die kostbaren Schätze von Verdiensten) which one has "through many years collected with effort and strain" (die man viele Jahre hindurch mit Mühe und Anstrengung gesammelt hat).[1] Thus, according to Scheeben, Trent rightly damned all who deny the doctrine of merit.[2]

About the turn of the twentieth century the polemic against Luther's teaching of meritless, consecutive justice of life reached a new high point through the beginning of Catholic research on Luther (Denifle, Grisar). Its subjective and aggressive theses are rejected by the Catholic research of today and are categorized as "moral and scientific execution" (moralische und wissenschaftliche Hinrichtung)[3] or as "demonization . . . which has no equal" (Verteufelung . . . die ihresgleichen nicht hat).[4] Nevertheless, as historical witnesses, they cannot be passed over in silence. For Hartmann Grisar, Luther's person and teaching are a psychopathological case. Luther was an "abnormal character."[5] His sickly spirit drove him into his teaching. His lack of appreciation of good works demonstrates surely a defective character.[6] No wonder, therefore, that Luther could not comprehend the Catholic principle of merit, that "wonderful edifice of doctrine, which corresponds to the reasonable

---

[1] Ibid., p. 185.   [2] Ibid., p. 279.

[3] Hubert Jedin, Die Erforschung der kirchlichen Reformationsgeschichte seit 1876 (Darmstadt: Wissenschaftliche Buchgesellschaft, 1975), p. 22.

[4] Otto H. Pesch, "Abenteuer Lutherforschung," NOrd 20 (1966):419.

[5] Grisar, Luthers Leben und Werk, p. 79.

[6] Ibid.

and free nature of humanity as well as to the goodness of God" (<u>jenes herrliche, der vernünftigen und freien Natur des Menschen ebenso wie der Güte Gottes entsprechende Lehrgebäude</u>).[1] On the other hand, Heinrich Denifle thought very differently. For him Luther and his teaching are a theological-moral case. In everything Luther's "damned half-knowledge" (<u>verfluchte Halbwisserei</u>)[2] and his "philosophy of the flesh" (<u>Philosophie des Fleisches</u>)[3] are at fault. The former hindered him from understanding the Catholic <u>habitus</u>-doctrine, and the latter made the effect of his teaching into a "seminar of sins and vices" (<u>Seminar von Sünden und Lastern</u>).[4] Denifle goes on to say that because Luther had a character of little worth (<u>Luther, in dir ist nichts Göttliches</u>),[5] with the rejection of the doctrine of merit he fell back on a teaching of little worth, the acceptance-doctrine of Ockham. With the teaching of "mere faith" (<u>blosser Glauben</u>)[6] and of the acceptance-necessity of works, he created a doctrine against "sound reason" (<u>gegen die gesunde Vernunft</u>)[7] and for covering up his immorality.[8] Thereby he separated life and teaching,[9] which led to catastrophic moral decadence in the life of the people. Since 1530 melancholy, heaviness of spirit, anguish of conscience,

---

[1] Ibid., p. 66.

[2] Heinrich Denifle, <u>Luther und Luthertum</u>, 2nd ed., 2 vols. (Mainz: F. Kirchheim, 1904), 1:666, 681.

[3] Ibid., 1:787. [4] Ibid., 1:799.

[5] Ibid., 1:797. [6] Ibid., 1:606.

[7] Ibid., 1:608, 612. [8] Ibid., 1:605.

[9] Ibid., 1:804.

despair, and suicide prevailed among his followers.[1]

At that same time, similar judgments raged among Catholic apologists and dogmatists. According to Paul Schanz, Luther's rejection of the doctrine of merit was a "peril to morality" (Gefährdung der Sittlichkeit).[2] With the Reformation, "a wholly new barbarity" (eine ganz neue Barbarei)[3] set in. The most beautiful flowers of Christian holiness were destroyed[4] and with the Reformation the lax elements of society won the upper hand.[5] On the other hand, the Catholic could point with pride to the holiness of his Church.[6]

With Heinrich and Gutberlet, the classical Catholic dogmatists in the area of the German language about the turn of the century, Luther's enslaved will is apostrophized as "inhuman doctrine" (unmenschliche Lehre).[7] The abiding root of sin, the sole agency of God, and the assurance of salvation did not get any better treatment. The first is an "unreasonable assertion that blasphemes God" (unsinnige, gotteslästerliche Behauptung),[8] the second a "horrible theory" (haarsträubende Theorie),[9] and the last "arrogance" (Anmassung).[10] Merit on the other hand appears as

---

[1] Ibid., 1:782.

[2] Paul Schanz, Apologie des Christentums, 3rd ed., 3 vols. (Freiburg i. Br.: Herder, 1906), 3:382.

[3] Ibid., 3:383. [4] Ibid., 3:381.

[5] Ibid., 3:379. [6] Ibid., 3:386.

[7] Heinrich and Gutberlet, Dogmatische Theologie, 8:483.

[8] Ibid., 8:484. [9] Ibid., 8:512.

[10] Ibid., 8:531.

justified "claim to payment" (<u>Anspruch auf Belohnung</u>)[1] and is a "return" (<u>Gegenleistung</u>)[2] of the person to God. Joseph Wilhelm and Thomas B. Scannell, the English revisers of Scheeben, can therefore describe Luther's struggle against the doctrine of merit only as "comical and perhaps tragical,"[3] since the merit of Christ and merits of the believer nevertheless complete each other harmoniously. Luther's denial of merits--thus the Italian dogmatician Tabarelli supplements--is simply an "immoral doctrine" (<u>immoralis doctrina</u>).[4]

Not a single one of the known Catholic theologians of the nineteenth century omitted a condemnation of Luther's teaching of justification, and all portrayed it as the very ground of separation of the confessions. And hardly any of the arguments with which Luther's teaching was already slandered at the time of the Reformation was omitted.

Thus, from Erasmus and Cochlaeus right on into recent times the thought continues that Luther's justification doctrine is Manichaean. Möhler used this label[5] and Scheeben repeated it.[6] Tabarelli speaks of the "mystical determinism."[7]

---

[1] Ibid., 8:644, 659.   [2] Ibid., 8:645.

[3] Joseph Wilhelm and Thomas B. Scannell, <u>A Manual of Catholic Theology</u>, 3rd ed., 2 vols. (London: Kegan, Trench, Trübner, 1908), 2:262.

[4] Tabarelli, <u>De gratia Christi</u>, p. 465.

[5] "Manichäistisch-gnostische Weltbetrachtung." <u>Symbolik</u>, pp. 248, 252.

[6] "Die Lehre der Reformatoren über die Beschaffenheit des Erbsünders . . . deckt sich fast ganz mit der manichäischen Lehre." <u>Dogmatik</u>, 6:172.

[7] "Mysticismus-deterministicus." <u>De gratia Christi</u>, p. 14.

Luther's ideas on justification were put down by his Catholic contemporaries as "vain delusions and puffed-up empty words" (eitel spiegelfechten mit aufgeblasenen leeren worten),[1] as "unapostolic and unprophetic opinion" (unapostolische und unprophetische opinion),[2] and as "pure vanity" (merae inaniae).[3] And there is no great difference between these opinions and the judgments of the nineteenth-century writers when, for example, Möhler speaks of "onesided and erroneous" (einseitig und irrig),[4] John Henry Newman of a "system of words without ideas,"[5] and Denifle of "confusion and emptiness of concepts" (Begriffsverwirrung und Begriffslosigkeit).[6]

The same is true concerning the accusation that Luther's justification doctrine is lax and lends impetus to immorality. The Edict of Worms already had charged against Luther, "he lives the life of a beast."[7] His theological opponents did not become tired of setting this immorality into connection with his teaching on justification, which they said brought forth all moral evils

---

[1] Johann Cochlaeus, "Ein nötig und christlich bedencken," in CCath 18, 9, 26.

[2] Georg Witzel, "Antwort auff Martin Luthers bekennete artickel," in CCath 18, 68, 7-8.

[3] Ambrosius Catharinus Politus, "Apologia pro veritate catholicae et apostolicae fidei," in CCath 27, 286, 17.

[4] Möhler, Symbolik, p. 139.

[5] John Henry Newman, Lectures on the Doctrine of Justification (Westminster, Md.: Christian Classics, 1966), p. 179.

[6] Denifle, Luther und Luthertum, 1:612.

[7] See Roland H. Bainton, Here I Stand (New York: Abingdon-Cokesbury Press, 1950), p. 189.

(leichtvertigkeit, vermessenheit und onbillicher frevel)[1] and made people hate the good.[2] The Catholic judgments of the nineteenth and the beginning of the twentieth centuries remain thoroughly in the realm of this characterization when Ignaz von Döllinger apostrophizes the Protestant doctrine of justification as "soul-murdering heresy of the time" (seelen-mörderische Häresie der Zeit)[3] which allows no true consciousness of sin to arise and stifles every arousal of conscience in the illusion of assurance of salvation.[4] Grisar seconds him, as he sets forth the thesis: Luther designed his doctrine of justification only in order to find appeasement in his own personal sad struggle (Beschwichtigung in seinem eigenen persönlichen traurigen Ringen).[5] Only rarely at that time was it mentioned by Catholics that the Reformation really had only arisen "because the Germans had the need to be pious" (C. M. Hofbauer).[6] The general opinion went toward the idea that the Lutheran doctrine of justification caused great damage and represented, from the Reformation on, the decisive and irreversible ground of separation. Döllinger expressed it clearly

---

[1] Johann Hoffmeister, "Wahrhafftige entdeckung unnd widerlegung," in CCath 18, 139, 1-3.

[2] Johann Eck, Enchiridion, trans. F. L. Battles, 2nd ed. (Grand Rapids, MI: Calvin Theological Seminary, 1978), p. 55.

[3] Ignaz von Döllinger, Kirche und Kirchen, Papsttum und Kirchenstaat, 2nd ed. (Munich: Cotta, 1861), p. 341.

[4] Idem, Die Reformation, 3 vols. (Frankfort/M.: Minerva, 1962), 3:43.

[5] Grisar, Luther's Leben und Werk, p. 99.

[6] See Loewenich, Der moderne Katholizismus, p. 18.

in his early ultramontanistic work Die Reformation:

> Denn nicht die bittere Stimmung und friedhässige Gesinnung einzelner, nicht die allerdings tief eingreifende Verkettung zeitlicher Interessen und Leidenschaften mit der Sache des Protestantismus--nicht diese Dinge waren es, welche die Unionsversuche vereitelten und die Trennung zu einer bleibenden machten, sondern der letzte und entscheidende Grund lag in dem Mittelpunkt der neuen Lehre--<u>der Lehre von der Rechtfertigung des Menschen</u>. Hier war jede Verständigung unmöglich, jede Annäherung schon illusorisch.[1]

How great a change of direction has taken place in the Catholic position since then, we could already ascertain from the first chapter. But there we were concerned with only one, though important, part of the question: Luther's Paulinism. Now we must ask whether this breakthrough and change in the Catholic theology of the twentieth century can also be shown for the teaching of justification as a whole--dogmatic, ethical, and historical.

We begin with four possible positions which should help us to answer the question: (1) Luther's teaching of justification is now, as it was then--judged from the Catholic standpoint--false and heretical: any change in the evaluation of his teaching cannot be established; the question about consensus must be answered with an unequivocal "No." (2) It is possible to perceive a rapprochement between the Catholic interpretation and that of Luther: Luther's doctrine of justification is in part orthodox, in part heretical; the question of a consensus must be answered with both "Yes" and "No." (3) If one interprets it correctly, Luther's teaching is Catholic: the question of a consensus can be affirmed in essence. (4) Luther's teaching of justification is

---

[1] Döllinger, Reformation, 3:3.

biblical-reformational: the Catholic Church must learn from it and integrate it into its thought and deed; the consensus is self-evident and allows no separation of churches, only at most that of schools. Magisterium and Church must, however, first internalize this knowledge.

<u>Luther's teaching is heretical</u>. For this viewpoint witnesses can be found both in the Catholic research in church history (Luther-research) and in the dogmatics of the twentieth century, most of them from the time before Vatican II.

While a large part of German research on Luther with F. X. Kiefl, S. Merkle, J. Lortz, A. Herte, and J. Hessen already in the 1930s and 1940s had moved away from Döllinger, Janssen, Grisar, and Denifle, their influence, especially that of Denifle, predominated for a long time in French circles (L. Cristiani, J. Paquier).[1]

Here the accusations of the Counter-Reformation and the ultramontanistic theology were simply repeated. For Cristiani, Luther's view of justification was only a comfortable teaching (<u>mystique commode</u>),[2] which gave impetus to moral irresponsibility and led to a cheap quieting of conscience.[3] Only immoral people, therefore, became followers of Luther.[4] According to Cristiani, Luther had learned of double justification in Italy with Giles of

---

[1] See Richard Stauffer, <u>Le catholicisme à la découverte de Luther</u> (Neuchâtel: Delachaux & Niestlé, 1966), pp. 19-38.

[2] <u>DTC</u>, s.v. "Réforme," by L. Cristiani.

[3] Cristiani, <u>Luther et le Luthéranisme</u>, p. 204.

[4] <u>DTC</u>, s.v. "Réforme," by L. Cristiani.

Viterbo and Seripando[1] and had made out of it an illogical system of romantic mysticism.[2] Luther's view is no doctrine but an autobiography.[3] If one wished to speak of a doctrine, then one must call the whole a curiosity (<u>doctrine bizzare</u>).[4]

For Paquier, also, the teaching is unacceptable. According to him it is Luther's own subjective view, a contradictory, vague mixture of Augustinianism and Platonism; from Nominalism Luther took over the contempt for reason, from Augustinianism the contempt for works. Luther's theology fluctuates from pessimism to optimism. He cannot be right, for he overlooks the logic of the idea of merit. Assurance of salvation is dangerous and immoral, trusting faith is dark and contradictory, and the rejection of the <u>gratia creata</u> is pantheistic idealism. With Luther's doctrine of justification, one could also justify murder, for indeed nothing could harm the believer.[5]

These theses were carried to the extreme by Jacques Maritain. Although he was a philosopher and neither a historian nor a theologian, in his work <u>Trois Réformateurs</u> he took the liberty of pronouncing judgment on Luther and his teaching. The work reached many educated people and was translated into Italian by later Pope Paul VI.[6]

What Maritain says about the person of Luther is not the

---

[1] Ibid.   [2] Ibid.

[3] Ibid.   [4] Ibid.

[5] <u>DTC</u>, s.v. "Luther," by J. Paquier.

[6] See John P. Dolan, <u>History of the Reformation</u> (New York: Desclee, 1965), p. 48.

object of our investigation; we can give attention only to his views about Luther's doctrine of justification. Maritain is also certain that Luther's teaching is the product of his experience, that it is a covering for immorality,[1] the result of a misunderstood Augustine,[2] pure egocentricity (égoïsme métaphysique),[3] and with its extrinsic understanding of grace, "despairing Pelagianism" (Pélagianisme de désespoir).[4] But Pelagianism is heresy. Luther, with his view of radical evil, prepared the way for the philosophy of Kant, Schelling, and Schopenhauer.[5] For a Thomist like Maritain, this was the sin par excellence!

Although, as indicated above, German Catholic scholarship on Luther was above all inclined toward a more objective interpretation of Luther himself, as well as of his thought, long before Vatican II, nevertheless, significant voices denied and continue to deny Luther's doctrine of justification. For Andreas Bigelmair it is a psychological result. In many ways it still shows connections with the teaching of the Catholic Church, but its deviations are better described with the word "revolution" than with "reformation." Luther's views are unacceptable to the Catholic Church.[6]

The historian Ernst Walter Zeeden in his work Martin Luther

---

[1] Jacques Maritain, Trois Réformateurs (Paris: Librairie Plon, 1925), p. 13.

[2] Ibid. [3] Ibid., pp. 19-23.

[4] Ibid., p. 25. [5] Ibid., p. 54.

[6] LTK, 1st ed., s.v. "Luther," by A. Bigelmair.

und die Reformation, which appeared after World War II, also deals marginally with Luther's justification doctrine. For him it is basically a new teaching,[1] a reduction of the gospel to justification,[2] the introduction of the subjectivity of conscience into theology.[3] Luther was driven to his teaching by his experience; the Catholic Church is led to her doctrine by the Holy Spirit.[4]

F. Richter, from whose work Martin Luther und Ignatius Loyola we have often cited already, expresses himself similarly. Luther's teaching of justification is contradictory,[5] a clear denial of the finality-character of works[6] and their meritoriousness,[7] an inadmissible reduction to the sola fide[8] and the overemphasis on a single doctrine.[9] It is not wholly capable of being united with the Catholic teaching.[10]

Here we must also mention the original, but wholly untenable, attempt by R. Weijenborg to explain the origin of the Reformation and Luther's teaching. Weijenborg attributes everything in Luther's Reformation back to Stotternheim. Luther, he says, fabricated this event in order to open the way for his entrance into the cloister. But because he could not find peace for his

---

[1] Ernst Walter Zeeden, Martin Luther und die Reformation, 2 vols. (Freiburg i. Br.: Herder, 1950), 1:20.

[2] Ibid., 1:16.   [3] Ibid., 1:18-19.

[4] Ibid.

[5] Richter, Luther and Loyola, pp. 75-76.

[6] Ibid., p. 80.   [7] Ibid., p. 82.

[8] Ibid., p. 93.   [9] Ibid., p. 96.

[10] Ibid., p. 79.

soul in the Catholic teaching, he established for himself a new doctrine. Thus, Luther's heresy began with the deception of Stotternheim![1]

But even in the immediate present--during and after Vatican II--some church historians and Luther-scholars characterize Luther's doctrine of justification as heretical. Hermann Tüchle, who himself can be reckoned with the Lortz school, speaks of a "heretical knowledge" of the Catholic in Luther. Why? Because the Reformer placed the good Catholic view of the given righteousness in a heretical connection with total human depravity, a consecutive way of salvation, the unmeritoriousness of works, and extrinsic grace.[2]

Paul Hacker also represents the view that Luther "disfigured" justification through his egocentric concept of faith.[3] This concept of faith, says Hacker, "opens a chasm between Catholicism and Luther's system."[4] The Catholic Church must insist on cooperation.[5] There cannot be any assurance of salvation for the Christian, because eternal salvation "is also dependent on his good works."[6] That the idea of merit was unfortunately given up by

---

[1] Reinoldus Weijenborg, "Miraculum a Martino Luthero confictum explicatne eius Reformationem?," Anton. 31 (1956):247-300. To the Lutheran scholar F. Lau, Weijenborg apologized for his brusque style but rescinded nothing as far as we can tell. See LuJ 33 (1966):118.

[2] Herman Tüchle, Geschichte der Kirche, 5 vols. (Einsiedeln: Benziger, 1963-77), 3:49-50.

[3] Paul Hacker, The Ego in Faith (Chicago: Franciscan Herald Press, 1970), p. 78.

[4] Ibid.   [5] Ibid.

[6] Ibid. p. 64.

Protestants and, in the present, also by "some progressive Catholics" is "a serious curtailment of the gospel," for it is "an essential part of the NT message."[1]

It is uncontended that the dogmaticians before Vatican II--we limit ourselves to Bartmann, Diekamp, Pohle and Gummersbach, Brinktrine, and Premm, as examples in the German-speaking realm--qualified Luther's teaching almost exclusively as heretical.[2]

The question, hotly debated in the late 50s whether one could speak of a consensus in Catholic theology with K. Barth on the basis of Küng's Rechtfertigung--the "good book" as K. Rahner called it--is also of importance for our investigation, since one can speak generally of a Reformation unity concerning justification.

K. Rahner, L. Bouyer, H. Fries, R. Grosche, E. Stakemeier, W. H. van de Pol, and others have confirmed Küng as giving the correct presentation of Catholic doctrine,[3] and since Barth has explained himself as basically in agreement with Küng's presentation, it was prematurely concluded that there was an agreement between Catholic and Reformation teaching concerning justification.

---

[1] Ibid., p. 81.

[2] "Unlösbare Antinomien." Bartmann, Dogmatik, 2:86. "Häretische . . . völlig veränderte Auffassung . . . der Rechtfertigung." Diekamp, Dogmatik, 2:432, 525. "Völlig neue Lehre . . . mit der Hlg. Schrift in offenem Widerspruch . . . Röm 3:28 gefälscht . . . absurde, allem gesunden Fühlen und Denken hohnsprechende Lehre . . . unsittlicher Antinomismus." Pohle and Gummersbach, Dogmatik, 2:688, 691, 694, 695. In justification there is "kein et-et, hier gibt es ein aut-aut: entweder ist die lutherische Rechtfertigungslehre richtig oder die katholische, die zugestandenermassen die der gesamten Tradition ist." Brinktrine, Lehre von der Gnade, p. 160. "Diese Lehre enthält eine Art Manichäismus." Premm, Glaubenskunde, 4:207.

[3] See Rahner, "Zur Theologie der Gnade," TQ 138 (1958):40-41.

Thereby the objections to which Bouillard and de Lubac have pointed, were and are overlooked, especially in the realm of the ontic making-righteous.[1] Johannes Witte, also on the basis of the difference between ontic and relational holiness, comes to the view that Barth's teaching does not basically agree with Catholic doctrine.[2] Heinrich Stirnimann formulated five points where he could see no consensus: Grace as gratia creata; justification as removal of sin; justification through love; justification not sola fide; and merit.[3] All these Catholic assertions, however, make Luther's teaching into heresy! It is therefore not to be wondered at if Catholic dogmaticians of today, with reference to Trent, reject Luther's justification as heretical.[4] We must ask, however, whether Luther's teaching is correctly reproduced, when Ott, for example, does not know anything else to say about Luther's doctrine of sanctification except that it is an external imputation of the righteousness of Christ![5]

Also in the present there is no lack of voices which remind us in their radicality of the polemic before Vatican II. According to Paul Toinet, for example, Luther's justification is "self-justification" (un système d'autojustification).[6] Here is a clear

---

[1] See Henri de Lubac, "Zum katholischen Dialog mit Karl Barth," Dok. 14 (1958):448-54.

[2] Johannes L. Witte, "Ist Barths Rechtfertigungslehre grundsätzlich katholisch?," MThZ 10 (1959):39, 48.

[3] Stirnimann, "Zur Rechtfertigung in dialektisch-katholischer Besinnung," SKZ 125 (1957):651-52.

[4] Ott, Dogmatik, p. 302.   [5] Ibid.

[6] Paul Toinet, Le problème de la vérité dogmatique (Paris: P. Téqui, 1973), p. 277.

continuation of Grisar! Luther is a false witness (faux témoin de la vérité évangélique),[1] the disputation with him is not ended, for Luther's teaching is unbiblical[2] and a protest of the autonomous, secular man[3] against the "motherly mediatorship" (médiation maternelle)[4] of the Catholic Church. Who does not recall, with these words, the aggressive criticism of Luther by the Popes (Leo XIII, Pius X)[5] about the turn of the century? The only thing that Toinet agrees with in Luther's teaching is Luther's subjective good will. Only with the passage of time have we come to understand what Luther really had done.[6] Similar words--as we have seen--have already been found in Möhler! Only the Catholic doctrine of justification, which needs the mediation of the Church, is correct--so Toinet says--for it unmasks the false arrogance of autonomy.[7]

Luther's teaching is partly orthodox. The astounding progress since Lortz of Catholic research on Luther could not remain without consequences in the judgment of Luther's doctrine of jusification. It not only set in motion a change in the assessment of the person of the Reformer, but in part also in the evaluation of his ideas, which O. H. Pesch has described excellently as "breakthrough of a 'new style'" (Durchbruch eines "neuen Stils").[8]

---

[1] Ibid., p. 276.   [2] Ibid., pp. 277-78.

[3] Ibid., p. 277.   [4] Ibid., p. 279.

[5] See Loewenich, Der moderne Katholizismus, pp. 303-04.

[6] Toinet, Vérité dogmatique, p. 278.

[7] "Elle démystifie la fausse prétention à l'autonomie." Ibid., p. 279.

[8] Pesch, "Abenteuer Lutherforschung," NOrd 20 (1966):420.

Those who dared to describe Luther as homo religiosus (Lortz),[1] homo propheticus (Hessen),[2] indeed, as "prophet" (Lortz, Olivier),[3] as well as "a theologian of the first rank" (Lortz)[4] and the "first evangelical theologian in the Church" (Brandenburg)[5] could not possibly reject his teaching wholesale. Werner Beyna has clearly indicated the change in the Catholic evaluation of the person of Luther.[6] We shall apply ourselves in brief to the new evaluation of Luther's doctrine of justification.

In the Reformer's teaching are contained essential elements that from the Catholic standpoint can be recognized as correct and true. This was already conceded by representatives of an ecumenically oriented polemical theology (A. and E. Stakemeier, P. Bläser, L. Bouyer, W. H. van de Pol, H. J. Schmidt, C. Moeller, Y. Congar) in the years immediately before Vatican II. At the same time, however, this position articulated still decisive reservations against Luther's teaching of justification. From its standpoint we could speak at most about a drawing nearer of views, but not of a consensus.

---

[1]Quoted in Johannes Hessen, Luther in katholischer Sicht, 2nd ed. (Bonn: Röhrscheid, 1949), p. 16.

[2]Ibid., p. 24.

[3]Lortz, "Grundzüge," in Reformata Reformanda, 1:220; Olivier, Le procès Luther, pp. 7-8.

[4]Lortz, "Grundzüge," in Reformata Reformanda, 1:220. Ein "Theologe von grossartigem Rang."

[5]Albert Brandenburg, Die Zukunft des Martin Luther (Münster i.W.: Aschendorff, 1977), p. 41. Der "erste evangelische Theologe in der Kirche."

[6]Werner Beyna, Das moderne katholische Lutherbild (Essen: Ludgerus Verlag, 1969).

A. and E. Stakemeier asserted that Luther's doctrine of the assurance of salvation was not rejected at the Council of Trent.[1] Stephanus Pfürtner some years later defended a far-reaching rapprochement between Thomistic hope of salvation and Lutheran assurance of salvation, so that in his view both confessions "have maintained basically the same understanding of the hope of salvation."[2]

Hessen convincingly proved that Luther's teaching was not self-appeasement, but that it meets the genuine thirst of the soul for salvation.[3] Schmidt, also, who seeks largely psychological explanations,[4] had to concede that Luther's doctrine of justification represented a "basic Christian concern" (Christliches Uranliegen).[5]

According to Bläser and Van de Pol, nobody can continue to assert that Luther's teaching is a matter of cheap grace. On the contrary! With Luther there is justitia realis[6] and genuine sanctification.[7]

---

[1] A. Stakemeier, Trient über Heilsgewissheit, p. 175; E. Stakemeier, "Trienter Lehrentscheidungen," in Weltkonzil von Trient, 1:102.

[2] Stephanus Pfürtner, Luther and Aquinas--a Conversation; our Salvation, its Certainty and Peril, trans. Edward Quinn (London: Darton, Longman & Todd, 1964), p. 113.

[3] Hessen, Luther in katholischer Sicht, p. 24.

[4] Schmidt, Brückenschlag, pp. 127, 130.

[5] Ibid., p. 163.

[6] Bläser, "Gesetz und Evangelium," Cath(M) 14 (1960):22.

[7] Van de Pol, Reformatorisches Christentum, pp. 419, 427.

Bouyer, again, calls attention to how Catholic the sola gratia of Luther is, that it is absolutely not heresy, for with Luther, as well as with the Catholics, when it comes to the question of salvation everything depends on grace.[1] Charles Moeller agreed with this view of Bouyer[2] and rebuked Catholics for their frequent misunderstanding of the Protestant doctrine of justification.[3] The reproach that Protestantism favors immorality comes rather close to being a caricature of the Protestant teaching.[4] Congar also emphasizes that Luther's concept of a righteousness which does not come from man himself is really a "Catholic-traditional truth" (une vérité catholique, traditionnelle).[5]

But this surely does not mean that these theologians were ready to admit that Luther was right. Basically, the representatives of this position also viewed Luther's teaching as heretical. They believed that Luther was lacking in ethics,[6] in the correct understanding of grace,[7] in Catholic fullness,[8] and in the idea of

---

[1] Bouyer, Du Protestantisme à l'Eglise, p. 55.

[2] Charles Moeller, "Théologie de la grâce et oecuménisme," Irén. 28 (1955):22.

[3] Ibid., p. 19.   [4] Ibid., p. 42.

[5] Yves M. J. Congar, Vraie et fausse réforme dans l'Eglise (Paris: Les Editions du Cerf, 1950), p. 451.

[6] E. Stakemeier, "Trienter Lehrentscheidungen," in Weltkonzil von Trient, 1:86; Bläser, "Gesetz und Evangelium," Cath(M) 14 (1960): 22-23; Hessen, Luther in katholischer Sicht, pp. 51, 54.

[7] Moeller, "Théologie de la grâce et oecuménisme," Irén. 28 (1955):34-35, 50; Congar, Vraie et fausse réforme, p. 451; Bouyer, Du Protestantisme à l'Eglise, p. 149; Van de Pol, Reformatorisches Christentum, pp. 398, 420; Schmidt, Brückenschlag, pp. 157-58.

[8] Schmidt, Brückenschlag, pp. 154, 160.

merit,[1] and they accused him of a lack of appreciation for the sacraments and the Church.[2] There are, in fact, in addition to the positive aspects, many negative sides to Reformation thought.[3]

Attempts to come to a dialogue with Luther and his Protestant interpreters continued in the days of Vatican II. They continue in the present. The positive-negative pattern is also applied chronologically by Catholic researchers on Luther. According to the Lortz school model, the homo catholicus is to be separated from the teacher of error. But while the late Lortz and some of his followers (Iserloh, Manns) already list the justification teaching of Luther almost wholly, or indeed entirely, on the positive side, others like Jedin still see differences.[4] J. Wicks, an American representative of the Lortz school, describes Luther's early work in "admiring tones," but he is not silent about "critical points."[5] In the early Luther, until 1517 before the break with Rome, there were "Christian, and even Catholic riches" which must impress Catholics--indeed, which can even enrich their thought and life.[6] Luther's theology is a theology of grace, not Nominalism. Luther has connections with Augustine and Bernard, but he is basically an independent thinker.[7] Of course, there are also

---

[1] Ibid., pp. 144-48; E. Stakemeier, "Trienter Lehrentscheidungen," in Weltkonzil von Trient, 1:101.

[2] Van de Pol, Reformatorisches Christentum, pp. 389-92, 400-05.

[3] Bouyer, Du Protestantisme à l'Eglise, p. 162.

[4] Jedin, Kirche des Glaubens, 2:550.

[5] Wicks, Man Yearning for Grace, p. 277.

[6] Ibid., pp. 14-15. [7] Ibid., p. 267.

negatives: the excessive dualistic anthropology (flesh-spirit), the doctrine of assurance of salvation which led to a new theology of sacrament, a weakening of the person's moral responsibility, the teaching on sin, and Luther's individualism.[1] Finally, however, both camps, Protestant and Catholic, can learn from the early Luther and thus draw nearer together with a view to a future unity.[2]

Somewhat less optimistically, but in a similar way, the Italian Dino Bellucci argues. The early Luther still shows in the First Lecture on Psalms a remarkable theological sense (un spiccato senso teologico).[3] The new interpretation of justification teaching appears in the Lecture on Romans.[4] Luther's error was to have radically separated the first and second justification, that is, justification from progress in righteousness, living faith from work of love, which in the eyes of God has value as righteousness. That the initial righteousness of justification rises to a higher holiness, Luther did not understand.[5] His teaching of law and gospel, in which the law only condemns, forestalled his having the possibility of an understanding of intrinsic grace.[6] A further error of Luther was that he revolted when the Church refused to accept his view of justification.[7] This doctrine brought enormous suffering to Christendom;[8] causing us to ask whether Lutheran and

---

[1] Ibid., pp. 273-77. [2] Ibid., p. 280.

[3] Dino Bellucci, Fede e giustificazione in Lutero (Rome: Libreria Editrice dell 'Universita' Gregoriana, 1963), p. 260.

[4] Ibid., p. 261. [5] Ibid., p. 217.

[6] Ibid., p. 236. [7] Ibid., p. 261.

[8] Ibid.

Catholic justification really lie so far apart. For what Luther expresses with the <u>simul justus et peccator</u> can be stated by the Catholic with the concept of actual sin. Both finally believe that justification by faith must lead to sanctification.[1]

We can summarize this position of the "yes, but" in the view of De Letter as follows: "Luther's theology of grace . . . has its own religious values, but it is basically a misinterpretation of both St. Paul and St. Augustine."[2] We can also express this antagonism with Friedrich Heer thus: Luther's teaching is at the same time "horrible <u>and</u> delightful" (schauerlich <u>und</u> beglückend).[3]

Thus, on the one hand it can be conceded that Luther stands much nearer to the Catholic view than was previously thought,[4] that the separation between the positions has diminished,[5] but that differences remain[6] and the dispute has not yet been decided.[7]

---

[1] Ibid.

[2] <u>CDT</u>, s.v. "Grace," by P. De Letter. Cf. Henri Rondet, <u>Gratia Christi</u> (Paris: Beauchesne, 1948), p. 260.

[3] Friedrich Heer, <u>Europäische Geistesgeschichte</u> (Stuttgart: Kohlhammer, 1953), p. 248, italics mine.

[4] Moeller, "Grace and Justification," <u>LV</u> 19 (1964):721; Beer, "Ausgangspositionen," <u>Cath(M)</u> 21 (1967):84.

[5] Schmidt, <u>Brückenschlag</u>, pp. 166, 172, 208; Jedin, <u>Kirche des Glaubens</u>, 2:550; Josef Finkenzeller, "Der Mensch im Glanz des göttlichen Lebens," in <u>Wahrheit und Zeugnis</u>, ed. Michael Schmaus and Alfred Läpple (Düsseldorf: Patmos, 1964), p. 817.

[6] Schmidt, <u>Brückenschlag</u>, pp. 208, 286-87; Van de Pol, <u>Reformatorisches Christentum</u>, p. 405; Jedin, <u>Kirche des Glaubens</u>, 2:550.

[7] Volk, <u>Gesammelte Schriften</u>, 3:197.

Luther's doctrine of justification is Catholic. To many Catholic theologians the "yes, but" does not seem to correspond any more to the results of modern Luther-research. Since Vatican II the voices of those are multiplying (many among whom, like Lortz and Schmaus himself, were once recommenders of the "yes, but") who can see in Luther's doctrine of justification a thoroughly Catholic variant of the justification event. The condition is that Luther's teaching is "properly understood"[1] and interpreted in <u>optimam partem</u>.[2] The Catholic interpretation will be all the easier if Luther is not compared with Thomas Aquinas but, following the opinion of Manns,[3] with Bernard or--as Dettloff thinks[4]--with Duns Scotus.

We can observe the progress of this position, for example, with Schmaus, who in the sixth edition of his <u>Dogmatik</u> (1965) sets forth the possibility of a Catholic interpretation of the <u>simul justus et peccator</u> which permits the formula to be viewed "correctly."[5] This can be the case only in assuming that the Protestant concept does not push forward into the metaphysical sense but remains in the realm of the personal-existential significance.[6] Here, Catholic theology could join in with its concept of a metaphysical removal of sin and the existential actual sin. In the fifth

---

[1] Tavard, <u>Protestantism</u>, p. 30.

[2] Heinz Schütte, <u>Protestantismus</u>, 2nd ed. (Essen: Fredebeul & Koenen, 1967), p. 468.

[3] See Wicks, ed., <u>Catholic Scholars</u>, p. 119.

[4] Werner Dettloff, "Rechtfertigung," in <u>HThG</u>, 2:390.

[5] Schmaus, <u>Dogmatik</u>, 3/2:156.   [6] Ibid., 3/2:123-24.

edition of the same work (1956), it was still asserted that the
Protestant explanation of the formula denied every metaphysical
reference and only allowed the existential. Since this, however,
comprises only relational holiness and not ontic holiness, Luther's
teaching of the remaining sin in the light of Trent is to be categorized as heresy.[1]

The development to the Catholic integration of Luther can
be most clearly shown in the way that Lortz has developed. In his
Geschichte der Kirche he still speaks of a complete contradiction
between Luther's Reformation teaching of justification and the
dogma of the Catholic Church.[2] In six points he finds Luther's
teaching heretical: (1) in the doctrine of the radical corruption;
(2) in the impotence of the will, which can contribute nothing to
salvation; (3) in the ineradicability of concupiscence; (4) in the
sole agency of God, which takes away all worth from good works;
(5) in the simul justus et peccator, which permits only a covering
of sin but not an inner transformation; and (6) in the sola fide,
which leads to the assurance of salvation, a concept that is sometimes rather unclear in Luther's teaching.[3]

At the same time, however, Lortz in his book Die Reformation
in Deutschland introduced the change in Catholic research through
his new evaluation of the person of Luther--Luther was not a morally
worthless character, but a genuine homo religiosus.[4] In judging

---

[1] Schmaus, Dogmatik, 3/2:104-05.

[2] "Luthers reformatorische Ansicht widerstreitet vollkommen der Lehre der Kirche." Joseph Lortz, Geschichte der Kirche, 11th-14th ed. (Münster/W.: Aschendorff, 1948), p. 274, italics mine.

[3] Ibid.   [4] Idem, Reformation, 1:191.

the teaching of Luther, Lortz, however, stayed with the positive-negative pattern.

From then on, the positive moved steadily into the foreground. In <u>Die Reformation als religiöses Anliegen heute</u> Lortz drew up ten points of agreement with Luther: (1) world and person are nothing before God; (2) no one can justify himself without God and the justified one remains an unprofitable servant; (3) all righteousness comes from faith; (4) God's grace is necessary for the whole Christian life; (5) God's grace is always a free gift; (6) in trust one draws nearer to God, in love one serves Him; (7) the Christian freedom is a distinguishing mark of one who is saved; (8) God, however, is also Judge and sets serious demands before the person; (9) in everything Christ is in first rank; (10) the Word of God contains the truth and the power for redemption.[1]

However, Lortz had still to raise two great objections against Luther's theology, namely, that it is subjective and one-sided. Because Luther was an "excitable type" (<u>Erregungstyp</u>),[2] who could only hear himself, and because he did not explain justification from the totally Catholic view,[3] he discovered Catholic teaching for himself and oversimplified it into heresy.[4] This finds expression especially in the denial of the will and of merit.[5]

---

[1] Joseph Lortz, <u>The Reformation: A Problem for Today</u>, trans. John C. Dwyer (Westminster, MD: Newman Press, 1964), pp. 213-14.

[2] Idem, <u>Reformation</u>, 1:162.   [3] Ibid., 1:183.

[4] Ibid., 1:434; idem, <u>The Reformation</u>, p. 136.

[5] Idem, <u>Reformation</u>, 1:183, 187.

Since, however--as Lortz's student, Manns, expresses it--
Luther's "basic concern" (<u>Grundanliegen</u>) is Catholic, there exists
nevertheless the possibility of integration.[1] In this integration
of items that can be interpreted in a Catholic manner, Lortz has
come a long way. At first he was concerned with the discovery of
the <u>homo catholicus</u> in the teacher of error, then with the discovery of the Catholic teaching in the erroneous doctrine--whereby
the theological stand of Luther in the <u>Lecture on Romans</u> seems to
him thoroughly Catholic[2]--then with the discovery that Luther is
"much more Catholic"[3] than Lortz had imagined at the time of his
book on the Reformation. Therefore the "wealth of Luther must be
gathered into the Catholic Church" (<u>Der Reichtum Luthers muss in die
katholische Kirche heimgeholt werden</u>).[4] In past centuries this was
not possible, for in the period of the Reformation there held sway
on the Catholic side the theology of the "stubborn denial" (<u>stures
Neinsagen</u>) and of the "hate-filled destruction" (<u>hasserfüllte
Vernichtung</u>).[5] Even Trent did not sufficiently listen to Luther
and wished only a "line of separation" (<u>Trennungsstrich</u>).[6] From

---

[1] Peter Manns, et al., "Das 'Reformatorische' bei Luther," in <u>Um Reform und Reformation</u>, ed. August Franzen (Münster/W.: Aschendorff, 1968), p. 39.

[2] Lortz, "Römerbriefvorlesung," <u>TThZ</u> 71 (1962):247.

[3] Idem, "Grundzüge," in <u>Reformata Reformanda</u>, 1:218.

[4] Ibid.

[5] Idem, "Wert und Grenzen der katholischen Kontroverstheologie in der ersten Hälfte des 16. Jh.," in <u>Um Reform und Reformation</u>, pp. 19, 21.

[6] Ibid., p. 29.

Barock und Neuscholastik likewise no bridges to Luther could be built.[1] The difficulties of those times, however, are in the past today.[2] The Catholic research on Luther has at least caught up with the Protestant.[3] The result is surprising: Luther is, in the doctrine of justification, so Catholic that this teaching today permits no longer any ecclesiastical separation: "We [Catholics] agree with Luther on the main point."[4]

In this Lortz makes an effort to set boundaries for himself on two sides: against the men of the past on both Catholic and Protestant sides, who, however, do not count in the research,[5] and against the radically progressive Catholics who wish to make not only the Catholic but also the reformational Luther at home in Catholicism.[6] Only so far as what is Catholic can be discovered in Luther is it capable of being integrated. If something in Luther's teaching were not Catholic, then, it would have to be eliminated.[7] For justification, however, this by no means seems to be necessary.

Erwin Iserloh, the best-known student of Lortz, expresses himself in a similar way. He agrees with the words of Cardinal

---

[1] Ibid., p. 30.

[2] Idem, "Grundzüge," in Reformata Reformanda, 1:217.

[3] Ibid.

[4] Ibid., 1:244. "Wir [die Katholiken] sind eins mit Luther im Hauptpunkt."

[5] Ibid., 1:217.

[6] "Derartige neuere katholische Elucubrationes sind eine Gefährdung der christlichen Lehre . . . sie kanonisieren den Relativismus." Idem, "Wert und Grenzen," in Um Reform und Reformation, p. 31.

[7] Ibid.

Willebrands, that Luther has retained a "noteworthy grasp of the ancient Catholic faith"[1] and that he can in justification be a "common teacher."[2] The Luther of 1514/15 was "an original Catholic" (urkatholisch).[3] However, the decree of the ban upon Luther happened rightly, because Luther had gone beyond the Urkatholische with his teaching on mass and office.[4] The doctrine of justification, however, is excepted from this; it is not a matter to separate the churches.[5]

Even theologians and historians who do not belong to Lortz's school are of this opinion. Fries, for instance, denies the church-separating character of the teaching of justification.[6] He asks whether one cannot regard the confessions in a way similar to the theological schools of the Middle Ages,[7] in order then to speak of the total Christendom as of a "unity in diversity" (Einheit in Vielfalt).[8] Heinz Schütte uses for it the expression proposed by Cardinal Ratzinger, "reconciled difference" (versöhnte Verschiedenheit).[9] Rahner is of the opinion that the theologians

---

[1] Erwin Iserloh, "Aufhebung des Lutherbannes?," in Lutherprozess und Lutherbann, ed. Remigius Bäumer (Münster/W.: Aschendorff, 1972), p. 70.

[2] Ibid., p. 71.   [3] Ibid., p. 72.

[4] Ibid., p. 79.

[5] Idem, Luther und die Reformation, pp. 60, 118.

[6] Fries, "Die Bedeutung der Konfessionen heute," in Neues Glaubensbuch, p. 644.

[7] Ibid., pp. 654-55.   [8] Ibid., p. 657.

[9] Heinz Schütte, "Anerkennung der Confessio Augustana als katholisch?," ÖR 27 (1978):24.

of both confessions could well unite, if they would, over the threefold sola.[1] Since the sense of faith of the people in the separated churches is the same today,[2] and since one does not need to reckon in the future with any substantial new ex cathedra decision of Rome,[3] the large churches could unite institutionally even today.[4] If this is not yet the case, at least the theologians are not the most guilty for the division.[5] Such an integration, which in the doctrine of justification is thoroughly possible,[6] would mean, according to the view of the English Catholic historian Todd, a change and revival of the Catholic tradition.[7] The result of Lortz's research is this: The doctrine of justification does not establish any separation of the churches! The prominent Church historian shares this view with a considerable number of important representatives of contemporary Catholic theology.[8] It is remarkable that on the occasion of the 450th anniversary of the Reformation--also celebrated in Rome--Cardinal Jäger could assert that Luther's teaching on justification has today "hardly any more meaning to separate the

---

[1] Karl Rahner, "Ist Kircheneinigung dogmatisch möglich?," TQ 153 (1973):112.

[2] Ibid., p. 113.   [3] Ibid., p. 117.

[4] Ibid., p. 118.   [5] Ibid.

[6] John M. Todd, Martin Luther (London: Burns & Oates, 1964), p. 82.

[7] Ibid., p. 216.

[8] See Otto Karrer, Die christliche Einheit - Gabe und Aufgabe (Lucerne: Räber, 1963), p. 17; Hans Urs von Balthasar, Karl Barth-- Darstellung und Deutung seiner Theologie, 2nd ed. (Cologne: J. Hegner, 1962), p. 389; Wacker, Ökumenischer Dialog, p. 269; Leo Scheffczyk, "Die Einheit des Dogmas und die Vielheit der Denkformen," MThZ 17 (1966):233.

churches" (kaum mehr kirchentrennende Bedeutung).[1]

Luther's doctrine of justification is biblical-reformational. That Luther's teaching can be interpreted as Catholic is not the last word of contemporary Catholic theology. Since at the Third International Congress for Luther Research in 1966 in Järvenpää (Finland), the Catholic camp of Luther experts became visibly split, there is a debate between the "historians" (Lortz school) and the "systematicians."

O. H. Pesch, one of the leading "systematicians," formulates his criticism of the Lortz school as follows: (1) Lortz and his followers have, in their search for the Catholic Luther, overlooked the real material questions of Luther's Reformation theology.[2] (2) What in Luther goes beyond the Catholic position (the reformational Luther!) is not evaluated and exonerated with Lortz.[3] (3) The "historians" therefore have made it impossible for themselves to discuss the real Luther. This discussion would automatically lead to the question whether that which for 450 years was uncatholic must still today be regarded as uncatholic.[4] (4) The "reformational Luther" is the challenge for Catholic theology. From him, one has to learn and to ask whether his "whole

---

[1] HK 21 (1967):566. The nominal Catholic and evangelical Lutheran theological commission judged in 1971 in the so-called "Maltabericht" (point 26) that today they mark out a far-reaching consensus in interpretation of justification. See HK 25 (1971): 539; Harding Meyer, "La doctrine de la justification dans le dialogue inter-confessionnel mené par l'église lutherienne," RHPR 57 (1977):27.

[2] Pesch, "Abenteuer Lutherforschung," NOrd 20 (1966):423.

[3] Ibid., p. 424.   [4] Ibid., p. 425.

theological thought structure" does not represent a "Catholic possibility."[1] (5) Thereby criticism must also be exercised concerning Trent. The council is to be interpreted according to the present-day Catholic consciousness.[2]

This massive challenge has been answered by Manns in the name of the Lortz school. He points out to Pesch that that which for 450 years was uncatholic cannot today be Catholic;[3] that Pesch shies away from measuring Luther unambiguously and clearly against "Catholic truth";[4] that those who already before Pesch dealt with Luther about doctrine, as for example Przywara, Congar, Bläser, Moeller, Volk, and Van de Pol, have rightly remained far behind the challenge to need to learn from Luther,[5] and that the replacement of polemical theology by an "ecumenical theology"--as Pfürtner has proposed--which would be common to all Christendom hides within it great dangers.[6]

In spite of these objections the position of the "systematicians" asserts itself. It calls itself most recently "Ökumeniker" and also demands, according to the principle of the ecclesia semper reformanda in Luther's sense, a reformation of the teaching of the Catholic Church and an elimination of the "uncatholic elements" (Ausscheidung des "Unkatholischen").[7]

The difference between these representatives and the

---

[1] Ibid., p. 430.   [2] Ibid., p. 427.
[3] Manns, Lutherforschung, p. 42.   [4] Ibid., p. 40.
[5] Ibid., p. 10.   [6] Ibid., p. 44.

[7] Otto Hermann Pesch, "Der gegenwärtige Stand der Verständigung," Conc(D) 12 (1976):540.

"historians" is most easily understood where it concerns the function of Luther as a teacher of the Church. According to Manns, only the final step is lacking in order for Luther to draw together with the Catholic doctrine of justification.[1] Finally, however, Luther lacks Catholic harmony and fullness! Therefore as a teacher of the Church he comes only conditionally into question.

The "systematicians" think entirely differently! They reach toward Luther--as Heer generalized for the whole Catholic Church of the present day--as toward an "elixir" (Biotikum) and a "massive dose of vitamins" (Vitaminstoss).[2] One must learn from Luther![3] He manifests a "tremendous presence" (unheimliche Präsenz)[4] and he must, if the accents are newly set, attain the "right of domicile" (Heimatrecht) in the Catholic Church.[5] Only with Luther will Christendom overcome its split and master the challenges of the future.[6]

Accordingly, Luther's doctrine of justification is also evaluated positively. It appears as the "return to the gospel"[7]

___

[1] Manns, "Fides absoluta--Fides incarnata," in Reformata Reformanda, 1:311.

[2] Friedrich Heer, "Martin Luther," in Die Wahrheit der Ketzer, ed. Hans Jürgen Schultz (Stuttgart: Kreuz Verlag, 1968), p. 100.

[3] Olivier, Foi de Luther, p. 14; Hasler, Luther in der katholischen Dogmatik, p. 348.

[4] Brandenburg, Martin Luther gegenwärtig, p. 61.

[5] Ibid., p. 90; Otto Hermann Pesch, Ketzerfürst und Kirchenlehrer (Stuttgart: Calwer Verlag, 1971), p. 42.

[6] Brandenburg, Die Zukunft des Martin Luther, p. 81.

[7] Küng, "Katholische Besinnung," in Theologie im Wandel, p. 464.

and the "rediscovery of the original Pauline teaching,"[1] as a "precious gift,"[2] as a "unique theology of Word and a splendid theology of event,"[3] and as "liberating help"[4] which can preserve theology from a new "Late Scholasticism."[5]

The followers of this position thus do not doubt in the least that theological consensus has been attained with Luther in the doctrine of justification[6] and that Christendom has already entered, in reference to this problem, into a "post-ecumenical stage" (post-ökumenisches Stadium).[7] This claim is sustained in spite of Trent and the Catholic doctrine of merit.[8] The only thing still lacking is that the Church leadership on both sides must finally accept this consensus and put it into practice.[9] However, regarding what the chances are for such an official acceptance, the opinions differ. Küng and Pesch have judged the prospects optimistically,[10] the former, in any case, before the withdrawal of

---

[1] Ibid., p. 467.

[2] Pesch, Theologie der Rechtfertigung, p. 956.

[3] Brandenburg, Martin Luther gegenwärtig, p. 18.

[4] Johannes Brosseder, "Die katholische Lutherrezeption," Conc(D) 12 (1976):521.

[5] Pesch, Theologie der Rechtfertigung, p. 956.

[6] Hans Küng, Christ sein, 6th ed. (Munich: R. Piper, 1975), p. 493; Pesch, "Gottes Gnadenhandeln," in Mysterium Salutis, 4/2: 897, 913; Brosseder, "Die katholische Lutherrezeption," Conc(D) 12 (1976):517.

[7] Küng, "Anfragen," Ref. 27 (1978):377.

[8] Pesch, "Der gegenwärtige Stand," Conc(D) 12 (1976):540.

[9] Küng, Christ sein, p. 493.

[10] Ibid., p. 494; Pesch, "Gottes Gnadenhandeln," in Mysterium Salutis, 4/2:907.

his missio canonica, the other before his transfer to a Protestant faculty. The late Hasler, who from 1967-71 could gather experiences with the Roman Curia in the Secretariat for the Unity of Christians, expressed himself skeptically in the face of the ruling "court theology." Rome has not yet accepted the consensus of the theologians; it fears a shaking of its structure of faith. In spite of verbal asseverations one still thinks in categories of the traditional School theology.[1] The one who judged most pessimistically some time ago is Olivier. Since, according to the "systematicians," the doctrine of justification must fulfill a critical function of the Church,[2] there can be no unity on the highest plane, for Rome views itself as standing above every criticism. "Luther's Christianity is irreconcilable with Roman doctrine."[3]

The Justification of Luther's Criticism of Merit

With the predominantly positive evaluation of Luther's doctrine of justification, present Catholic theology sees itself facing a delicate question: If Luther in the article of justification truly is supposed to have been right in part or wholly, is then his criticism of the Catholic doctrine of works and merit justified or not?

---

[1] August Hasler, "Luther in der katholischen Schultheologie," Conc(D) 12 (1976):524.

[2] See Pesch, "Der gegenwärtige Stand," Conc(D) 12 (1976):541.

[3] Olivier, "Warum hat man Luther nicht verstanden?," Conc(D) 12 (1976):477. "Das Christentum Luthers ist unvereinbar mit der römischen Doktrin."

Still in the latest Catholic works on dogmatics many anti-Reformation echoes of past theological controversies can be heard, which reject Luther's criticism as unjustified and heretical. The reproach raised by Cochlaeus that Luther criticized the worth of the person (<u>dignitas hominis</u>) from the standpoint of Manichaeism (<u>Marcionica Manichaea blasphemia</u>),[1] still echoes, here and there through dogmatic textbooks.[2] Protestantism unjustly sees in the doctrine of merit a degradation of the grace of Christ.[3] While Pelagianism exaggerated its human monergism, Luther fell into the other extreme and exaggerated God's sole agency.[4]

Beside these, however, the thesis is also brought forward that Luther's criticism in relation to the teaching of High Scholasticism and the doctrine of the Council of Trent is more a question of language than of substance. Luther had only started with a different formulation of the problem; his answer would not be different from that of the Catholic Church, only with the one distinction that the Catholic concept is complete because it adds the parenetic aspect of human cooperation to the dogmatic statement of <u>sola gratia</u>.[5] Luther apparently wished to express in un-

---

[1] Johann Cochlaeus, <u>De libero arbitrio hominis libri duo</u> (1525), Lib. 1. The accusation appears to have been raised for the first time in 1520 by Latomus and then later was repeated by Erasmus, Cochlaeus, and others. See Alfred Adam, "Die Herkunft des Lutherwortes vom menschlichen Willen als Reittier Gottes," <u>LuJ</u> 29 (1962): 33.

[2] Premm, <u>Glaubenskunde</u>, 4:207; Auer and Ratzinger, <u>Dogmatik</u>, 5:216.

[3] Ott, <u>Dogmatik</u>, p. 320.   [4] Stevens, <u>Life of Grace</u>, p. 64.

[5] Auer and Ratzinger, <u>Dogmatik</u>, 5:234-35.

founded formulation the same thing as the Catholic Church.[1] If Protestants like Pierre-Yves Emery of Taizé categorize the struggle concerning the doctrine of merit in the Reformation as a misunderstanding on both sides (<u>La controverse reposait de part et d'autre sur des malentendus</u>)[2] and today a rapprochement of these Protestants towards the formulations and solutions of the Catholic doctrine can be observed, then this is greeted by many Catholic theologians with agreement[3] and satisfaction.[4] It, of course, confirms the thesis that the criticism of merit by the Reformers finally was unneedful and therefore, the main hindrance to mutual understanding no longer exists.[5]

The fact that there still remains a continuing Protestant criticism of the doctrine of merit would rest upon a continued misunderstanding on the Protestant side.[6] This fact is felt as "vexatious." O. H. Pesch attributes it to an inadequate, that is, "synergistic," interpretation on the Catholic side. Thus, unfortunately, the concept of "merit" can still become a match that can inflame the controversy again.[7] Gérard Philips, on the other hand,

---

[1] Schmidt, <u>Brückenschlag</u>, p. 201.

[2] Pierre-Yves Emery, <u>Le Christ notre récompense</u> (Neuchâtel: Delachaux & Niestlé, 1962), p. 209.

[3] Maurizio Flick, "Dialogo sul merito," <u>Gr</u>. 45 (1964):345-46.

[4] Eraldo Quarello, "Cattolici e Protestanti reiuniti di fronte al valore meritorio delle opere buone?," <u>Sal</u>. 26 (1964):151-52.

[5] Ibid., p. 152.

[6] Brinktrine, <u>Lehre von der Gnade</u>, p. 231.

[7] Pesch, "Freiheitsbegriff," <u>Cath(M)</u> 17 (1963):242-43.

sees the fault on the Protestant side. Protestants keep chasing
the idea of merit, like a scapegoat into the wilderness. They
would do better, however, to study the theology of the great
classical theologians (Albertus Magnus, Thomas Aquinas); then they
would receive a different impression of the Catholic doctrine.[1]

In agreement with the positive evaluation of the Lutheran
doctrine of justification, there are, however, many contemporary
Catholic voices that categorize Luther's criticism both for the
time of the Reformation and for today as justified.

It is conceded that Luther's position goes back to the
Augustinian tradition,[2] and that Thomas already in his teaching on
grace and merit anticipated Luther's pessimism.[3] In view of the
overemphasis and the practice of the Church of that time, Luther's
polemic against merit appears understandable and even to a certain
extent justified.[4] The motives that drove Luther to the struggle
are definitely acknowledged. Schmaus speaks of a biblical concern,
for the obedience of the Christian will always be imperfect.[5]
Lortz stresses the genuineness of the Lutheran experience of sin.
Luther stressed the immense weight of sin, as few had done before.[6]

---

[1] Gérard Philips, L'union personnelle avec le Dieu vivant (Gembloux: J. Duculot, 1974), p. 271.

[2] Adolar Zumkeller, "Die Augustinertheologen Simon Fidati von Cascia und Hugolin von Orvieto und Martin Luthers Kritik an Aristoteles," ARG 54 (1963):22, 36.

[3] Schütte, Wiedervereinigung, p. 68.

[4] Hessen, Luther in katholischer Sicht, p. 57.

[5] Schmaus, Dogmatik, 3/2:513.

[6] Lortz, Reformation, 1:192.

Manns states that the Ockhamistic topos of a love for God from natural powers (ex naturalibus viribus) is completely sufficient to make Luther's polemic understandable. But Luther's struggle also pertained to High Scholasticism, for its caritas-doctrine must have seemed to him, with his understanding of consecutive work, as camouflaged work-righteousness (Werkerei), since he saw in the final character (Finalcharakter) of love the restoration of the righteousness of the law.[1] Sartory is also of the opinion that Luther's struggle against the meritoriousness of good works was legitimately motivated by the fantastic over-evaluation of human power in Late Scholasticism.[2] Luther's pessimism--writes Baumgartner--becomes understandable in part through the excessive ethical optimism of the Nominalists.[3]

Only the ecumenical avant-garde, however, succeeds in achieving complete agreement with Luther. While Pesch speaks of a "new discovery of the Pauline doctrine of justification,"[4] Küng states that Luther's teaching stands in "continuity with the theology of the preceding time" and represents "no positively new beginning."[5]

---

[1] Manns, "Fides absoluta--Fides incarnata," in Reformata Reformanda, 1:289-92.

[2] Thomas Sartory, "Martin Luther in katholischer Sicht," US 16 (1961):45.

[3] Baumgartner, Grâce du Christ, p. 107.

[4] Pesch, "Gottes Gnadenhandeln," in Mysterium Salutis, 4/2: 839. It appears noteworthy that O. H. Pesch originally rejected the thesis of the rediscovery: "Luther ist Wiederentdecker und Vollender des NT--das kann kein Katholik hinnehmen." "Ein katholisches Anliegen an evangelische Darstellungen der Theologie Luthers," Cath(M) 16 (1962):309, italics mine.

[5] Küng, "Katholische Besinnung," in Theologie im Wandel, pp. 456-57.

For both, however, Luther's protest was unrestrictedly correct, for Luther with his teaching has the NT, and especially Paul, behind him (Küng);[1] indeed, his views became a "key position" against an ecclesiastical authority which had "turned away from" the "principal witnesses Paul and Augustine, or had domesticated them" (Pesch).[2]

However, the majority of dogmaticians and scholars on Luther are not ready to go so far. Luther's criticism can only be seen as justified against the optimism of Nominalism and against the extreme work-holiness of the people on the eve of the Reformation. A lasting character is to be refused to it because Luther did not attain to the "true doctrine of good works."[3] Similar limitations are made with reference to the "pedagogical meaning of the idea of reward and merit,"[4] to the natural moral performance-capability of the human being,[5] and to the finality-character of love.[6] Luther simply had the tendency to absolutize his existential-personal approach to the problem and to forge it into a theological doctrine.[7]

Nevertheless, it is conceded that the "faith-revolt" of the

---

[1] Ibid., p. 465.

[2] Pesch, "Gottes Gnadenhandeln," in Mysterium Salutis, 4/2: 841.

[3] Auer and Ratzinger, Dogmatik, 5:238-39.

[4] Hessen, Luther in katholischer Sicht, p. 57.

[5] Baumgartner, Grâce du Christ, p. 107; Lortz, Reformation, 1:192.

[6] Manns, "Fides absoluta--Fides incarnata," in Reformata Reformanda, 1:292.

[7] Schmaus, Dogmatik, 3/2:513.

Reformation represented a new "way to be a Christian" and a "radical new understanding of the gospel." "New" is no longer understood in a derogatory sense as formerly, but in a reformational sense. The Reformation wished to free the Church of all historical deformations. It was therefore a tragic error that the Church wished to give no opportunity to this "evangelical call to wake up," and to sidetrack Luther's criticism only defensively as schism and heresy.[1] Schütte speaks of a twofold fault in regard to the Church's attitude toward Luther: first, his reformational premises were not taken seriously and, second, he was handled in an unchristian manner by the Catholic Church.[2] One must demand from Rome a more clear and concrete mea culpa, mea maxima culpa than it has given up to now.[3]

Progressive Catholic theologians ask themselves above all whether it is sufficient to concede the historical justification of Luther's criticism and simply to deny its present function, because the Catholic Church of today ostensibly stands cleansed and no longer offers points to be attacked. This is above all the criticism given by Beyna[4] to Cardinal Bea, and by Hasler[5] to Paul VI. Rome either acts as if everything were already settled or it remains silent. Küng discerns various motives in Luther's understanding of the doctrine of justification. He can detect in it a reaction against Nominalism and a return to the Scripture and

---

[1] Fiolet, Die Zweite Reformation, p. 29.

[2] Schütte, Protestantismus, p. 508.   [3] Ibid., p. 370.

[4] Beyna, Das moderne katholische Lutherbild, pp. 205-06.

[5] Hasler, "Luther in der katholischen Schultheologie," Conc(D) 12 (1976):524.

Augustine as well as the personal experience of Luther. But above
all he sees a contradiction to the Catholic work-righteousness
(Werklerei).[1] In spite of 400 years of Catholic reform, this
problem has not yet been solved, for "much still remains to be
done today in the struggle against the practical work-righteousness."[2]
Olivier, for example, expressly emphasizes that especially Catholic
Christianity stands in danger of fostering legalism and scrupulosity.[3] The Catholic obsession with the law (l'obsession de la loi)
is detrimental to the gospel.[4] What Lucas Cranach showed in his
famous picture at the time of the Reformation, Catholicism even to
this day has not overcome. Over against the Catholic who groans
under the burden of the law and is referred to the intercession of
the saints in heaven stands the Protestant Christian who trustfully
looks to the cross, from whence all grace flows.[5] It is doubtless
true that the biblical doctrine of justification was a forgotten
teaching (doctrine oubliée)[6] at the time of the Reformation, but
Luther not only lifted it up on the lampstand but also, with his
polemic against the righteousness of law, pointed out a constant
and always present danger for Christendom.[7] Karrer speaks, therefore, of the Protestant criticism as a "thorn" which has a necessary

---

[1] Küng, Rechtfertigung, p. 215; idem, Christ sein, p. 398.

[2] Idem, Rechtfertigung, p. 273. "Es bleibt im Kampf gegen die praktische Werklerei auch heute noch sehr viel zu tun."

[3] Olivier, Foi de Luther, p. 238.   [4] Ibid., p. 239.

[5] Ibid., p. 241.   [6] Ibid., p. 132.

[7] Ibid., p. 136.

function in correcting defects.[1] The resistance against Luther, according to the view of Adam, has frequently led to an overemphasis on "work-holiness" and formalism. The "being in Christ" which motivates in trust, gratitude, and joy seems to "sink back in broad stretches into Jewish law-righteousness."[2] But that Luther today "is more and more present" (O. H. Pesch)[3] in Catholic theology really appears to be the best proof that he, along with his criticism, advanced into timeless dimensions. The phrase of the Lutherus praesentissimus (Brandenburg)[4] surely has its justification in this connection.

Catholic exegetes today indirectly agree with Luther when they characterize the doctrine of reward of Jesus and Paul as an ethic of obedience and gratitude. Good works occur because they have to occur because thereby God is glorified. An ethic of speculation, which performs only good works because one can thereby earn a reward, is unbiblical.[5] Dogmatic and historical theologians on the Catholic side today are quite unanimous in the view that much of what is time-bound and unevangelical has slipped into the biblical idea of reward. Tertullian and Cyprian developed a doctrine of merit which was more indebted to the thinking and

---

[1] Karrer, Galaterbrief, p. 32, quoted in Küng, Rechtfertigung, p. 265.

[2] Adam, Una Sancta, pp. 112-13.

[3] Pesch, "Der gegenwärtige Stand," Conc(D) 12 (1976):541.

[4] Brandenburg, Martin Luther gegenwärtig, p. 61.

[5] Josef Schmid, Das Evangelium nach Matthäus, 5th ed. (Regensburg: F. Pustet, 1965), p. 294; Didier, Désintéressement du chrétien, p. 221.

speaking of legal life and the world of business than to the gospel.[1] The word "merit" thus received a "Roman and legal flavour."[2] Thereby, likewise, at least to a certain degree, Luther has been rehabilitated, since the Reformation above all was concerned with eliminating everything that had historically been superimposed on the gospel!

Not a few among the contemporary Catholic theologians recognize today the "danger of activism" in theological thinking and religious piety. Molinski indicates a few "cliffs" when he says:

> The danger of the doctrine [of merit] is that it easily leads to Phariseeism and Pelagianism, since the notion of merit is very easily linked with the notion of claims which can be asserted, and also readily suggests that man is in some way independent of God. It can thus promote a fundamental misunderstanding of religion. Further the doctrine can easily obscure the sense of the ambivalent character of the content of the formally good moral act, since it determines the merit of the moral act merely according to formal aspects. It may thus possibly promote a one-sided ethic confined to attitudes, to the detriment of an ethic with a considered sense of responsibility, which must always bear clearly in mind the materially bad effects of even formally good actions.[3]

Fiolet also points out the danger that the human answer to God's call in the Catholic doctrine of merit leads to an independence (Verselbständigung) of the creature. This theology of the Counter-Reformation cannot escape a twofold danger: (1) the infringement on God's transcendence and the total graciousness of His will for salvation, and (2) the under-evaluation of the human

---

[1] Schmaus, Dogmatik, p. 520.

[2] Charles Moeller and Gérard Philips, The Theology of Grace, trans. R. A. Wilson (London: A. R. Mowbray, 1961), p. 27.

[3] SM(E), s.v. "Merit," by W. Molinski.

powerlessness in regard to sin and the tendency to make a trifle of sin.[1] From these a movement toward self-righteousness can arise.[2] The problem of the "clean slate" (weisse Weste), of which Küng speaks, comes here to expression. Since popular Catholicism thinks of grace anthropocentrically and materialistically--as "fluid" or "thing" man is tempted to misplace the purity in himself instead of in the verdict and dealing of God. Through this arises the danger of forgetting the personal relation to God and of the conception of oneself as a "pure soul."[3] However, since the interest which people receive from this soul-capital may be very different, the temptation of spiritual class consciousness arises. The teaching of the saints and the evangelical councils presses directly toward apprehension of an "elite position," a "special category of being Christian" (Sonderkategorie von Christsein).[4] When Trent defined the celibate position as more meritorious (melius ac beatius),[5] reflection on the extent of self-merits was directly provoked. It is only a short step from this idea to that of adding and counting merits. Joseph Pascher clearly points out this danger in his book Inwendiges Leben in der Werkgefahr. He speaks of a formal "greed" (Gewinnsucht) which sets the sense of true religiosity upside down.[6]

---

[1] Fiolet, Die zweite Reformation, p. 54.

[2] Lortz, The Reformation, p. 232.

[3] Küng, Rechtfertigung, p. 198.

[4] Friedrich Wulf, "Theologische Phänomenologie des Ordenslebens," in Mysterium Salutis, 4/2:472.

[5] DS 1810.

[6] Joseph Pascher, Inwendiges Leben in der Werkgefahr (Krailling vor Munich: E. Wewel, 1940), p. 11.

This striving for reward is dangerous for faith. Christendom must let itself be guided by the criticism from the gospels and the Epistle to the Romans.[1] Schmaus also affirms the danger of collecting merits. Such a position, however, is that of an "unenlightened believer in Christ."[2] Thereby it is easy for the high feeling of spiritual quality to be followed by the <u>anxiety</u> of spiritual insufficiency. Hessen reminds us that anxiety of conscience and scrupulosity accompanies like a shadow every religion of law and that, on the eve of the Reformation, Catholicism itself represented a "fruitful soil" for that. Therefore Luther in his experience and, in part, in his criticism is to be rehabilitated.[3] But since legalism is a constant danger of the Catholic doctrine,[4] the "putting into works" (<u>Verwerklichung</u>) must be reformed by a "getting out of works" (<u>Entwerklichung</u>).[5] A clearer agreement with the abiding justification of Luther's criticism of merit can hardly be imagined! The question is, how far does this agreement reach? Is it an ecumenical tactic or an ecumenical turn? Is it applied Catholicity, in which the contradictions are resolved dialectically in a kind of higher synthesis, or is it an outbreak of reformation? Is it an expression of the good will of a few, or is it a movement becoming ever more intensive in Catholic theology? In both camps it is emphasized that rank

---

[1] Ibid., p. 66.   [2] Schmaus, <u>Dogmatik</u>, 3/2:526.

[3] Hessen, <u>Luther in katholischer Sicht</u>, p. 23.

[4] Otto Hermann Pesch, <u>Die Rechtfertigungslehre Luthers in katholischer Sicht</u> (Berlin: Evangelische Verlagsanstalt, 1967), p. 52.

[5] Pascher, <u>Inwendiges Leben</u>, p. 12.

and interpretation of the doctrine of merit today represent a kind of proof in the question of consensus with Luther.[1] First, therefore, we must ask, What role does the doctrine of merit still play in Catholic theology today? To this question we now turn our attention.

The Place of the Doctrine of Merit in Modern Catholic Theology

People of today's secular meritocracy are surely no less reward-and-gain oriented than people in past times, but the philosophical criticism of the Christian morality of reward, the religious indifference of the dechristianized masses, and the ecumenical dialogue in theology have contributed not a little to the fact that the word "merit" has become a "sore word"[2] in the opinion of many contemporary Catholic theologians, a word of which Catholics are often even ashamed of in ecumenical conversations.[3] The concept is also felt as "problematic,"[4] and thus in current theology little attention is given to it. In the pastorate it is often unmentioned, as though it were--as some Catholic theologians complain--a matter of a theologoumenon without foundation in the Scriptures.[5] One no longer likes to speak of the doctrine of merit, Rahner asserts; only in

---

[1] Dantine, Gerechtmachung des Gottlosen, p. 39; Pesch, Theologie der Rechtfertigung, p. 772.

[2] Charles Journet, Entretiens sur la grâce (Paris: Desclée de Brouwer, 1959), p. 99.

[3] Maurizio Flick and Zoltan Alszeghy, Il vangelo della grazia (Florence: Libreria Editrice Fiorentina, 1967), p. 666.

[4] SM(E), s.v. "Merit," by W. Molinski.

[5] Flick, "Dialogo sul merito," Gr. 45 (1964):339.

dogmatical textbooks does it continue to exist.[1] Indeed the problematic issue contained in the word "merit" is discussed even today, but to many theologians the question is not pressing.[2]

When we consider some of the newest Catholic positions on the doctrine of merit, we probably receive the impression that the old idea of merit has finally been overcome and the dogma of merit has been reinterpreted in such a way that the road to Luther is really open.

Fransen, for instance, is of the opinion that the thought of merit "is disappearing more and more"[3] as there is a growing love for God. Merit is final union with Christ and with the Father. "Whoever concretely experiences this reality is no longer able to talk of merits!"[4] Rahner sees in the wonderful prayer of Theresa of Lisieux--"I do not wish to gather merits for heaven . . . in the evening of this life I will appear before Thee with empty hands. For in no way, O Lord, do I ask that my good works be counted. I therefore wish to be clothed with Thy righteousness and to receive from Thy love the eternal possession of Thyself"--something thoroughly good-Catholic and absolutely nothing heretical.[5] Pesch states that with the biblical idea of reward which indeed Luther

---

[1] Rahner, Schriften zur Theologie, 3:170.

[2] Schmaus, Glaube der Kirche, 2:651; LThK, 2nd ed., s.v. "Verdienst-Systematisch," by A. Forster.

[3] Fransen, "Das neue Sein," in Mysterium Salutis, 4/2:980.

[4] Ibid. "Wer diese Wirklichkeit aber konkret erfährt, ist nicht mehr imstande, von Verdiensten zu reden!"

[5] Rahner, Schriften zur Theologie, 3:172.

also affirms one can regard the doctrine of merit, in spite of its tradition and Trent, as a "dispensable theologoumenon" (entbehrliches Theologoumenon).[1] This "unhappy analogy" (unglückliches Analogat)[2] can be left out and be replaced by the biblical concept of "hope" and "gratitude."[3] The "sober, critical Catholic exegesis" (nüchterne, kritische katholische Exegese), which is not led by dogmatic a prioris, "arrives ever more by beautiful inevitability and self-evident truth at clearly "Lutheran' formulations" (gelangt in schöner Zwangsläufigkeit und Selbstverständlichkeit zu deutlich 'lutherischen' Formulierungen).[4] It would be enough that this Catholic interpretation be tolerated by the Magisterium to attain consensus with Luther. Since it is not to be expected that Rome would publicly proclaim such a consensus in a solemn doctrinal decision, but would silently accept it by the breadth of variation of possibilities for Catholic interpretation,[5] we could already say that today the doctrine of merit is no longer a "matter of dispute" (Gegenstand des Streites).[6] Only the lack of Protestant understanding would allow the controversy about merit to break out again and again, and for this the "synergistic" interpretations of Catholic theology would be, indeed, mostly to blame.[7]

Of course, only some of the theologians interested in an

---

[1] Pesch, "Die Lehre vom Verdienst," in Wahrheit und Verkündigung, 2:1867, 1901, 1905.

[2] Ibid., 2:1905.   [3] Ibid., 2:1907.

[4] Ibid., 2:1902.   [5] Ibid., 2:1901.

[6] Idem, "Der Gegenwärtige Stand," Conc(D) 12 (1976):540.

[7] Idem, "Freiheitsbegriff," Cath(M) 17 (1963):242-43.

ecumenical dialogue go this far. A majority wish to hold fast to the concept of merit as a "helpful motive" (Hilfsmotiv)[1] or as a "crutch" (béquille)[2] with which the spiritually elite but not the masses could dispense. Joyce, speaking from the Catholic view, expresses how important the drive toward merit appears to be for the majority of people:

> It is hardly necessary to point out what fatal effects the Protestant teaching must have on Christian life and practice. To labour without regard for the reward belongs to the highest sanctity alone. <u>The great majority of men need to be stimulated to virtue.</u>[3]

Baumgartner, citing de Montcheuil, expresses himself similarly:

> A côté des chrétiens d'élite et des saints, il y a la masse de ceux qui ont encore souvent besoin d'être détournés du mal par la crainte de l'enfer ou encouragés au bien par la pensée de la récompense, avant de s'élever au stade parfait de l'amour et surtout d'y demeurer. Même les chrétiens fervents n'arrivent pas toujours à s'y maintenir: <u>le souvenir du ciel ou de l'enfer leur donne alors la force de rester fidèles.</u>[4]

If these statements would be understood as a remembrance of God's promise, then--as we have shown in the presentation of Luther's teaching--one could not object to such an interpretation from the Reformation standpoint. But since they are interpreted in the framework of dogma as the final-meritorious seeking for reward (<u>recherche de la récompense</u>),[5] as remuneration (<u>rétribution des</u>

---

[1] Karrer, Galaterbrief, p. 32, quoted in Küng, Rechtfertigung, p. 265.

[2] Baumgartner, Grâce du Christ, p. 225.

[3] Joyce, Catholic Doctrine of Grace, p. 171, emphasis mine.

[4] Y. de Montcheuil, Problèmes de vie spirituelle, p. 77, quoted in Baumgartner, Grâce du Christ, p. 225, emphasis mine.

[5] Ibid.

efforts de l'homme)[1] and as a claim on reward (une récompense due "ex titulo justitiae"),[2] there arises an indubitable chasm in relation to Luther and not a drawing closer, as Baumgartner thinks.[3]

Therefore theologians less radical than Pesch have the opinion that one does not serve the "delicate matter" (idée délicate)[4] of the thought of merit if one tries to place a calculating Christian morality opposite the selfless ethic of many non-Christians.[5] The idea of merit can only be defended when it is "purified."[6] Opinions differ, however, about how that must be done. Schillebeeckx wishes to hold fast to the content of the Thomistic principle of proportion but possibly to renounce the term.[7] Nicolas wishes to hold fast to the term, but wants to elevate the concept from the legal sphere to the plane of love[8] and, thereby, to spiritualize it (transfigurer par l'amour),[9] although he must concede that the concept does not allow a complete

---

[1] Ibid., p. 115.   [2] Ibid., p. 207.

[3] "Les protestants modernes continuent d'ordinaire à critiquer le langage de l'Eglise catholique; en ce qui concerne la doctrine elle-même, on peut parfois se demander s'ils sont tellement éloignés de la position catholique." Ibid., p. 210.

[4] Gustave Thils, Sainteté chrétienne (Tielt: Ed. Lannoo, 1958), p. 144.

[5] Ibid., p. 145.

[6] Jean Hervé Nicolas, Les profondeurs de la grâce (Paris: Beauchesne, 1969), p. 522.

[7] Schillebeeckx, "Tridentinisches Rechtfertigungsdekret," Conc(D) 1 (1965):454.

[8] Nicolas, Profondeurs de la grâce, pp. 534, 538.

[9] Ibid., p. 547.

withdrawal from legalistic thinking.[1] Molinski wishes to hold fast to the term and the concept, but through a connection with the teaching of creation and grace he wishes to grant the idea of merit a "subordinate position, which is proper to it."[2] Wicks, on the other hand, attempts to help himself with Luther. The Reformer's manner of speaking of the Christ working in man (<u>Christus actuosissimus in nobis</u>)[3] "would prohibit merit from playing any extensive role in a Christian's conscious self-estimate."[4] The logical consequence of the <u>Christus actuosissimus</u> is, however, the sole agency and the annulling of the doctrine of merit, as Luther has concluded (cf. Part I, chapter 2)! Wishing to borrow from Luther, indeed speaks in favor of the openness of contemporary Catholic theologians, but it still must be left open whether one can harmonize Luther's concept with the traditional doctrine of merit! In this situation most theologians are left only with the "method of explanation," as, for instance, Journet proposes. One must hold unconditionally to the idea of merit, for it indeed underlies a "splendid doctrine" (<u>doctrine splendide</u>).[5] In order to come into conversation with Protestants, one must help them to overcome the problematic character of their tactic. Protestant polemical theology, in its criticism of merit, builds up a false

---

[1] Ibid., pp. 547-48.

[2] <u>SM(E)</u>, s.v. "Merit," by W. Molinski.

[3] WA 1, 140, 20-21.

[4] Wicks, <u>Man Yearning for Grace</u>, p. 278.

[5] Journet, <u>Entretiens sur la grâce</u>, p. 104.

enemy image from which it then derives the justification for the existence of its polemic.[1] Therefore Catholics should avoid the word and explain the matter to them. It would then be clear that with the word nothing more or different is meant than what they have always believed (il pourra leur sembler qu'elle exprime ce qu'ils ont toujours cru).[2]

From this to the traditional high evaluation of the doctrine of merit is only a step. We have to agree with Rahner that this high evaluation is not pressed in mission or pastorate today. But it is, nevertheless, alarming to discover what an important dimension the doctrine of merit has in relation to the teaching of justification in the Catholic School dogmatics and not only before Vatican II! The authors of the dogmatic handbooks which give more space to the doctrine of justification--and sometimes then only in connection with the doctrine of grace--than to the doctrine of merit can be named as follows (the approximate ratio of space devoted to justification to that devoted to merit is given in parentheses): Schmaus, 1965 (8:1); Lercher, 1951 (4:1); Bozzola and Greppi, 1948; de Aldama, Gonzalez, and Solano, 1953; Pohle and Gummersbach, 1956; and Flick and Alszeghy, 1967 (3:1); de Abárzuza, 1956; Diekamp, 1959; and Auer and Ratzinger, 1972 (2:1).

More alarming is the fact that in some works the doctrine

---

[1] "Ils sont obligés de défigurer cette splendide doctrine, si grande, pour pouvoir l'attaquer." Ibid.

[2] Journet, Entretiens sur la grâce, p. 99; cf. "Tandem recentiores protestantes, etsi vocem impugnent, videntur aliquod meritum admittere." De Aldama, Gonzalez, and Solano, Sacrae theologiae summa, 3:693.

of merit is given as much space as that of justification. This is
true of Van Noort, 1920; Boyer, 1946; Daffara, 1950; Premm, 1953;
Tabarelli, 1962; and Muldoon, 1965.

Even more problematic, of course, are those authors with
whom the doctrine of merit takes up more space than the doctrine
of justification itself (without the chapter on preparation for
justification): Hervé, 1943 (3:1); Lumbreras, 1947; and
Baumgartner, 1963 (2:1).

Here then flows a broad stream of Catholic theology which
has not yet smoothed out its anti-Reformation waves. The principle
of cooperation is seen as the very basis of the Catholic dogma
(la base même de tout dogme catholique)[1] and the merits derived from
it as the "most powerful"[2] and "most noble effect"[3] of grace. The
doctrine of merit is, on the basis of the decision of Trent, a
Catholic "fundamental doctrine" (doctrine fondamentale).[4] It belongs to the religion of revelation[5] and is unrenounceable because
it has a broad biblical foundation[6] and represents an important
part of the NT.[7] Believers must therefore be reminded of the
privilege of merits: "Let us never forget . . . this privilege

---

[1] DTC, s.v. "Mérite," by J. Rivière; cf. Auer and Ratzinger:
"Kern der katholischen Gnadenlehre," Dogmatik, 5:227.

[2] Richardo Tabarelli, Opere teologiche, 5 vols. (Rome:
Pontificia universitas Lateranensis, 1962), 4:354.

[3] Billot, De gratia Christi, p. 244.

[4] Rondet, Gratia Christi, p. 283.

[5] Auer and Ratzinger, Dogmatik, 5:229.

[6] Ibid., p. 228.   [7] Hacker, The Ego in Faith, p. 81.

of accumulating merits," for "dipped in grace, the base metal of our actions is changed into pure gold, and is made capable of purchasing heaven."[1]

The doctrine of merit is important for the following reasons:

1. It holds the middle ground between the heresies of Manichaeism and Pelagianism.[2]

2. It makes possible the personal relation of the believer to God[3] and expresses his independence from God (das Gefühl einer gewissen--Gott ebenbildlichen--Eigenmächtigkeit und freien Selbständigkeit).[4]

3. It is the necessary boundary against Protestants[5] and makes clear the great difference in relation to them.[6]

4. It is an expression of the communio sanctorum, for the saints can apply their merits in an intercessory way for the believers.[7]

5. Because it was so painfully elaborated, it is an important dogma of the Council of Trent and therefore a part of contemporary Catholic doctrine also.[8]

---

[1] William Joseph Doheny, The Marvels of Divine Grace (Notre Dame, IN: Ave Maria Press, 1977), pp. 103-04, italics mine.

[2] Auer and Ratzinger, Dogmatik, 5:227.

[3] Hacker, The Ego in Faith, p. 82.

[4] Auer and Ratzinger, Dogmatik, 5:234, italics mine.

[5] Hervé, Manuale theologiae dogmaticae, 3:243.

[6] Journet, Entretiens sur la grâce, pp. 108-09.

[7] Peters, "Der Begriff Meritum in der liturgischen Sprache," TThZ 65 (1956):114.

[8] Jedin et al., "Das 'Reformatorische' bei Luther," in Um Reform und Reformation, p. 42.

With respect to these considerations, the weakening of the doctrine of merit by progressive ecumenical scholars seems a "serious curtailment of the gospel" and, in Hacker's view, one can only deplore it when "some progressive Catholics today" have taken the road of Protestantism.[1] These tones, of course, sounded still more radical before Vatican II, for then the Protestant criticism of the doctrine of merit was still rejected in the sense of the Counter-Reformation, as the voice of the deepest moral depravity.[2] But even after Vatican II, Luther's teaching of a freely given salvation (<u>misericordia et miseratione es iustus</u>)[3] can be rejected sometimes as arrogance, for according to conservative Catholic theology the fact remains: increase of grace and salvation must be earned.

> Attendre de Dieu la grâce, et la gloire, sans aucunement les mériter, <u>c'est encore présomption</u>. Car Dieu ne donne les accroissements de grâce et leur consommation dans la gloire <u>qu'à ceux qui les méritent</u>.[4]

The Council of Trent in the Conflict of Opinions

The conflict over the evaluation of the doctrine of merit in contemporary Catholic thinking forces the decisions of Trent to the front. Did not the Catholic Church then and there infallibly

---

[1] Hacker, The Ego in Faith, p. 81.

[2] "Ecce typicam objectionem eorum, qui, solis desideriis contenti et nihil boni facientes, <u>immo saepe more suino viventes</u>, bono quod alii operantur, ad superbissimam et infelicissimam sui excusationem et consolationem, detrahere cupiunt." Baisi, Institutiones theologiae scholasticae, 3:507, italics mine.

[3] WA 40II, 353, 3.

[4] Nicolas, Profondeurs de la grâce, p. 544, italics mine.

and unambiguously explain through a universal council what is truth, and what is not? Has one not heard even recently that the Tridentine decree on justification, together with its decisions on the question of merit, represents a "theological masterpiece" (Pius XII)[1] which was composed with "unique care"[2] and far exceeds Luther in truth and clarity[3] and assures the "surpassing significance of the council for centuries"?[4] Did not the council itself express as its purpose the need to overcome the "darkness of erroneous teachings" in order that "the light of Catholic truth . . . might stream forth in glorious purity"?[5]

Where this boundary between light and darkness runs becomes clear in the rejection of Seripando's teaching about double justification[6] by the Council fathers: The doctrine of merit had to be safeguarded. For, if Luther's teaching of acceptance by mercy was

---

[1] See Grabmann, "Trient als Fortschrittsprinzip," in Weltkonzil von Trient, 1:38; cf. Tüchle, Geschichte der Kirche, 3:142.

[2] Stakemeier, "Trienter Lehrentscheidungen," in Weltkonzil von Trient, 1:97.

[3] "The teaching of the Council of Trent on justification is much clearer and more convincing than Luther's." Richter, Luther and Loyola, p. 91.

[4] Tüchle, Geschichte der Kirche, 3:139.

[5] See Eduard Stakemeier, "Die theologischen Schulen auf dem Trienter Konzil während der Rechtfertigungsverhandlungen," TQ 117 (1936):189.

[6] Although Seripando rejected Italian evangelicalism, his teaching on justification was based on the Bible and Augustine (Augustinian view of concupiscence and emphasis on the justice of Christ). Thus, at the Council of Trent, he advocated very forcefully the concept of "double justification." This teaching was a compromise between the Scholastic view of "inherent justice" and the Reformers' view of "imputed justice." Double justification combined the personal, imperfect and inherent justice of the believer with God's perfect and imputed justice in the judgment. Although

accepted even in only a most weakened form, this would have catastrophic results for the Catholic doctrines of grace, of merit, and of purgatory.[1]

Since the Reformers themselves were not united in their position on the doctrine of merit--Melanchthon wished to maintain a relative concept of merit, while Calvin rejected even the very term except for Christ--clarity, according to Catholic viewpoint, had to be created. That occurred in Trent![2] Of course, the council did not tackle the inner-Catholic concerns but it did clarify the matter against the Reformers![3]

The great majority of Catholic dogmaticians saw, and still see, in the decisions of Trent concerning justification and merit, a clear condemnation of Luther, even though his name does not appear at all in the decrees. For when the council, for example, condemned the "vain trust" (_inanis fiducia_) of heretics (_haeretici_), who believe themselves justified _sola fide_,[4] it thereby (and for centuries neither Catholics nor Protestants have doubted this) condemned Luther and the other Reformers.[5] For it was exactly through

---

Seripando retained the concept of merit, it soon became clear that the idea of an imperfect inherent justice was an attack on the doctrine of merit.

[1] See Jedin, _Konzil von Trient_, 2:216.

[2] The council emphasized strongly the role of grace in the believer's merits (_DS_ 1546, 1547). However, merits are considered --due to free will (_DS_ 1529) and inherent grace (_DS_ 1547)--as man's own and true merits (_DS_ 1546, 1582).

[3] _NCE_, s.v. "Merit," by C. S. Sullivan.

[4] _DS_ 1533, 1534, 1559, 1562.

[5] Diekamp, _Dogmatik_, p. 543.

the doctrine of merit, according to the Catholic view, that Trent succeeded in repelling the reformational <u>sola fide</u>.[1] When the council condemned "adversaries of the true doctrine of religion" (<u>adversari orthodoxae religionis doctrinae</u>) who assert that works of the righteous are also sinful,[2] then it condemned Luther.[3] When the council spoke out in favor of the doctrine of increasing jusification[4] and condemned those who rejected such an increase of grace by good works,[5] then it rejected Luther's viewpoint and that of all Protestants.[6] When one finds in the decrees and canons decisions regarding the final and meritorious character of the works of grace and regarding the justification of the reflexion on reward,[7] then the council without any doubt turned against Luther.[8] The same is true concerning "inherent righteousness" (<u>iustitia inhaerens</u>)[9] and the "weakened and bent will" (<u>liberum arbitrium . . . attenuatum et inclinatum</u>).[10]

---

[1] <u>NCE</u>, s.v. "Justification," by P. de Letter.

[2] <u>DS</u> 1538, 1539, 1581.

[3] <u>LThK</u>, 1st ed., s.v. "Verdienst," by K. Feckes; Pohle and Preuss, <u>Grace</u>, p. 401; <u>CathEnc</u>, s.v. "Merit," by J. Pohle.

[4] <u>DS</u> 1535.   [5] <u>DS</u> 1574.

[6] Berthier and Raemers, <u>Compendium of Theology</u>, p. 359.

[7] <u>DS</u> 1546, 1581.

[8] "This is <u>of faith</u> against Martin Luther." Berthier and Raemers, <u>Compendium of Theology</u>, p. 361; cf. Matthias Premm, <u>Dogmatic Theology for Laity</u>, trans. O. Heimann (Staten Island, NY: Alba House, 1967), p. 263.

[9] <u>DS</u> 1547, 1561; Baisi, <u>Institutiones theologiae scholasticae</u>, p. 313; Diekamp, <u>Dogmatik</u>, 2:432.

[10] <u>DS</u> 1521, 1554, 1555; <u>Dictionary of Dogmatic Theology</u>, s.v. "Merit," by P. Parente, A. Piolanti, and S. Garofalo.

In spite of all positive judgments of Protestant critics from Harnack[1] to Barth,[2] the Reformation camp was always conscious that Trent signified a determined, "radical condemnation"[3] of the evangelical doctrine of justification and that "there can however be no honest compromise between the Roman and Reformed doctrine of justification."[4]

However, the very thesis, accepted up to now by both sides --Trent has spoken, any further discussion is fruitless--is now being questioned not only by radical but also by many moderate, Catholic ecumenical scholars. Hasler formulates the concerns in this direction with the cutting sentence: "Trent cannot be the last word on the doctrine of justification" (<u>Trient kann in der Rechtfertigungslehre nicht das letzte Wort sein</u>).[5] It is naive to think, so Küng says, that Trent is the "peak of Catholic wisdom" (<u>der Gipfel katholischer Weisheit</u>).[6]

What is the ground for such hopes? First of all is the fact that the council did not mention the name of Luther or of any other Reformer. Luther is thus not condemned by name; his

---

[1] Harnack, <u>Dogmengeschichte</u>, 3:711.

[2] Barth, <u>KD</u> 4/1:697.

[3] Berkouwer, <u>Faith and Justification</u>, pp. 96-97.

[4] Martin Smyth, "Differences between the Roman and Reformed Doctrines of Justification," <u>EvQ</u> 36 (1964):47.

[5] Hasler, <u>Luther in der katholischen Dogmatik</u>, p. 291.

[6] Küng, "Katholische Besinnung," in <u>Theologie im Wandel</u>, p. 464.

cause can continue.[1] The council was timebound[2] like any other historical event and can, indeed must, be completed.[3] Fransen even says that the canons, on account of their time conditioning, do not belong at all unconditionally and formally to the content of faith (Offenbarungsgut).[4] The council was not at all acquainted with Luther's teaching--or only insufficiently--and therefore has understood it falsely.[5] Many an item--so, for example, Luther's concept of concupiscence--was not seen at all (trat nicht ins

---

[1] Of course, that never deceived anyone up to the present that with the haeretici only the Reformers could have been meant, since Trent, like the ancient councils, was wholly aimed at the theological conflicts of its time. Olivier even says that names were not called because Luther was to suffer the damnatio memoriae ("il est voué à l'oubli"), since one hoped that Protestants would leave him and return to the Catholic Church. Foi de Luther, p. 227. Jedin, the most important expert on research on the Council of Trent today, sees even without calling of names the anathemas of the canons directed anyway against Luther and the CA. Konzil von Trient, 2:260-63. Cf. Gotthold Hasenhüttl, Kritische Dogmatik (Graz: Styria, 1979), p. 142.

[2] Küng, "Katholische Besinnung," in Theologie im Wandel, p. 465; Schmaus, Glaube der Kirche, 2:577.

[3] Jedin, Kirche des Glaubens, 2:552; Tüchle, Geschichte der Kirche, 3:153; Schillebeeckx, "Tridentinisches Rechtfertigungsdekret," Conc(D) 1 (1965):453.

[4] Fransen, "Entfaltung der Gnadenlehre," in Mysterium Salutis, 4/2:715. Jedin on the contrary sees in the canons the "Nerv der Trienter Lehrdekrete," welche die "Lehre der Kirche fixieren und absichern." The canons are "fundamental," they repel the "stark differierenden Lehrbegriffe des Protestantismus." Hubert Jedin, Vaticanum II und Tridentinum (Cologne: Westdeutscher Verlag, 1968), p. 9.

[5] Hasler, Luther in der katholischen Dogmatik, pp. 159-60, 277; Pesch, "Abenteuer Lutherforschung," NOrd 20 (1966):417. Jedin, on the contrary, points out that the Council fathers had a certain knowledge of the original Protestant confessions and writings of the Reformers. Kirche des Glaubens, 2:549.

Blickfeld),[1] so that the council really fought against a distorted enemy image (karikierter Gegner).[2] Trent offers in any case no genuine representation of the teaching of Luther.[3]

A. Stakemeier soon after the second World War attempted to prove that Luther's teaching on the assurance of salvation had not really been touched in Trent.[4] At the time of Vatican II Pfürtner took another step forward. He not only asked whether Trent had understood and countered Luther,[5] but he also raised the problem of the freedom of opinion, time conditioning, and the incompleteness of the council.[6]

A. Stakemeier had also reproached the Council fathers with simply failing to speak to Luther's concept of sola fide.[7] Hasler agreed with this opinion and saw the distorted picture, indicated by Stakemeier, overwhelmingly confirmed in the Catholic School

---

[1] Hasler, Luther in der katholischen Dogmatik, p. 128. Fransen calls this, of course, "an oversimplification that does not tally with historical facts." Piet Fransen, The New Life of Grace, trans. Georges Dupont (London: G. Chapman, 1971), p. 214.

[2] Hasler, Luther in der katholischen Dogmatik, p. 285.

[3] Fries, "Grundanliegen der Theologie Luthers," in Wandlungen des Lutherbildes, p. 160.

[4] Stakemeier, Trient über Heilsgewissheit, pp. 73-74.

[5] Pfürtner, Luther and Aquinas, p. 31.

[6] Ibid., pp. 32-33. Ansgar Ahlbrecht, of course, clearly uncovers the weaknesses of Pfürtner's argumentation when he points to the difference between the future hope-assurance of Thomas and the present salvation-assurance of Luther. Therefore Luther in spite of everything does not escape the anathema at all. "Neuere katholische Versuche zur Würdigung der theologischen Anliegen Luthers," US 18 (1963):178.

[7] Stakemeier, Trient über Heilsgewissheit, p. 91.

dogmatics.[1] According to Fransen, the Council fathers basically misunderstood the Lutheran fides specialis, for it has in it nothing of an "arrogant fiducia".[2]

Likewise Luther's formula simul justus et peccator--if it is rightly understood--was not condemned in Trent.[3] R. Grosche propounded this thesis even before the second World War[4] and since then he has found many followers. If the formula is understood as "dialektisch" (Grosche), "existentiell" (Fries), "psychologisch" (Adam), "ethisch-asketisch" (Brandenburg), "konkret-geschichtlich" (Schmaus), "zeitlich-heilsgeschichtlich" (Schütte), "persönlich-erfahrungsmässig" (Rahner), "dynamisch-geschichtlich" (Kösters), then it can become integrated as Catholic.[5] Then also Luther has not been condemned by Trent. Only the "ontologisch-metaphysisch-dogmatisch-objektive" meaning must be rejected.[6]

Concerning the teaching about the unfree will, Pesch has

---

[1] Hasler, Luther in der katholischen Dogmatik, p. 192.

[2] Fransen, "Entfaltung der Gnadenlehre," in Mysterium Salutis, 4/2:724.

[3] Schmaus, Dogmatik, 3/2:154.

[4] Robert Grosche, "Simul peccator et iustus," Cath(M) 4 (1935):137.

[5] See Bogdahn, Rechtfertigungslehre Luthers, p. 193.

[6] How difficult it is to unite Luther's total aspect of the simul formula with the Catholic doctrine of removal of sin is shown by the twisted judgments of Kösters ("Luthers These, 'Gerecht und Sünder zugleich'," Cath[M] 18 [1964]:77) and of Pesch. "Gottes Gnadenhandeln," in Mysterium Salutis, 4/2:886-90. Rahner explains such a compromise also as impossible. Trent has in truth rejected the total aspect of the formula. Schriften zur Theologie, 6:265-68.

attempted to point out that there is in Thomas Aquinas also a teaching of the "bondage of will" which does not stand far away at all from Luther's conviction.[1] McSorley, at the fringe of his work, arrived at the same conclusion regarding the relationship of Trent to Luther, as far as Luther's concept being biblically founded is concerned:

> Luther's biblical concept of <u>servum arbitrium</u> is very close to the concept of the captive free will (<u>liberum arbitrium captivatum</u>) of Augustine and Peter Lombard. It is unquestionably a Catholic concept <u>that is in complete harmony with the concept of liberum arbitrium captivatum of the Council of Trent.</u>[2]

When we now turn to our real object, the doctrine of merit, it is confirmed that here also similar attempts have been undertaken to bring Luther and Trent closer together. Schmaus concedes that Trent had to turn against Luther because he had dogmatically absolutized the existential-personal conviction about the insufficiency of works.[3] However, he says that the council integrated into the Catholic doctrine Luther's concerns that the human can make no claim upon God and must not rely on his works.[4] The

---

[1] Pesch, "Freiheitsbegriff," Cath(M) 17 (1963):198.

[2] McSorley, Luther: Right or Wrong?, p. 355, italics mine; cf. Eduard Stakemeier, "Luthers de servo arbitrio," Cath(M) 22 (1968):133. The Protestant Vorster affirms the nearness between Luther's servum arbitrium and Thomas' view, which one must call servum liberum arbitrium. Freiheitsverständnis, p. 229. Vorster, however, sees an important difference between Thomas and Trent. The Trent decisions sound Thomistic, but they are not. Ibid., p. 318. Pesch concedes that Trent paid homage to a "humanistischen Freiheitsbegriff." "Gottes Gnadenhandeln," in Mysterium Salutis, 4/2:855. Seen thus, the claim of an agreement with Luther appears richly dared.

[3] Schmaus, Dogmatik, 3/2:513.

[4] Ibid., 3/2:514; idem, Glaube der Kirche, 2:652.

dogmatic denial of the doctrine of merit is, of course, "error."[1] According to the view of Beer, we could even go another step further. Since the authors of the canons did not have sufficient documentation of Luther's teaching at their disposal, "Luther was not countered in most of the points" (wurde Luther in den meisten Punkten nicht getroffen).[2] Because the Reformer knew not only the grace concept of the favor of God (favor Dei) but also of the power of God (donum Dei), and had not rejected cooperation and merit even after his break with Rome,[3]--although not absolutely in the traditional Catholic sense--there is a greater "substantial rapprochement" (substantielle Annäherung) than one usually assumes.[4]

If we now ask what result comes from the many new interpretations of Trent, we must distinguish two basically different standpoints.

1. If the Tridentine decisions are uncritically accepted--as really corresponds to the Catholic dogmatic understanding--if they are not questioned on limitations of time and situation, then the overwhelming majority of dogmaticians are right: Luther's teaching on justification and criticism of merit were unambiguously rejected by the council. Even the church historian who is concerned

---

[1] Idem, Dogmatik, 3/2:513.

[2] Beer, "Ausgangspositionen," Cath(M) 21 (1967):84.

[3] We have attempted in the second chapter of Part I to show how far this thesis is pertinent or not.

[4] Beer, "Ausgangspositionen," Cath(M) 21 (1967):84. De Letter, on the other hand, sees right in the Tridentine doctrine of merit a distinct rejection of the Lutheran justification sola fide. NCE, s.v. "Merit," by P. de Letter.

with compromise--Jedin here is the best example--for whom a revision of the decrees of Trent is impossible, because as papally accredited decisions of a universal council they are "infallible,"[1] must then frankly state that the harmonizing of Luther with Trent has failed.[2]

2. But if one begins the venture of questioning Trent and of thinking beyond Trent, then the Catholic theologian sees himself facing the delicate question as to what method he should choose in order, on the one hand, to maintain the dogma and, on the other hand, to demonstrate the desired or even already claimed consensus with Luther.

The <u>method of explanation</u> seems the simplest. Since Trent did not wish total renunciation (Jedin),[3] indeed, even strove for a "réconciliation" (Congar),[4] one could with closer elucidation of the positions, distinguishing the essential from the unessential, the rhetoric from the content (Auer), find a compromise of both standpoints (<u>der Sache nach können beide Lehren als "rechtgläubig" verstanden werden</u>).[5] Protestants like Emery also follow this

---

[1] Jedin, <u>Kirche des Glaubens</u>, 2:552.

[2] "Der Versuch, das Trienter Rechtfertigungsdekret mit Luther zu harmonisieren, ist meines Erachtens missglückt." Idem, "Wandlungen des Lutherbildes in der katholischen Kirchengeschichtsschreibung," in <u>Wandlungen des Lutherbildes</u>, p. 95.

[3] Hubert Jedin, "Historische Randbemerkungen zum Thema: Tridentinum und Wiedervereinigung," in <u>Begegnung der Christen</u>, p. 460.

[4] <u>Jean Puyo interroge le "Père Congar</u> (Paris: Le Centurion, 1975), p. 63. According to Fransen it was not the Pope and the council that obeyed him who strove to hold the door open, but the emperor. Pope and council wished to condemn the reformational teachings. "Entfaltung der Gnadenlehre," in <u>Mysterium Salutis</u>, 4/2:712.

[5] Auer and Ratzinger, <u>Dogmatik</u>, pp. 148, 234.

method and believe that Trent has proved that the problem of justification and merit was and is a great misunderstanding (La controverse reposait de part et d'autre sur des malentendus).[1] But is this method really leading to the goal? Barth[2] and Berkouwer[3] have announced their objection as to whether one could annul 400 years of controversy, that has so sharply split Christendom, with irenic and surely well-intentioned explanations as to language and content, as simply misunderstanding. This method seems to offer a possibility of an evasion rather than of an explanation!

The method of completion seems to be a more serious attempt. It is represented by Jedin,[4] Tüchle,[5] Stirnimann,[6] and Schillebeeckx.[7] The more moderate theologians who pursue the ecumenical dialogue can with this method combine their fidelity to the dogma with their ecumenical engagement. The decisions of Trent can, according to this position, be taken as "incomplete" (Schillebeeckx).[8] They must not be the last word (Tüchle);[9]

---

[1] Emery, Le Christ notre récompense, p. 209.

[2] Barth, "Ein Brief an den Verfasser," quoted in Küng, Rechtfertigung, p. 12.

[3] Gerrit C. Berkouwer, Recent Developments in Roman Catholic Thought, trans. J. J. Lamberts (Grand Rapids, MI: Eerdmans, 1958), p. 62.

[4] Jedin, Kirche des Glaubens, 2:552.

[5] Tüchle, Geschichte der Kirche, 3:153.

[6] Stirnimann, "Zur Rechtfertigung in dialektisch-katholischer Besinnung," SKZ 125 (1957):650.

[7] Schillebeeckx, "Das tridentinische Rechtfertigungsdekret in neuer Sicht," Conc(D) 1 (1965):453.

[8] Ibid.

[9] Tüchle, Geschichte der Kirche, p. 153.

nothing stands in the way to "further develop" the Tridentine formulations (Stirnimann).[1] A revision[2] or correction[3] is of course completely excluded, for Catholic dogmas are irreformable.[4] This method surely makes allowance for a certain rapprochement with Luther, but no complete consensus can be attained. Jedin consented to this publicly.[5]

    The method of correction appears more radical and daring. It is represented by some of the "Systematiker" or "Ökumeniker." Naturally it is not a matter of a public correction of the content of Trent or its definitions. This would be theological suicide! But by cautious criticism of Trent, as Pfürtner dared for the first time,[6] and by a new interpretation according to today's consciousness of faith (Pesch),[7] one goes beyond Trent. The council is questioned on the basis of time-conditioning and limitation of understanding.[8] Had some of Luther's concerns even come in the council's vision? Hasler courageously answers this with "No."[9] Trent battled against a caricature of its opponent.[10] Pesch

---

[1] Stirnimann, "Zur Rechtfertigung in dialektisch-katholischer Besinnung," SKZ 125 (1957):650.

[2] Jedin, Kirche des Glaubens, 2:552.

[3] Schillebeeckx, "Das tridentinische Rechtfertigungsdekret in neuer Sicht," Conc(D) 1 (1965):453.

[4] DS 3074.   [5] Jedin, Kirche des Glaubens, 2:550.

[6] Pfürtner, Luther and Aquinas, pp. 30-34.

[7] Pesch, "Abenteuer Lutherforschung," NOrd 20 (1966):427.

[8] Pfürtner, Luther and Aquinas, pp. 31-33.

[9] Hasler, Luther in der Katholischen Dogmatik, p. 128.

[10] Ibid., p. 285.

says that one must pay attention to the purpose of definition and horizon of thinking of the council and from there dialogue anew with Luther.[1] In the doctrine of merit this means that the <u>substance</u> is binding, but not the <u>concept</u> and the <u>teaching</u>.[2] The substance would be better represented by the biblical concepts "fruit," "answer," "hope," and "gratitude."[3] Küng states that basically a council must be open for criticism and its definitions must be able to be corrected:

> Doctrinal statements . . . are <u>human</u> formulations. As human and historical formulations, it is of the very nature of the Definitions of the Church to be <u>open to correction</u> and to stand <u>in need of correction</u>. Progress in dogma is not always necessarily just an organic development. Dogmas can even lead to a certain petrification of faith.[4]

These are bold words which to date have not yet been heard in Catholic theology. Can the revision of Trent, already demanded by Leibniz, be attained in this way? The followers of this position claim in any case to be able to prove that with their method of interpretation Luther has not been condemned by Trent.[5]

The Lutheran, Erdmann Schott, has classified these tendencies in Catholic theology of today, as they are represented, for example, by Küng, as at the same time "delightful and frighten-

---

[1] Pesch, Theologie der Rechtfertigung, p. 954.

[2] Idem, "Lehre vom Verdienst," in Wahrheit und Verkündigung, 2:1902.

[3] Ibid., 2:1907.

[4] Hans Küng, The Council in Action, trans. Cecily Hastings, p. 205, quoted in Jaroslav Pelikan, Development of Christian Doctrine (New Haven: Yale University Press, 1969), p. 145.

[5] Pesch, "Abenteuer Lutherforschung," NOrd 20 (1966):417; idem, "Der gegenwärtige Stand," Conc(D) 12 (1976):540.

ing" (beglückend und beängstigend).[1] Delightful because such self-criticism does not even stop at Trent, the pride of the Counter-Reformation. But why frightening? Surely not because the Protestant scholar on Luther, who wrote this word at the time of the "affable and tolerant" John XXIII, could foresee that the "affable but unyielding" John Paul II would withdraw the missio canonica from the theology professor Küng at Tübingen! So, frightening because one must ask himself whether Trent really can be interpreted in such a "minimalistic" way and whether Luther's teaching of consecutive, unmerited sola fide-granted salvation comes into its right!

We do not yet wish to regard this as the conclusion. Before we feel ready for that we wish to investigate, in the last chapter, in what way modern Catholic exegesis, dogmatics, and Vatican II interpret the doctrine of merit today in order that we may then be able to answer the question: United with Luther in justification in spite of the doctrine of merit?

Summary

1. At the beginning of the Reformation stands the discussion about indulgence, sacrament of penance, power of the keys, and purgatory. But as soon as it became apparent that the struggle really concerned justification, Catholic polemical theology set up the traditional doctrine of merit as a weapon against Luther's new view of justification. The definitions of the Council of Trent

---

[1] Erdmann Schott, "Einig in der Rechtfertigungslehre?," LuJ 26 (1959):1.

concerning the doctrine of merit are to be understood as countering Luther's justification sola fide (De Letter).

2. Thus, the problem of justification and merit became a main controversy (Bellarmine). Catholic controversialists saw in the past, in the doctrine of merit, an unbridgeable chasm between Protestants and Catholics (Bossuet). In the same proportion in which the doctrine of merit was lifted up, Luther's teaching of justification was put down as Manichaeism and as morally destructive (from Cochläus to Bellarmine, Bossuet, Möhler, Perrone, Döllinger, Scheeben, Denifle, and Grisar). This thesis was also represented even into the most recent past (Cristiani, Paquier, Pohle and Gummersbach, Premm).

3. This uniform rejection of the Lutheran doctrine of justification yields in modern Catholic theology to a broadly divergent pluralism. Beside the traditional view of Luther as a heretic, represented by Luther scholars (Hacker, Richter, Weijenborg) and dogmaticians (Bartmann, Brinktrine, Diekamp, Ott, Pohle and Gummersbach, Premm), other views can be found. Thus, e.g., the position that Luther's teaching is partly heretical, partly orthodox (Bläser, Bouyer, Congar, Jedin, De Letter, Moeller, Van de Pol, Schmidt, A. and E. Stakemeier). The early Luther until the Lecture on Romans (Bellucci) or until the outbreak of the Reformation (Wicks) is worthy of note. This position is exceeded by the "historians" in the Luther research (Iserloh, Lortz, Manns) and an integration of the "Catholic Luther" is demanded. Since Luther proves himself in justification to be much more Catholic than had been perceived, unity exists with Luther in the main

point (Lortz). The thesis of the "Catholic Luther" is nevertheless rejected by the progressive position of the "systematicians" (Brandenburg, Hasler, O. H. Pesch). They are interested in the "reformational Luther" from whom it is valid to learn and who must receive "right of domicile" (<u>Heimatrecht</u>) in the Catholic Church (Brandenburg). The question about the consensus with Luther in justification must be unambiguously answered with "Yes" (Pesch).

4. The same pluralism is evident in the judgment about Luther's criticism of merit. The opinion can still be heard that Luther's criticism was unjustified (Ott) and his position extreme (Stevens). Beside this the opinion is represented that the criticism lives only from Protestant misunderstanding of the Catholic doctrine of merit (Philips). Nevertheless today there are voices that acknowledge the justification of Luther's criticism for the time of the Reformation (Baumgartner, Fiolet, Lortz, Manns, Sartory, Schmaus) and even for today, for Luther's teaching must be applied as a church-critical function (Hasler, Küng, Olivier, Pesch).

5. Although the problem of the doctrine of merit in the life of the Church and in the thinking of open-minded theologians is not felt as pressing forward today (Rahner, Schmaus), it is still being discussed in dogmatics. Thereby different reactions are shown in the ecumenical dialogue on the Catholic side: One feels that term and concept are problematic (Molinski) and wishes to allow the teaching only as a "helpful concept" (<u>Hilfsbegriff</u>) which the spiritually elite can renounce (Baumgartner, Karrer). The idea of merit must be purified (Nicolas, Schillebeeckx) or it

could completely fall away because in growing love thinking about merit disappears (Fransen) and, furthermore, because it represents a "dispensable theologoumenon" (entbehrliches Theologoumenon) which should be replaced by the biblical concepts of "hope" and "gratitude." In this case the doctrine of merit would be no longer an object of controversy (Pesch). For others, this "splendid" (Journet) and "fundamental doctrine" (Rondet) is now as before a necessary boundary against Protestants (Journet). The giving up of the doctrine of merit by some progressive theologians must be disapproved (Hacker), for it is a part of Catholic dogma (Jedin). To see redemption as an unmerited gift is arrogance (Nicolas).

6. If the decrees and canons of the Council of Trent represent the last word in the controversy, then the attempt to harmonize Luther with the council has failed (Jedin). Progressive Catholic theologians however try to think beyond Trent. They discover the "Sitz im Leben" of the council and relativize its pronouncements by references to limited horizons of thought, to certain purposes of definitions, to time-bound situations, and to the differences between substance and formulation. The council must be able to be completed (Jedin, Schillebeeckx) and should not stand above criticism (Pfürtner). It must be interpreted according to today's faith-consciousness of the Church (Pesch). Trent did not at all take into consideration the totality of Luther's teaching (Hasler); therefore, Luther's genuine teaching on justification was not really touched at the council (Pesch). Basically, council decisions must also be open to correction (Küng). This radical view is decisively rejected by other theologians. Dogmatic

decisions are not in need of revision; they are according to the doctrine of the Catholic Church--irreformable and infallible (Jedin).

CHAPTER IV

THE DOCTRINE OF MERIT IN MODERN CATHOLIC
THEOLOGY: ITS THEOLOGICAL FOUNDATIONS

Exegesis and the Doctrine of Merit

The fact that the idea of merit is foreign to the OT[1] and that reward in the Old Covenant is a reward of grace[2] has permeated contemporary Catholic theology more and more. This influence has reduced School dogmatics to an outmoded concept which even in most recent times maintained that the idea of merit was anchored in the OT and saw it established as a principle of reward,[3] especially in passages (e.g., Sir 16:14) of the so-called deuterocanonical books.[4]

Commentators today deny the idea that the thought of

---

[1] LTK, 2nd ed., s.v. "Verdienst--Altes Testament," by V. Hamp.

[2] "If God rewards good works, that is reward of grace." Ibid. "In the OT the reward granted by God is always understood as reward of grace." Schmaus, Glaube der Kirche, 2:651. "Actually they did call Yahweh's justice a ḥesed, mercy." P. Zerafa, "Retribution in the Old Testament," Ang. 50 (1973):489.

[3] See Brinktrine, Lehre von der Gnade, p. 227; Diekamp, Dogmatik, 2:571.

[4] Brinktrine (Lehre von der Gnade, pp. 226-27) cites according to the Vulgate: "Omnis misericordia faciet locum unicuique secundum meritum operum suorum . . . ;" the statement that the verse is lacking in the LXX does not prove true; it only sounds significantly different there: πάσῃ ἐλεημοσύνῃ ποιήσει τόπον, ἕκαστος κατὰ τὰ ἔργα αὐτοῦ εὑρήσει. The Hebrew text differs from that: כל הצדקה יש לו שכר.

retribution in the OT is determined by a legal claim.¹ Indeed, one may find an abundance of expressions in the OT expressing the thought of retribution,² so that the latter becomes a most important moral motivating force,³ but nowhere does a kind of juridism adhere to the theology of retribution, for the biblical covenant idea rests upon God's freedom and one's due obedience.⁴

Initially, Israel understood retribution as purely earthly and collective⁵ until with the development of religious individualism after the Exile (Jeremiah, Ezekiel) it interpreted the idea of retribution as eternal and individual.⁶ According to Schmid the latter view was even operational in earlier times.⁷ The Catholic view⁸ denies a purely anthropocentric meaning of retribution in the sense of a law of immanence, each deed necessarily drawing from itself the corresponding consequence as postulated by the Protestant Klaus Koch.⁹ Retribution goes forth from God and is

---

¹LTK, 2nd ed., s.v. "Verdienst--Altes Testament," by V. Hamp; Zerafa, "Retribution," Ang. 50 (1973):486, 494.

²As the most important Zerafa names שכר (reward), שלם (retribution), גמל (fruit), פקדה (punishment), נקמה (revenge), פעלה (deed and consequence), חטא (sin and punishment) and און (sin and punishment); ibid., pp. 466-70.

³Schmid, Evangelium nach Matthäus, p. 287.

⁴Zerafa, "Retribution," Ang. 50 (1973):487.

⁵Schmid, Evangelium nach Mätthaus, p. 287.

⁶Ibid.; DSp, s.v. "Mérite," by A. Solignac; Baumgartner, Grâce du Christ, p. 213.

⁷Schmid, Evangelium nach Matthäus, p. 287.

⁸Zerafa, "Retribution," Ang. 50 (1973):485.

⁹Klaus Koch, "Gibt es ein Vergeltungsdogma im Alten Testament?," ZTK 52 (1955):3, 7, 19.

therefore theocentric; it is God's gift, which He distributes without being indebted (Job 33).[1] It is recognized that both the idea of equivalence of work and reward and the principle of claim do not come from the OT but from the theology of Late Judaism.[2]

In view of this, modern Catholic theology sees its task in having to interpret the struggle of Jesus against the Rabbinic concept of merit in the NT. Contemporary exegetes have clearly demonstrated that Jesus rejected any kind of reward-reckoning and in so doing denied the Pharisaic teaching of reward.[3] However, Catholic theologians draw completely different conclusions from this: growth in faith, promise of reward, good works, righteousness of the Judge, and just punishment are evaluated as proofs for a Christian doctrine of merit from the mouth of Jesus and the Apostles.[4] Jesus is supposed to have expressed clearly two main elements of the Catholic teaching of merit--the cooperation between God and man, and the believer's right to a heavenly reward.[5]

On the other hand, a number of contemporary exegetes have expressed their doubts about such an interpretation: (1) Since

---

[1] Zerafa, "Retribution," Ang. 50 (1973):483.

[2] Schmid, Evangelium nach Matthäus, pp. 288-89; Schmaus, Glaube der Kirche, 2:651.

[3] Paul Gaechter, Das Matthäusevangelium (Innsbruck; Tyrolia, 1962), p. 202; Schmid, Evangelium nach Matthäus, pp. 284-86; Wilhelm Pesch, Der Lohngedanke in der Lehre Jesu (Munich: K. Zink, 1955), pp. 22, 52.

[4] SM(E), s.v. "Merit," by W. Molinski; DSp, s.v. "Mérite," by A. Solignac.

[5] M. François Berrouard, "Le mérite dans les Evangiles Synoptiques," IsL. 3 (1956):192, 200.

Jesus compares the true disciple with a child (Mk 10:15), he requires a disposition to renounce reward and to confess its impotence before God.[1] Man is never a partner of God.[2] (2) Out of the sovereignty of God, under which man is cast as "child," "slave," "servant," and "steward," it follows that there can be no kind of right or claim before God.[3] The same conclusion can be drawn from the believer's love for God. Love which wishes to make a claim in expectation of a gift in return is worthless.[4] God's coming to man first with His gift precludes any thought of merit. And nowhere does Jesus speak of such merit.[5] Man as a cooperator with God, who can transfer "surplus merit from his account in the hereafter" to the benefit of a fellow believer is not the disciple but the Pharisee.[6] Jesus, however, clearly stated that reward-seeking and anxiety about salvation are foreign to the gospel since God's salvation (the preceding kingdom, the already existing treasure, the prepared meal, the proposed adoption as son) precedes every work of man.[7] Consequently, obedience and expectation of reward are separate.[8]

This radical result, of course, does not coincide with the

---

[1] W. Pesch, *Lohngedanke*, pp. 56-57.

[2] Engelbert Neuhäusler, *Anspruch und Antwort Gottes* (Düsseldorf: Patmos, 1962), p. 36.

[3] Ibid., pp. 36, 66. Cf. Meinertz, *Theologie des NT*, 1:104.

[4] Neuhäusler, *Anspruch und Antwort*, p. 45.

[5] Ibid., p. 97.　　　　[6] Ibid., pp. 66-67.

[7] Ibid., pp. 44, 55, 61, 76.　　[8] Ibid., p. 72.

dogmatic claim that Jesus' teaching of reward establishes the doctrine of merit. This claim, already present in Thomas Aquinas' coupling of merit and reward (<u>meritum et merces ad idem referuntur</u>),[1] is maintained even into the present.[2] Jesus is supposed to have expressly taught a "morality of reward"[3] and to have especially emphasized the thought of reward in the Sermon on the Mount.[4] This fact is said to have thrown Protestants into great embarrassment (<u>ce qui ne cause pas peu d'ennui au protestantisme</u>).[5]

These statements, however, are strongly challenged by exegetes and even by some dogmaticians. Since Jesus only seldom[6] or hardly ever[7] speaks of reward, the thought of reward is not a central teaching of Jesus,[8] but only a "secondary phenomenon" (<u>Begleiterscheinung</u>).[9] When Jesus speaks of reward, he means

---

[1] <u>S. Th.</u> la2ae. 114, 1.

[2] Bartmann, Dogmatik, 2:117; Brinktrine, <u>Lehre von der Gnade</u>, p. 227; Billot, <u>De gratia Christi</u>, p. 245; Diekamp, <u>Dogmatik</u>, 2:571; Herman F. Fiolet, <u>Ecumenical Breakthrough</u> (Pittsburgh: Duquesne University Press, 1969), pp. 389-99; Robert W. Gleason, <u>Grace</u> (New York: Sheed & Ward, 1962), p. 175; Lange, <u>De gratia</u>, p. 565; Mausbach, <u>Moraltheologie</u>, 1:304; Ott, <u>Dogmatik</u>, p. 320; Premm, <u>Glaubenskunde</u>, 4:299; idem, <u>Dogmatic Theology</u>, p. 262; Schmaus, <u>Dogmatik</u>, 3/2:514; idem, <u>Glaube der Kirche</u>, 2:651; Schmidt, <u>Brückenschlag</u>, pp. 145-47; <u>DSp</u>, s.v. "Mérite," by A. Solignac.

[3] Schmidt, <u>Brückenschlag</u>, p. 147.

[4] Brinktrine, <u>Lehre von der Gnade</u>, p. 228.

[5] Marie-Joseph Lagrange, <u>Evangile selon Saint Matthieu</u>, 4th ed. (Paris: Lecoffre, 1927), p. 87.

[6] W. Pesch, <u>Lohngedanke</u>, p. 2.

[7] Neuhäusler, <u>Anspruch und Antwort</u>, p. 97.

[8] Dettloff, "Rechtfertigung," in <u>HThG</u>, 2:393. Schmid, <u>Evangelium nach Matthäus</u>, p. 293.

[9] Meinertz, <u>Theologie des NT</u>, 1:104.

neither "payment owed,"[1] nor reward of accomplishment but of grace.[2] This fact precludes any thought of a just legal claim to reward. Reward is only a "metaphore" (<u>Bild</u>)[3] for the promise of God.[4] The only thing man merits is the judgment.[5] Since everything depends on God's goodness, there can be no pursuit of reward.[6] The teaching of merit is one of the "most disputed themes of polemical theology."[7] The factor primarily responsible for this controversy is the change from the biblical concept of reward to one of law (<u>Verrechtlichung</u>). The application of the concept of merit to the eternal reward is therefore "problematic."[8] Thus, it is understandable that to the Reformers the thought of merit seemed unacceptable.[9]

Can one say, on the basis of this surprising similarity to Luther's teaching of reward with its rejection of the idea of merit, that contemporary Catholic theology is also ready to accept a teaching of reward that lacks merit? Evidences of this are undeniably at hand in a few representatives, above all with those who

---

[1] W. Pesch, <u>Lohngedanke</u>, p. 2.

[2] Dettloff, "Rechtfertigung," in <u>HThG</u> 2:393; Schelkle, <u>Theologie des NT</u>, 3:71; Meinertz, <u>Theologie des NT</u>, 1:104; Küng, <u>Christ sein</u>, p. 201; Schmid, <u>Evangelium nach Matthäus</u>, p. 293.

[3] Schmid, <u>Evangelium nach Matthäus</u>, p. 293.

[4] Neuhäusler, <u>Anspruch und Antwort</u>, p. 45.

[5] W. Pesch, <u>Lohngedanke</u>, p. 52.

[6] Neuhäusler, <u>Anspruch und Antwort</u>, pp. 44, 55, 61.

[7] Dettloff, "Rechtfertigung," in <u>HThG</u>, 2:393.

[8] Ibid.   [9] Ibid.

relativize or deny the equation: reward=merit. Thus, e.g., Schelkle affirms that the idea of reward emphasizes the responsibility of the person before God, but that the person has no claim to a reward that the obedience of the believer will always be defective, and the true Christian will not wish at all to heap up merits because discipleship, as a matter of course, motivates one to act.[1] Küng states it even more clearly: Neither does the word "reward" have in the NT the meaning of merit, nor is the matter of merit biblical in itself.[2] In the Scripture the morality of merit is the morality of the Pharisee.[3] For Jesus there is no merit at all, for by "reward" He means the gift of God which God freely bestows without any claim by man. God always gives more than the person merits. "Reward" simply means that God truly gives a retribution.[4]

O. H. Pesch speaks most clearly. The idea that reward and merit coincide pertains only to Rabbinic theology and not to Jesus.[5] Here, in his view, the Catholic (W. Pesch) and the Protestant (G. Bornkamm) specialists agree. In five points one can demonstrate the contradiction between the biblical view of reward and the extrabiblical concept of merit.[6]

1. In Scripture punishment alone is merited, not reward.

---

[1] Schelkle, Theologie des NT, 3:71.

[2] Küng, Rechtfertigung, p. 263.   [3] Ibid.

[4] Idem, Christ sein, p. 201.

[5] O. H. Pesch, "Lehre vom Verdienst," in Wahrheit und Verkündigung, 2:1868-69.

[6] Ibid., 2:1870-72.

2. Even if it were otherwise, every merit is forfeited on account of man's sin. Jesus blesses those who are conscious of their unworthiness.

3. Reward is promised to those who act selflessly and not for the sake of reward.

4. God dissolves and challenges the human concepts of justice and merit (parable of the workers in the vineyard; parables about the lost coin, sheep, and son).

5. The theme of the kingdom permits neither a reification nor a reckoning of the reward.

In addition to denying the equation of reward and merit, the attempt by several Catholic theologians to separate the biblical concept of reward from a legal context is noteworthy. We illustrate this attempt in connection with the explication of the parable of the workers in the vineyard (Mt 20:1-16).

In more recent Catholic exegesis there has been no lack of interpreters who have attempted to harmonize this parable with the judicial structures of the teaching of merit. Perhaps this is the reason why Schmid speaks of a parable which "in spite of its clarity belongs to the most misunderstood parables of Jesus."[1]

Typical of the juridical exegesis of the parable is the explanation of Karl Weiss. According to him, the emphasis of the declaration of the parable lies not on the generous kindness of the owner of the vineyard, but on his justice.[2] All workers, even

---

[1] Schmid, Evangelium nach Matthäus, p. 285. "Die Parabel gehört trotz ihrer Klarheit zu den am meisten missdeuteten Gleichnissen Jesu."

[2] Karl Weiss, "Die Frohbotschaft Jesu über Lohn und Vollkommenheit," NTA 12 (1927):80, 97.

those who have worked the least, could expect the same reward on the basis of a "title of right" (Rechtstitel).[1] How is this to be explained? Weiss works with the concept of "habitual diligence" (habitueller Fleiss)[2] or of "the will to work" (Arbeitswille).[3] He assumes that all workers were equally willing and that the master rewarded according to this.[4] The inner will was the basis of the equality of the workers.[5] Actually the first worked longest, but in disposition there was no difference.[6] Thus, the payment of the last-hired was not an act of kindness but of right,[7] for there must be equal reward for equal endeavour.[8] The willingness to work is the main merit[9] and the payment--not merely according to actual performance and diligence, but also according to habitual diligence--is the "most perfect canon of reward" (volkommenster Lohnkanon).[10] The parable therefore also speaks not of the righteous and sinners, but only of the righteous.[11]

Contemporary Catholic commentators are hardly comfortable with this explanation. W. Pesch describes Weiss as an "untypical outsider" (untypischer Aussenseiter)[12] and Schmid calls his explanation "destruction of the basic thought of the parable" (Zerstörung des Grundgedankens der Parabel),[13] for every meaning

---

[1] Ibid., p. 90.   [2] Ibid., pp. 82, 88.
[3] Ibid., p. 87.   [4] Ibid., pp. 75, 87, 89.
[5] Ibid., p. 79.   [6] Ibid., p. 88.
[7] Ibid., p. 80.   [8] Ibid., p. 87.
[9] Ibid., p. 80.   [10] Ibid., p. 86.
[11] Ibid., p. 94.   [12] W. Pesch, Lohngedanke, p. 11.
[13] Schmid, Evangelium nach Matthäus, pp. 285-86.

ought to proceed from verse 15, that is, from the "sovereign freedom . . . of God's rulership" (<u>souveränen Freiheit . . . des Waltens Gottes</u>).[1] Immediately after its publication, Weiss' work was subjected to a thorough critique by Urban Holzmeister. The latter refers to the fact that Weiss' thesis of the habitual willingness to work has shifted the equalizing factor--which was always attributed to God's kindness--from God's side to the side of man.[2] The kernel of the parable however is not verse 7 (the lacking opportunity), but verse 15 (the free will of the giver of work and his kindness).[3] Nowhere in the whole parable is there any mention that the inner will can displace the outer work.[4] Holzmeister pleads for the explanation of Fonck,[5] who, as one of the best-known exegetes at the turn of this century, had already demonstrated clearly that the main idea of the parable is God's freedom and kindness.[6]

In more recent times Johann B. Bauer has attempted to explain the parable anew from the juridical standpoint. For him the "juridical aspect" is precisely the key to the parable.[7] Bauer defends the thesis that the last-hired workers also had claim to a full day's wage, because according to contemporary Roman law,

---

[1] Ibid., p. 286.

[2] Urban Holzmeister, "Zum Gleichnis von den Arbeitern im Weinberg (Mt 20, 1-16)," <u>ZKT</u> 52 (1928):407.

[3] Ibid., p. 409.   [4] Ibid., p. 411.   [5] Ibid., p. 408.

[6] Leopold Fonck, <u>Die Parabeln des Herrn im Evangelium</u>, 3rd ed. (Innsbruck: F. Rauch, 1909), pp. 354, 356.

[7] Johann B. Bauer, "Gnadenlohn oder Tageslohn (Mt 20, 8-16)?," <u>Bib</u>. 42 (1961):225.

the laborer who worked only part of the day was still to be paid a full day's wage.[1] Therefore, it was not a matter of the freedom and kindness of the master, but of the right of the worker.[2] The kindness of the master was thought evidenced in the fact that he had hired workers late in the day (those ignorant of the Law), and against this the first workers (the Scribes and Pharisees) murmured.[3] The question of payment of wage, however, was decided according to "legal requirement" (Rechtsordnung) and not according to kindness.[4]

Among renowned contemporary Catholic commentators, however, not one--so far as we have been able to determine--seems ready to follow Bauer. New Testament scholars (Schmid, Dillersberger, Gaechter, W. Pesch, Schelkle, Meinertz)[5] as well as dogmaticians (Küng, O. H. Pesch)[6] affirm that in this parable it is a matter of the overturning of the order of human law. Schmid states that the meaning must not proceed from the first part (invitation to the work), but from the second part (sovereign freedom of the owner).[7] The accent lies on the kindness of the master[8] and the whole parable

---

[1] Ibid., pp. 225-26.   [2] Ibid., pp. 227.

[3] Ibid., pp. 227-28.   [4] Ibid., p. 228.

[5] Schmid, Evangelium nach Matthäus, p. 286; Josef Dillersberger, Matthäus (Salzburg: O. Müller, 1953), p. 154; Gaechter, Matthäusevangelium, p. 636; W. Pesch, Lohngedanke, p. 12; Schelkle, Theologie des NT, 3:71; Meinertz, Theologie des NT, 1:104.

[6] Küng, Christ sein, p. 201; O. H. Pesch, "Lehre vom Verdienst," in Wahrheit und Verkündigung, 2:1871.

[7] Schmid, Evangelium nach Matthäus, p. 286.

[8] Ibid.

stands in "sharp contradiction to the reckoning of reward and merit" (<u>in scharfem Gegensatz zur Lohn- und Verdienstrechnerei</u>).[1] With Lk 17 (parable of the servant) this parable--according to Schmid--is the "most important document for the understanding of the thought of reward in Jesus' teaching."[2]

One can well say that this is an unconfessed abandonment of the doctrine of merit. The nearness to Luther is not to be overlooked. We have already stated that not all commentators draw the same conclusions from the texts. Nevertheless, it is astonishing to see how near some contemporary exegetes come to Luther's teaching on work and reward! Whether contemporary dogmaticians are able to use these approaches, and just how far these new interpretations diverge from the traditional ones, we now investigate in the following section.

Dogmatics and the Doctrine of Merit

A survey of dogmatic textbooks which were considered representative of Catholic teaching before Vatican II, easily demonstrates the almost complete absence of presentations of the doctrine of merit which in any measure resemble what modern exegesis has affirmed.

School dogmatics sees the idea of merit exclusively from the viewpoint of the <u>legal claim</u>. Even if one allows that absolute right (<u>de rigore</u>) pertains only to Christ's merit, nevertheless the merit of the believer--on the basis of his co-worthiness (<u>de</u>

---

[1] W. Pesch, <u>Lohngedanke</u>, p. 22.

[2] Schmid, <u>Evangelium nach Matthäus</u>, p. 286.

condigno)--likewise becomes a right in accordance with God's ordinance.[1] Hence, in the Latin works there are the formulations: "true right to reward" (verum ius ad praemium),[2] "right to supernatural compensation" (ius ad supernaturalem retributionem),[3] and "right to reward" (ius ad praemium).[4]

The definitions in other languages are similar. French, for instance, speak of the "right to supernatural reward" (droit à une récompense surnaturelle),[5] "right to reward" (droit à une récompense),[6] "right to the heavenly inheritance" (droit à l'héritage céleste),[7] and "right to glory" (droit à la gloire).[8] Likewise the German dogmatic handbooks read: "proper claim, title to reward" (Eigentlicher Rechtsanspruch, Rechtstitel auf Lohn),[9] "claim of right" (Rechtsanspruch),[10] and "right to reward" (Recht

---

[1] Eduardo Hugon, Tractatus dogmatici, 10th ed. 3 vols. (Paris: Lethielleux, 1935), 2:251.

[2] Tabarelli, De gratia Christi, p. 458.

[3] Tanquerey, Synopsis, 3:130.

[4] Garrigou-Lagrange, De gratia, p. 288.

[5] Idem, Les trois âges de la vie intérieure, 2 vols. (Paris: Les Editions du Cerf, 1938), 1:177.

[6] Jacques Leclercq, Les grandes lignes de la philosophie morale (Louvain: Editions de l'Institut Supérieur de Philosophie, 1946), p. 426.

[7] Odon Lottin, Morale fondamentale (Paris: Desclée & Co., 1954), p. 512.

[8] E. Neveut, "Des conditions de la plus grande valeur de nos actes méritoires," DT(P) 34 (1931):354.

[9] Pohle and Gummersbach, Dogmatik, 2:788, 794.

[10] Premm, Glaubenskunde, 4:294.

auf eine Belohnung).[1] In English works, aside from the definition, "Merit is the right to a reward due for a morally good action,"[2] one even finds such formulations as "strict claim to a reward"[3] and "strict right to a reward."[4]

The idea of right makes the reward appear as a debt owed by God (<u>Deus enim tq. supremus mundi gubernator debet reddere praemia pro operibus benefactis</u>).[5] That this is a divine debt which God owes primarily to Himself and in a further expanded sense only to humankind commentators frequently dilute.[6] This allows, however, the one earning merit to present his works to the rewarder for the reward.[7]

Is this way of thinking and speaking of "legal relationship" (<u>rechtsartiges Verhältnis</u>)[8] between God and man merely a relic from a past era that has long since been overcome in the ecumenical age? Anyone investigating current Catholic textbooks on dogmatics and theological lexicons can confirm that it is not

---

[1] Brinktrine, <u>Lehre von der Gnade</u>, p. 224.

[2] <u>Dictionary of Dogmatic Theology</u>, s.v. "Merit," by P. Parente, A. Piolanti, and S. Garofalo.

[3] Pohle and Preuss, <u>Grace</u>, p. 397.

[4] Berthier and Raemers, <u>Compendium of Theology</u>, 1:363.

[5] Mors, <u>Institutiones theologiae dogmaticae</u>, 4:189; cf. CathEnc., s.v. "Merit," by J. Pohle.

[6] Premm, <u>Glaubenskunde</u>, 4:294; Pohle and Gummersbach, <u>Dogmatik</u>, 2:794.

[7] "<u>Merens</u> enim movet <u>iustitiam</u> retribuentis ad <u>mercedem</u> vel praemium dandum, exhibens illi opus. . . ." Tabarelli, <u>De gratia Christi</u>, p. 457.

[8] Pohle and Gummersbach, <u>Dogmatik</u>, 2:794.

an outmoded concept. For example, in some French writings the
matter is still discussed as it was before Vatican II. Thus,
Baumgartner defines the relationship between merit and reward
expressly as right--and not as a relationship of benevolence.[1]
The reward is owed on the basis of the principle of right (la
récompense est dûe "ex titulo justitiae").[2] Nicolas asserts that
even love cannot exclude the dimension of right[3] because a "certain
right" (une sorte de droit) remains even with love.[4] German
sources do not disagree: Ott defines the meritum de condigno as
"rightful claim" (Rechtsanspruch)[5] and Auer distinguishes the
meritum de congruo from the meritum de condigno, in that he
characterizes the first as a "moral" and the second as a "legal
claim."[6] English works share these views too; indeed they often
speak more optimistically. The condign merit "acquires a claim to
supernatural reward from God,"[7] "the right to a reward,"[8] "a title
to the reward,"[9] and "a strict right to a reward."[10] Italian

---

[1] "La relation entre le mérite et la rétribution a pour fondement nécessaire la justice, ou du moins une certaine justice, et non la pure bienveillance ou la miséricorde." Baumgartner, Grâce du Christ, p. 207.

[2] Ibid.

[3] Nicolas, Profondeurs de la grâce, p. 547.

[4] Ibid., p. 548.   [5] Ott, Dogmatik, p. 321.

[6] Auer and Ratzinger, Dogmatik, 5:228.

[7] Modern Catholic Dictionary, s.v. "Merit," by J. A. Hardon.

[8] The Maryknoll Catholic Dictionary, s.v. "Merit," by A. J. Nevins, ed.

[9] NCE, s.v. "Merit," by C. S. Sullivan; The Catholic Encyclopedia, s.v. "Merit," by R. C. Broderick.

[10] Dictionary of Theology, s.v. "Merit," by L. Bouyer.

theology also uses juridical language (<u>il giusto merita la vita eterna</u>),[1] although Flick says that the concept of merit in Italian has only a weakened juridical sense.[2]

Following Thomas Aquinas who speaks only of a "certain kind of justice" (<u>quidam justitiae modus</u>),[3] Catholic dogmatics again and again attempts to distinguish the idea of merit from the stigma of juridism and with weakened definitions to make it more bearable. Thus, Pohle denies, on the one hand, the juridical character of the concept of merit;[4] and, on the other hand, he reestablishes it within the divine ordinance,[5] even describing it as <u>do ut des</u>.[6] In order to become free from the juridical constraint, one must employ such formulas as: The reward is not rooted in righteousness per se (<u>in eigentlicher Gerechtigkeit</u>);[7] merit bestows only a "certain right" (<u>certain droit</u>;[8] <u>ius quoddam</u>[9]);

---

[1]Flick, "Dialogo sul merito," <u>Gr.</u> 45 (1964):346.

[2]"Non ci sembra che in italiano il termine 'merito' abbia quel senso strettamente giuridico." Ibid.

[3]<u>S. Th.</u> 1a2ae. 114, 1.

[4]"The virtue of justice cannot be brought forward as the basis of a real title for a Divine reward either in the natural or in the supernatural order." <u>CathEnc</u>, s.v. "Merit," by J. Pohle.

[5]"Merit in the strict sense (<u>meritum de condigno</u>) gives a right to a threefold reward: increase of sanctifying grace, heavenly glory, and the increase thereof." Ibid.

[6]Ibid.   [7]<u>LThK</u>, 1st ed., s.v. "Verdienst," by K. Feckes.

[8]Henri D. Noble, <u>L'amitié avec Dieu</u> (Paris: Desclée de Brouwer, 1932), p. 363.

[9]Prudentio de Letter, "De ratione meriti secundum Sanctum Thomam," <u>AnGr</u> 19 (1939):XV.

condign merit is not a strict but a relative merit (Ne parlons pas . . . de mérite strict, mais seulement de mérite fort relatif).[1] It is only a matter of "a certain notion of justice" (une certaine notion de justice),[2] the "juridical framework" of which must be completed by a "psychological framework,"[3] so that "man, therefore, has some rights with God acquired through good works;"[4] but one must speak about this right very carefully and may comfortably overlook its juridical origin.[5]

The concept of "reward" as a metaphor for gift is, of course, incompatible with the most moderate definition of right. Hence, the work of the School dogmaticians and polemical theologians frequently disallows the concept of gift because man "offers God an accomplishment of his own" (er bietet eine eigene Leistung an). In this way, one can speak of merit and deny the idea of a gift.[6] Pure mercy on the part of the giver and nothing but selflessness on the part of the doer would destroy the principle of justice.[7] If good works--as in Luther--were only works of God, then one could view salvation as an "unmerited gift;" but since it is a matter of reward and retribution, the works must also comprise man's own accomplishment.[8] Consequently, the "measure of gain and merit"

---

[1] Noble, L'amitié avec Dieu, p. 361.

[2] Philips, L'union personnelle, p. 272.

[3] Gleason, Grace, p. 174. [4] Ibid., p. 175.

[5] Ibid., p. 176. [6] Premm, Glaubenskunde, 4:295.

[7] "The guiding norm can be only the virtue of justice and not disinterested kindness or pure mercy; for it would destroy the very notion of reward to conceive of it as a free gift or bounty." CathEnc, s.v. "Merit," by J. Pohle.

[8] Schmidt, Brückenschlag, p. 205.

(Mass des Gewinnes und Verdienstes) is formed according to the degree of cooperation (Grad der Mitwirkung).[1] This idea of human capability of accomplishment before God compels the relationship of work and reward under the yoke of merit and payment, complicating the effort of Catholic dogmaticians to remove legalism from the thought of merit. If it is a matter of one's own accomplishment,[2] one's own tiring efforts,[3] and of one's own calculations[4] then it is also close to being a matter of one's own demand for the reward.[5] From this, it follows that reward acquires the character of a quid pro quo (Gegenleistung).[6]

The juridical structure of the idea of merit also leads to subtle systematizing and over-systematizing, as carried on with predilection in the handbooks, especially in the older ones. There one finds, beside the classical division of meritum de condigno ex iustitia and meritum de congruo non ex justitia, the further subdivision of the former into a de rigore iustitiae (equivalent merit of Christ) and into a de condignitate tantum (proportional merit of the believer), and of the latter into a de congruo stricte dictum (quasi-merit for the believer in the state of grace) and into a de congruo late dictum (quasi-merit for the preparation of grace).[7]

---

[1] Bartmann, Gnadenleben, p. 379.

[2] Brinktrine, Lehre von der Gnade, p. 104.

[3] Bartmann, Gnadenleben, p. 412.

[4] Leo A. Coressel, "Merit for Others," RR(StM) 5 (1946):163.

[5] Tabarelli, De gratia Christi, p. 457.

[6] WWKL, 2nd ed., s.v. "Verdienst," by Kirschkamp.

[7] Garrigou-Lagrance, De gratia, p. 291.

Other divisions result from the difference between the natural and supernatural ordinace of right. Thus, one may comprehend merit as not only <u>meritum sive in concreto</u>--that is, according to the totality of the act (such as almsgiving)--but also as <u>meritum sive in abstracto</u>--that is, only according to the meritorious aspect in the act (that which is worth a reward in almsgiving). A merit can be <u>meritum in actu primo</u>; that means, to possess an indigenous moral worth, whereby the idea of retribution may be excluded; but it can also be <u>meritum in actu secundo</u>, whereby the accomplishment performed is accepted for reward. The supernatural merit before God is conceived as such a <u>meritum in actu secundo</u>.[1] This can now be seen again as <u>meritum de condigno</u>, which is to be rewarded out of "justice" (<u>ex iustitia</u>), because a certain (moral) equivalence exists between accomplishment and reward (<u>es besteht eine gewisse [moralische] Gleichheit</u>). If such an accomplishment were to go unrewarded, one would "do injury to justice" (<u>sonst würde die Gerechtigkeit verletzt</u>). If the work is seen from the viewpoint of grace, then this reasoning must prove right. However, it can also be seen from the viewpoint of man as <u>meritum de congruo</u>. In this case the reward follows out of "fairness" (<u>ex decentia</u>). Accomplishment and reward are weighed against each other, and reward is given according to the principle of benevolence (<u>ex liberalitate</u>).[2] In some handbooks, merit is subdivided into a dozen subconcepts, which are compartmentalized, weighed against each other, and differentiated.[3]

---

[1] Premm, <u>Glaubenskunde</u>, 4:293.   [2] Ibid.

[3] Cf. Alexio M. Lepicier, <u>Tractatus de gratia</u> (Paris: P. Lethielleux, 1907), pp. 366-67; Garrigou Lagrange, <u>De gratia</u>, p. 291.

One can only dispense with this juridism if the idea of right and claim is given up. This insight struggles for recognition in contemporary Catholic dogmatics. Heribert Mühlen blames the traditional School dogmatics for having represented the teaching of merit so synergistically that Protestant "misunderstandings" were almost impossible to avoid.[1] Fransen, therefore, demands a "pure doctrine of merit," as "religion demands it."[2] It is actually impossible to unite the religious principle with the juridical. The juridical interpretation of the teaching of merit was a "reaction to Protestantism . . . in an unsatisfactory way."[3] If there must be any talk of "right" in the kingdom of God, then only of such as "God deigns to give us."[4] In this sense, some contemporary Catholic dogmaticians reject the concept of "right" or "claim." Schmaus, for example, says: "Reward is grace; man is not entitled to claim anything before God."[5] Küng contrasts "Leistungslohn" (reward of achievement) with "Gnadenlohn" (reward of grace), which will be given to man "on the basis of His will, without any claim" (aufgrund seines Willens ohne allen Anspruch),[6] and O. H. Pesch states categorically: "The NT separates reward and

---

[1] Heribert Mühlen, "Gnadenlehre," in Bilanz der Theologie im 20. Jh., ed. Herbert Vorgrimmler and Robert van der Gucht, 2nd ed. 4 vols. (Freiburg i. Br.: Herder, 1970), 3:185.

[2] Fransen, New Life of Grace, p. 206.

[3] Ibid., p. 210.   [4] Ibid., p. 212.

[5] Schmaus, Dogmatik, 3/2:515, 518; idem, Glaube der Kirche, 2:651. "Der Lohn is kein Anspruch, den der Mensch bei Gott geltend machen kann, sondern Gnade."

[6] Küng, Christ sein, p. 201.

claim" (Das NT scheidet Lohn und Anspruch).[1] Flick repels the traditional comparison with the do ut des,[2] Rahner, Forster, and Molinski deny or relativize the juridical structure in the idea of merit,[3] and Philips apostrophizes the concept "debt" (debitum) in the relationship of God to man as "Pharisaic error" (C'est l'erreur des pharisiens).[4] Idesbald Ryelandt proposes using the concepts "title" or "right" only with "a certain mental reservation."[5] "The words 'title' and 'right' must be explained and modified."[6] Many Catholic dogmaticians take this warning very seriously and attempt to speak in personalist rather than juristic categories. Some time ago, Malevez proposed forgetting the juridical sound of the word "merit," retaining only the term since it received its consecration in Trent (un vocable que le concile de Trente a consacré).[7] This challenge did not go unheard. Contemporary dogmatic thinking struggles with this warning. Thus, for example, Fransen insists on a purely personalist interpretation: God and man cannot be viewed

---

[1] Pesch, "Lehre vom Verdienst," in Wahrheit und Verkündigung, 2:1905.

[2] ". . . la fede cristiana nella ricompensa dell'altra vita è assai più complessa e non può essere ridotta ad una semplice relazione del 'do ut des' tra la creatura e il Creatore" (Flick and Alszeghy, Il vangelo della grazia, p. 639).

[3] Rahner, Schriften zur Theologie, 3:173; LThK, 2nd ed., s.v. "Verdienst-Systematisch," by A. Forster; SM(E), s.v. "Merit," by W. Molinski.

[4] Philips, L'union personnelle, p. 272.

[5] Idesbald Ryelandt, The Life of Grace, trans. M. Dillon (Dublin: Clonmore & Reynolds, 1964), p. 114.

[6] Ibid.

[7] Léopold Malevez, "Histoire et réalités dernières," EThL 19 (1942):75.

as equal "partners" and "co-workers" enjoying the same rights.[1] The doctrine of merit must be changed into a "living dialectic."[2] It is not a matter of a static right, but of "an active existential relationship"[3] between God, the Father, and us, His children. However, if one still wished to speak of right, it would be rather a "right of honor,"[4] similar to the granting of the Nobel Prize to worthy scientists and artists. Thus, according to Gleason, the idea of merit would be freed from the character of the "automatic magic." This concept can, in any case, only be described as "puerile."[5] Relying on reward would also be void, for neither love[6] nor friendship[7] do any reckoning. In love and friendship, the laws of mathematics cease.[8] Thils warns that too many Catholics have a "quantitative-mathematical" understanding of merit and do not yet think "qualitatively-dynamically."[9] The trend of the times runs toward the idea of what is free and given. Earlier times were perhaps more pious but also more formalistic. It would be catastrophic if the Catholic Church were to transmit the idea of a "'commercialized' piety" (spiritualité 'commerciale')[10] to the modern Christian, who is so much attracted by the evangelical message of grace. Lortz also speaks in a similar way when he says

---

[1] Fransen, New Life of Grace, pp. 206-07.   [2] Ibid., p. 201.
[3] Ibid., p. 207.   [4] Ibid., p. 204.
[5] Gleason, Grace, p. 178.
[6] Fransen, New Life of Grace, p. 225.
[7] Noble, L'amitié avec Dieu, p. 413.   [8] Ibid.
[9] Thils, Sainteté chrétienne, p. 145.   [10] Ibid.

that Catholic practice does not always correspond to the height of this "magnificent and consoling doctrine."[1] Too often the idea of merit is interpreted in "a crude sense," that is, in a reckoning manner. This "mathematical approach to good works and merits . . . smacks of moralism and at times of self-righteousness."[2] But if one should succeed--so Fransen thinks--in interpreting merit purely personalistically, that is, as a love obligation, as a symbol of the mutual devotion, then the idea of merit as "right" would completely disappear, for "love does away with 'merit' by the very intensity which it attains. Achievement, too, disappears; it makes room for the person himself. Man henceforth disposes of nothing better than symbols to express his love."[3]

There is an intensive struggle in Catholic dogmatics concerning this new meaning and new formulation. The juridical content of the word creates a "malaise"[4] and is sensitive (délicat).[5] The concept is ambiguous (une notion ambiguë).[6] The difficulty is two-fold: (1) of semantic nature, because it is a matter of overcoming the juridical connotations of meritum, especially as modern man equates, wages and reward (in German, der Verdienst [wages] instead of das Verdienst [merit]) and with wages respects more the personal worthiness than the achievement itself (right to basic wages, social

---

[1] Lortz, The Reformation, p. 232.   [2] Ibid.

[3] Fransen, New Life of Grace, p. 205.

[4] Gleason, Grace, p. 173.

[5] Thils, Sainteté chrétienne, p. 144.

[6] Edmond Chavaz, Catholicisme romain et protestantisme (Tournai: Casterman, 1958), p. 75.

security, bonus).¹ Where it is a matter of distinction and not of claim, "one can no longer speak of commutative or distributive justice."² (2) It is also of a systematic nature, because the complexity of the life of grace defies a rigid classification, and difficulties only arise from systematization (<u>les difficultés commencent lorsque les théologiens cherchent à systématiser les conditions du mérite</u>).³ Fransen thinks that one would avoid many superfluous controversies if one could find a "more suitable expression" to paraphrase the teaching of how the entrance into eternal life follows the keeping of the commandments.⁴ The efforts of most recent Catholic theology are directed to this. In spite of the danger of falling, ourselves, into the trap of systematizing, we nevertheless attempt to group these new ideas and formulations for the sake of an overview:

1. <u>The Idea of Participation</u>: Charles Meyer indicates that the Latin word <u>meritum</u> comes from the Greek μέρος (part). That is, one could translate merit simply with participation in the divine life through love. Thereby the works of man become divine, "in some limited way theandric." The love of God becomes the love of the believer and thereby acquires value. This value signifies "a pledge and guarantor of divine grace and protection."⁵ Thus,

---

[1] Fransen, "Das neue Sein," in <u>Mysterium Salutis</u>, 4/2:977.

[2] Ibid., 4/2:978.

[3] <u>DSp</u>, s.v. "Mérite," by A. Solignac.

[4] Fransen, "Das neue Sein," in <u>Mysterium Salutis</u>, 4/2:978.

[5] Charles R. Meyer, <u>A Contemporary Theology of Grace</u> (Staten Island, NY: Society of St. Paul, 1971), p. 144.

according to O'Brien, we are confronted with a "juridical concept" which "expresses the personalist aspect of the growth and fulfillment of the life of grace."[1] One could therefore see the juridical element as purely formal, although the real sense is a thoroughly unjuridical-personal one. It simply expresses a relationship. Merit then would mean nothing else but man's "Yes" to God;[2] and between man's works of grace and the fellowship with God (eternal life) an "immanent relation"[3] arises, which one could characterize as a "response cycle"[4] or an "engaged freedom."[5] In this relationship work is less important than the person. In view of this, Fransen says:

> In our phenomenological analysis, we drew attention to the fact that merit is to be estimated less by performance or achievement than by the dignity of the person who freely expresses himself in the achievement. . . . Much less importance is attached to deeds than to love expressed in life.[6]

Here, an agreement with Luther seems possible because he continually emphasized: "Good works are done by a person, who already has been justified through faith, just as good fruits come from a tree which already is good by nature."[7]

---

[1] Corpus Dictionary of Western Churches, s.v. "Merit," by T. C. O'Brien, ed.

[2] Journet, Entretiens sur la grâce, p. 101.

[3] LTK, 2nd ed., s.v. "Verdienst," by A. Forster.

[4] The Catholic Encyclopedia, s.v. "Merit," by R. C. Broderick.

[5] Wacker, Ökumenischer Dialog, p. 270.

[6] Fransen, New Life of Grace, p. 222, italics mine. Cf. DSp, s.v. "Mérite," by A. Solignac.

[7] "Sed bona opera fiunt a persona iam ante iustificata per fidem, sicut fructus boni fiunt ab arbore iam ante bona per naturam." WA 39I, 46, 33-34, italics mine. Cf. WA 7, 231, 16-17.

However, it seems to us that the real distinction arises right here. It is not by chance that the Catholic theologian speaks of the "dignity of the person" and Luther speaks of "faith," for the former means by grace the "ontic quality" of the person, the proprium; the latter, the "forensic acquittal and the sanctifying Lordship of Christ," therefore the alienum. For faith, although I experience it as my faith, can never fall into the possession of man, since it is identical with Christ (ipsa comprehendit Christum),[1] and only thereby are forgiveness and victory realized (et ignoscitur et vincitur).[2]

While Luther must speak from the viewpoint of his understanding of sole agency of God and experienced partnership of man, Catholic personalism can speak of "cooperation," "not [as] a mere passive openness or receptivity, [but as] an active engagement in the life of justice and righteousness. . . . The doctrine of merit . . . is the definition of a property or quality inherent in the good works."[3] In the Catholic view, personalism can go beyond the realm of analogy and become "full partnership." The person is, of course, no "independent partner,"[4] but since "the Catholic doctrine of justification . . . affirms that man is intrinsically changed by justification, he has been taken into full partnership with God."[5] Schmaus interprets the ontic quality in the sense of

---

[1]WA 39I, 83, 27.   [2]Ibid., 40.

[3]Stevens, Life of Grace, pp. 62-63, italics mine.

[4]SM(E), s.v. "Merit," by W. Molinski.

[5]Ibid., italics mine.

the Franciscan light streaming into the soul (<u>Der Mensch ist durchglüht und durchleuchtet von Gottes Licht und Glut</u>),[1] but this meaning, built more on relation than on possession, also permits one to speak of God as "chiefly active" (<u>Haupttätiger</u>)[2] and hence of man still as "secondarily active" (<u>Nebentätiger</u>). The merits of man, at least in a secondary way (<u>comme cause seconde</u>),[3] are therefore his own merits. Accordingly, in the framework of the <u>gratia creata or inhaerens</u> the Catholic personalist meaning has great difficulties in overcoming the autonomous aspect[4] in the principle of merit!

2. <u>The Idea of Fruit</u>: Some Catholic theologians attempt to identify the concept of merit with the biblical idea of fruit: "Merit a fruit;"[5] merit is to be supplanted by the "deeper concept of fruit;"[6] grace and merit are related to each other "as the blossom prepares the fruit" (<u>comme la fleur prépare le fruit</u>).[7]

---

[1] Schmaus, <u>Dogmatik</u>, 3/2:518. [2] Ibid.

[3] Journet, <u>Entretiens sur la grâce</u>, p. 101.

[4] "Good works of the supernatural order . . . do not mean in any way that the reality of man's causality is diminished. . . . The reality of merit [is] indicating . . . the reality of man's action in the order of salvation. . . . Man is enabled to work for his own eternal beatitude." Stevens, <u>Life of Grace</u>, pp. 62-63. "The danger of the doctrine is that it . . . readily suggests <u>that man is in some way independent of God.</u>" <u>SM(E)</u>, s.v. "Merit," by W. Molinski, italics mine. Cf. Hasenhüttl's definition: "Entfaltung der <u>Eigentätigkeit</u>." <u>Kritische Dogmatik</u>, p. 143, italics mine.

[5] Gleason, <u>Grace</u>, p. 183.

[6] Hans Urs von Balthasar, <u>Schleifung der Bastionen</u>, p. 28, quoted in Pöhlmann, <u>Rechtfertigung</u>, p. 208.

[7] Malevez, "Histoire et réalités dernières," <u>EThL</u> 19 (1942): 69.

The idea of fruit permits the actions of the believer to be defined as "simple and obvious" (einfach und selbstverständlich)[1] and without any reckoning of a reward. One can then say:

> Meritorious obedience is a human condition, which, in His love of goodness and of mankind, the Father wills to regard (though He gains nothing) as man's fulfillment of the covenant founded by and on God's love that man has not earned.[2]

Thus, if one speaks of natural fruit that <u>must</u> grow, it is clear that one again stands very near Luther. For in the view of the Reformer, God's commandments must be fulfilled[3] and indeed as a natural consequence of faith.[4] He can even--as we have seen--describe this as cooperation,[5] because he understands this experientially as a working of God through us.[6] When Lortz refers to "meriting" (<u>mereri</u>) as "receiving" (<u>accipere</u>),[7] then the consensus with Luther seems truly to have been reached.

But is it really so? Is the "human condition" of which Most speaks not a telelogically oriented condition (final

---

[1] Schelkle, Theologie des NT, 3:71.

[2] NCE, s.v. "Grace (in the Bible)," by W. G. Most.

[3] "Steht dan die gerechtickeit im glauben, szo ists klar, das er allein alle gebot erfullet und alle yhre werck rechtfertig macht, <u>seint dem mal niemant rechtfertig ist, er thu dan alle gottis gebot.</u>" WA 6, 211, 4-6, italics mine.

[4] "Dan das erst werck ist glauben, ein gut hertz und zuversicht zu got haben. Ausz dem fleust das ander gute werck, gottis namen preysen." WA 6, 249, 14-16.

[5] ". . . das er mit uns und durch uns sein werck wil wircken." WA 6, 227, 31.

[6] ". . . das wir allein got in uns wircken lassen unnd wir nichts eygens wircken in allen unsern krefften." Ibid., 244, 5-6.

[7] Lortz, "Grundzüge," in Reformata Reformanda, 1:245.

ausgerichtete Bedingung), while it is for Luther a consecutive result (konsekutive Auswirkung)? One can indeed with Thomas Aquinas see fruit also from the standpoint of a teleological process (seed--tree)[1] and not as with Luther of a consecutive process (tree--fruit)! If our works occur in view of salvation (en vue du salut),[2] then this interpretation of the idea of fruit is the Thomistic and not the Lutheran one!

3. <u>The Idea of the Dynamic of Life</u>: This synonym for merit ("God's dynamic action in us")[3] proceeds from the dynamic of grace in order to overcome the static nature of juridism. Once God has grasped man, and man remains under God, a process begins which can be called a "qualitatively intensified"[4] and a "positive perfection of himself."[5] Küng explains this process simply in the sense of the Scripture as a denial of passivity.[6] Here one would surely also be very near to Luther, for we remember the words of faith as a lively and active attitude (lebendig, schefftig . . . ding).[7] And yet this view of the perfection of the person is at the same time very far removed from Luther since for the Reformer this is not an ontic

---

[1] S.Th. 1a2ae. 114, 3 ad 3.

[2] Malevez, "Histoire et réalités dernières," <u>EThL</u> 19 (1942):69.

[3] Peter Riga, <u>Catholic Thought in Crisis</u> (Milwaukee: Bruce Publishing Co., 1963), p. 156.

[4] Stevens, <u>Life of Grace</u>, p. 63.

[5] <u>SM(E)</u>, s.v. "Merit," by W. Molinski.

[6] "Wie in der Schrift geht es allein darum, dass der Mensch nicht in träger sittlicher Passivität sitzen bleibe." Küng, <u>Rechtfertigung</u>, pp. 264-65.

[7] DB 7, 11, 9.

process, in which the person in himself becomes better ("a healing from within,"[1] "a partner . . . with intrinsic value"[2]), but rather Christ gains greater and greater control over the life of the believer because faith increases.[3] The dynamic of faith is, however, something essentially different from that which even today is called in Catholic dogmatics "increase in grace."[4] Fransen indeed states that contemporary Catholic theology renounces the concept of "ontological growth" (ontologisches Wachstum).[5] He proposes to speak of a life developing towards God. He calls this life-dynamic "intensification of the basic option" (Verstärkung der Grundoption).[6] In so doing, he succeeds in focusing on grace from a more actual-dynamic than from a habitual-ontic view. He does not, however, rid himself of the idea of merit; he only relativizes it, when he says that every intensification of the basic option for God "merits" a further intensification of grace.[7] Thus, even the principle of life-dynamic is unable to break through the bipolar-causal structure of human devotion as a pre-condition and means for God's ultimate gift. For Luther, however, it is exactly the opposite. Only from

---

[1] Stevens, Life of Grace, p. 63.

[2] SM(E), s.v. "Merit," by W. Molinski.

[3] Christus "quotidie venit ad me, quia hoc agit, ut crescat fides et conscientia de die in diem perfectius apprehendat Christum et in dies minuatur lex carnis, peccati, pavor mortis et quidquid lex habet." WA 40I, 536, 8-537, 1.

[4] Riga, Catholic Thought, p. 156; Stevens, Life of Grace, p. 63.

[5] Fransen, "Das neue Sein," in Mysterium Salutis, 4/2:980.

[6] Ibid.   [7] Ibid.

the totality of the gift is it possible for the devotion of man to increase without thereby "meriting" anything.

4. *The Principle of Love*. With the concept of "basic option," love for God is brought into play. What would be more suitable for eliminating the juridical bonds than the power of love? Therefore, it seems to modern Catholic theologians that precisely the biblical love-relationships between God and man and that between man and God are suited for making the idea of merit more comprehensible, or indeed, as Fransen says, to effect its disappearance.[1] But such a "disappearance" is not quite so easy, because apparently for Catholic thinking love also can be "merited." Von Rudloff sees the process as follows: Through justification man becomes "inwardly better" (innerlich besser). This "nobility of the soul" (Adel der Seele) finds its expression in works of love to God. God *must* respond to this love likewise with His "reciprocating love" (Gegenliebe). Thus, the works carried out in a state of grace earn an increase of grace and finally salvation. The love of man and God's "Gegenliebe" form a reciprocal game of "surrender" (Hingeben) and "conferment" (Austeilen), whereby God's "Gegenliebe" can be viewed as "reward" for man.[2]

This presentation for laymen, written before Vatican II, is definitely not outdated. Even today one reads similar formulations. The juridical idea of contract remains; it is merely applied, not to two trade partners, but to two love partners. Thus, for example, Nicolas says:

---

[1] Ibid.

[2] Leo von Rudloff, Kleine Laiendogmatik, 2nd ed. (Regensburg: F. Pustet, 1934), p. 99. Cf. Ryelandt, Life of Grace, p. 119.

> Le contrat, même s'il conserve un caractère foncièrement juridique, n'est plus une stipulation portant sur des objets, mais l'ensemble des relations établies par l'amour entre deux sujets. Il reste que, lorsque ces liens ont été établis par un amour réciproque, <u>celui qui aime mérite l'amour de l'être aimé</u> et toutes ses manifestations.[1]

In his book about grace, Fransen also speaks of an "unquestionable 'right'" to merited love: "He who bestows his love and knows that it is accepted, acquires an unquestionable 'right' to a return of love."[2]

The Dutch Catechism too refuses commercial juridism without abandoning merit. God's relationship to us rests not upon a "work contract," and the reward is no "payment" but "acceptance in love."[3] Nevertheless it includes the idea of merit even if it is only a relativized ("No one knows how many merits he collects") and a subordinated concept ("Therefore no person can live solely for the sake of the merits, but in love").[4]

In <u>Mysterium Salutis</u>, Fransen first breaks wholly with every kind of juridism: "We no longer see in it [= the concept of the Covenant] the slightest juridical relationship, not even in a sense of analogy."[5] He places the theme of grace wholly upon the biblical

---

[1] Nicolas, <u>Les profondeurs de la grâce</u>, pp. 538-39, italics mine.

[2] Fransen, <u>New Life of Grace</u>, p. 205, italics mine.

[3] <u>Glaubensverkündigung für Erwachsene--Dt. Ausgabe des Holländischen Katechismus</u> (Nijmegen: Dekker & van de Vegt, 1968), p. 149.

[4] Ibid.

[5] Fransen, "Das neue Sein," in <u>Mysterium Salutis</u>, 4/2:979. "Wir erblicken darin nicht mehr das geringste Rechtsverhältnis, selbst nicht in einem analogen Sinn."

basis of divine Covenant and promise.¹ Only here can the idea of merit with its implied "concept of reciprocity" (<u>Aspekt der Gegenseitigkeit</u>)² be realized. But is not Luther closer to the idea of Covenant when he places everything on God's side and ascribes to man's obedience only salvation-witnessing and salvation-preserving value, instead of the character of a "movement which leads us to heaven" (<u>eine Bewegung, die uns zum Himmel führt</u>)?³ The aspect of reciprocity is surely biblical, but according to the Reformer in such a way that man should not fall away from the Covenant with God; but according to the Catholic interpretation, in such a way that God provides for man the possibility to reach Him completely.

5. <u>The Principle of Dignity</u>: Already in the section about the idea of man's participation in the divine life, the attempt was made to bind the idea of merit less to works and much more to the individual. This thought recurs in the interpretation: merit=to receive dignity.⁴ Since, however, merit is a gift (<u>Verdienst [ist das], was Gottes Gnade uns gibt</u>),⁵ the concept of dignity seems at first to be safeguarded against any misunderstanding that would lead to asserting one's autonomy before God. The definition: "Merit means . . . the arrival of grace" (<u>Verdienst sagt . . . Angekommensein der Gnade</u>)⁶ also sounds completely harmless until one begins to ask

---

¹Ibid.   ²Ibid.   ³Ibid.

⁴Heinrich Fries, <u>Antwort an Asmussen</u>, pp. 885-87, quoted in Pöhlmann, <u>Rechtfertigung</u>, p. 208; Wacker, <u>Ökumenischer Dialog</u>, p. 270.

⁵Rahner, <u>Schriften zur Theologie</u>, 3:171.

⁶Ibid.; idem, <u>Theological Investigations</u>, trans. Karl-H. and Boniface Kruger (Baltimore: Helicon Press, 1967), 3:143.

the question, what does the expression "arrival of grace" really mean? Rahner wishes to go beyond the scope of ontologism and speaks of "ontological self-communication of God" (seinshafter Selbstmitteilung Gottes),[1] which ought not to be understood in an "objectified and reified" manner (gegenständlich-sachhaft).[2] Other theologians like Baumgartner speak of an "ontological transformation" (transformation ontologique)[3] or, like Molinski, of "supernatural transformation."[4] Until a short time ago, School dogmatics still proudly insisted on the "material character" (Dinglichkeitscharakter) in this event.[5] But even if one prefers Rahner's personalist interpretation, which contemporary Catholic theology recommends,[6] it is still a matter of man's perfection having "intrinsic value."[7] "Alien justice" is not sufficient.[8]

This conceptualization is based--as we have seen--upon the teaching of Thomas Aquinas, for whom grace determines the dignity

---

[1] Idem, Grundkurs des Glaubens, 9th ed. (Freiburg i. Br.: Herder, 1976), p. 122; idem, Foundations of Christian Faith, trans. William V. Dych (New York: Seabury Press, 1978), p. 116.

[2] Ibid. Cf. Hasenhüttl: Gnade ist das, was den Menschen "zu seiner Identität bringt." Kritische Dogmatik, p. 143.

[3] Baumgartner, Grâce du Christ, p. 206.

[4] SM(E), s.v. "Merit," by W. Molinski.

[5] "Dass die rationalistischen Protestanten eine 'dingliche Gnade' nicht annehmen wollen, ist nicht zu verwundern. Denn sie wollen ja überhaupt nichts Übernatürliches zugeben, keine göttliche Offenbarung, keine Sakramente, die eben dann die dingliche Gnade hervorbringen." Premm, Glaubenskunde, 4:220, italics mine.

[6] Cf. Mühlen, "Gnadenlehre," in Bilanz der Theologie, pp. 148-159.

[7] SM(E), s.v. "Merit," by W. Molinski.

[8] Hasenhüttl, Kritische Dogmatik, p. 143.

of man,[1] yet at the same time, because grace enters into the soul, grace constitutes the intrinsic value of man himself, for he now possesses grace.[2] Consequently, merits are his merits, at least in so far as he is a participant in them as a second cause.[3] The dignity of grace is inseparable from the dignity of man and his works.[4]

This leads to the possibility of completely contrary confessions of faith, derived from two of the most famous Catholic saints. We have already referred to the avowal of Theresa of Lisieux. Other statements of hers sound similar in emphasizing human insufficiency: "I have never sought anything other than to please the dear Lord. If I had striven to accumulate merits, I would be without any hope at this hour."[5] This quotation reveals a dignity wholly embedded in the thought of divine love and divine mercy. One can, however, with equal justification view dignity from the standpoint of human works of grace. Theresa of Avila does precisely this, when she says: "Don't allow me to step up to You with empty hands, for the reward must correspond to the works."[6] Surely, even these works do not come into existence without grace

---

[1] S.Th. 1a2ae. 114, 3.   [2] Ibid., 1a. 43, 3.

[3] Ibid., 3a. 19, 3. Cf. Baumgartner, Grâce du Christ, p. 219.

[4] "L'azione meritoria consta quindi come di due parti, distinte ma non separabili." Antonio Piolanti, Il mistero della communione dei Santi (Rome: Desclée & Co., 1957), p. 632.

[5] "Je n'ai jamais desiré que faire plaisir au Bon Dieu. Si j'avais cherché à amasser des mérites, à l'heure qu'il est, je serais désespérée." Quoted in DSp, s.v. "Mérite," by A. Solignac.

[6] Ibid., italics mine.

but also not without human cooperation. In this sense, Luther would probably not have subscribed to the formula proposed by Fries: sola gratia--non sine homine.[1]

      6. The Idea of the Eschatological Prolepsis: One can also attempt to circumvent the juridical character in merit by viewing the whole life of grace as a process in time initiated by God in man and developing towards eternity. This process results in making eternity proleptically present. In such a process there is no claim, but only development. Let us recall Fransen's definition of the "movement which leads to heaven."[2] Baumgartner speaks of a "divine life which develops."[3] Malevez calls it a "slow ripening in the soul," and "heaven in the true process of becoming."[4] What is eventually to be is already present inceptively. The driving force of this movement is the cooperation between God and man, the working together of the divine gift (grace) and the free action of man (free will).[5] The result of this cooperation is merit, appearing as the "essential principle of this continuity" (le mérite est un principe essentiel de cette continuité).[6] Thus, Rahner calls merit "eternity in time" (Ewigkeit in der Zeit)[7] and Gleason characterizes it as the beginning of heaven: "Merit is

---

[1] Quoted in Pöhlmann, Rechtfertigung, p. 208.

[2] Fransen, "Das neue Sein," in Mysterium Salutis, 4/2:979.

[3] Baumgartner, Grâce du Christ, p. 117.

[4] Malevez, "Histoire et réalités dernières," EThL 19 (1942): 71.

[5] Baumgartner, Grâce du Christ, p. 117.   [6] Ibid.

[7] Rahner, Schriften zur Theologie, 3:171.

... a real beginning of heaven."[1] The works of the Christian are not signs of the justification that has taken place and been completed, but are the cause (des causes)[2] of the developing justification (progrès de la justification).[3] As far as these works correspond to the commandments of God and of the Church, they are set up as final (zweckgerichtet) and are "linked together with the idea of reward" (mit dem Lohngedanken verbunden).[4] Only the opera supererogatoria are really not connected with reward; they come spontaneously into being for the service of God and one's neighbor.[5] Therefore, the Catholic teaching of merit, viewed positively, is a "further growth through one's own, although totally dependent, supernatural activity" (ein Weiterwachsen durch eigene, obwohl total abhängige, übernatürliche Tätigkeit).[6]

There is no doubt that the idea of the proleptic completion through the development of the supernatural life relativizes the idea of claim, for if in the development the end is already anticipated, it is a matter of process-thinking which can never be wholly grasped by juridical concepts. "Juristic thinking" today is, therefore, not useful any more in Catholic theology.[7] If merit represents

---

[1] Gleason, Grace, p. 177.

[2] Baumgartner, Grâce du Christ, p. 117.   [3] Ibid.

[4] Auer and Ratzinger, Dogmatik, 5:238.   [5] Ibid.

[6] Witte, "Ist Barths Rechtfertigungslehre katholisch?," MThZ 10 (1959):45.

[7] "The 'economic' metaphor of reward for services rendered may well be regarded as a way of talking . . . which no longer proves as helpful as it once seems to have done." Cornelius Ernst, The Theology of Grace (Notre Dame, IN: Fides Publishers, 1974), p. 85.

"successive stages of growth,"[1] then out of this organic-final process-thinking even a kind of assurance of salvation, an "incontrovertible guarantee and pledge of our initial transformation into the glory of God"[2] can be attained; for what God has begun and man has assented to must arrive at its goal.[3] The human answer makes the process into a "growth in the order of response"[4] and thereby distinguishes it from the "biological order of birth, aging and death."[5] Despite failure and deviation it is, however, a "continuous curve with a definite sense."[6]

Does the Catholic dogma with this kind of assurance concur with Luther's view? Here one should note that the concept of the eschatological prolepsis is developed in the framework of a first and second justification, even if this is not always explicitly stated, and that man's acquiescence is realized in the form of the Scholastic <u>actus salutares</u>, that is, in salvation-achieving and salvation-obtaining works. In the first justification, God has begun the process of grace. Including an active cooperation developed by man, the process of the second eschatological justification unfolds carrying over the prolepsis to its fulfillment on the basis of merits. Towards this fulfillment works are performed. They are therefore done in order to procure future salvation, not to witness to present salvation. This reduces--in our view--Luther's assurance of salvation to the Thomistic assurance of

---

[1] Ibid., pp. 84-85.   [2] Ibid., p. 85.

[3] "The repeated 'We know' of 1 John evokes the realized gift of God's love which anticipates its consummation in glory." Ibid.

[4] Ibid., p. 84.   [5] Ibid.   [6] Ibid., p. 85.

hope. Between the two lie perhaps points of contact, but not of agreement.

But should one not at least admit that the endeavour to overcome juridical thinking attempts a "purification" of the teaching of merit? Does it not at least hint at reformational shores, even if it does not successfully reach them?

At first glance one surely would not answer these questions negatively. Whoever explains merit in the framework of participation, fruit, life-dynamic, love, dignity and eschatological prolepsis is thinking in personalistic and not in juristic categories. It is clear that one approximates Luther in this approach, for O. H. Pesch has pointed out that unlike the "objectivizing" character of Thomistic theology, Luther's thinking by faith is unambiguously "existential."[1] But the personalistic trait is not so intensive in the latest Catholic dogmatics, that there would not still remain concepts of right and claim. The final-meritorious way of salvation is apparently inseparable from juridism! Where goal-oriented meritorious actions--including human activity--come into being, many still see at least a "certain kind" of claim upon reward established, for "if a reward is not given for a meritorious act, for something earned, for something that is mine, the word loses its meaning."[2] So Gleason speaks of "some rights with God acquired through good works"[3] and Philips speaks of a "certain concept of righteousness" which conducts itself like

---

[1] Pesch, Theologie der Rechtfertigung, p. 937.

[2] Lortz, The Reformation, p. 231.   [3] Gleason, Grace, p. 175.

a chain reaction and sets in motion continuous giving on the part of God.[1] Malevez says that one can forget the juristic origin, but not wholly, only _almost_ wholly (_presque_ complètement),[2] and Schmaus believes that one should value the merits "not merely" as a claim upon salvation.[3] Flick and Alszeghy help themselves with the distinciton between "strict juridical sense" (_l'espressione . . . non ha un significato strettamente giuridico_) and "claim to honor" (_un titulo che rende una persona degna_).[4] Merit would thus become at least a "right to honor." Fransen speaks in his book about grace still as of "some sort [of] 'right'"[5] and only in _Mysterium Salutis_ does he renounce any relationship of right even in the sense of an analogy.[6] The assertion, however, that only a few Scholastic-oriented theologians like de Letter had interpreted the doctrine of merit juridically[7] is—to say it gently—rather an understatement: Until recently the entire School dogmatics has interpreted

---

[1] "Le mérite a pour unique conséquence qu'une certaine notion de justice enchaîne le premier don de Dieu à un don subséquent." Philips, _L'union personnelle_, p. 272.

[2] Malevez, "Histoire et réalités dernières," _EThL_ 19 (1942): 75, italics mine.

[3] Schmaus, _Dogmatik_, 3/2:523.

[4] Flick and Alszeghy, _Il vangelo della grazia_, p. 667.

[5] Fransen, _New Life of Grace_, p. 204.

[6] "Den Begriff 'Verdienst vor Gott', wenn auch in einem sehr analogen Sinn, auf Beziehungen kommutativer oder distributiver Gerechtigkeit einzuschränken, wie dies einzelne scholastische Theologen versucht haben, ist ganz einfach ein semantischer Irrtum. . . . Wir erblicken darin nicht mehr das geringste Rechtsverhältnis, selbst nicht in einem analogen Sinn." Idem, "Das neue Sein," in _Mysterium Salutis_, 4/2:978-79.

[7] Ibid., 4/2:978.

the doctrine of merit juridically, and we have seen how difficult it is for contemporary Catholic dogmatics to rid itself of it.[1]

It is equally difficult for them to overcome the systematic structures which in the past had been derived from juristic thinking, such as in the distinction between congruous and condign merits. Only O. H. Pesch, who attempts to think biblically, does not engage in a discussion about these Scholastic distinctions at all. The fact that there can be no meritum de congruo in the preparation for justification was asserted before Vatican II only by inveterate Thomists like Diekamp. And even he allowed as valid a congruous merit "in an improper sense" (im uneigentlichen Sinn).[2] To attain first justification the overwhelming majority of School dogmaticians accepted a meritum de congruo and to attain the second, a meritum de condigno.[3] Only seldom did they leave the question open.[4] Contemporary dogmaticians apparently have difficulties in extricating

---

[1] Flick and Alszeghy, for example, do not wish absolutely to renounce the analogous sense when they say: "In questo senso, il rendere la vita eterna come premio agli atti buoni del giusto, ha une certa analogia con un atto di giustizia, la quale esige appunto che a ciascuno sia dato il suo." Il vangelo della grazia, p. 668.

[2] Diekamp, Dogmatik, 2:585. Garrigou-Lagrange calls it "late dictum." De gratia, p. 293.

[3] Thus, for example, De Aldama, González and Solano, Sacrae theologiae summa:3:698; de Abárzuza, Manuale theologiae dogmaticae, 3:518, 533; Berthier and Raemers, Compendium of Theology, 1:367; Billot, De gratia, p. 288; Dander, Summarium tractatus dogmatici, 2:22; LTK, 1st ed., s.v. "Verdienst," by K. Feckes; Lange, De gratia, p. 579; Mors, Institutiones theologiae dogmaticae, 4:195; Premm, Glaubenskunde, 4:316; Pohle and Gummersbach, Dogmatik, 2:821; Schmidt, Brückenschlag, p. 197; Towers, "Sanctifying Grace," in Teaching of the Catholic Church, 1:580; Tabarelli, De gratia Christi, p. 505.

[4] Brinktrine, Lehre von der Gnade, pp. 250-51.

themselves from this kind of traditional thinking. Gleason[1] and Ott[2] still affirm congruous merit for justification. Baumgartner contents himself with the statement that the meritum de condigno is "theologically certain" (théologiquement certain), but that its explanation and everything associated with the meritum de congruo is subject to free theological opinion (sont des opinions théologiquement libres).[3] Lais and Fransen opt, on the contrary, for a rejection of the meritum de congruo as merit for attaining justification, Lais, on the basis that the meritum de congruo represents no merit at all in a real sense[4] and Fransen, because here "all initiative rests with God"[5] and because one may probably prepare himself for justification but cannot earn it. The basic option of those not yet justified is actually not yet filled with the totality of love, but only with its beginning.[6]

Criticism of the meritum de condigno is articulated even more cautiously. This is not surprising, since until the recent past almost everybody in Catholic theology applied the Tridentine statement of vere mereri to condign merit.[7] At the present time this

---

[1] Gleason, Grace, p. 182.   [2] Ott, Dogmatik, p. 325.

[3] Baumgartner, Grâce du Christ, p. 212.

[4] Hermann Lais, Dogmatik, pt. 1 (Kevelaer: Butzon & Bercker, 1965), p. 241.

[5] Fransen, New Life of Grace, p. 227.

[6] Idem, "Das neue Sein," in Mysterium Salutis, 4/2:981.

[7] See Hugon, Tractatus dogmatici, 2:260; CathEnc, s.v. "Merit," by J. Pohle; Tanquerey, Synopsis, 3:138; Brinktrine, Lehre von der Gnade, p. 243.

view is represented, among others, by Baumgartner[1] and Sullivan.[2] Dettloff, on the other hand, uses Duns Scotus' opinion that <u>vere mereri</u> need not absolutely mean a true <u>meritum de condigno</u>, because the Council of Trent did not at all wish to decide the controversy between Thomists and Scotists on this point.[3] Schmaus likewise seems to deny the concept of strict condign merit. For him this merit is not grounded so much in the quality of the deed, but in the mercy of God which lets it stand as merit.[4] Fransen characterizes the concept <u>meritum de condigno</u> as "abstract and not very elegant" (<u>abstrakt und nicht sehr elegant</u>).[5] He is satisfied with the concept <u>vere mereri</u> alone.[6] The Scholastic view of the revival of merits after the loss of sanctifying grace--an opinion that was supported even by Pius XI[7] and was advocated by representatives of the School dogmatists[8]--is called by Fransen a "strange concept" (<u>seltsame Auffassung</u>).[9] But even he allows a "revival," although not in a juridical sense (restitution of the collected merits), but

---

[1] Baumgartner, <u>Grâce du Christ</u>, pp. 115, 210-11.

[2] <u>NCE</u>, s.v. "Merit," by C. S. Sullivan.

[3] Dettloff, "Rechtfertigung," in <u>HThG</u>, 2:394.

[4] Schmaus, <u>Dogmatik</u>, 3/2:511.

[5] Fransen, "Das neue Sein," in <u>Mysterium Salutis</u>, 4/2:981.

[6] Ibid.

[7] Pius XI, "Indictio universalis iubilaei anni sancti," <u>AAS</u> 16 (1924):210.

[8] See Diekamp, <u>Dogmatik</u>, 2:588; <u>LTK</u>, 1st ed., s.v. "Verdienst," by K. Feckes.

[9] Fransen, "Das neue Sein," in <u>Mysterium Salutis</u>, 4/2:981.

in a personalistic sense (in re-conversion, God acknowledges our past again).

Thus, one can see efforts to overcome the old structures, especially the structures of juridical imprint; of course, this has not yet succeeded fully. Even if it had succeeded in fully doing away with juridism, the idea of merit would still have been so theologically structured that one could not possibly speak of agreement with Luther's doctrine of justification. We see the bases for the incongruity in the very different form of Catholic theology of reason, grace, and work. We shall briefly establish this in the following:

1. <u>The Catholic Rationalism</u>: Because natural theology plays a major role in Catholicism, the doctrine of merit is also seen from the viewpoint of reason. What <u>coram hominibus</u> seems reasonable cannot be unreasonable <u>coram Deo</u>! The society in which we live requires a constant effort of one who wishes to increase his achievements. Only in this way can there be greater reward and reputation. Why, according to reason, should it be otherwise with God? In the final analysis, it is a matter of those "simple truths" which to the ordinary man ("If you work, you'll get somewhere!") as well as to the sophisticated minds ("The one who diligently strives, that one we can redeem")[1] appear thoroughly plausible. Did not Luther also praise reason[2] and give it highest

---

[1] <u>Faust</u> 2. 5. 11936-37. "Wer immer strebend sich bemüht, den können wir erlösen."

[2] "Vernunfft ist auch ein Liecht und ein schönes Liecht." WA 48, 76, 2.

priority in art, medicine, and law?[1] Yes, but at the same time he also made us aware that its parameters are thereby circumscribed. In divine matters, reason is blind[2] and seductive. It is therefore not only a "beautiful light" (schönes Licht) but also a "whore" (Hure).[3] The theology of reason (Scholasticism) would have to "first be led to the bath"[4] because metaphysical speculation does not belong in Christian thinking.[5] Christian thinking occurs only and solely from faith. If therefore Christendom speaks of works, it is never in a "moral" but in a "theological" sense. That is, they never stem from natural thinking but from faith.[6]

Very little of this distinction is evident in Catholic dogmatics. Instead it allows the greatest latitude to that which appears "so reasonable." The doctrine of merit "accords fully with natural ethics," for just as in society, so there are likewise in religion sanctions (demeritum) and distinctions (meritum).[7] Thereby one can appeal either to the study of comparative religions

---

[1] WA 39I, 175, 11-13.

[2] "Drumb ist sie alhier zwejmahl blind und spricht: Hastu gesundigt, so thue busse und gute werck, auff das du diese Sunde bezalest, werde ein Monch und Nonnen und thue gott die drej gelubde, der keuscheit, armuths und gehorsams. Dan bezalestu nicht allein deine Sunde, sondern auch ander leuthe Sunde, den du hast gute werck ubrig, die du andern kanst mittheilen." WA 47, 169, 30-35; cf. WA 48, 76, 2-9.

[3] "Die doll, blindt huer, di vernunfft." WA 9, 559, 28; "Die vernunfft, des teuffels hure." WA 18, 164, 25-26.

[4] WA 39I, 229, 24-25.   [5] Ibid., 228, 14-16.

[6] WA 40I, 412, 14-24.

[7] CathEnc, s.v. "Merit," by J. Pohle.

or to philosophical speculation.[1]

In "speculative reflection" (<u>spekulative Betrachtung</u>)[2] the teaching of merit appears "highly suitable" (<u>hoch angemessen</u>).[3] "Theological reason" (<u>der theologische Vernunftgrund</u>)[4] perceives the fundamental agreement of natural and supernatural order.[5] The Catholic view "corresponds more to the natural sense of human morality and that confirms its correctness."[6] Thus, one can rely on moral-philosophical considerations: Since merit must be conceived in relation to the ethical good and not to eudaemonistic advantages, the concept of merit comes close to Kant's categorical imperative.[7] But according to the Catholic view, Kant overlooked the aspect of merit. For, even if the good is done for the sake of the good, every free-will moral action constitutes nevertheless a personal merit.[8] But since the good is not only the moral good

---

[1] "Le varie descrizioni del giudizio dei morti, tanto diffuse nelle mitologie, rispecchiano l'idea che le opere buone danno un certo titolo, un certo diritto ad una remunerazione. Anche la filosofia popolare considera spesso come un postulato dell'esistenza di Dio e dell'immortalità dell'anima, il premio dell'altra vita, per le opere buone." Flick and Alszeghy, <u>Il vangelo della grazia</u>, p. 638.

[2] Diekamp, <u>Dogmatik</u>, 2:573.

[3] Ibid.; cf. Mausbach, <u>Moraltheologie</u>, 1:304.

[4] Pohle and Gummersbach, <u>Dogmatik</u>, 2:798.

[5] Ibid.; cf. Jean Daujat, <u>The Theology of Grace</u>, trans. by a nun of Stanbrook Abbey (New York: Hawthorn Books, 1959), pp. 103, 108.

[6] "Zweifellos entspricht die katholische Auffassung mehr dem natürlichen Moralempfinden des Menschen, und das spricht für ihre Richtigkeit." Schmidt, <u>Brückenschlag</u>, p. 153.

[7] Leclercq, <u>Philosophie morale</u>, p. 427.

[8] Ibid., pp. 430-31.

(deeds accomplished on the basis of the moral law), but also the religious good (deeds accomplished on the basis of the promise of heavenly reward), morality and the search for happiness coincide again.[1] Such striving is not of inferior value, it is rather a duty.[2] If one's own salvation takes priority over love for God, this striving is not immoral.[3] If God appears only on the periphery, even a mediocre work can be meritorious.[4] It is of great importance to impress this on the mind of the believer because many Catholics have been influenced by Reformation or Kantian ideas.[5] Such individuals must recognize that Catholic ethics cannot be understood without the doctrine of merit.[6]

According to Catholic opinion, psychology also supports the doctrine of merit. The merit motive is psychologically necessary for the masses[7] and is a legitimate motive.[8] The believer can depend on his works.[9] On the one hand, he should be motivated by anxiety

---

[1] Schmidt, Brückenschlag, p. 148.   [2] Ibid.

[3] Schmaus, Dogmatik, 3/2:525; Brinktrine, Lehre von der Gnade, p. 232; Baumgartner, Grâce du Christ, p. 225.

[4] Brinktrine, Lehre von der Gnade, p. 248; Diekamp, Dogmatik, 2:584.

[5] Mausbach, Moraltheologie, 1:304.

[6] "Cette doctrine des oeuvres méritoires explique toute la vie catholique." Léon Cristiani, Du Luthéranisme au Protestantisme (Paris: Bloud & Cie., 1911), p. 381.

[7] CathEnc, s.v. "Merit," by J. Pohle; Pohle and Gummersbach, Dogmatik, 2:800; Baumgartner, Grâce du Christ, p. 225.

[8] Theological Dictionary, s.v. "Merit," by K. Rahner and H. Vorgrimler; Baumgartner, Grâce du Christ, p. 226.

[9] Bartmann, Gnadenleben, p. 364; NCE, s.v. "Merit," by C. S. Sullivan.

that he might be lost[1] and, on the other hand, by love for God and for his own salvation.[2] Bartmann says that the Christian should be more "inventive," in order to increase his holiness,[3] while Rahner speaks of a kind of "self-forgetting" accumulation of merits.[4] At any rate, the believer cannot avoid collecting merits!

The principle of merit also appears reasonable from the standpoint of social life, for God and man can be regarded as contract partners. God's promise is not fulfilled simply out of faithfulness to man; it is like a promise that may be equated with a "contract."[5] If man realizes the required supernatural acts, then God will reward them according to their immanent quality.[6] Even on the horizontal level from person to person, the idea of merit has its validity. The Christian can intercede for his fellow man, earning for others de congruo that which for himself he earns de condigno. Indeed above and beyond that he can earn for another de congruo a first actual grace, something he cannot do for himself.[7] Thus, prayer[8] and work[9] become a "daily round of meritorious actions."[10] In so doing, however, one need not think that we should give "all our

---

[1] Schmidt, Brückenschlag, p. 130; Baumgartner, Grâce du Christ, p. 225.

[2] Daniel Feuling, Glaubenslehre, p. 851.

[3] Bartmann, Gnadenleben, p. 426.

[4] Rahner, Schriften zur Theologie, 3:172.

[5] Pohle and Gummersbach, Dogmatik, 2:793.   [6] Ibid.

[7] Coressel, "Merit for Others," RR(StM) 5 (1946):164.

[8] Ibid., p. 165.   [9] Ibid., p. 163.   [10] Ibid.

merit to some one else,"¹ but we participate with our merits in the "apostolate for the salvation of souls."² Thus, the idea of merit appears to the Catholic as highly reasonable from all vantage points: from the history of religion, from moral teaching, from psychology, and from social life.

2. The Catholic Concept of Grace: A basic grasp of the Catholic doctrine of merit requires a few remarks on the Catholic doctrine of grace. Both stand in closest correlation to each other, for the idea of merit fostered the theology of grace³ and conversely grace, as "property or quality inherent in the good works," is the foundation of merit.⁴ Merit is the effect of grace (nobillissimus gratiae cooperantis effectus).⁵

The scholastic references to grace as a "created gift" (donum creatum)⁶ and the dogma of "inherent justice" (iustitia inhaerens, gratia inhaerens)⁷ have been very frequently understood in a "reified manner" (in dinglicher Weise)⁸ until the present. Some

---

¹Ibid., p. 169.   ²Ibid., p. 163.

³LTK, 2nd ed., s.v. "Verdienst," by A. Forster.

⁴Stevens, Life of Grace, p. 63.

⁵Billot, Gratia Christi, p. 244.

⁶S.Th. 1a. 43, 3 ad 1; 1a2ae. 110, 2 ad 3.

⁷DS 1547, 1561.

⁸". . . uber die Nachlassung der Sünden hinaus [wird] ein übernatürliches Etwas, eine 'dingliche Gnade' der Seele im Augenblick der Rechtfertigung von Gott eingegossen." Premm, Glaubenskunde, 4:207, italics mine. "Gnade . . . ist ein geschaffenes Gut." Bartmann, Dogmatik, 2:11, italics mine. "Die Gnade ist ein überaus himmlisches Ding." Idem, Gnadenleben, p. 72, italics mine. "Man kann das Göttliche . . . nur erfassen, wenn man dafür ein Organ besitzt." Schmidl, Brückenschlag, p. 191, italics mine.

time ago, Catholic polemical theology still conceived "reified grace" like a <u>shibboleth</u>, separating Catholic truth from Protestant error (Ancient and New Protestantism).[1] Grace was defined as something physical,[2] as something created apart from God,[3] which is qualitatively inherent in man,[4] effectively removing sin from the person,[5] becoming man's personal possession.[6] Actually,

---

[1] Premm, <u>Glaubenskunde</u>, 4:207, 220.

[2] "Etwas Moralisches und Physisches." Ibid., 4:220. "Physischer Influxus . . . etwas Physisches." Brinktrine, <u>Lehre von der Gnade</u>, pp. 92, 186. "Physische . . . Qualität." Bartmann, <u>Dogmatik</u>, 2:99. "'Physische' Qualitäten." Feuling, <u>Glaubenslehre</u>, p. 225. "Something physically inherent." Pohle and Preuss, <u>Grace</u>, p. 332. "Power . . . through the sacraments, which physically produces grace." Aegidius Dolan, <u>Sanctifying Grace</u> (Cork: Mercier Press, 1953), p. 97. "Assimilatio physica." Van Noort, <u>Tractatus de gratia</u>, p. 127. "Physische Gemeinschaft." Ott, <u>Dogmatik</u>, p. 310.

[3] "Grace [is] a created reality, distinct from God Himself." Stevens, <u>Life of Grace</u>, p. 59. "Gnade . . . [ist] an sich wesentlich von Gott verschieden." Bartmann, <u>Dogmatik</u>, 2:11.

[4] "Une réalité interne . . . dans l'âme juste qui lui demeure attachée." Baumgartner, <u>Grâce du Christ</u>, p. 113. ". . . die der Seele als bleibende Qualität inhäriert." Ott, <u>Dogmatik</u>, pp. 272, 309. "Permanent quality in the soul." Towers, "<u>Sanctifying Grace</u>," in <u>Teaching of the Church</u>, 1:550. "Divine quality inherent in the soul." Pohle and Preuss, <u>Grace</u>, p. 333. "Catholics believe in an embodiment of grace." Thomas Sartory, <u>The Oecumenical Movement and the Unity of the Church</u>, trans. Hilda C. Graef (Oxford: B. Blackwell, 1963), p. 112.

[5] "Die Sünde ist ausgelöscht . . . die Sünde ist vollkommen ausgetrieben." Schmidt, <u>Brückenschlag</u>, pp. 123, 157. "Objective, ontological modification of man." <u>Theological Dictionary</u>, s.v. "Existential, Supernatural," by K. Rahner and H. Vorgrimler. "Grace wipes out sin . . . grace remits sin by his own intrinsic power." Berthier and Raemers, <u>Compendium of Theology</u>, 1:356. "Grace . . . effaces all the stains of our soul." Pohle and Preuss, <u>Grace</u>, p. 333. "Ontologische Sanierung." Witte, "Ist Barths Rechtfertigungslehre katholisch?," MThZ 10 (1959):42. "Übermenschentum." Karl Adam, <u>Das Wesen des Katholizismus</u>, 13th ed. (Düsseldorf: Patmos, 1957), p. 265. "Die Mariologie ist . . . konkrete Gnadenlehre." Ludwig Hödl, "Lumen Gratiae," in <u>Mysterium der Gnade</u>, ed. H. Rossmann and J. Ratzinger (Regensburg: F. Pustet, 1975), p. 245.

[6] See Bartmann, <u>Gnadenleben</u>, p. 148; Berthier and Raemers,

only the <u>gratia creata</u> counted as grace.[1] A certain human autonomy (<u>Selbstand, Selbstmächtigkeit</u>)[2] results from this possession, making cooperation[3] and merit[4] possible. In this way Catholic dogmatics thought itself to have chosen the middle ground between rationalistic naturalism and reformational supernaturalism. In any case, it was taken for granted that the Catholic and the Reformation teachings on grace could not be united and that the Catholic view greatly surpassed that of Luther.

Whether the latter proves true must be determined, however, from the viewpoint of faith of the individual. But that Luther's teaching of grace differs basically from the Catholic interpretation is undeniable in view of Luther's fundamental ideas about grace. Grace never means to Luther a <u>proprium</u> (possessed habit or quality) but always an <u>alienum</u>. Either it is God's gracious attitude

---

<u>Compendium of Theology</u>, 1:352; Rudloff, <u>Laiendogmatik</u>, p. 97. Noble, <u>L'amitié avec Dieu</u>, p. 359.

[1] "Nur die <u>gratia supernaturalis</u> [=gratia creata] ist Gnade im eigentlichen Sinn." Brinktrine, <u>Lehre von der Gnade</u>, p. 31.

[2] Grace "emaniert," "beeigenschaftet," "west" and "durchgnadigt" the person. Feuling, <u>Glaubenslehre</u>, pp. 224, 228, 232, 259.

[3] "Wenn wir den Glauben die erste Brücke zu Gott nennen, dann bauen an dieser Brücke . . . <u>zwei</u> Werkmeister: Gott und der Mensch. Die <u>Hauptarbeit</u> aber leistet . . . Gott mit seiner Gnade." Bartmann, <u>Gandenleben</u>, p. 100, italics mine. "Alle Gottesursächlichkeit . . . geht darauf, diese Tat <u>ersursächlich</u> so zu wirken, dass sie <u>zweitursächlich</u> vom Menschen selbst gewirkt sei. . . . Das ist ja eben der letzte Kern der Freiheit unserer Gnadentaten, dass wir die Handlung nicht nur in ihrem Sosein, sondern überhaupt in ihrem Sein <u>selbstmächtig</u> setzen." Feuling, <u>Glaubenslehre</u>, pp. 249, 247, italics mine.

[4] "A man who possesses this grace becomes a saint, . . . capable of works meritorious for salvation." Berthier and Raemers, <u>Compendium of Theology</u>, 1:352.

(Gottis hulde odder gunst),[1] on the basis of which God provides forgiveness to the sinner, or God's gracious Lordship (Christus, der geyst mit seynen gaben),[2] with which He rules over the life of the Christian. Man does not possess grace, but grace possesses him. But if grace touches our lives, then "it consumes sin" (frisst sie die Sünde auf),[3] i.e., it procures forgiveness of sin through Christ's sacrifice and death to sin through the Spirit, in order that sin may no longer rule our life, until in eternity we finally become entirely free from it.[4] Thus, for Luther grace always expresses itself in the form of a personal relationship and never in the form of an ontic quality.[5] Therefore, in contrast to Aristotelian static quality, the Reformer can bring to bear the dynamic of the biblical creation- and Covenant idea.[6] Just as the creature and the Covenant partner in the Scriptures constantly and wholly depend on God, and do not bring anything from themselves into this relationship, so also for Luther grace means the same as "mercy without merit" (Barmherzigkeit ohne Verdienst).[7] The sinner who has been given salvation by God must not fall out of salvation.

---

[1] DB 7, 8, 11. [2] Ibid., 12.
[3] WA 22, 94, 11-13. [4] Ibid., 22, 96, 1-7.

[5] "Sophistae nostri in eo errore sunt, ut somnient satis esse semel coepisse, sic enim docent, gratiam esse qualitatem latentem in corde, quam si quis habeat tanquam gemmam inclusam in cor, eum respici a Deo, si cooperetur cum libero arbitrio." WA 40II, 422, 23-26.

[6] "Sed nos de gratia aliter docemus et credimus, nempe quod Gratia sit continua et perpetua operatio seu exercitatio, qua rapimur et agimur Spiritu Dei, ne simus increduli promissionibus eius et cogitemus atque operemur, quicquid Deo gratum est et placet." Ibid., 27-30.

[7] WA 33, 50, 14-18.

Accordingly, he may confidently expect God's eschatological redemption. He need not earn this future salvation with divided grace, i.e., sacramental justification as making future salvation possible on condition of cooperation in a final-meritorious process of an increasingly effective justification. The realm of grace is one kingdom both in faith and sight.[1] What man has now by faith will someday unfold for him visibly!

Modern Catholic theologians have learned much from Luther in this respect and attempt to substitute the biblical way of thinking in personal categories for the Aristotelian-Scholastic concept of form and matter.[2] Like Luther, they view grace as favor Dei,[3] as a relationship[4] and not as a possession[5] of something

---

[1] WA 2, 457, 27-30.

[2] "La nostra comunione con il Cristo è una comunione personale." Flick, "Dialogo sul merito," Gr 45 (1964):347. "Der Begriff . . . der Überformung durch die Gnade erhält nun einen eindeutig personalen Sinn." Hödl, "Lumen Gratiae," in Mysterium der Gnade, p. 250. "'Gnade' ist also nicht in erster Linie eine physische Entität im menschlichen Subjekt, sondern sie ist etwas durch und durch Personales." Küng, Rechtfertigung, p. 196. "Sanctifying grace is . . . the intimate, personal relationship of God to me." Anthony T. Wilhelm, Christ Among Us (New York: Newman Press, 1967), p. 30.

[3] "'Gnade' ist nach dem NT nicht eine von verschiedenen physischen übernatürlichen Entitäten, die in Substanz und Fakultäten der Seele sukzessive eingegossen werden, sondern ist Gottes lebendige Gunst und Huld, sein personales und gerade so den Menschen wirkkräftig bestimmendes und wandelndes Verhalten, wie es in Jesus Christus offenbar geworden ist." Küng, "Katholische Besinnung," in Theologie im Wandel, p. 465, italics mine. Cf. Edward Schillebeeckx, Christ. The Experience of Jesus as Lord, trans. John Bowden (New York: Seabury Press, 1980), pp. 86, 87, 89, 90, 116.

[4] "We might call 'grace' . . . a wholly new dimension of rleationship between God and his creation." Ernst, Theology of Grace, p. 29.

[5] "Es geht nicht um mein Gnade-Haben, sondern um sein Gnädig-Sein." Küng, Rechtfertigung, p. 197. Grace is "too often

material.[1] Grace is identical with God Himself,[2] with the Self-communication of God,[3] with Jesus Christ,[4] with being in the Spirit of Jesus.[5] Already long before Vatican II Catholic theologians had been searching for compromise formulas, in order to be able to do justice to both the personal and the reified aspect in the Catholic concept of grace. The best known was the formula of Maurice de la Taille: <u>Actuation créée par acte incréé</u>,[6] which one could translate as "God's uncreated act supplies a created actualizing to the creature." De la Taille is still, however, much indebted to the <u>nécessités métaphysiques</u> but attempts to make the Scholastic thinking of form and matter more dynamic. God as <u>Etre incréé</u> is not changeable, but He strives for a <u>union</u>, which is "a gift of Himself" (<u>un don de soi</u>).[7] This occurs through "something

---

misunderstood, and confused with the recovery of a lost object!" Moeller, "Grace and Justification," <u>LV</u> 19 (1964):727.

[1] "<u>Gnade</u> . . . ist im ersten und letzten Gott selber, . . . also kein <u>Ding</u>." Karl Rahner, "Natur und Gnade in der katholischen Kirche," in <u>Theologie heute</u>, ed. Leonhard Reinisch (München: C. H. Beck, 1959), p. 100.

[2] "Ce don de Dieu, c'est Dieu lui-même (la 'grâce incréée') . . . l'état et la vie d'une personne suscités par l'action d'une autre Personne . . . (grâce 'créée')." Chavaz, <u>Catholicisme romain et protestantisme</u>, p. 136.

[3] Grace is "göttliche Selbstmitteilung." Rahner, "Natur und Gnade," in <u>Theologie heute</u>, p. 92.

[4] "Jesus Christus ist <u>die</u> Gnade Gottes." Küng, <u>Rechtfertigung</u>, p. 198. "In the experience of Jesus Christ in faith, . . . we wish to locate grace." Ernst, <u>Theology of Grace</u>, p. 69.

[5] "Die Gnade lässt sich erfahren als ein Sein im Geiste Jesu Christi." Schmaus, <u>Glaube der Kirche</u>, 2:567.

[6] Maurice de la Taille, "Actuation créée par acte incréé," <u>RechSR</u> 18 (1928):253-68.

[7] Ibid., p. 253.

created" (quelque chose de créé),[1] which one can call "actuation créée par acte incréé," that is, a dynamic infusion, informing or qualifying, through which the "force created . . . imperfect in itself" (puissance créée . . . de soi imparfaite) becomes disposed towards a "wholly divine perfection" (perfection toute divine).[2] In this way the idea of personal union is to be united with the Aristotelian principle of form: "The inhabitation is therefore an actualizing presence or a presence of a quasi-form" (L'inhabitation est donc une présence d'actuation ou une présence quasi formelle).[3]

Although De la Taille's definition is still often used today,[4] nevertheless more and more the biblical-reformational aspect of the gratia increata is stressed[5] and the problem is recognized, which Aristotelianism--"the event of most serious consequences in theological history"[6]--represents for the Catholic teaching of grace.[7]

---

[1] Ibid., p. 254.   [2] Ibid., p. 257.

[3] Robert Morency, L'union de grâce selon Saint Thomas (Montreal: Les Editions de l'immaculée Conception, 1950), p. 50. Cf. The different definitions of grace as "favor" and as "created gift" in R. D. Lawler, ed., The Teaching of Christ (Huntington, IN: OSV, 1976), pp. 370-73.

[4] See Moeller and Philips, Theology of Grace, p. 29; Gleason, Grace, p. 142; Henri Rondet, Essais sur la théologie de la grâce (Paris: Beauchesne, 1964), pp. 76-80.

[5] "Der Primat des lebendigen Gottes als der 'ungeschaffenen Gnade' muss so hervorgehoben werden, dass alles, was als 'geschaffene Gnade' bezeichnet werden kann, ihm unterstellt wird. Dies ist möglich, wenn wir die lebendige, liebende, schöpferische Gegenwart als Vorstellungsmodell verwenden. Die 'geschaffene Gnade' bringt innerhalb dieser Sicht den Sachverhalt zum Ausdruck, dass diese göttliche Gegenwart wirklich an unser Innerstes rührt." Fransen, "Das neue Sein," in Mysterium Salutis, 4/2:928.

[6] Mühlen, "Gnadenlehre," in Bilanz der Theologie, 3:161.

[7] "Dans ce sens, on peut se demander si le terme 'grâce créée . . . est tellement heureux: . . . ces termes doivent être

However, since Catholic theology today is beginning to dissociate itself from the "clasp of the Greek-Scholastic understanding of being"[1] and to discover the biblical personalism of Luther, there is no lack of Catholic voices that already see a rapprochement to the Reformer in the doctrine of grace.[2] However, one cannot help asking whether the Thomistic teaching of grace as "something" (aliquid)--man "possesses,"[3] qualifying[4] him as donum creatum,[5] as habituale donum infusum,[6] can so simply be equated with the concept of Luther, who expressly rejected the teaching of grace as a quality.[7] In addition, there is also the question whether the Tridentine dogma of the gratia inhaerens,[8] which as causa formalis makes righteous[9] and changes intrinsically-ontologically, not extrinsically-pneumatically, can simply be equated[10] with the Pauline ἐνεργεῖν[11] and interpreted as "divine

---

'dédouanés.'" Moeller, "Théologie de la grâce," Irén. 28 (1955):40. "This 'reification' of grace . . . could not but lead to an impoverished theology of the life of grace." CDT, s.v. "Grace," by P. de Letter.

[1]Mühlen, "Gandenlehre," in Bilanz der Theologie, 3:161.

[2]"Divinisation, grâce créée, grâce extrinsèque: ces termes caractérisent le point de vue respectif de l'Orthodoxie, du catholicisme et de la Réforme . . . ces trois visions de la grâce ne sont pas si inconciliables qu'il y paraît." Moeller, "Théologie de la grâce," Irén. 28 (1955):19.

[3]S.Th. 1a2ae. 110, 1. [4]Ibid., 110, 2.

[5]Ibid., 1a. 43, 3 ad 1. [6]Ibid., 1a2ae. 110, 2.

[7]WA 40II, 422, 23-26. [8]DS 1530, 1561.

[9]DS 1529.

[10]Moeller and Philips, Theology of Grace, p. 41.

[11]The passages in Paul that come into question (1 Cor 12:6; Gal 3:5; Eph 1:11, 19; 3:20; Php 2:13; Col 1:29; 1 Th 2:13) all point in the direction of an endowment (gift) from the direct

presence which touches our innermost part" (göttliche Gegenwart, die an unser Innerstes rührt).[1] The admission that Luther "was a voice of the future, while the rejoinder of the Council of Trent was undoubtedly a voice of the Christian past,"[2] is indeed impressive, but it changes very little, precisely because Trent implies not only the past but also the present. In this sense, the interpretations of other contemporary Catholic theologians appear much more sober, who say that grace as an inherent quality is unavoidable,[3] that Trent depends primarily on "reification,"[4] and represents a different kind of teaching of grace than does that of Luther.[5]

3. <u>The Catholic Concept of Works</u>: From the Catholic teaching of grace a direct line leads to the teaching of works: Work follows being (<u>operari sequitur esse</u>).[6] At first this sounds quite

---

Creator-creature relationship through the inworking and indwelling of the Spirit.

[1] Fransen, "Das neue Sein," in <u>Mysterium Salutis</u>, 4/2:928.

[2] Ernst, <u>Theology of Grace</u>, p. 55.

[3] "Der Begriff der Gnade als einer dem Gerechtfertigten inhärierenden Realität, einer 'Qualität' . . . ist nicht zu umgehen." <u>LTK</u>, 2nd ed., s.v. "Aktualismus in der Gnadenlehre," by H. Volk.

[4] "Das Konzil hat . . . primär das 'Dingliche' an der Gnade (die heiligmachende Gnade) im Auge." Schmaus, <u>Glaube der Kirche</u>, 2:656.

[5] "Without giving a detailed theological explanation of formal causality, the Council affirms that the inner structure of the justification of man <u>is not something identical with God or Christ</u> . . . it is <u>something proper to man</u> transformed in Christ. The whole Catholic theology of grace as a <u>created reality</u>, distinct from God himself . . . is here stated by the Council. . . . What theology calls 'sanctifying grace' is here determined and defined as <u>opposite to the Lutheran teaching of justification</u>." Stevens, <u>Life of Grace</u>, p. 59, italics mine.

[6] Baisi, <u>Institutiones theologiae</u>, 3:493.

similar to the Lutheran statement: "Good, pious works never make a good, pious man, but a good, pious man does good, pious works."[1] Actually, these two statements are worlds apart. For Luther the being of the believer is a being in relationship to God. Man is placed <u>before</u> God (justification) and <u>under</u> God (sanctification); each of his works <u>witnesses</u> to this:

> Und das keyn werck, keyn gepott eynem Christen nott sey zur seligkeit, sondern er frey ist von allen gepotten, und auss lauterer freyheit umb sonst thut alls, was er thut, <u>nichts damit gesucht seyness nutzs oder selickeyt</u>, Denn er schon satt und selig ist durch seynenn glaubenn und gottis gnaden, sondern <u>nur gott darynnen gefallen</u>.[2]

In Catholic teaching being is an infused quality (first justification), making salvation possible (second justification). Works <u>attain</u> this salvation. While Luther--as we have already seen--removes works from the process of salvation and sees them only from the viewpoint of witnessing to genuine faith, works have in Catholic teaching an important position in attaining salvation. They have a fourfold power: as <u>impetratio</u> (power of acceptance) through the act of prayer; as <u>propitiatio</u> (power of expiation) through salvific acts which are able to cancel the debt of sin; as <u>satisfactio</u> (power of satisfaction) for the lessening of the punishment of sin; and as <u>meritum</u> (power of merit) for increasing grace and meriting eternal life.[3]

This difference is so significant that one must wonder at

---

[1] WA 7, 32, 5-6. "Gute, fromme Werke machen niemals einen guten, frommen Mann, sondern ein guter, frommer Mann macht gute, fromme Werke."

[2] WA 7, 32, 30-34, italics mine.

[3] Premm, <u>Glaudenskunde</u>, 4:292.

the apparent disregard of this "classical controversy" in current polemical theology.[1] The common Christian concern that works must occur--in a post-Christian world like ours, more necessary than ever--should not obscure the fact that we face here two diametrically opposed positions.

According to Catholic understanding, man is a genuine co-worker in achieving his salvation. Accordingly, dogmaticians speak of cooperatio and cosatisfactio, for man is "himself co-active in the work of redemption" (Die Menschheit ist mittätig im Erlösungswerk) and a "partner in expiation" (mittragend an der Sühne).[2] Christ is the "first co-redeeming person" (der erste miterlösende Mensch).[3] Works are therefore an element of justification, of merit, of satisfaction, and of perfection.[4] Salvation depends upon them[5] and is claimed through them.[6] Even if this does not occur in the form of the Semi-Pelagian completion of grace and work, but in the form of the Scholastic inclusion of work in grace, it still marks

---

[1] See Franz Courth, "Gerechtfertigt von Gott--frei für das Leben," TThZ 83 (1974):90.

[2] Feuling, Glaubenslehre, pp. 341, 846; Cf. Hasenhüttl: "Selbstentfaltung . . . Selbstvollzug [mit] Orientierungspunkten (Z. B. Jesus)." Kritische Dogmatik, p. 146.

[3] Feuling, Glaubenslehre, p. 341.

[4] "Un élément de justification, de mérite, de satisfaction, de perfection." DTC, s.v. "Surérogatoires (oeuvres)," by A. Michel.

[5] "Final and eternal salvation is also dependent on . . . good works." Hacker, Ego in Faith, p. 64.

[6] "Anspruch auf das Heil." LTK, 2nd ed., s.v. "Verdienst," by A. Forster. "Schlüssel zum Himmelreich." Bartmann, Gnadenleben, p. 363.

Catholic teaching with the stamp of legalism,[1] which seems to us incompatible with Luther's thinking on salvation. That heaven should "cost us something,"[2] that it must be "earned" (<u>verdient</u>)[3] and "gained" (<u>erdient</u>),[4] is impossible to harmonize with Luther's teaching on justification and works. The same is true also of the hierarchy of works, which rates the same performance higher for a saintly person than for a less saintly one.[5]

In view of this thought-structure, we must consider the idea of merit an integral part of Catholic teaching, even when it is interpreted more and more personalistically.[6] The final performance of works and the cooperational element in works necessarily lead to the doctrine of merit. Since Luther fought against both, the doctrine of merit had no significance for him in the teaching of justification. To say that it is merely a matter in differences of "conceptual formulation," that those differences are "more verbal

---

[1] Feuling speaks of "Segnungen der Gesetzlichkeit" and of superiority of the active achievement-redemption over the "passive Erlöstheit." <u>Glaubenslehre</u>, pp. 846, 340.

[2] Brinktrine, <u>Lehre von der Gnade</u>, p. 232.

[3] Schmidt, <u>Brückenschlag</u>, p. 120; Ryelandt, <u>Life of Grace</u>, p. 111.

[4] Premm, <u>Glaubenskunde</u>, 4:293.

[5] See Brinktrine, <u>Lehre von der Gnade</u>, p. 238.

[6] Cf. Hasenhüttl: "Die guten Werke sind jedoch echtes 'Verdienst' des Menschen . . . und sind entscheidend für die Befreiung von der Entfremdung." <u>Kritische Dogmatik</u>, p. 144. "It is a prime duty of the Catholic to retain and develop this relationship with God. Only in the state of grace can one merit further blessings and eternal life" Lawler, ed. <u>Teaching of Christ</u>, p. 374.

than real"[1] and that there exists a "possibility of union" (Vereinbarkeit) between the teaching of Luther and that of Trent,[2] does simply not do justice to the matter. We think that those Catholic theologians judge more soberly and correctly who regard the idea of merit not as an "afterthought," but as the very crown of their teaching of works ("Totality of the Catholic affirmation of grace") and see in the element of cooperation a "direct refutation" of the Lutheran teaching of the sole agency of God.[3]

The Question: Justification/Merit and Vatican II

Everything discussed thus far stands under reservation of the Roman Magisterium. For hundreds of years both Catholics and Protestants could point to the Tridentine dogma and, with good reason, assert that the question at issue concerning justification and merit had been definitely settled by Rome against Luther and the Reformation.

With the present ecumenical openness of Catholic theology to the Reformation, however, the old debate has entered a new arena and once again the question must be posed, after the fronts have broached the issue anew: What does Rome say to this?

---

[1] Corpus Dictionary of Western Churches, s.v. "Merit," by T. C. O'Brien, ed.

[2] O. H. Pesch, "Lehre vom Verdienst," in Wahrheit und Verkündigung, 2:1900. In that Pesch places the idea of merit in the distinction between human achievement-merit and divine grace-merit, he does not do justice to the complexity of the final and the cooperation aspects. Right in the latter Schillebeeckx, for example, sees the continuing difference with the Reformation. "Tridentinisches Rechtfertigungsdekret," Conc(D) 1 (1965):453.

[3] Stevens, Life of Grace, p. 63.

Many expected Rome to give an answer at the Second Vatican Council. Although it became clear very quickly that the council would not be a union council but a reform council,[1] the catchwords aggiornamento,[2] dogmatic council,[3] dialogue,[4] mirabile spectaculum veritatis,[5] progress in the understanding of the fullness of divine truth[6] and hierarchy of truths[7] raised the expectation that the problem of "justification" with its additional dimension of "merit" would be so discussed that in the future one would have to take notice, not only of a dialogue of theologians, but also of an official position taken by the Magisterium.

The optimistic commentaries of some Protestant observers,[8] who at that time described Vatical II as a "divine event"[9] that

---

[1] See Skydsgaard and Pedersen, "The Coming Council, Its Purpose and Problems," in Papal Council and Gospel, pp. 96, 122.

[2] "Aggiornamento also stresses ecumenism. . . . There is no longer talk of reunion with Rome. . . . This is now replaced by emphasis on the common Christian search for the activity of the Spirit . . . with the hope that eventually the mutual mistakes of the past will cease to influence the present and the future." Corpus Dictionary of Western Churches, s.v. "Aggiornamento," by O'Brien, ed.

[3] Skydsgaard and Pedersen, "The Coming Council," p. 107.

[4] Unitatis redintegratio 1. 4.

[5] Skydsgaard and Pedersen, "The Coming Council," p. 121.

[6] Dei verbum 2. 8.   [7] Unitatis redintegratio 2. 11.

[8] "Konzil evangelischer Erneuerung" . . . "Konzil ökumenischer Öffnung." Max Lackmann, Mit evangelischen Augen, 4 vols. (Graz: Styria, 1963-65), 2:284, 286.

[9] Roger Schutz, Die Dynamik des Vorläufigen (Freiburg i. Br.: Herder, 1978), p. 66.

would justify Luther's main concerns,[1] reveal that such an expectation was in the air. In the meantime, a practical realism has penetrated both Protestant and Catholic sides. Vatican II was only in part a council of dialogue. The real soul of this "council of ecclesiology"[2] was the "theandric"[3] self-representation of the Catholic Church, which as "fullness of Christ" (plenitudo eius),[4] "universal help towards salvation" (generale auxilium salutis),[5] and "universal sacrament of salvation" (universale salutis sacramentum)[6] transmits truth and grace[7] and whose hierarchical-sacramental mediation is an important factor in salvation.[8] On the meaning of the doctrine of justification in general and for the ecumenical dialogue in particular came no word.[9] It is hard to

---

[1] "Wie oft musste ich während der Konzilssitzungen unter der Kuppel der Peterskirche an M. Luther denken. Ich sagte mir: Wäre dieser Mann hier, wie würde er sich freuen, zu hören, dass seine wesentlichsten Anliegen, die Zielvorstellungen, die ihn im Anfang im Innersten bewegt haben, hier ausgesprochen werden." Ibid., p. 63, italics mine.

[2] Maron, Kirche und Rechtfertigung, p. 6.

[3] Ibid., p. 27. [4] Lumen gentium 1. 7.

[5] Unitatis redintegratio 1. 3. [6] Lumen gentium 7. 48.

[7] Ibid., 1. 8. [8] Ibid., 3. 26.

[9] "'Expressis verbis' enthalten die Texte des 2. Vatikanums nun allerdings so gut wie keine Aussage über die Rechtfertigung." Maron, Kirche und Rechtfertigung, p. 6. "Da macht also ein Konzil . . . ein umfassendes ekklesiologisches Dokument . . .--und von Rechtfertigung des Sünders als Massstab für die Kirche fällt darin kein Wort!" O. H. Pesch, "Gottes Gnadenhandeln," in Mysterium Salutis, 4/2:902. Cf. Hermann Dietzfelbinger, "Konzil und Kirche der Reformation," in Dialog unterwegs, ed. George A. Lindbeck (Göttingen: Vandenhoeck & Ruprecht, 1965), p. 262. Pfürtner's statement that the council had respected Luther's concern by its teaching of christocentricity, of the common priesthood of the believer, and of the difference between Church and Christ is relativized by its acknowledgment of a totally different "kirchliches

unite the Catholic view still represented after Vatican II that Luther had "found his council"[1] with this sobering fact. On the other hand, the complaint of Catholic ecumenists that Vatican II unfortunately produced only a completion of Vatican I and not of Trent[2] appears to us more understandable. Similarly, one cannot easily dismiss Protestant criticisms that for Rome iustificatio remains a "suspicious word" (suspektes Wort) and one which since Trent appears only in connection with condemnations, while greater and greater latitude is allowed for ecclesiology in the proclamation of the Magisterium.[3] Maron[4] points to Harnack's statement that Trent--only incited by the challenge of the Reformation--felt obligated to face the problem of justification, but that at this time the tendency to assert itself as "sacramental Church" (Sakramentskirche)[5] was already dominant. Although at Vatican II much was said about reform,[6] the council really did not muster the courage to follow John XXIII in distinguishing between substance

---

Selbsverständnis." Stephanus Pfürtner, "Reformation und Reform des zweiten Vatikanums," in Strukturen christlicher Existenz, ed. Heinrich Schlier et al. (Würzburg: Echter, 1968), pp. 116-26.

[1]"Es ist hier nicht zu bestreiten, dass Luther sein Konzil gefunden hat." Brandenburg, Martin Luther gegenwärtig, p. 146.

[2]"Ökumenisch gesehen, wäre es deshalb ein Segen gewesen, wenn das 2. Vatikanum nicht nur eine Ergänzung zum 1. Vatikanischen Konzil, sondern auch zum Konzil von Trient gegeben hätte." Schillebeeckx, "Tridentinisches Rechtfertigungsdekret," Conc(D) 1 (1965): 453.

[3]Maron, Kirche und Rechtfertigung, p. 160.

[4]Ibid., p. 157.   [5]Harnack, Dogmengeschichte, 3:699.

[6]In any case, not what pertains to doctrine, but only what pertains to moral life and the kind of teaching-proclamation (Unitatis redintegratio 2. 6). The dogmas are irreformable definitions! (Lumen gentium 3. 25).

and *formulation* in the transmitted dogma.[1]

The council did of course indicate that the "hierarchy of truths" is derived from the closeness of its connection with Christ[2] and that the Scripture must form the foundation for dialogue with the "separated brethren,"[3] but it left completely open what this means for the problem of justification and merit. The council only tersely stated that between the Catholic Church and the "separated brethren" there exist "considerable differences concerning the work of redemption.[4] Of the differences themselves, the Council decrees say nothing. The words *iustificatio* and *iustificare* are used only infrequently, the former twice, the latter three times:[5] Two of them in a general sense and secular context,[6] and only three in passages that focus on the theology of justification. One of them is a Bible citation (Rom 4:25) without further comment,[7] so that really only two texts remain. One[8] is of a very general nature and speaks of justification by faith through baptism also of those who

---

[1] See Maron, Kirche und Rechtfertigung, p. 96. Only in Gaudium et spes 2. 2. 62 is there found a weak allusion to it.

[2] Unitatis redintegratio 2. 11. Cf. LTK, 2nd ed. (Das 2. Vatikanische Konzil), 2:89 by J. Feiner. Schlink recognizes from the Protestant side the "wichtige Hilfe" of the formula of the hierarchy of truths for the ecumenical dialogue, but calls it "mehr Aufgabe als Lösung." Edmund Schlink, "Die Hierarchie der Wahrheiten und die Einigung der Kirchen," KuD 21 (1975):2-3.

[3] Unitatis redintegratio 3. 21.   [4] Ibid., 3. 20.

[5] Philippe Delhaye, Michel Gueret, and Paul Tombeur, Concilium Vaticanum II (Louvain: Cetedoc, 1974), p. 359.

[6] Gaudium et spes 2. 3. 67; 2. 4. 74.

[7] Lumen gentium 2. 9.

[8] Unitatis redintegratio 1. 3.

are outside the Catholic Church; on the basis of this justification, they can be designated as "Christians" and "brothers in the Lord." The other[1] contains a short definition, indeed an extremely short definition, of the Catholic doctrine of justification: The follower of Christ is called by God, not on the basis of his works, but on the basis of God's gracious decision. Justification occurs in Jesus Christ through the baptism of faith and bestows holiness.

    The background of this statement is found in Thomas Aquinas[2] and furnishes the necessary explanation: Baptism points to the sacramental character of justification, for the act of baptism cancels sin. Therefore the comparison with a medicine! Since, however, the sick person must also be a participant in the process of healing, faith is required. This faith is the <u>fides caritate formata</u>, the sum total of dogmatic faith and of love, through which the person cooperates in his justification. The result is inner holiness (new quality of being). Other passages in the Council decrees complete this statement in a revealing way. Man, merely "wounded by sin," (<u>libertas hominis, a peccato vulnerata</u>)[3] starts, moved by God's grace, to "liberate himself from the bondage of the passions" (<u>sese ab omni passionum captivate liberans</u>).[4] In

---

[1] <u>Lumen gentium</u> 5. 40.   [2]<u>S.Th.</u> 3a. 68, 4.

[3] <u>Gaudium et spes</u> 1. 1. 17.

[4] Ibid. Even so conservative a theologian as Joseph Ratzinger comments on this passage as the "least satisfying" of the text. According to him here lies a mingling of Christian and philosophical ideas. "Theologisch lässt sie [die Stelle] jenen ganzen Problemkomplex beiseite, den Luther polemisch-einseitig in den Begriff des <u>servum arbitrium</u> gefasst hat; von jenem den Menschen durchziehenden Zwiespalt, den Röm 7:13-25 so dramatisch schildert, lässt der ganze Text kaum etwas ahnen. Er verfällt in eine geradezu

this way, man cooperates[1] with grace infused by the church sacraments (qua [ecclesia] veritatem et gratiam diffundit).[2] The holiness thereby bestowed must be increased.[3] The person who accomplishes this by practising the evangelical counsels in a monastic order reveals a "greater love for God,"[4] proclaims the eschatological completion,[5] and belongs in the "state of perfection."[6] Generally speaking, however, every Christian should increase his state of holiness through cooperation with grace.[7] Thus, through good deeds eternal life will be attained.[8]

If one asks how much of the wide-ranging dialogues of modern Catholic theology with Luther--discussed in chapters 1 and 3 of this work--has penetrated the Council decrees, the answer is disappointing. The problem of human nature was passed over lightly by the council with the Scholastic term "wounded by sin" (a peccato vulnerata);[9] on the other hand, free will,[10] in the framework of a "Semi-Pelagian concept," (Semipelagianisches Vorstellungsschema)[11]

---

pelagianische Terminologie." LTK, 2nd ed. (Das 2. Vatikanische Konzil), 3:331-32, by J. Ratzinger.

[1] Lumen gentium 5. 41.   [2] Ibid. 1. 8.

[3] Apostolicam actuositatem 1. 4.   [4] Perfectae caritatis 12.

[5] Lumen gentium 6. 44.   [6] Ibid., 6. 45.

[7] Ibid., 5. 41.

[8] Dei verbum 1. 3. The Pauline passage cited (Rom 2:6-7) is to be understood, in the context of the traditional teaching on justification which was repeated by the council, in the Catholic-final and surely not in the Lutheran-consecutive sense.

[9] Gaudium et spes 1. 1. 14; 1. 1. 17.   [10] Ibid.

[11] LTK, 2nd ed. (Das 2. Vatikanische Konzil), 3:332, by J. Ratzinger.

was glorified, for grace is understood as a help which brings the will to its "full potential."[1] Although the concept <u>supernaturalis</u> was avoided,[2] the traditional scheme of the teaching of grace concerning the wounded nature and the lost supernatural status looms in the background.[3] There is, of course, a reference to a "reign of sin"[4] in us, but the Lutheran concept of radical sin is only an "inducement to sin"[5] and the idea of <u>simul justus et peccator</u> is indicated only in connection with actual sin.[6] Faith is indeed sometimes seen as decision,[7] but nevertheless in the majority of contexts it is defined as agreement with doctrine[8] or as the content of faith.[9] Salvation is--as we have already seen--brought into connection with works while the problem of "law and gospel" is excised.[10] Here one cannot find the slightest connection to Luther.

---

[1] <u>Gaudium et spes</u> 1. 1. 17.

[2] <u>LTK</u>, 2nd ed. (<u>Das 2. Vatikanische Konzil</u>), 2:515, by J. Ratzinger.

[3] Ibid., 3:321, by J. Ratzinger.   [4] <u>Lumen gentium</u> 4. 36.

[5] <u>Gaudium et spes</u> 1. 1. 13; 1. 2. 25.   [6] <u>Lumen gentium</u> 5. 40.

[7] <u>Gravissimum educationis</u> 4; <u>Dignitatis humanae</u> 9.

[8] <u>Dei verbum</u> 1. 5.

[9] <u>Unitatis redintegratio</u> 3. 22; <u>Presbyterorum ordinis</u> 2. 4; <u>Dei verbum</u> 2. 10.

[10] <u>Dei verbum</u> 1. 3. To this Ratzinger remarks: "Hier wird man freilich die Frage nicht unterdrücken können, ob das Konzil bei seiner Zeichnung von Offenbarung und Heilsgeschichte nicht doch von einer zu ausschliesslich optimistischen Sicht ausgegangen ist, der die Tatsache aus dem Auge entschwindet, dass göttliches Heil wesentlich als <u>Rechtfertigung des Sünders</u> ergeht, dass die Gnade durch das Gericht des Kreuzes hindurch sich vollzieht und so selbst immer auch Gerichtscharakter trägt, dass deshalb auch das <u>eine</u> Wort Gottes in der doppelten Weise von <u>Gesetz und Evangelium</u> auftritt." <u>LTK</u>, 2nd ed. (<u>Das 2. Vatikanische Konzil</u>), 2:509.

At most one could see a relation in the rejection of any work-righteousness in man's calling.[1] Works of love as witness of being a Christian[2] for the glory of God[3] could also be mentioned here, as well as the religious value of secular works.[4] But there is no doubt that in so doing only the first incitement of actual grace in the calling is meant, not the human contribution to justification and to salvation, namely, cooperation.[5] In addition to this, everything stemming from tradition, such as the "pious exercises among the people,"[6] asceticism,[7] and ecclesiastical laws,[8] is included in works. With such things evangelical Christendom has, of course, long since broken. Because grace is sacramental grace (<u>sacramenta . . . gratiam conferunt</u>)[9] and is "infused" into the believer (<u>gratia divina manante</u>),[10] the council was not concerned with the justification of the sinner before God's judgment seat, but rather with man's continual transformation by the sacraments, i.e., with the justification of the pious. Not <u>iustificatio</u>, but <u>transmutatio</u>. The model of such an individual is Mary, exalted by tradition.[11]

---

[1] <u>Lumen gentium</u> 5. 40.

[2] <u>Apostolicam actuositatem</u> 2. 6; 4. 19; 6. 31.

[3] <u>Sacrosanctum concilium</u> 1. 9; <u>Ad gentes</u> 2. 11.

[4] <u>Gaudium et spes</u> 1. 3. 34.   [5] <u>Lumen gentium</u> 5. 41.

[6] <u>Sacrosanctum concilium</u> 1. 13. "Dabei ist vor allem an Formen wie <u>Kreuzweg</u> und <u>Rosenkranz</u> gedacht, die vom Hlg. Stuhl so vielfach empfohlen sind, dann aber auch an die Vielfalt der Gebete . . . die zum Teil mit <u>Ablässen</u> versehen wurden." <u>LTK</u>, 2nd ed. (<u>Das 2. Vatikanische Konzil</u>), 1:26 by J. A. Jungmann, italics mine.

[7] <u>Sacrosanctum concilium</u> 5. 105.   [8] <u>Lumen gentium</u> 4. 37.

[9] <u>Sacrosanctum concilium</u> 3. 59.   [10] Ibid., 3. 61.

[11] See Maron, <u>Kirche und Rechtfertigung</u>, p. 225.

The effectuation of this transformation occurs liturgically, for the liturgy being carried on in the Church is the priestly office of Jesus Christ.[1] Therefore the Church is comparable to the incarnated Redeemer;[2] His mystery continues in the mystery of the Church,[3] which was instituted as a "universal sacrament of salvation" (universale salutis sacramentum).[4] Assurance of salvation, which the Protestant gains through faith in Christ, becomes therefore for the Catholic an assurance of hope in the Church.[5]

Likewise, none of the bold words from many progressive theologians concerning the problematic or inopportune character of the idea of merit, have been incorporated into the documents of the council. We admit that this teaching stands as far out on the margin of Vatican II as justification, but where it is hinted, it is handled just as traditionally as is the other. One gets the impression that the aggiornamento went past those classical points of controversy, carefully avoiding any contact. The historical and ecumenical implications are nowhere visible. In this sphere

---

[1] Sacrosanctum concilium 1. 7.

[2] Lumen gentium 1. 8. The "theandrism" of Christ mirrors itself again in the Church. LTK, 2nd ed. (Das 2. Vatikanische Konzil), 1:16 by J. A. Jungmann.

[3] Sacrosanctum concilium 1. 5.

[4] Lumen gentium 7. 48; Gaudium et spes 1. 4. 45; Ad gentes 1. Hence the Church is interpreted as "Ursakrament" (original sacrament). See LTK, 2nd ed. (Das 2. Vatikanische Konzil), 1:16, 20, by J. A. Jungmann.

[5] See Maron, Kirche und Rechtfertigung, p. 200. Whether one can speak of a belief in the Church (O. Semmelroth, H. Bacht) or only of an: I believe the Church (H. de Lubac, K. Rahner, H. Küng), is an object of inner Catholic discussion. Ibid., pp. 186-89.

Vatican II simply presupposed Trent, without in the least taking into account the progress of modern ecumenical theology.

In the Council documents mereri(e) and meritum appear seven and eight times, respectively.[1] In a theological sense these words are used three or six times, respectively. Initially, reference is made to the merits of Christ. By His sacrifice Christ has "merited life"[2] for us. These merits Christ acquired in "superabundance."[3] The believers should not ascribe their transfer into the state of grace to their own merits, but must attribute this to the grace of Christ.[4] He who perseveres in grace, however, proves it by demonstrating Christian life.[5] Here one can state positively that the sola gratia can dimly be perceived; negatively, that faith is separated from love, for obviously only love--not faith--is the sign of the state of grace. Faith is here seen in a purely traditional way as fides dogmatica.[6] But also that which is said of grace does not supersede the traditional teaching. Grace ennables human participation in salvation. Believers must "merit" their fellowship with the glory of Christ (ut gloriae Eius mereantur esse consortes),[7] and they must strive to merit eternal life.[8] But he who is already glorified and now sees God can apply his merits,

---

[1] Delhaye, Gueret, and Tombeur, Concilium Vaticanum II, p. 393.

[2] Gaudium et spes 1. 1. 22; Lumen gentium 8. 53; Sacrosanctum concilium 5. 102.

[3] Lumen gentium 8. 60.   [4] Ibid., 2. 14.   [5] Ibid.

[6] "Durch Gottes Gnade [können] Glaube und Hoffnung auch in Sündern leben, in denen die Liebe erstorben ist." LTK, 2nd ed. (Das 2. Vatikanische Konzil), 1:200, by A. Grillmeier.

[7] Lumen gentium 5. 41.   [8] Ibid., 7. 48.

attained through Christ, intercedingly before God for fellow brothers who are still pilgrims on earth.[1] This especially refers to the saints, who by God's grace have attained perfection on earth.[2]

When one reflects on these few passages which contain only allusions, one surely cannot say that the council has restated the traditional doctrine of merit or even explained it more fully. According to the original intentions of the council this could not be expected even by the most unyielding champions of tradition. On the contrary! From a council of opening, of renewal, of ecumenism, and of dialogue one might expect that it would at least take a stance regarding the problems of its ecumenical specialists. This simply did not happen. On the other hand, it alluded clearly enough to the traditional teaching on justification and merit that we cannot avoid making two statements:

1. Although no one could really expect that Vatican II would correct Trent, nothing, however, occurred in the realm of the doctrine of justification to complement it. The doctrinal tolerances in this question are probably much more narrow than believed and claimed in practice by many Catholic theologians.

2. The claimed consensus with Luther on justification cannot be supported by any official decision or interpretation of Vatican II. The ecclesiological self-consciousness of the council apparently suppressed the problem of justification and indirectly disassociated itself from the controlling function of this doctrine. The same can be said of the idea of merit. By way of allusion, the

---

[1] Ibid., 7. 49.   [2] Sacrosanctum concilium 5. 104.

council repeated the traditional doctrine of merit and thus ignored and indirectly rejected the central concern of the Reformation.

The only positive position taken by Rome regarding Luther as a teacher of justification is the explanation given by Cardinal Willebrands a few years after Vatican II, which we cited in the Introduction. In a refreshing way it contrasts with the silence of the council and could be assessed as an approaching move of Rome to the main concern of Luther. However, it is known today that with this explanation Willebrands encountered a considerable unwillingness in the Curia,[1] and the Pope himself remained as silent as the council. The Cardinal's word thus had at most semi-official character and expressed the opinion of a thin layer of Catholic ecumenists rather than the official position of Rome.[2] But even the explanation of the Cardinal is today interpreted rather soberly by Catholic theologians: Willebrands expressed himself freely and politely on Luther, but in the matter itself indicated no concession whatsoever.[3] Official Catholicism cannot openly accept Luther's criticism without running the danger of destroying its own raison d'être.[4] O. H. Pesch therefore still observes an unbridgeable chasm between theology and the Magisterium:

> Das kirchenamtliche Urteil über Luther hat die Entwicklung der katholischen Lutherforschung in Historie und Theologie nicht

---

[1] Hasler, "Luther in der katholischen Schultheologie," Conc(D) 12 (1976):524.

[2] O. H. Pesch, "Der gegenwärtige Stand," Conc(D) 12 (1976): 537.

[3] Olivier, "Warum hat man Luther nicht verstanden?," Conc(D) 12 (1976):477.

[4] Ibid., pp. 477-78.

mitvollzogen. Abgesehen von einer kurzen, wohlwollenden Stillhaltephase zur Konzilszeit steht das Leitungszentrum der Kirche in Sachen Luther auf den Standpunkten von 1939, als Lortz mit seiner <u>Reformation in Deutschland</u> ins Feuer innerkirchlicher Kritik geriet.[1]

What has happened since then is not very likely to retract anything from this judgment. After no progress had been made under Paul VI, a step backward took place with John Paul II. According to Küng we are experiencing an "epoch of restoration" (<u>Epoche der Restauration</u>), a "stationary ecumenical depression" (<u>stationäres ökumenisches Tief</u>) and a "freezing-in of the council" (<u>Einfrieren des Konzils</u>).[2] Neither the 450th anniversary of the Diet of Worms[3] nor the 450th anniversary of the Augsburg Confession[4] could entice official Rome out of its reserve. The ecumenical climate suffers from this, as the polemics on both sides on the occasion of the Papal visit to the country of the Reformation demonstrated. If there is again talk of the "dark sides in Luther's personality (<u>Schattenseiten der Persönlichkeit Luthers</u>), of his "blindness for the Catholic truth" (<u>Blindheit für die katholische Wahrheit</u>), and his "heretical doctrines" (Remigius Bäumer),[5] can one actually refer to a willingness on the part of Rome or on the part of a number of Catholic theologians to settle the core issue in the

---

[1] Pesch, "Der gegenwärtige Stand," <u>Conc(D)</u> 12 (1976):537.

[2] "Nur noch Mutige protestieren," <u>Die Zeit</u>, 21 November 1980; idem, "Where I Stand," <u>CaC</u> 41 (1981):3-11.

[3] O. H. Pesch, "Gottes Gnadenhandeln," in <u>Mysterium Salutis</u>, 4/2:902.

[4] "Kirchentag des Bekennens," <u>Evangelische Kommentare</u>, August 1980.

[5] "Nicht mit Engelszungen," <u>Die Zeit</u>, 7 November 1980.

controversy over the question of justification?

Summary

1. Present-day Catholic exegesis strives to appreciate Jesus' struggle against the Pharisaical doctrine of merit (Neuhäusler, W. Pesch). That Jesus' mentioning of reward establishes a Christian teaching of merit is partly affirmed (Berouard, Molinski, Solignac) but strongly relativized by the statement that it concerns a reward of grace (Meinertz, Schelkle, Schmid). The equation reward=merit must be denied (W. Pesch). The juridism that in the past was read into the text is today rejected (W. Pesch, Schmid).

2. In the dogmatic literature this recognition progresses only with difficulty. In the handbooks before Vatican II merit was always interpreted by the idea of legal right (Brinktrine, Garrigou-Lagrange, Pohle and Gummersbach, Tabarelli, Tanquerey). But this standpoint is also represented in current dogmatics (Auer and Ratzinger, Baumgartner, Ott). Other dogmaticians seek a "pure (purified) doctrine of merit" (Fransen) and therefore reject any principle of claim (Küng, O. H. Pesch, Schmaus). Merit is understood in the framework of the personal relationship God-man as honorable distinction. Accordingly, the principle of commutative and distributive righteousness is annulled (Fransen).

3. In order to eliminate the idea of legal right, one refers to participation, fruit, life-dynamic, basic option (principle of love), dignity, and eschatological prolepsis. These expressions, derived from religious experience, are supported,

however, not by the Lutheran principle of _sola fide_ but by the principle of inherent quality and of final cooperation.

    4. The old Scholastic structures (_meritum de congruo_, _meritum de condigno_) are hardly modified by present-day School-dogmatics (Baumgartner, Ott). Some ecumenically minded dogmaticians distance themselves from the traditional terminology (Fransen) or no longer give it any consideration (O. H. Pesch).

    5. Intertwining the idea of merit with natural theology and with the doctrine of grace and works constitutes a formidable obstacle in the new interpretation of the doctrine of merit.

    6. Every judgment on a rapprochement or consensus of Catholic theology with Luther stands under the power of reservation of the Magisterium. Contrary to the expectation of many, Vatican II remained silent over the ecumenical meaning of the article of justification. This "ecclesiological council" only alluded to the points of teaching on justification and merit and referred to them only in the traditional sense. So far, the Roman Magisterium has never, neither during nor after Vatican II, by an official declaration recognized or even encouraged the theological strivings toward a consensus with Luther over the question of justification.

GENERAL SUMMARY AND CONCLUSION

It is an unquestionable fact that Catholic theology has made great strides forward in doing justice both to the person and to the teaching (doctrine of justification) of Luther--much more than was the case at the beginning of this century and even until the Second World War. Due to the work of Lortz, Herte, Hessen, Iserloh, and Manns, we possess today a more balanced and correct Catholic picture of Luther than at the turn of the century (Janssen, Denifle, Grisar).

As has been unfolded, the center of gravity of Catholic research on Luther moved after the Second World War from the Reformer's life to his teaching. Following the pre-Vatican II discussions by Bläser and Congar, an intensive Catholic dialogue concerning Luther's teaching on justification developed, particularly during and after the council. Single aspects such as law and gospel, simul justus et peccator, unfree will, assurance of salvation, and faith were investigated anew and presented by Catholic scholars like McDonough, Kösters, McSorley, Pfürtner, and Manns. Both the "Catholic Luther" (Lortz, Bellucci, Wicks) as well as the "Reformation Luther" (Brandenburg, O. H. Pesch, Hasler, Olivier) were studied penetratingly. As a consequence, one can say that Catholic research on Luther has caught up with that of the Protestant scholars. Both "Historiker" (Lortz) and "Systematiker"

(O. H. Pesch) have reached the conclusion that Catholic theology is in basic agreement with Luther in the doctrine of justification. This claim was perceived on the Lutheran side as "most highly positive and pleasing" (äusserst positiv und erfreulich)[1] and the "possibility" of such a consensus was conceded.[2]

In all this, the doctrine of merit was viewed, however, only peripherally as an oversensitive point (neuralgischer Punkt)[3] or as a "scratch test" (Nagelprobe)[4] of the problem. The reasons for this neglect may be found in the fact that in the ranks of ecumenically minded Catholic theologians the problem of the doctrine of merit is felt as an issue of "minimal impact"[5] and is evaluated as a "dispensable theologoumenon."[6] On the Protestant side, one is not sure whether the Catholic reticence or the new interpretations represent a genuine overcoming of the idea of merit or is nothing but a theological manipulation (theologische Spitzfindigkeit).[7]

We have endeavored to show that the claim of unity between Luther and Rome in the doctrine of justification is opposed by the Catholic dogma of merit. This obstacle could be overcome only if one of the two dialoguing partners were to relinquish fundamental

---

[1] Bogdahn, Rechtfertigungslehre, p. 271.

[2] Pöhlmann, Rechtfertigung, p. 378.

[3] Vajta, "Sine meritis," Oec. 3 (1968):148.

[4] Dantine, Gerechtmachung des Gottlosen, p. 39.

[5] Schmaus, Glaube der Kirche, 2:651.

[6] O. H. Pesch, "Lehre vom Verdienst," in Wahrheit und Verkündigung, 2:1905.

[7] Vajta, "Sine meritis," Oec. 3 (1968):194-95.

structures of his historical and dogmatic position. Since it seems impossible to harmonize Luther's teaching of justification <u>sola fide sine operibus et meritis</u> with the Tridentine dogma of the attainment of eternal life through one's own works and merits,[1] this would mean either a disregarding of Luther or an interpreting of the Catholic doctrine in such a way that it can be brought into conformity with the Reformer.

The major part of contemporary Catholic polemical theology has chosen once again to dialogue with Luther and to initiate a new process of theological reflection. In the course of this work, we have assessed a significant closeness to Luther attained by modern Catholic Luther research. Wherever the doctrine of merit has been drawn into the dialogue on justification, Catholic scholars acknowledge that Luther's criticism of the idea of merit was historically, and to a certain degree also dogmatically, justified. In their teaching, contemporary Catholic theologians stress that both the preparation for justification and the first justification itself come about wholly unmerited and that the merits with reference to the second justification are always merits of grace. Thus, current Catholic theology can concede a <u>sola gratia</u>, which--in our opinion--is not identical with the Lutheran one but approximates it. Since faith is viewed more and more in the sense of the Lutheran fiducia, and its primary position in the process of salvation is conceded, one can even speak of a Catholic <u>sola fide</u>. The majority of theologians on both sides would probably

---

[1] DS 1582.

admit, however, that this sola fide means something different from the Lutheran term.

In spite of the self-evident congeniality, we think that the claim to a consensus with Luther in justification, as it is raised especially by Lortz and O. H. Pesch, does not prove to be correct. Not only because this claim is made merely by a minority of ecumenically minded scholars, while the other Catholic dogmaticians still think in the forms of traditional School theology and not only because the teaching office represents a "factor of uncertainty" (Unsicherheitsfaktor),[1] but above all because we think that the matter itself with its unresolved questions reduces the claimed consensus to pious wishful thinking. We see these unresolved questions now as before in the Catholic teaching of works and merit--questions which to us seem impossible to harmonize with the structure of Luther's sola fide principle--for the following reasons:

1. Although works of the believer are required both by Luther and in Catholic doctrine, they have a wholly different character in the process of justification. With Luther they are excluded from justification and have validity only in the framework of the lived faith as a sign and witness that justification has occurred. Works clearly have a consecutive, salvation-witnessing character. In the Catholic doctrine, works are included

---

[1] Bogdahn, Rechtfertigungslehre, p. 272. One must actually speak of a "factor of opposition," for the Reformation views on justification and merit still stand under the condemnation of Trent. Cf. Ernst Benz, "Das 2. Vatikanische Konzil in protestantischer Sicht," ÖR 15 (1966):157.

in the process of justification and intensify this process for the attainment of eternal life. Works thus have clearly a _final_, salvation-attaining character.

2. With Luther the believer can ascribe nothing of the lived faith to himself. On the basis of the _aptitudo passiva_ he can experience the mystery of the sole agency of God as a personal deed. But it remains always an _alienum_ according to its origin and its value. In Catholic doctrine, too, the believer must ascribe everything to grace. But since one's own free will, activated by grace, can become operative not only _coram mundo_ as with Luther, but also _coram Deo_, human cooperation is effective in God's all-encompassing agency. Hence, the deed is also a _proprium_ according to its origin and value.

3. Because with Luther salvation is received simultaneously with faith established, preserved, and lived by grace (_sola fide numquam sola_), man himself does not contribute anything to his redemption. The _alienum_ hinders the _meritum_. One cannot express this better than with Luther's last words: "We are beggars, that is true." (_Wir sind Bettler, das ist wahr_).[1] Man lives before God only through God's mercy (_sola misericordia_). In Catholic doctrine this is otherwise! Grace as an inherent quality creates the possibility of salvation, as far as the believer brings himself into the process of salvation with a new but self-possessed quality of achievement. The _proprium_ makes the _meritum_ possible. Man lives before God through his own worthiness and merit included in grace.

---

[1] Quoted in Fausel, _Martin Luther_, 2:311.

We have observed that in the most recent past both Protestant and Catholic theologians have expended great efforts to assess the controversial problem of justification as being solved. As worthy of recognition as this irenic dialogue is, it is also equally as problematical, for it leads sometimes to hasty, unjustified conclusions. As long as the problem of the final-meritorious works is not solved, we come in Luther and in Catholicism face to face with two different interpretations of the gospel. It is not a matter of indifference whether man is only a receiver or also a contributor, whether he can stand before God with nothing of his own or whether he is worthy of salvation on the basis of his merits. Here it is a matter of faith-righteousness which is confronted with a "work-righteousness that has become humble" (demütig gewordene Werksgerechtigkeit) or, in other words, a question of "solely" or of "both . . . and."[1]

We do not believe that the attempts at bridging the gap justify the speaking of an essential rapprochement or of even of reconciliation. The proposed "compromise of doctrine" (Lehrkompromiss)[2] seems to us to be the least appropriate to lead to the goal of unity. As necessary as compromises may be in the social-political realm, they are untenable in the area of personal conscience. Throughout his life Luther spoke out against such, and the character of Catholic dogma resists the idea contained in the compromise of a partial

---

[1] Karl Barth, "Der römische Katholizismus als Frage an die protestantische Kirche," ZZ 6 (1928):302.

[2] Max Seckler, "Über den Kompromiss in Sachen der Lehre," in Begegnung, ed. Max Seckler et al. (Graz: Styria, 1972), p. 50.

relinquishment of binding positions. In this regard, the remarks that for modern man--as long as he is still a Christian at all--traditional controversial issues have lost their meaning[1] and what separates is often viewed today as a dispensable theologoumenon, which basically has no longer any justifiable existence,[2] do not help. Such a capitulation to the Zeitgeist would neither be fair to the message of the gospel nor be useful to the necessary inter-confessional dialogue. Minimizing doctrinal differences does not get us anywhere. Whether it is sufficient to base an agreement only on the fact that both Luther and the Catholic dogma require good works[3] is highly questionable, if the final-meritorious character of these works remains without consideration. Similarly it seems to us equally questionable whether one makes capital out of the statement that the history of dogma is not only a history of "progress" but also of "forgetting." This statement of K. Rahner in connection with christological questions has been carried over by Küng to the problem of justification.[4] Because Luther attributed to the sola fide concept a central and controlling function, while the Council of Trent not only intended to point out errors on this point but also wished to define the "true and healthy doctrine" (veram sanamque doctrinam)[5] of the Catholic Church against the

---

[1] Albert Brandenburg, "Eine theologische Urspaltung?," in Begegnung, p. 187.

[2] Ibid., p. 189.

[3] See Bellucci, Fede e giustificazione, p. 261.

[4] Küng, Rechtfertigung, p. 112.   [5] DS 1520.

Reformers--as Küng himself has to admit[1]--this concession regarding "forgetting" provides no benefit to the solution of the problem.

In connection with the modern interpretation of Trent (see chapter 3) we have pointed out a second possibility: The "completion of doctrine" (Lehrergänzung). Such completions undoubtedly have their value. They have enabled ecumenically minded persons in both camps to bring their standpoints to an undeniable rapprochement. But even this method cannot finally lead to the goal of unity. In this connection, it is not at all decisive that such completions have found in Rome no official encouragement or approval, but it is decisive that a completion can never lead to a full consensus and easily falls into the justified reproach of furthering a double-level theology.[2]

Something similar may also be said of the attempt to solve the problem by the Catholic interpretation of Luther's doctrine. Approaches can undoubtedly be accomplished by an interpretation in optimam partem. But the doctrine of merit effectively shows the boundaries of this method. Luther's teaching of the sole agency of God and of the freely given salvation counteracts all Catholic interpretations. Where it is nevertheless attempted, the impression arises of a flight into theological subtlety or into an unjustified dialectic.

The attempt to solve the problem by the reformational

---

[1] Küng, Rechtfertigung, p. 113.

[2] This double-level theology already existed at Trent. W. v. Loewenich rightly calls the Tridentine doctrine of merit from grace and achievement a "gefährliche Dialektik." Der moderne Katholizismus, p. 23.

interpretation seems the most courageous and radical, since it challenges the Catholic partner in the dialogue with the demand of providing validity for Luther's way of thinking in the Catholic Church. As admirable as this attempt may appear, it is nevertheless unrealistic. Does, for instance, the assertion that the doctrine of merit is a matter of a "dispensable theologoumenon"[1] really take its character of dogma into account? As far as we can see, this standpoint also is represented only by a minority of Catholic theologians.

In view of these facts, in any case with reference to Luther and Catholic dogma, the claim does not seem justified that consensus has been reached on justification and that the dispute over the doctrine of merit can be given up. But is the unmistakable rapprochement in the dialogue sufficient at least to remove the split between the churches?[2] This question cannot be answered from the standpoint of the doctrine of justification only, even if one can point to Luther as a witness for it.[3] One should not forget, of course, that the Reformer saw justification sola fide endangered also in the doctrine of the mass and the Papacy, and therefore had to state: "Therefore we are and remain forever separated" (Also

---

[1] O. H. Pesch, "Die Lehre vom Verdienst," in Wahrheit und Verkündigung, 2:1905.

[2] ". . . die in den letzten Jahren um die Rechtfertigung geführte Diskussion . . . hat meines Erachtens aber keine irreduktibel kirchenspaltende Unterschiede zwischen der evangelischen und der katholischen Rechtfertigungslehre zutage gefördert." Küng, "Katholische Besinnung," in Theologie im Wandel, p. 466.

[3] "Hoc impetrato, scilicet quod solus Deus ex mera gratia per Christum iustificet, non solum volumus Papam in manibus portare, imo etiam ei osculari pedes." WA 40I, 181, 11-13.

sind und bleiben wir ewiglich geschieden).¹

K. Rahner tries to break through this firm front by saying that one could only live in separated churches if one <u>definitely</u> knew that one is "<u>unambiguously</u> separated in the truth."² As far as Luther is concerned--and on him above all this research has focused--we think we can draw an unmistakable conclusion: The Reformer was for himself "unambiguously certain" that his understanding of justification by faith could not be united with the final-meritorious principle of salvation in Catholic doctrine.³ In order to aim at a consensus or to abolish the split of the churches on this point, the kernel of Luther's teaching would have to be given up, for "how do endeavor and merit accord with a righteousness freely bestowed?"⁴

---

¹WA 50, 204, 19-20.

²K. Rahner, <u>Schriften zur Theologie</u>, 4:245, italics mine.

³"Quia <u>certus sum</u> doctrinam meam esse veram et divinam. . . . Quare Deo dante mea frons durior erit fronte omnium. Hic durus et esse et haberi volo, hic gero titulum: <u>Cedo nulli</u>." WA 40I, 180, 21; 181, 22-24, italics mine.

⁴"Quomodo conatus et meritum conveniunt cum gratuita et donata iustitia?" <u>WA</u> 18, 769, 26-27; <u>LW</u> 33, 266.

BIBLIOGRAPHY

BIBLIOGRAPHY

Abárzuza, Francisco X. de. Manuale theologiae dogmaticae. 2nd ed. 4 vols. Madrid: Ediciones Studium, 1956.

Adam, Alfred. "Die Herkunft des Lutherwortes vom menschlichen Willen als Reittier Gottes." Luther-Jahrbuch 1962. Hamburg: F. Wittig, 1962.

_____. Lehrbuch der Dogmengeschichte. 2nd ed. 2 vols. Gütersloh: G. Mohn, 1970.

Adam, Karl. Una Sancta in katholischer Sicht. Düsseldorf: Patmos, 1948.

_____. Das Wesen des Katholizismus. 13th ed. Düsseldorf: Patmos, 1957.

Ahlbrecht, Ansgar. "Neuere katholische Versuche zur Würdigung der theologischen Anliegen Luthers." Una Sancta 18 (1963):174-83.

Aland, Kurt, ed. Lutherlexikon. Stuttgart: E. Klotz, 1957.

_____. Die Reformatoren. Gütersloh: G. Mohn, 1976.

Albertus Magnus. Opera omnia. Edited by Stephanus C. A. Borgnet. Paris: L. Vivès, 1894.

Aldama, Josepho A. de; Gonzalez, Severino; and Solano, Jesu. Sacrae theologiae summa. 4 vols. Madrid: Biblioteca de autores cristianos, 1953.

Alexander Halesius. Summa theologica. Ad claras Aquas (Quaracchi): Typographia Collegii S. Bonaventurae, 1948.

Alfeld, Augustin von. Wider den wittenbergischen Abgot Martin Luther. Vol. 11 of Corpus Catholicorum. Edited by Käthe Büschgens. Münster/W.: Aschendorff, 1926.

Algermissen, Konrad. Konfessionskunde. 8th ed. Paderborn: Bonifacius, 1969.

Althaus, Paul. Die christliche Wahrheit. 7th ed. Gütersloh: Bertelsmann, 1966.

_____. "Gottes Gottheit als Sinn der Rechtfertigungslehre Luthers." Luther-Jahrbuch 1931. Amsterdam: J. Benjamins, 1967.

_____. Paulus und Luther über den Menschen. 2nd ed. Gütersloh: Bertelsmann, 1951.

_____. "Die Rechtfertigung allein aus dem Glauben in Thesen Martin Luthers." Luther-Jahrbuch 1961. Berlin: Lutherisches Verlagshaus, 1961.

_____. Die Theologie Martin Luthers. 4th ed. Gütersloh: G. Mohn, 1975.

Amiot, François. L'enseignement de saint Paul. 6th ed. 2 vols. Paris: Lecoffre, 1946.

Aner, Karl. "Glaube-Dogmengeschichtlich." Religion in Geschichte und Gegenwart. 2nd ed. Vol. 2. Tübingen: J. C. B. Mohr (Paul Siebeck), 1928.

Asmussen, Hans. Sola fide - das ist lutherisch! Munich: Chr. Kaiser, 1937.

Asmussen, H.; Fincke, E.; Lackmann, M.; Lehmann, W.; and Baumann, R. The Unfinished Reformation. Translated by R. J. Olsen. Notre Dame, IN: Fides, 1961.

Atzberger, Leonhard. Geschichte der christlichen Eschatologie. Graz: Akademische Druck- und Verlagsanstalt, 1970.

Auer, Johann. Die Entwicklung der Gnadenlehre in der Hochscholastik. 2 vols. Freiburg i. Br.: Herder, 1951.

_____. "Zur Geschichte der Gnadenlehre." Lexikon für Theologie und Kirche. 2nd ed. Vol. 4. Freiburg i. Br.: Herder, 1960.

Auer, Johann, and Ratzinger, Joseph. Kleine katholische Dogmatik. 2nd ed. Vol. 5. Regensburg: A. Pustet, 1972.

Bäumer, Remigius. Die Erforschung der kirchlichen Reformationsgeschichte seit 1931. Darmstadt: Wissenschaftliche Buchgesellschaft, 1975.

Bainton, Roland H. Here I Stand. New York: Abingdon-Cokesbury Press, 1950.

Baird, Robert. Sketches of Protestantism in Italy. Boston: B. Perkins, 1845.

Baisi, Conradus. Institutiones theologiae scholasticae. 3 vols. Milan: Editrice Ancora, 1949.

Bakhuizen van den Brink, Jan Nicolaas. "Mereor and meritum in some Latin Fathers." Texte und Untersuchungen zur Geschichte der altchristlichen Literatur. Vol. 78. Edited by O. v. Gebhardt and A. v. Harnack. Berlin: Akademie Verlag, 1961.

Balthasar, Hans Urs von. Karl Barth. Darstellung und Deutung seiner Theologie. 2nd ed. Cologne: J. Hegner, 1962.

Bardenhewer, Otto; Schermann, Th.; and Weyman, K., ed. Bibliothek der Kirchenväter. Kempten: Kösel, 1911-38.

Barth, Karl. Die Botschaft von der freien Gnade Gottes. Stuttgart: Kohlhammer, 1948.

_____. Kirchliche Dogmatik. Vol. 4/1 and 4/2. Zurich: Evangelischer Verlag, 1964.

_____. "Der römische Katholizismus als Frage an die protestantische Kirche." Zwischen den Zeiten 6 (1928):274-302.

Barth, Karl, and Thurneysen, Eduard. Briefwechsel. 2 vols. Zurich: Theologischer Verlag, 1973-74.

Bartmann, Bernhard. Des Christen Gnadenleben. 3rd ed. Paderborn: Bonifacius, 1922.

_____. Lehrbuch der Dogmatik. 8th ed. 2 vols. Freiburg i. Br.: Herder, 1932.

Battenhouse, Roy W., ed. A Companion to the Study of St. Augustine. Grand Rapids, MI: Baker Book House, 1979.

Bauer, Johann Baptist, ed. Bibeltheologisches Wörterbuch. Graz: Styria, 1959.

_____. "Gnadenlohn oder Tageslohn." Biblica 42 (1961):224-28.

Baumgartner, Charles. La grâce du Christ. Tournai: Desclée, 1963.

Bautz, Josef. Grundzüge der katholischen Dogmatik. Vol. 3. Mainz: F. Kirchheim, 1890.

Bavaud, Georges. "Luther, commentateur de l'épître aux Romains." Revue de théologie et de philosophie 20 (1970):240-61.

Beer, Theobald. "Die Ausgangspositionen der lutherischen und der katholischen Lehre von der Rechtfertigung." Catholica 21 (1967):65-84.

_____. "Lohn und Verdienst bei Luther." Münchener theologische Zeitschrift 28 (1977):258-84.

Bekenntnischriften der evangelisch-lutherischen Kirche. 2nd ed.
Göttingen: Vandenhoeck & Ruprecht, 1955.

Bellarmin, Robertus. Opera omnia. 12 vols. Paris: L. Vivès, 1870-74.

Bellucci, Dino. Fede e giustificazione in Lutero. Rome: Libreria Editrice dell' Università Gregoriana, 1963.

Benrath, Gustav Adolf, ed. Reformtheologen des 15. Jahrhunderts. Gütersloh: G. Mohn, 1968.

Benrath, Karl. Bernardino Ochino von Siena. 2nd ed. Brunswick: Schwetschke & Sohn, 1892.

Benz, Ernst. "Das 2. Vatikanische Konzil in protestantischer Sicht." Ökumenische Rundschau 15 (1966):137-61.

Benz, Karl. Die Ethik des Apostels Paulus. Freiburg i. Br.: Herder, 1912.

Berkouwer, Gerrit Cornelius. The Conflict with Rome. Translated by D. H. Freeman. Grand Rapids, MI: Baker Book House, 1958.

_____. "Convergentie in de Rechtvaardigingsleer?" Gereformeerd theologisch Tijdschrift 72 (1972):129-57.

_____. Faith and Justification. Translated by L. B. Smedes. Grand Rapids, MI: Eerdmans Publishing Co., 1954.

_____. Gehorsam und Aufbruch. Munich: Chr. Kaiser, 1968.

_____. Das Konzil und die neue katholische Theologie. Munich: Chr. Kaiser, 1968.

_____. Recent Developments in Roman Catholic Thought. Translated by J. J. Lamberts. Grand Rapids, MI: Eerdmans Publishing Co., 1958.

_____. Verdienste of genade? Kampen: J. H. Kok, 1958.

Berrouard, M. François. "Le mérite dans les évangiles synoptiques." Istina 3 (1956):191-209.

Berthier, Jean, and Raemers, Sidney A. A Compendium of Theology. Translated by S. A. Raemers. Vol. 1. St. Louis, MO: Herder, 1931.

Beyna, Werner. Das moderne katholische Lutherbild. Essen: Ludgerus, 1969.

Biel, Gabriel. Quaestiones de justificatione. Edited by C. Feckes. Münster/W.: Aschendorff, 1929.

Bigelmair, Andreas. "Luther." Lexikon für Theologie und Kirche. 1st ed. Vol. 6. Freiburg i. Br.: Herder, 1934.

Billot, Ludovico. De gratia Christi. 2nd ed. Rome: In Universitate Gregoriana, 1920.

Bizer, Ernst. "Die Entdeckung des Sakraments durch Luther." Evangelische Theologie 17 (1957):64-90.

_____. Fides ex auditu. 3rd ed. Neukirchen-Vluyn: Neukirchener Verlag, 1966.

Bläser, Peter. "Gesetz und Evangelium." Catholica 14 (1960):1-23.

_____. Rechtfertigungsglaube bei Luther. Münster/W.: Verlag der Hiltruper Missionare, 1953.

Böttger, Paul Christoph. "Lohn." Theologisches Begriffslexikon zum Neuen Testament. Vol. 2/1. Wuppertal: Brockhaus, 1969.

Bogdahn, Martin. Die Rechtfertigungslehre Luthers im Urteil der neueren katholischen Theologie. Göttingen: Vandenhoeck & Ruprecht, 1971.

Bonaventure. Liber Sententiarum. 4 vols. Ad claras Aquas (Quaracchi): Typographia Collegii S. Bonaventurae, 1891.

Bonsirven, Joseph. Les idées juives au temps de notre Seigneur. Mayenne: Bloud & Gay, 1933.

_____. Théologie du Nouveau Testament. Paris: Aubier-Montaigne, 1951.

Bornkamm, Günther. Der Lohngedanke im Neuen Testament. Göttingen: Vandenhoeck & Ruprecht, 1961.

_____. "Verdienst im Neuen Testament." Religion in Geschichte und Gegenwart. 3rd ed. Vol. 6. Tübingen: J. C. B. Mohr (Paul Siebeck), 1962.

Bornkamm, Heinrich. Luther, Gestalt und Wirkungen. Gütersloh: G. Mohn, 1975.

_____. Luther im Spiegel der deutschen Geistesgeschichte. Heidelberg: Quelle & Meyer, 1955.

_____. Luthers geistige Welt. 4th ed. Gütersloh: G. Mohn, 1962.

Bossuet, Jacques Bénigne. Oeuvres. Vol. 4. (Histoire des variations des églises Protestantes). Paris: F. Didot Frères, 1870.

Bouillard, Henri. Conversion et grâce chez S. Thomas d'Aquin. Paris: Aubier-Montaigne, 1944.

_____. *Karl Barth*. 2 vols. Paris: Aubier-Montaigne, 1957.

Bouyer, Louis. *La décomposition du Catholicisme*. Paris: Aubier-Montaigne, 1968.

_____. *Dictionary of Theology*. Translated by Ch. U. Quinn. Tournai: Desclée, 1965.

_____. *Du Protestantisme à l'Eglise*. 3rd ed. Paris: Les Editions du Cerf, 1959.

Bover, José M. *Teologia de San Pablo*. Madrid: Biblioteca de autores cristianos, 1946.

Bovis, André de. "Foi." *Dictionnaire de spiritualité, ascétique et mystique*. Vol. 5. Paris: Beauchesne, 1964.

Boyer, Carolo. *Tractatus de gratia divina*. Rome: Apud aedes Universitatis Gregorianae, 1938.

Bozzola, Carolus, and Greppi, Crescentius. *Cursus theologicus*. 4 vols. Naples: M. D'Auria, 1948.

Brandenburg, Albert. "Auf dem Wege zu einem ökumenischen Lutherverständnis." *Reformata Reformanda*. Vol. 1. Edited by E. Iserloh and K. Repgen. Münster/W.: Aschendorff, 1965.

_____. *Gericht und Evangelium*. Paderborn: Bonifacius, 1960.

_____. "Die Lutherstudien Rudolf Hermanns." *Catholica* 14 (1960):315-16.

_____. *Martin Luther gegenwärtig*. Munich: F. Schöningh, 1969.

_____. "Um die Deutung der Theologie Luthers." *Theologische Revue* 60 (1964):82-86.

_____. *Die Zukunft des Martin Luther*. Münster/W.: Aschendorff, 1977.

Brandon, Samuel G. F., ed. *Dictionary of Comparative Religion*. London: Weidenfeld & Nicolson, 1970.

Braun, Herbert. "Beobachtungen zur Tora-Verschärfung im häretischen Spätjudentum." *Theologische Literatur Zeitung* 79 (1954): 347-52.

Brecht, Martin. "Der rechtfertigende Glaube an das Evangelium von Jesus Christus als Mitte von Luthers Theologie." *Zeitschrift für Kirchengeschichte* 89 (1978):45-77.

Brinktrine, Johannes. Die Lehre von der Gnade. Paderborn: F. Schöningh, 1957.

Broderick, Robert C. "Merit." The Catholic Encyclopedia. Nashville, NY: Th. Nelson, 1976.

Brosché, Fredrik. Luther on Predestination. Stockholm: Almqvist & Wiksell, 1978.

Brosseder, Johannes. "Die katholische Lutherrezeption." Concilium 12 (1976):515-21.

Brox, Norbert. Understanding the Message of Paul. Translated by Joseph Blenkinsopp. Notre Dame, IN: University of Notre Dame Press, 1968.

Brunner, Peter. Pro Ecclesia. Vol. 2. Berlin: Lutherisches Verlagshaus, 1966.

Bultmann, Rudolf. "Πιστεύω." Theologisches Wörterbuch zum Neuen Testament. Vol. 6. Stuttgart: W. Kohlhammer, 1959.

_____. Theologie des Neuen Testamentes. Tübingen: J. C. B. Mohr (Paul Siebeck), 1953.

Burnaby, John. Amor Dei, A Study of the Religion of St. Augustine. London: Hodder & Stoughton, 1938.

Cantinat, Jean. Les épîtres de saint Paul expliquées. Paris: Lecoffre, 1960.

Carlson, Charles P., Jr. Justification in Earlier Medieval Theology. The Hague: M. Nijhoff, 1975.

Cerfaux, Lucien. Le chrétien dans la théologie paulinienne. Paris: Les Editions du Cerf, 1962.

Charles, Robert Henry. The Apocrypha and Pseudepigrapha of the Old Testament. 2 vols. Oxford: Clarendon Press, 1913.

Chavaz, Edmond. Catholicisme Romain et Protestantisme. Tournai: Casterman, 1958.

Cochlaeus, Johannes. Adversus cucullatum Minotaurum Wittenbergensem. De sacramentorum gratia iterum. Vol. 3 of Corpus Catholicorum. Edited by J. Schweiser. Münster/W.: Aschendorff, 1920.

_____. Aequitatis discussio super consilio delectorum cardinalium. Vol. 17 of Corpus Catholicorum. Edited by H. Walter. Münster/W.: Aschendorff, 1931.

_____. Commentaria de actis et scriptis Martini Lutheri Saxonis. Farnborough. Greggs Press, 1968.

_____. De libero arbitrio hominis, libri duo. 1525.

_____. Ein nötig und christlich bedencken. Vol. 18 of Corpus Catholicorum. Edited by H. Volz. Münster/W.: Aschendorff, 1932.

Confutatio Confessionis Augustanae. Vol. 33 of Corpus Catholicorum. Edited by H. Immenkötter. Münster/W.: Aschendorff, 1979.

Congar, Yves. "Luther vu par les Catholiques." Revue des Sciences Philosophiques et Théologiques 34 (1950):507-17.

_____. "Regards et réflexions sur la christologie de Luther." Das Konzil von Chalkedon. Vol. 3. Edited by Alois Grillmeier and Heinrich Bacht. Würzburg: Echter, 1954.

_____. Vraie et fausse réforme dans l'Eglise. Paris: Les Editions du Cerf, 1950.

Conzelmann, Hans. "Χάρις." Theologisches Wörterbuch zum Neuen Testament. Vol. 9. Stuttgart: W. Kohlhammer, 1973.

Coressel, L. A. "Merit for Others." Review for Religious 5 (1946): 161-69.

Courth, Franz. "Gerechtfertigt von Gott - frei für das Leben." Trierer theologische Zeitschrift 83 (1974):81-97.

Cristiani, Léon. "Réforme." Dictionnaire de théologie catholique. Vol. 13/2. Paris: Letouzey & Ané, 1937.

_____. Du Luthéranisme au Protestantisme. Paris: Bloud et Cie., 1911.

_____. Luther et Luthéranisme. Paris: Librairie Bloud, 1908.

Crossan, Dominic M. "Justification." New Catholic Encyclopedia. Vol. 8. New York: McGraw-Hill, 1967.

Daffara, Marcolinus. De gratia Christi. Turin: Marietti, 1950.

Dander, Franciscus. Summarium tractatus dogmatici. 3 vols. Innsbruck: F. Rauch, 1949-54.

Dantine, Wilhelm. Die Gerechtmachung des Gottlosen. Munich: Chr. Kaiser, 1959.

_____. "Die Rechtfertigungslehre in der gegenwärtigen systematischen Arbeit der evangelischen Theologie." Evangelische Theologie 23 (1963):245-65.

Daujat, Jean. The Theology of Grace. Translated by a nun of Stanbrook Abbey. New York: Hawthorn Books, 1959.

Deharbe, Joseph. *Katholischer Katechismus*. Regensburg: F. Pustet, 1912.

Delhaye, Philippe; Gueret, Michel; and Tombeur, Paul. *Concilium Vaticanum II*. Louvain: Cetedoc, 1974.

Denifle, Heinrich. *Luther und Luthertum*. 2nd ed. 2 vols. Mainz: F. Kirchheim, 1904.

Dettloff, Werner. *Die Entwicklung der Akzeptations- und Verdienstlehre von Duns Scotus bis Luther*. Münster/W.: Aschendorff, 1963.

_____. "Rechtfertigung." *Handbuch theologischer Grundbegriffe*. Vol. 2. Munich: Kösel, 1963.

Didier, Georges. *Désintéressement du chrétien*. Paris: Aubier-Montaigne, 1955.

Diekamp, Franz. *Katholische Dogmatik nach den Grundsätzen des hlg. Thomas*. 11th & 12th eds. 3 vols. Münster/W.: Aschendorff, 1959.

Dietzfelbinger, Hermann. "Konzil und Kirche der Reformation." *Dialog unterwegs*. Edited by G. A. Lindbeck. Göttingen: Vandenhoeck & Ruprecht, 1965.

Dillersberger, Josef. *Matthäus*. 6 vols. Salzburg: O. Müller, 1953.

Dockx, Stanislas I. *Fils de Dieu par grâce*. Paris: Desclée de Brouwer, 1948.

Döllinger, Ignaz von. *Kirche und Kirchen. Papsttum und Kirchenstaat*. 2nd ed. Munich: Cotta, 1861.

_____. *Die Reformation*. 3 vols. Frankfort/M.: Minerva, 1962.

Doheny, William J. *The Marvels of Divine Grace*. Notre Dame, IN: Ave Maria Press, 1977.

Dolan, Aegidius. *Sanctifying Grace*. Cork: Mercier Press, 1953.

Dolan, John P. *History of the Reformation*. New York: Desclee Co., 1965.

Ebeling, Gerhard. *Luther - Einführung in sein Denken*. 2nd ed. Tübingen: J. C. B. Mohr (Paul Siebeck), 1964.

_____. *Lutherstudien*. Vol. 1. Tübingen: J. C. B. Mohr (Paul Siebeck), 1971.

_____. "Luther - Theologie." *Religion in Geschichte und Gegenwart*. 3rd ed. Vol. 4. Tübingen: J. C. B. Mohr (Paul Siebeck), 1960.

_____. "Zur Lehre vom triplex usus legis in der reformatorischen Theologie." *Theologische Literaturzeitung* 75 (1950):235-46.

Eck, Johann. *Enchiridion*. Edited and translated by F. L. Battles. 2nd ed. Grand Rapids, MI: Calvin Theological Seminary, 1978.

_____. *Gegen Martin Luthers Anklage wider das Konzil von Konstanz*. Vol. 14 of *Corpus Catholicorum*. Edited by K. Meisen and F. Zoepfe. Münster/W.: Aschendorff, 1929.

_____. *In primum Librum Sententiarum annotatiunculae*. Edited by W. L. Moore, Jr. Leiden: E. J. Brill, 1976.

Ehrlich, Rudolf E. *Rome. Opponent or Partner?* Philadelphia: Westminster Press, 1965.

Elert, Werner. *Das christliche Ethos*. 2nd ed. Hamburg: Furche, 1961.

_____. *Der christliche Glaube*. 2nd ed. Berlin: Furche, 1941.

_____. *Morphologie des Luthertums*. 2 vols. Munich: C. H. Beck, 1958.

Emery, Pierre-Yves. *Le Christ notre récompense*. Neuchâtel: Delachaux & Niestlé, 1962.

Emser, Hieronymus. *A venatione Lutheriana aegocerotis assertio*. Vol. 4 of *Corpus Catholicorum*. Edited by F. X. Thurnhofer. Münster/W.: Aschendorff, 1921.

Epstein, Isidore, ed. *The Babylonian Talmud*. 35 vols. London: Soncino Press, 1948-52.

Ernst, Cornelius. *The Theology of Grace*. Notre Dame, IN: Fides Publishers, 1974.

Esser, Hans-Helmut. "Gnade." *Theologisches Begriffslexikon zum Neuen Testament*. Vol. 2/1. Wuppertal: Brockhaus, 1969.

Evangelisch-lutherisch/römisch-katholische Studienkommission. Maltabericht. "Das Evangelium und die Kirche." *Herder Korrespondenz* 25 (1971):536-44.

Fausel, Heinrich. *D. Martin Luthers Leben und Werk*. 2 vols. Munich: Siebenstern, 1966.

Feckes, Karl. "Verdienst." *Lexikon für Theologie und Kirche*. 1st ed. Vol. 10. Freiburg i. Br.: Herder, 1938.

Feiner, Johannes, and Löhrer, Magnus, eds. Mysterium Salutis.
   5 vols. Einsiedeln: Benziger, 1969-78.

Feiner, Johannes, and Vischer, Lukas, eds. Neues Glaubensbuch.
   8th ed. Freiburg i. Br.: Herder, 1973.

Feuling, Daniel. Katholische Glaubenslehre. 3rd ed. Salzburg:
   O. Müller, 1950.

Finkenzeller, Josef. "Der Mensch im Glanz des göttlichen Lebens."
   Wahrheit und Zeugnis. Edited by M. Schmaus and A. Läpple.
   Düsseldorf: Patmos, 1964.

Fiolet, Hermanus A. Ecumenical Breakthrough, an Integration of the
   Catholic and the Reformational Faith. Pittsburgh:
   Duquesne University Press, 1969.

_____. Die zweite Reformation. Graz: Styria, 1971.

Fisher, Johannes. Sacri sacerdotii defensio contra Lutherum.
   Vol. 9 of Corpus Catholicorum. Edited by Hermann Klein
   Schmeink. Münster/W.: Aschendorff, 1925.

Flick, Maurizio. "Dialogo sul merito." Gregorianum 45 (1964):
   339-48.

Flick, Maurizio, and Alszeghy, Zoltan. Il vangelo della grazia.
   Florence: Libreria Editrice Fiorentina, 1967.

Fonck, Leopold. Die Parabeln des Herrn im Evangelium. 3rd ed.
   Innsbruck: F. Rauch, 1909.

Forster, Anselm. "Verdienst - Systematisch." Lexikon für Theologie
   und Kirche. 2nd ed. Vol. 10. Freiburg i. Br.: Herder,
   1965.

Forster, Karl, ed. Wandlungen des Lutherbildes. Würzburg: Echter,
   1966.

Fransen, Piet. "Dogmengeschichtliche Entfaltung der Gnadenlehre."
   Mysterium Salutis. Vol. 4/2. Edited by J. Feiner and
   M. Löhrer. Einsiedeln: Benziger, 1973.

_____. The New Life of Grace. Translated by G. Dupont.
   London: G. Chapman, 1971.

Franzen, August, ed. Um Reform und Reformation. Münster/W.:
   Aschendorff, 1968.

Freedman, Harry, and Simon, Maurice, eds. Midrash Rabbah. 10 vols.
   London: Soncino Press, 1939.

Fries, Heinrich. "Hans Küng. Rechtfertigung." Theologische
   Quartalschrift 136 (1956):356-57.

_____. Ökumene statt Konfessionen? Frankfurt/M.: J. Knecht, 1977.

Gaechter, Paul. Das Matthäusevangelium. Innsbruck: Tyrolia, 1962.

Garrigou - Lagrange, Reginaldus. "L'augmentation de la charité et les actes imparfaits." La vie spirituelle 6 (1925):321-34.

_____. De gratia. Turin: Casa Editrice Marietti, 1946.

_____. Les trois âges de la vie intérieure. Vol. 1. Paris: Les Editions du Cerf, 1938.

Gatterer, M., ed. Cathechismus Romanus. Innsbruck: F. Rauch, 1930.

Gerest, Régis. "Du serf arbitre à la liberté du chrétien. Les cheminements de Martin Luther." Lumière et vie 12 (1963): 75-120.

Glaubensverkündigung für Erwachsene. Deutsche Ausgabe des Holländischen Katechismus. Nijmwegen: Dekker & Van de Vegt, 1968.

Gleason, Robert W. Grace. New York: Sheed & Ward, 1962.

Gogarten, Friedrich. Luthers Theologie. Tübingen: J. C. B. Mohr (Paul Siebeck), 1967.

Goppelt, Leonhard. "Grace." Baker's Dictionary of Christian Ethics. Grand Rapids, MI: Baker Book House, 1973.

Grabmann, Martin. Die Geschichte der katholischen Theologie seit dem Ausgang der Väterzeit. Darmstadt: Wissenschaftliche Buchgesellschaft, 1974.

_____. "Das Konzil von Trient als Fortschrittsprinzip der katholischen Dogmatik." Das Weltkonzil von Trient. Edited by G. Schreiber. Vol. 1. Freiburg i. Br.: Herder, 1951.

Grane, Leif. Contra Gabrielem. Luthers Auseinandersetzung mit Gabriel Biel in der Disputatio contra scholasticam theologiam 1517. Copenhagen: Gyldendal, 1962.

Grass, Hans. "Gespräch über die Rechtfertigungslehre." Glaube, Geist, Geschichte. Edited by G. Müller and W. Zeller. Leiden: E. J. Brill, 1967.

Green, Lowell C. "The Influence of Erasmus upon Melanchthon, Luther and the Formula of Concord in the Doctrine of Justification." Church History 43 (1974):183-200.

Grisar, Hartmann. Martin Luthers Leben und sein Werk. 2nd ed. Freiburg i. Br.: Herder, 1927.

Grosche, Robert. "Simul peccator et iustus." Catholica 4 (1935):132-39.

Gross, Heinrich. "Gnade im Alten Testament." Mysterium Salutis. Vol. 4/2. Edited by J. Feiner and M. Löhrer. Einsiedeln: Benziger, 1973.

Gross, Julius. Entwicklungsgeschichte des Erbsündendogmas. 4 vols. Munich: E. Reinhardt, 1960-72.

Guggisberg, Kurt. Die römisch - katholische Kirche. Zurich: Zwingli Verlag, 1946.

Gyllenkrok, Axel. Rechtfertigung und Heiligung in der frühen evangelischen Theologie Luthers. Uppsala: A. B. Lundequistka Bokhandeln, 1952.

Hacker, Paul. The Ego in Faith: Martin Luther and the Origin of Anthropocentric Religion. Chicago: Franciscan Herald Press, 1970.

Hägglund, Bengt. The Background of Luther's Doctrine of Justification in Late Medieval Theology. Philadelphia: Fortress Press, 1971.

_____. History of Theology. Translated by G. J. Lund. St. Louis, MO: Concordia, 1968.

_____. "Luther und die Mystik." The Church, Mysticism, Sanctification and the Natural in Luther's Thought. Edited by I. Asheim. Philadelphia: Fortress Press, 1967.

Häring, Bernhard. The Law of Christ. 6th ed. Vol. 1. Translated by E. G. Kaiser. Westminster, MD: Newman Press, 1965.

Hamm, Berndt. Promissio, Pactum, Ordinatio. Tübingen: J. C. B. Mohr (Paul Siebeck), 1977.

Hamp, Vinzenz. "Verdienst im Alten Testament." Lexikon für Theologie und Kirche. 2nd ed. Vol. 10. Freiburg i. Br.: Herder, 1965.

Hampe, Johann Christoph, ed. Die Autorität der Freiheit. Gegenwart des Konzils und Zukunft der Kirche im ökumenischen Disput. 3 vols. Munich: Kösel, 1967.

Hardon, John A. "Merit." Modern Catholic Dictionary. Garden City, NY: Doubleday & Co., 1980.

Harent, Stéphane. "Foi." Dictionnaire de théologie catholique. Vol. 6/1. Paris: Letouzey & Ané, 1947.

Harnack, Adolf von. "Geschichte der Lehre von der Seligkeit allein durch den Glauben in der alten Kirche." Zeitschrift für Theologie und Kirche 1 (1891):82-178.

―――――. Lehrbuch der Dogmengeschichte. 4th ed. 3 vols. Darmstadt: Wissenschaftliche Buchgesellschaft, 1964.

Harnack, Theodosius. Luthers Theologie. 2 vols. Munich: Chr. Kaiser, 1927.

Hase, Karl von. Evangelisch Protestantische Dogmatik. 5th ed. Leipzig: Breitkopf & Härtel, 1860.

―――――. Handbook to the Controversy with Rome. 2nd ed. 2 vols. Translated by A. W. Streane. London: Religious Tract Society, 1909.

Hasenhüttl, Gotthold. Kritische Dogmatik. Graz: Styria, 1979.

Hasler, August. Luther in der katholischen Dogmatik. Munich: M. Hueber, 1968.

―――――. "Luther in der katholischen Schultheologie." Concilium 12 (1976):522-25.

Haspecker, Josef. "Der Begriff der Gnade im Alten Testament." Lexikon für Theologie und Kirche. 2nd ed. Vol. 4. Freiburg i. Br.: Herder, 1960.

Heer, Friedrich. Europäische Geistesgeschichte. Stuttgart: Kohlhammer, 1953.

Heiler, Friedrich. Der Katholizismus. Munich: E. Reinhardt, 1923.

Heinrich, Johann Baptist, and Gutberlet, Constantin. Dogmatische Theologie. 10 vols. Mainz: F. Kirchheim, 1896-1904.

Heinrichs, Maurus. Theses dogmaticae. 2nd ed. Vol. 2. Hong Kong: Studium Biblicum O.F.M., 1954.

Herborn, Nikolaus. Locorum communium adversus huius temporis haereses enchiridion. Vol. 12 of Corpus Catholicorum. Edited by P. Schlager. Münster/W.: Aschendorff, 1927.

Hermann, Rudolf. Gesammelte Studien zur Theologie Luthers und der Reformation. Göttingen: Vandenhoeck & Ruprecht, 1960.

―――――. Luthers Theologie. Göttingen: Vandenhoeck & Ruprecht, 1967.

―――――. Luthers These Gerecht und Sünder zugleich. 2nd ed. Gütersloh: G. Mohn, 1960.

_____. "Rechtfertigung." Religion in Geschichte und Gegenwart. 3rd ed. Vol. 5. Tübingen: J. C. B. Mohr (Paul Siebeck), 1961.

Hermes, Georg. Christkatholische Dogmatik. 3 vols. Frankfort/M.: Minerva, 1968.

Herms, Eilert. "Explikationsprobleme des Rechtfertigungsthemas und der Prinzipien des wissenschaftlichen Dialogs zwischen protestantischen und röm. kath. Theologen." Kerygma und Dogma 21 (1975):277-314.

Herte, Adolf. Das katholische Lutherbild im Bann der Lutherkommentare des Cochläus. 3 vols. Münster/W.: Aschendorff, 1943.

Hervé, Jean Marie. Manuale theologicae dogmaticae. 18th ed. 4 vols. Westminster, MD: Newman Press, 1943.

Hess, M. Whitcomb. "The Quest for the Historical Luther." The Catholic World 196 (1962):73-79.

Hessen, Johannes. Luther in katholischer Sicht. 2nd ed. Bonn: Röhrscheid, 1949.

Heyer, Friedrich. Konfessionskunde. Berlin: W. de Gruyter, 1977.

Hirsch, Emanuel. Hilfsbuch zum Studium der Dogmatik. 4th ed. Berlin: W. de Gruyter, 1964.

Hödl, Ludwig. "Lumen gratiae - ein Leitgedanke der Gnadentheologie des Thomas von Aquin." Mysterium der Gnade. Edited by H. Rossmann and J. Ratzinger. Regensburg: F. Pustet, 1975.

Hoffmeister, Johann. Wahrhaftige Entdeckung und Widerlegung. Vol. 18 of Corpus Catholicorum. Edited by H. Volz. Münster/W.: Aschendorff, 1932.

Holböck, Ferdinand. Credimus. Kommentar zum Credo Pauls VI. 3rd ed. Salzburg: A. Pustet, 1973.

Holl, Karl. Gesammelte Aufsätze zur Kirchengeschichte. 7th ed. Vol. 1. Tübingen: J. C. B. Mohr (Paul Siebeck), 1948.

_____. Gesammelte Aufsätze zur Kirchengeschichte. Vol. 3. Darmstadt: Wissenschaftliche Buchgesellschaft, 1965.

Holzmeister, Urban. "Zum Gleichnis von den Arbeitern im Weinberg." Zeitschrift für katholische Theologie 52 (1928):407-12.

Hugon, Eduardo. Tractatus dogmatici. 10th ed. 3 vols. Paris: P. Lethielleux, 1935.

Hus, Joannis. Opera omnia. Edited by W. Flajšhans and M. Kominkova. 3 vols. Osnabrück: Biblio, 1966.

Ihmels, Ludwig. "Rechtfertigung." Realenzyklopädie für protestantische Theologie und Kirche. 3rd ed. Vol. 16. Leipzig: J. C. Hinrich, 1905.

Iserloh, Erwin. "Aufhebung des Lutherbannes?" Lutherprozess und Lutherbann. Edited by R. Bäumer. Münster/W.: Aschendorff, 1972.

_____. "Luther und die Mystik." The Church, Mysticism, Sanctification and the Natural in Luther's Thought. Edited by I. Asheim. Philadelphia: Fortress Press, 1967.

_____. Luther und die Reformation. Aschaffenburg: Paul Pattloch, 1974.

_____. Luther zwischen Reform und Reformation. Münster/W.: Aschendorff, 1966.

Iwand, Hans Joachim. Glaubensgerechtigkeit nach Luthers Lehre. Munich: Evangelischer Verlag A. Lempp, 1941.

_____. Rechtfertigungslehre und Christusglaube. 3rd ed. Munich: Chr. Kaiser, 1966.

_____. "Studien zum Problem des unfreien Willens." Zeitschrift für systematische Theologie 8 (1930):216-50.

Jedin, Hubert, ed. Die Erforschung der kirchlichen Reformationsgeschichte seit 1876. Darmstadt: Wissenschaftliche Buchgesellschaft, 1975.

_____. Geschichte des Konzils von Trient. Vol. 2. Freiburg i. Br.: Herder, 1957.

_____. Handbuch der Kirchengeschichte. Vol. 4. Freiburg i. Br.: Herder, 1967.

_____. "Historische Randbemerkungen zum Thema: Tridentinum und Wiedervereinigung." Begegnung der Christen. Edited by M. Roesle and O. Cullmann. Stuttgart: Evangelisches Verlagshaus, 1959.

_____. Kirche des Glaubens, Kirche der Geschichte. 2 vols. Freiburg i. Br.: Herder, 1966.

_____. Kleine Konziliengeschichte. Freiburg i. Br.: Herder, 1959.

_____. "Das Konzil von Trient und der Protestantismus." Catholica 3 (1934):137-56.

_____. Vatikanum II und Tridentinum. Cologne: Westdeutscher Verlag, 1968.

_____. "Wo sah die vortridentinische Kirche die Lehrdifferenzen mit Luther?" <u>Catholica</u> 21 (1967):85-100.

Jeremias, Joachim. <u>Neutestamentliche Theologie</u>. Vol. 1. Gütersloh: G. Mohn, 1971.

Joest, Wilfried. <u>Gesetz und Freiheit</u>. 2nd ed. Göttingen: Vandenhoeck & Ruprecht, 1956.

_____. <u>Die katholische Lehre von der Rechtfertigung und von der Gnade</u>. Lüneburg: Heliand, 1954.

_____. "Paulus und das Luthersche simul justus et peccator." <u>Kerygma und Dogma</u> 1 (1955):269-320.

_____. "Rechtfertigung - Dogmengeschichte." <u>Religion in Geschichte und Gegenwart</u>. 3rd ed. Vol. 5. Tübingen: J. C. B. Mohr (Paul Siebeck), 1961.

_____. "Die tridentinische Rechtfertigungslehre." <u>Kerygma und Dogma</u> 9 (1963):41-69.

Jonas, Hans. <u>Augustin und das paulinische Freiheitsproblem</u>. Göttingen: Vandenhoeck & Ruprecht, 1930.

Journet, Charles. <u>Entretiens sur la grâce</u>. Paris: Desclée de Brouwer, 1959.

Joyce, George H. <u>The Catholic Doctrine of Grace</u>. Westminster, MD: Newman Press, 1950.

Kadai, Heino O., ed. <u>Accents in Luther's Theology</u>. St. Louis, MO: Concordia, 1967.

Kähler, Ernst. "Prädestination - Dogmengeschichtlich." <u>Religion in Geschichte und Gegenwart</u>. 3rd ed. Vol. 5. Tübingen: J. C. B. Mohr (Paul Siebeck), 1961.

Kautzsch, Emil. <u>Die Apokryphen und Pseudoepigraphen des Alten Testamentes</u>. 2 vols. Hildesheim: G. Olms, 1962.

Kawerau, Peter. <u>Luther - Leben, Schriften, Denken</u>. Marburg: N. G. Elwert, 1969.

Kelly, John N. D. <u>Early Christian Doctrines</u>. 5th ed. New York: Harper & Row, 1978.

Kertelge, Karl. <u>Rechtfertigung bei Paulus</u>. Münster/W.: Aschendorff, 1967.

Kinder, Ernst. <u>Die Erbsünde</u>. Stuttgart: Schwabenverlag, 1959.

_____. Die evangelische Lehre von der Rechtfertigung. Lüneburg: Heliand, 1957.

_____. "Rechtfertigung - Dogmengeschichte II." Religion in Geschichte und Gegenwart. 3rd ed. Vol. 5. Tübingen: J. C. B. Mohr (Paul Siebeck), 1961.

Kinder, Ernst, and Haendler, Klaus., eds. Gesetz und Evangelium. Darmstadt: Wissenschaftliche Buchgesellschaft, 1968.

Kirchner, Victor. Der "Lohn" in der alten Philosophie, im bürgerlichen Recht, besonders im Neuen Testament. Gütersloh: C. Bertelsmann, 1908.

Kirn, Otto. "Glaube." Realenzyklopädie für protestantische Theologie und Kirche. 3rd ed. Vol. 6. Leipzig: J. C. Hinrich, 1899.

_____. "Gnade." Realenzyklopädie für protestantische Theologie und Kirche. 3rd ed. Vol. 6. Leipzig: J. C. Hinrich, 1899.

Kirschkamp. "Verdienst." Kirchenlexikon von Wetzer - Welte. 2nd ed. Vol. 12. Edited by J. Hergenröther and F. Kaulen. Freiburg i. Br.: Herder, 1901.

Klein, Günter. "Rechtfertigung im Neuen Testament." Religion in Geschichte und Gegenwart. 3rd ed. Vol. 5. Tübingen: J. C. B. Mohr (Paul Siebeck), 1961.

Klooster, Fred H. "Merit." Baker's Dictionary of Christian Ethics. Grand Rapids, MI: Baker Book House, 1973.

Koch, Klaus. "Gibt es ein Vergeltungsdogma im Alten Testament?" Zeitschrift für Theologie und Kirche 52 (1955):1-42.

Koehler, Walter. Dogmengeschichte. 3rd ed. 2 vols. Zurich: M. Niehans, 1951.

Kösters, Reinhard. "Die Lehre von der Rechtfertigung unter besonderer Berücksichtigung der Formel 'Simul justus et peccator'." Zeitschrift für katholische Theologie 90 (1968):309-24.

_____. "Luthers These 'gerecht und Sünder zugleich'." Catholica 18 (1964):48-77.

_____. "Zur Theorie der Kontroverstheologie." Zeitschrift für katholische Theologie 88 (1966):121-62.

Köstlin, Julius. Luthers Theologie. 3rd ed. 2 vols. Darmstadt: Wissenschaftliche Buchgesellschaft, 1968.

Kolping, Adolf. *Katholische Theologie, gestern und heute.* Bremen: C. Schünemann, 1964.

Kommission für spätantike Religionsgeschichte der deutschen Akademie der Wissenschaften zu Berlin, ed. *Die griechischen christlichen Schriftsteller der ersten drei Jahrhunderte.* Berlin: Akademie Verlag, 1897 -.

Kouwenhoven, H. J. *Simul justus et peccator in de nieuwe Roomskatholicke Theologie.* Delft: W. D. Weinema, 1969.

Kraus, Georg. *Vorherbestimmung.* Freiburg i. Br.: Herder, 1977.

Kreck, Walter. *Grundfragen der Dogmatik.* Munich: Chr. Kaiser, 1970.

Kroeger, Matthias. *Rechtfertigung und Gesetz.* Göttingen: Vandenhoeck & Ruprecht, 1968.

Kühn, Ulrich. "Ist Luther Anlass zum Wandel des katholischen Selbstverständnisses?" *Theologische Literaturzeitung* 93 (1968):881-98.

_____. *Die Rechtfertigungslehre des Thomas von Aquin in evangelischer Sicht.* Berlin: Evangelische Verlagsanstalt, 1967.

_____. "Die Rechtfertigungslehre in heutiger Sicht." *Evangelische Welt* 20 (1966):647-48.

Küng, Hans. "Anfragen an die Reformation heute." *Reformatio* 27 (1978):374-93.

_____. *Christ sein.* 6th ed. Munich: R. Piper, 1975.

_____. "Katholische Besinnung auf Luthers Rechtfertigungslehre heute." *Theologie im Wandel.* Edited by Katholische theologische Fakultät an der Universität Tübingen. Munich: E. Wewel, 1967.

_____. *Rechtfertigung. Die Lehre Karl Barths und eine katholische Besinnung.* Einsiedeln: Johannes Verlag, 1957.

_____. "Rechtfertigung und Heiligung nach dem Neuen Testament." *Begegnung der Christen.* Edited by M. Roesle and O. Cullmann. Stuttgart: Evangelisches Verlagswerk, 1959.

_____. "Response." *Union Seminary Quarterly* 27 (1971):143-47.

_____. "Where I Stand." *Christianity and Crisis* 41 (1981): 3-11.

_____. "Zur Diskussion um die Rechtfertigung." *Theologische Quartalschrift* 143 (1963):129-35.

Kuhn, Johannes von. Die christliche Lehre von der göttlichen Gnade. Frankfort/M.: Minerva, 1968.

Kunze, Johannes. "Merit." The New Schaff-Herzog Encyclopedia of Religious Knowledge. Vol. 7. New York: Funk & Wagnalls, 1910.

_____. "Verdienst." Realenzyklopädie für protestantische Theologie und Kirche. 3rd ed. Vol. 20. Leipzig: J. C. Hinrich, 1908.

Kuss, Otto. Der Römerbrief. Regensburg: F. Pustet, 1957 -.

Lackmann, Max. Credo Ecclesiam Catholicam. Graz: Styria, 1960.

_____. Mit evangelischen Augen. 4 vols. Graz: Styria, 1963-65.

Lagrange, Marie Joseph. "Le commentaire de Luther sur l'épître aux Romains." Revue Biblique 12 (1915):456-84 and 13 (1916): 90-120.

_____. Evangile selon Saint Matthieu. 4th ed. Paris: Lecoffre, 1927.

_____. Saint Paul: Epître aux Romains. Paris: Lecoffre, 1950.

Lais, Hermann. Dogmatik. Kevelaer: Butzon & Bercker, 1965.

Landeen, William M. Martin Luther's Religious Thought. Mountain View, CA: Pacific Press, 1971.

Landgraf, Arthur Michael. Dogmengeschichte der Frühscholastik. 4 vols. Regensburg: F. Pustet, 1952-56.

Lange, Hermannus. De gratia. Freiburg i. Br.: Herder, 1929.

Lau, Franz. Luther. Translated by R. H. Fischer. Philadelphia: Westminster Press, 1963.

Lauterbach, Jacob Z., ed. Mekilta de - Rabbi Ishmael. 3 vols. Philadelphia: Jewish Publication Society of America, 1933-35.

Lawler, Ronald D.; Wuerl, Donald; and Lawler, Thomas C., eds. The Teaching of Christ. Huntington, IN: OSV, 1976.

Leaver, Robin A. Luther on Justification. St. Louis, MO: Concordia, 1975.

Leclercq, Jacques. Les grandes lignes de la philosophie morale. Louvain: Editions de l'Institut supérieur de philosophie, 1946.

Lemmonnyer, Antoine. "La doctrine de la justification dans la Sainte Ecriture." Dictionnaire de théologie catholique. Vol. 8/2. Paris: Letouzey & Ané, 1925.

Lépicier, Alexio Maria. Tractatus de gratia. Paris: P. Lethielleux, 1907.

Lercher, Ludovicus. Institutiones theologiae dogmaticae. 4 vols. Oeniponte (Innsbruck): F. Rauch, 1948-51.

Le Senne, René. Traité de morale générale. Paris: Presses Universitaires de France, 1947.

Letter, Prudentius de. "De ratione meriti secundum Sanctum Thomam." Analecta Gregoriana 19 (1939):1-151.

_____. "Grace." A Catholic Dictionary of Theology. Vol. 2. London: Thomas Nelson & Sons, 1967.

Lilje, Hans, ed. Didache. Berlin: Furche, 1938.

Lindbeck, George A., ed. Dialog unterwegs. Göttingen: Vandenhoeck & Ruprecht, 1965.

_____. The Future of Roman Catholic Theology. Philadelphia: Fortress Press, 1970.

_____. "Der Zusammenhang von Kirchenkritik und Rechtfertigungslehre." Concilium 12 (1976):481-86.

Link, Wilhelm. Das Ringen Luthers um die Freiheit der Theologie von der Philosophie. Berlin: Evangelische Verlagsanstalt, 1954.

Lipgens, Walter. Kardinal Johannes Gropper. Münster/W.: Aschendorff, 1951.

Löfgren, David. Die Theologie der Schöpfung bei Luther. Göttingen: Vandenhoeck & Ruprecht, 1960.

Loewenich, Walter von. Duplex iustitia. Wiesbaden: F. Steiner, 1972.

_____. "Evangelische und katholische Lutherdeutung der Gegenwart im Dialog." Luther-Jahrbuch 1967. Hamburg: F. Wittig, 1967.

_____. Luther als Ausleger der Synoptiker. Munich: Chr. Kaiser, 1954.

_____. Der moderne Katholizismus vor und nach dem Konzil. Witten: Luther Verlag, 1970.

_____. Von Augustin zu Luther. Witten: Luther Verlag, 1959.

Lohse, Bernhard. "Die Bedeutung Augustins für den jungen Luther." Kerygma und Dogma 11 (1965):116-35.

_____. "Warum hat man Luther nicht verstanden? Lutherische Antwort." Concilium 12 (1976):474-77.

Lohse, Eduard. "Verdienst im Judentum." Religion in Geschichte und Gegenwart. 3rd ed. Vol. 6. Tübingen: J. C. B. Mohr (Paul Siebeck), 1962.

Lonergan, Bernard J. F. Grace and Freedom. London: Darton, Longman & Todd, 1971.

Loofs, Friedrich. Leitfaden zum Studium der Dogmengeschichte. 6th ed. Tübingen: M. Niemeyer, 1959.

Lortz, Joseph. Geschichte der Kirche. 11th-14th eds. Münster/W.: Aschendorff, 1948.

_____. How the Reformation Came. Translated by O. M. Knab. New York: Herder & Herder, 1964.

_____. "Luthers Römerbriefvorlesung." Trierer theologische Zeitschrift 71 (1962):129-53/216-47.

_____. "Martin Luther, Grundzüge seiner geistigen Struktur." Reformata Reformanda. Vol. 1. Edited by E. Iserloh and K. Repgen. Münster/W.: Aschendorff, 1965.

_____. The Reformation a Problem for Today. Translated by J. C. Dwyer. Westminster, MD: Newman Press, 1964.

_____. Die Reformation in Deutschland. 5th ed. 2 vols. Freiburg i. Br.: Herder, 1962.

Lortz, Joseph, and Iserloh, Erwin. Kleine Reformationsgeschichte. Freiburg i. Br.: Herder, 1969.

Lottin, Odon. Morale fondamentale. Paris: Desclée, 1954.

Lubac, Henri de. "Zum katholischen Dialog mit Karl Barth." Dokumente 14 (1958):448-54.

Lubac, Henri de, and Daniélou, Jean, ed. Sources chrétiennes. Paris: Editions du Cerf, 1941 -.

Lumbreras, Petrus. De gratia. Rome: Edizioni A. Arnoldo, 1946.

Luthardt, Christoph Ernst. Kompendium der Dogmatik. 13th ed. Leipzig: Dörffling & Franke, 1933.

Luther, Martin. Werke (Kritische Gesamtausgabe - Weimarer Ausgabe). Weimar: H. Böhlau, 1883 -.

Lutheran World Federation. Justification Today. New York: National Lutheran Council, 1965.

Lynn, William D. "Christ's Redemptive Merit." Analecta Gregoriana 115 (1962):1-168.

Lyonnet, Stanislaus. Quaestiones in Epistolam ad Romanos. Rome: Pontificio Istituto Biblico, 1955.

McCue, James F. "Ecumenical Reflection on Justification." The Ecumenist 18 (1980):49-53.

McDonough, Thomas M. The Law and Gospel in Luther. London: Oxford University Press, 1963.

McSorley, Harry J. Luther: Right or Wrong? An Ecumenical-Theological Study of Luther's Major Work, "The Bondage of the Will". New York: Newman Press, 1969.

Malevez, Léopold. "Histoire et réalités dernières." Ephemerides theologicae Lovanienses 19 (1942):47-90.

_____. Pour une théologie de la foi. Paris: Desclée de Brouwer, 1969.

Manns, Peter. "Fides absoluta - Fides incarnata." Reformata Reformanda. Vol. 1. Edited by E. Iserloh and K. Repgen. Münster/W.: Aschendorff, 1965.

_____. Lutherforschung heute. Wiesbaden: F. Steiner, 1967.

Maritain, Jacques. Trois Réformateurs. Paris: Plon, 1925.

Marmorstein, Arthur. The Doctrine of Merits in Old Rabbinical Literature. New York: KTAV Publishing House, 1968.

Maron, Gottfried. Kirche und Rechtfertigung. Göttingen: Vandenhoeck & Ruprecht, 1969.

Mau, Rudolf. Der Gedanke der Heilsnotwendigkeit bei Luther. Berlin: Evangelische Verlagsanstalt, 1969.

_____. "Zur Frage der Begründung von Heilsgewissheit beim jungen Luther." Theologische Literaturzeitung 92 (1967): 742-48.

Mausbach, Joseph. Die Ethik des Hlg. Augustinus. 2 vols. Freiburg i. Br.: Herder, 1909.

_____. Katholische Moraltheologie. 9th ed. 3 vols. Münster/W.: Aschendorff, 1959.

Mayer, Cornelius. "Rechtfertigung durch Werke?" Theologische Quartalschrift 154 (1974):118-36.

Meersch, Joseph van der. "Grâce." Dictionnaire de théologie catholique. Vol. 6/2. Paris: Letouzey & Ané, 1947.

Meinertz, Max. <u>Theologie des Neuen Testamentes</u>. 2 vols. Bonn: P. Hanstein, 1950.

Meissinger, Karl August. <u>Der katholische Luther</u>. Munich: L. Lehnen, 1952.

Metz, Johann Baptist. "Konkupiszenz." <u>Handbuch theologischer Grundbegriffe</u>. Vol. 1. Edited by H. Fries. Munich: Kösel, 1962.

_____. <u>Reform und Gegenreformation heute</u>. Mainz: M. Grünewald, 1969.

Meyer, Charles R. <u>A Contemporary Theology of Grace</u>. Staten Island, NY: Society of St. Paul, 1971.

Meyer, Harding. "La doctrine de la justification dans le dialogue interconfessionnel mené par l'Eglise luthérienne." <u>Revue d'histoire et de philosophie religieuses</u> 57 (1977):19-51.

Michel, Marie Albert. "Surérogatoires (Oeuvres)." <u>Dictionnaire de théologie catholique</u>. Vol. 14/2. Paris: Letouzey & Ané, 1941.

Michel, Otto. "Der Lohngedanke in der Verkündigung Jesu." <u>Zeitschrift für systematische Theologie</u> 9 (1932):47-54.

Migne, Jacques Paul, ed. <u>Patrologiae cursus completus, series Graeca</u>. Paris, 1857-66.

_____., ed. <u>Patrologiae cursus completus, series Latina</u>. Paris, 1841-55.

Minear, Paul S. <u>And Great Shall Be Your Reward--The Origin of Christian Views of Salvation</u>. New Haven: Yale University Press, 1941.

Minges, Parthenius. <u>Joannis Duns Scoti: Doctrina philosophica et theologica</u>. 2 vols. Ad Claras Aquas: Typographia Collegii S. Bonaventurae, 1930.

Modalsli, Ole. <u>Das Gericht nach den Werken</u>. Göttingen: Vandenhoeck & Ruprecht, 1963.

Moeller, Charles. "Grace and Justification." <u>Lumen Vitae</u> 19 (1964):719-30.

_____. "Théologie de la grâce et oecuménisme." <u>Irénikon</u> 28 (1955):19-56.

Moeller, Charles, and Philips, Gérard. <u>The Theology of Grace</u>. Translated by R. A. Wilson. London: A. R. Mowbray, 1961.

Moffat, James. <u>Grace in the New Testament</u>. London: Hodder & Stoughton, 1931.

Möhler, Johann Adam. Symbolik. 5th ed. Mainz: F. Kupferberg, 1838.

Molinski, Waldemar. "Merit." Sacramentum Mundi. Vol. 4. Edited by Karl Rahner et al., New York: Herder & Herder, 1969.

Montague, George T. Growth in Christ. Kirkwood, MO: Maryhurst Press, 1961.

Morency, Robert. L'union de grâce selon Saint Thomas. Montreal: Les Editions de l'Immaculée Conception, 1950.

Mors, Iosepho. Institutiones theologiae dogmaticae. Vol. 4. Petropolis: Editora Vozes, 1939.

Most, William George. "Grace in the Bible." New Catholic Encyclopedia. Vol. 6. New York: McGraw-Hill, 1967.

Mühlen, Karl Heinz zur. Nos extra nos. Tübingen: J. C. B. Mohr (Paul Siebeck), 1972.

Mühlen, Heribert. "Gnadenlehre." Bilanz der Theologie im 20. Jahrhundert. 2nd ed. 4 vols. Edited by Herbert Vorgrimler and Robert van der Gucht. Freiburg i. Br.: Herder, 1970.

Müller, Gerhard. Die Rechtfertigungslehre. Gütersloh: G. Mohn, 1977.

Müller, Hanfried. Evangelische Dogmatik im Überblick. Berlin: Evangelische Verlagsanstalt, 1978.

Muldoon, Thomas. Theologicae dogmaticae praelectiones. 5 vols. Rome: Catholic Book Agency, 1958-65.

Mulert, Hermann, and Schott, Erdmann. Konfessionskunde. 3rd ed. Berlin: A. Töpelmann, 1956.

Mussner, Franz. "Der Begriff der Gnade im Neuen Testament." Lexikon für Theologie und Kirche. 2nd ed. Vol. 4. Freiburg i. Br.: Herder, 1960.

_____. "Die neutestamentliche Gnadentheologie in Grundzügen." Mysterium Salutis. Vol. 4/2. Edited by J. Feiner and M. Löhrer. Einsiedeln: Benziger, 1973.

Neuhäusler, Engelbert. Anspruch und Antwort Gottes. Düsseldorf: Patmos, 1962.

Neveut, E. "Des Actes méritoires." Divus Thomas(P) 33 (1930): 386-408.

_____. "Des conditions de la plus grande valeur de nos actes méritoires." Divus Thomas(P) 34 (1931):353-75.

_____. "Du mérite de convenance." *Divus Thomas(P)* 35 (1932): 1-29.

_____. "Du mérite de convenance chez le juste." *Divus Thomas(P)* 36 (1933):337-59.

Nevins, Albert J. "Merit." *The Maryknoll Catholic Dictionary*. New York: Grosset & Dunlap, 1965.

Newman, John Henry. *Lectures on the Doctrine of Justification*. Westminster, MD: Christian Classics, 1966.

Nicolas, Jean Hervé. *Les profoundeurs de la grâce*. Paris: Beauchesne, 1969.

Niesel, Wilhelm. *The Gospel and the Churches*. Translated by D. Lewis. Philadelphia: Westminster Press, 1962.

Noble, Henri Domenique. *L'amitié avec Dieu*. Paris: Desclée de Brouwer, 1932.

Noort, Gerardus Cornelis van. *Tractatus de gratia Christi*. 3rd ed. Bussum: Sumptibus Societatis Editricis Anonymae, 1920.

Normann, Sigurd. "De servo arbitrio als Ausdruck lutherischen Christentums." *Zeitschrift für systematische Theologie* 14 (1937):303-38.

Nygren, Anders. "Simul justus et peccator bei Augustin und Luther." *Zeitschrift für systematische Theologie* 16 (1939):364-79.

Nygren, Gotthard. *Das Prädestinationsproblem in der Theologie Augustins*. Göttingen: Vandenhoeck & Ruprecht, 1956.

Oberman, Heiko Augustinus. "Facientibus quod in se est Deus non denegat gratiam." *Harvard Theological Review* 55 (1962): 317-42.

_____. *Forerunners of the Reformation*. New York: Holt, Rinehart & Winston, 1966.

_____. *The Harvest of Medieval Theology*. Cambridge, MA: Harvard University Press, 1963.

_____. "'Iustitia Christi' and 'Iustitia Dei'. Luther and the Scholastic Doctrines of Justification." *Harvard Theological Review* 59 (1966):1-26.

_____. "The Reformation: Proclamation of Grace." *God and Man in Contemporary Christian Thought*. Edited by Charles Malik. Beirut: American University, 1970.

_____. "Das tridentinische Rechtfertigungsdekret im Lichte der spätmittelalterlichen Theologie." Zeitschrift für Theologie und Kirche 61 (1964):251-82.

_____. Werden und Wertung der Reformation. Tübingen: J. C. B. Mohr (Paul Siebeck), 1977.

O'Brien, Thomas C., ed. Corpus Dictionary of Western Churches. Washington, D.C.: Corpus Publications, 1970.

Oesterley, William O. E., ed. Pirke Aboth--The Sayings of the Fathers. London: Society for Promoting Christian Knowledge, 1919.

Olivier, Daniel. La foi de Luther. Paris: Beauchesne, 1978.

_____. Le procès Luther. Paris: Fayard, 1971.

_____. "Warum hat man Luther nicht verstanden? Katholische Antwort." Concilium 12 (1976):477-81.

Ott, Heinrich. Die Antwort des Glaubens. Berlin: Kreuz Verlag, 1972.

Ott, Ludwig. Grundriss der Dogmatik. 7th ed. Freiburg i. Br.: Herder, 1965.

Pannenberg, Wolfhart. "Der Einfluss der Anfechtungserfahrung auf den Präedestinationsbegriff Luthers." Kerygma und Dogma 3 (1957):109-39.

Paquier, Jules. "Luther." Dictionnaire de théologie catholique. Vol. 9/1. Paris: Letouzey & Ané, 1926.

Parente, Pietro; Piolanti, Antonio; and Garofalo, Salvatore. Dictionary of Dogmatic Theology. Translated by E. Doronzo. Milwaukee: Bruce Publishing Co., 1951.

Pascher, Joseph. Inwendiges Leben in der Werkgefahr. Krailling vor Munich: E. Wewel, 1940.

Perrone, Joannis. Praelectiones theologicae. 49th ed. 2 vols. Rome: H. Marietti, 1901.

Persson, Per Erik. "The Reformation in Recent Roman Catholic Theology." Dialog 2 (1963):24-31.

Pesch, Otto Hermann. "Abenteuer Lutherforschung." Die neue Ordnung 20 (1966):417-30.

_____. "Freiheitsbegriff und Freiheitslehre bei Thomas von Aquin und Luther." Catholica 17 (1963):197-244.

_____. "Der gegenwärtige Stand der Verständigung." Concilium 12 (1976):534-43.

_____. "Gottes Gnadenhandeln als Rechtfertigung des Menschen." Mysterium Salutis. Vol. 4/2. Edited by J. Feiner and M. Löhrer. Einsiedeln: Benziger, 1973.

_____. "Ein katholisches Anliegen an evangelische Darstellungen der Theologie Luthers." Catholica 16 (1962):304-16.

_____. Ketzerfürst und Kirchenlehrer. Stuttgart: Calwer Verlag, 1971.

_____. "Die Lehre vom 'Verdienst' als Problem für Theologie und Verkündigung." Wahrheit und Verkündigung. Vol. 2. Edited by L. Scheffczyk, W. Dettloff, and R. Heinzmann. Munich: F. Schöningh, 1967.

_____. Die Rechtfertigungslehre Luthers in katholischer Sicht. Berlin: Evangelische Verlagsanstalt, 1967.

_____. Theologie der Rechtfertigung bei Martin Luther und Thomas von Aquin. Mainz: M. Grünewald, 1967.

_____. "Twenty Years of Catholic Luther Research." Lutheran World 13 (1966):303-16.

Pesch, Wilhelm. Der Lohngedanke in der Lehre Jesu. Munich: K. Zink, 1955.

_____. "Der Sonderlohn für den Verkündiger des Evangeliums." Neutestamentliche Aufsätze. Edited by Josef Blinzler, Otto Kuss, and Franz Mussner. Regensburg: F. Pustet, 1963.

Peters, Albrecht. Glaube und Werk. Berlin: Lutherisches Verlagshaus, 1962.

_____. "Luthers Rechtfertigungslehre in der Interpretation der modernen katholischen Theologie." Neue Zeitschrift für systematische Theologie und Religionsphilosophie 12 (1970): 267-93.

_____. "Reformatorische Rechtfertigungsbotschaft zwischen tridentinischer Rechtfertigungslehre und gegenwärtigem evangelischen Verständnis der Rechtfertigung." Luther-Jahrbuch 1964. Hamburg: F. Wittig, 1964.

Peters. "Der Begriff Meritum in der liturgischen Sprache." Trierer theologische Zeitschrift 65 (1956):114-16.

Pfeiffer, Gerhard. "Das Ringen des jungen Luther um die Gerechtigkeit Gottes." Luther-Jahrbuch 1959. Berlin: Lutherisches Verlagshaus, 1959.

Pfnür, Vinzenz. Einig in der Rechtfertigungslehre? Wiesbaden: F. Steiner, 1970.

Pfürtner, Stephanus. Luther and Aquinas--A Conversation. Translated by E. Quinn. London: Darton, Longman & Todd, 1964.

_____. "Reformation und Reform des 2. Vatikanums." Strukturen christlicher Existenz. Edited by H. Schlier, E. von Severus, J. Sudbrack, and A. Pereira. Würzburg: Echter, 1968.

Philips, Gérard. L'union personnelle avec le Dieu vivant. Gembloux: J. Duculot, 1974.

Pinomaa, Lennart. Faith Victorious: An Introduction to Luther's Theology. Translated by W. J. Kukkonen. Philadelphia: Fortress Press, 1963.

_____. "Unfreier Wille und Prädestination bei Luther." Theologische Zeitschrift 13 (1957):339-49.

Piolanti, Antonio. Il mistero della comunione dei Santi. Rome: Desclée & Co., 1957.

Pöhlmann, Horst Georg. Abriss der Dogmatik. 2nd ed. Gütersloh: G. Mohn, 1975.

_____. Rechtfertigung. Gütersloh: G. Mohn, 1971.

Pohle, Joseph. "Merit." The Catholic Encyclopedia. Vol. 10. New York: R. Appleton, 1911.

Pohle, Joseph, and Gummersbach, Josef. Lehrbuch der Dogmatik. 10th ed. 3 vols. Paderborn: F. Schöningh, 1956.

Pohle, Joseph, and Preuss, Arthur. Grace, Actual and Habitual. 11th ed. St. Louis, MO: Herder, 1945.

Pohlmann, Hans. Hat Luther Paulus entdeckt? Berlin: A. Töpelmann, 1959.

Pol, Willem Hendrik van de. Das reformatorische Christentum in phänomenologischer Betrachtung. Einsiedeln: Benziger, 1956.

Politus, Ambrosius Catharinus. Apologia pro veritate catholicae et apostolicae fidei. Vol. 27 of Corpus Catholicorum. Edited by J. Schweizer. Münster/W.: Aschendorff, 1956.

Prat, Fernand. The Theology of Saint Paul. Translated by J. L. Stoddard. 2 vols. London: Burns, Oates & Washbourne, 1945.

Preisker, Herbert. "Μισθός." Theologisches Wörterbuch zum Neuen Testament. Vol. 4. Stuttgart: Kohlhammer, 1942.

Premm, Matthias. Dogmatic Theology for Laity. Translated by O. Heimann. Staten Island, NY: Alba House, 1967.

----------. Katholische Glaubenskunde. 4 vols. Vienna: Herder, 1953.

Prenter, Regin. "Luthers Lehre von der Heiligung." Lutherforschung heute. Edited by V. Vajta. Berlin: Lutherisches Verlagshaus, 1958.

----------. Spiritus Creator - Studien zu Luthers Theologie. Munich: Chr. Kaiser, 1954.

Puyo, Jean, ed. Jean Puyo interroge le Père Congar. Paris: Le Centurion, 1975.

Quadt, Anno. Gott und Mensch. Munich: F. Schöningh, 1976.

Quarello, Eraldo. "Cattolici e Protestanti riuniti di fronte al valore meritorio delle opere buone?" Salesianum 26 (1964):134-52.

Rahner, Karl. Grundkurs des Glaubens. 9th ed. Freiburg i. Br.: Herder, 1976.

----------. "Ist Kircheneinigung dogmatisch möglich?" Theologische Quartalschrift 153 (1973):103-18.

----------. Schriften zur Theologie. 12 vols. Einsiedeln: Benziger, 1954-75.

----------. "Zur Theologie der Gnade." Theologische Quartalschrift 138 (1958):40-77.

Rahner, Karl; Cullmann, Oscar; and Fries, Heinrich. Sind die Erwartungen erfüllt? Munich: M. Hueber, 1966.

Rahner, Karl, and Vorgrimler, Herbert. Kleines Konzilskompendium. 3rd ed. Freiburg i. Br.: Herder, 1966.

Rahner, Karl, and Vorgrimler, Herbert. Theological Dictionary. Translated by R. Strachan. New York: Herder, 1965.

Reicke, Bo Ivar. "The New Testament Conception of Reward." Aux sources de la tradition chrétienne (Mélanges M. Goguel). Neuchâtel: Delachaux & Niestlé, 1950.

Reinisch, Leonhard. Theologie heute. Munich: C. H. Beck, 1959.

Richter, Friedrich. *Martin Luther and Ignatius Loyola.* Translated by L. F. Zwinger. Westminster, MD: Newman Press, 1960.

Riga, Peter. *Catholic Thought in Crisis.* Milwaukee: Bruce Publishing Co., 1963.

Rivière, Jean. "Justification." *Dictionnaire de théologie catholique.* Vol. 8/2. Paris: Letouzey & Ané, 1925.

_____. "Mérite." *Dictionnaire de théologie catholique.* Vol. 10/1. Paris: Letouzey & Ané, 1928.

_____. "Quelques antécédents patristiques de la formule: 'Facienti quod in se est'." *Revue des sciences religieuses* 7 (1927):93-97.

Rondet, Henri. *Essais sur la théologie de la grâce.* Paris: Beauchesne, 1964.

_____. *Gratia Christi.* Paris: Beauchesne, 1948.

Rost, Gerhard. *Der Prädestinationsgedanke in der Theologie Martin Luthers.* Berlin: Evangelische Verlagsanstalt, 1966.

Rousselot, Pierre. "La grâce d'après Saint Jean et d'après Saint Paul." *Recherches de science religieuse* 18 (1928):87-104.

Rudloff, Leo von. *Kleine Laiendogmatik.* 2nd ed. Regensburg: F. Pustet, 1934.

Rückert, Hanns. *Die Rechtfertigungslehre auf dem Tridentinischen Konzil.* Bonn: Marcus & Weber, 1925.

_____. *Vorträge und Aufsätze zur historischen Theologie.* Tübingen: J. C. B. Mohr (Paul Siebeck), 1972.

Rupp, Gordon. *The Righteousness of God.* New York: Philosophical Library, 1953.

Ryelandt, Idesbald. *The Life of Grace.* Translated by M. Dillon. Dublin: Clonmore & Reynolds, 1964.

Ryrie, Charles C. *The Grace of God.* Chicago: Moody Press, 1963.

Saarnivaara, Uuras. *Luther Discovers the Gospel.* St. Louis, MO: Concordia, 1951.

Saint-Martin, Jules. "Prédestination - Saint Augustin." *Dictionnaire de théologie catholique.* Vol. 12/2. Paris: Letouzey & Ané, 1935.

Sandmel, Samuel. *Judaism and Christian Beginnings.* New York: Oxford University Press, 1978.

Sartory, Thomas. *The Ecumenical Movement and the Unity of the Church*. Translated by H. C. Graef. Oxford: B. Blackwell, 1963.

_____. "Martin Luther in katholischer Sicht." *Una Sancta* 16 (1961):38-54.

_____. "Das Mysterium der Kirche in reformatorischer Sicht." *Mysterium Kirche*. Vol. 2. Edited by F. Holböck and Th. Sartory. Salzburg: O. Müller, 1962.

Schanz, Paul. *Apologie des Christentums*. 3rd ed. 3 vols. Freiburg i. Br.: Herder, 1906.

Scheeben, Matthias Joseph. *Gesammelte Aufsätze*. Freiburg i. Br.: Herder, 1967.

_____. *Handbuch der katholischen Dogmatik*. 3rd ed. 6 vols. Freiburg i. Br.: Herder, 1961.

_____. *Die Herrlichkeiten der göttlichen Gnade*. 17th ed. Freiburg i. Br.: Herder, 1949.

_____. *Die Mysterien des Christentums*. 3rd ed. Freiburg i. Br.: Herder, 1958.

Scheel, Otto. *Martin Luther. Vom Katholizismus zur Reformation*. 3rd and 4th eds. 2 vols. Tübingen: J. C. B. Mohr (Paul Siebeck), 1930.

Scheffmacher, Johann J. *Kontroverskatechismus*. Strassburg: Le Roux, n. d.

Scheffczyk, Leo. "Die Einheit des Dogmas und die Vielheit der Denkformen." *Münchener theologische Zeitschrift* 17 (1966): 228-42.

Schell, Hermann. *Katholische Dogmatik*. 3 vols. Paderborn: F. Schöningh, 1892.

Schillebeeckx, Edward. *Christ--The Experience of Jesus as Lord*. Translated by J. Bowden. New York: Seabury Press, 1980.

_____. "Das tridentinische Rechtfertigungsdekret in neuer Sicht." *Concilium* 1 (1965):452-54.

Schilling, Otto. *Lehrbuch der Moraltheologie*. 2 vols. Munich: M. Hueber, 1928.

Schinzer, Reinhard. *Die doppelte Verdienstlehre des Spätmittelalters und Luthers reformatorische Entdeckung*. Munich: Chr. Kaiser, 1971.

Schlier, Heinrich. *Der Römerbrief*. Freiburg i. Br.: Herder, 1977.

Schlink, Edmund. "Gesetz und Evangelium als kontroverstheologisches Problem." Kerygma und Dogma 7 (1961):1-35.

_____. "Die Hierarchie der Wahrheiten und die Einigung der Kirchen." Kerygma und Dogma 21 (1975):1-12.

_____. "Pneumatische Erschütterung?" Kerygma und Dogma 8 (1962):221-35.

_____. Theologie der lutherischen Bekenntnisschriften. Munich: Chr. Kaiser, 1948.

Schloenbach, Manfred. Heiligung als Fortschreiten und Wachstum des Glaubens in Luthers Theologie. Helsinki: Luther-Agricola Gesellschaft, 1963.

Schmaus, Michael. Der Glaube der Kirche. 2 vols. Munich: M. Hueber, 1970.

_____. Katholische Dogmatik. 5th ed. Vol. 4/1. Munich: M. Hueber, 1956.

_____. Katholische Dogmatik. 6th ed. 5 vols. Munich: M. Hueber, 1965.

Schmid, Josef. Das Evangelium nach Matthäus (Regensburger Neues Testament). 5th ed. Regensburg: F. Pustet, 1965.

_____. "Verdienst im Judentum und Neuen Testament." Lexikon für Theologie und Kirche. 2nd ed. Vol. 10. Freiburg i. Br.: Herder, 1965.

Schmidt, Hermann Joseph. Brückenschlag zwischen den Konfessionen. Paderborn: F. Schöningh, 1951.

Schnackenburg, Rudolf. Christliche Existenz nach dem Neuen Testament. 2 vols. Munich: Kösel, 1967.

_____. Neutestamentliche Theologie. 2nd ed. Munich: Kösel, 1965.

Schoeps, Hans Joachim. Das Judenchristentum. Berne: Francke, 1964.

Schoof, Mark. Der Durchbruch der neuen katholischen Theologie. Vienna: Herder, 1969.

Schott, Erdmann. "Christus und die Rechtfertigung allein durch den Glauben in Luthers Schmalkaldischen Artikeln." Zeitschrift für systematische Theologie 22 (1953):192-217.

_____. "Einig in der Rechtfertigungslehre?" Luther-Jahrbuch 1959. Berlin: Lutherisches Verlagshaus, 1959.

_____. "Luthers Lehre vom servum arbitrium in ihrer theologischen Bedeutung." Zeitschrift für systematische Theologie 7 (1929): 399-430.

_____. Rechtfertigung und Zehn Gebote nach Luther. Stuttgart: Calwer Verlag, 1971.

_____. "Verdienst." Religion in Geschichte und Gegenwart. 3rd ed. Vol. 6. Tübingen: J. C. B. Mohr (Paul Siebeck), 1962.

Schreiber, Georg, ed. Das Weltkonzil von Trient. 2 vols. Freiburg i. Br.: Herder, 1951.

Schütte, Heinz. Protestantismus. 2nd ed. Essen: Fredebeul & Koenen, 1967.

_____. Um die Wiedervereinigung im Glauben. Essen: Fredebeul & Koenen, 1958.

Schultz, Hans Jürgen, ed. Tendenzen der Theologie im 20. Jahrhundert. Stuttgart: Kreuz Verlag, 1966.

Schultz, Hermann. "Der sittliche Begriff des Verdienstes und seine Anwendung auf das Verständnis des Werkes Christi." Theologische Studien und Kritiken 67 (1894):7-50.

Schulz, F. "Benedikt Stattler." Katholische Theologen Deutschlands im 19. Jahrhundert. Vol. 1. Edited by H. Fries and G. Schwaiger. Munich: Kösel, 1975.

Schulz, Siegfried. "Katholisierende Tendenzen in Schliers Galater-Kommentar." Kerygma und Dogma 5 (1959):23-41.

Schutz, Roger. Die Dynamik des Vorläufigen. Freiburg i. Br.: Herder, 1978.

Schwarz, Reinhard. Fides, spes und caritas beim jungen Luther. Berlin: W. de Gruyter, 1962.

_____. Vorgeschichte der reformatorischen Busstheologie. Berlin: W. de Gruyter, 1968.

Seckler, Max, et al., eds. Begegnung. Graz: Styria, 1972.

Seebass, Horst. "Gerechtigkeit." Theologisches Begriffslexikon zum Neuen Testament. Vol. 1. Wuppertal: R. Brockhaus, 1967.

Seeberg, Erich. Luthers Theologie. Vol. 2. Darmstadt: Wissenschaftliche Buchgesellschaft, 1969.

Seeberg, Reinhold. Grundriss der Dogmengeschichte. 4th ed. Leipzig: Deichertsche Verlagsbuchhandlung W. Scholl, 1919.

_____. Die religiösen Grundgedanken des jungen Luther und ihr Verhältnis zu dem Ockhamismus und der deutschen Mystik. Berlin: W. de Gruyter, 1931.

_____. Textbook of the History of Doctrines. 7th ed. 2 vols. Translated by Ch. E. Hay. Grand Rapids, MI: Baker Book House, 1966.

_____. Die Theologie des Johannes Duns Scotus. Aalen: Scientia, 1971.

Seils, Martin. Der Gedanke vom Zusammenwirken Gottes und des Menschen in Luthers Theologie. Gütersloh: G. Mohn, 1962.

Seripando, Girolamo. De iustitia et libertate christiana. Vol. 30 of Corpus Catholicorum. Edited by A. Forster. Münster/W.: Aschendorff, 1969.

Sheerin, John B. "Canonize Martin Luther?" Catholic World 197 (1963):84-87.

Simpson, James G. "Justification." Encyclopedia of Religion and Ethics. Vol. 7. New York: Charles Scribner's Sons, 1915.

Skydsgaard, Kristen E. The Papal Council and the Gospel. Minneapolis: Augsburg Publishing House, 1961.

Smyth, Martin. "Differences between the Roman and Reformed Doctrines of Justification." The Evangelical Quarterly 36 (1964): 42-48.

Söhngen, Gottlieb. Gesetz und Evangelium. Freiburg i. Br.: K. Alber, 1957.

Solignac, Aimé. "Mérite et vie spirituelle." Dictionnaire de spiritualité, ascétique et mystique. Vol. 10. Paris: Beauchesne, 1979.

Stakemeier, Adolf. Das Konzil von Trient über die Heilsgewissheit. Heidelberg: F. H. Kerle, 1947.

Stakemeier, Eduard. "Luthers de servo arbitrio." Catholica 22 (1968):132-35.

_____. "Die theologischen Schulen auf dem Trienter Konzil während der Rechtfertigungsverhandlungen." Theologische Quartalschrift 117 (1936):188-207/322-50.

_____. "Trienter Lehrentscheidungen und reformatorische Anliegen." Weltkonzil von Trient. Vol. 1. Edited by G. Schreiber. Freiburg i. Br.: Herder, 1951.

Stange, Carl. "Luther im katholischen Urteil von vier Jahrhunderten." Zeitschrift für systematische Theologie 20 (1943):332-36.

Stapleton, Thomas. A Fortresse of the Faith. Antwerpe: Laet, 1565.

Stauffer, Richard. Le catholicisme à la découverte de Luther. Neuchâtel: Delachaux & Niestlé, 1966.

Steck, Karl Gerhard. "Die christliche Wahrheit und der Streit der Konfessionen." Protestantismus heute. Edited by F. H. Ryssel. Frankfort/M.: Ullstein, 1959.

_____. Die christliche Wahrheit zwischen Häresie und Konfession. Munich: Chr. Kaiser, 1974.

Stevens, Gregory. The Life of Grace. Englewood Cliffs, NJ: Prentice Hall, 1963.

Stirnimann, Heinrich. "Zur Rechtfertigung in dialektisch - katholischer Besinnung." Schweizerische Kirchenzeitung 125 (1957):650-52.

Stoebe, H. J. "חסד" Theologisches Handwörterbuch zum Alten Testament. Edited by E. Jenni and C. Westermann. Vol. 1. Munich: Chr. Kaiser, 1971.

Strack, Hermann, and Billerbeck, Paul. Kommentar zum Neuen Testament aus Talmud und Midrasch. 4 vols. Munich: C. H. Beck, 1922-28.

Strohl, Henri. Luther jusqu'en 1520. Paris: Presses Universitaires de France, 1962.

Stufler, Johann. "Die entfernte Vorbereitung auf die Rechtfertigung nach dem hlg. Thomas." Zeitschrift für katholische Theologie 47 (1923):1-23/161-83.

Sullivan, C. Stephen. "Merit." New Catholic Encyclopedia. Vol. 9. New York: McGraw-Hill, 1967.

Tabarelli, Richardo. Opere teologiche. 5 vols. Rome: Pontificia Universitas Lateranensis, 1962.

_____. De gratia Christi. Rome: M. Bretschneider, 1908.

Taille, Maurice de la. "Actuation créée par acte incréé." Recherches de sciences religieuses 18 (1928):253-68.

Tanquerey, Adolphe-Alfred. Synopsis theologiae dogmaticae. 13th ed. 3 vols. Cincinnati: Benziger, 1911.

Tavard, Georges. Protestantism. Translated by R. Attwater. New York: Hawthorn Books, 1959.

Thein, John. Ecclesiastical Dictionary. New York: Benziger, 1900.

Theodorou, Andreas. "Die Lehre von der Vergottung des Menschen bei den griechischen Kirchenvätern." Kerygma und Dogma 7 (1961):283-310.

Thielicke, Helmut. Theologische Ethik. 4th ed. 3 vols. Tübingen: J. C. B. Mohr (Paul Siebeck), 1972.

_____. Leiden an der Kirche. Hamburg: Furche, 1965.

Thils, Gustave. Sainteté chrétienne. Tielt: Ed. Lannoo, 1958.

Thomas Aquinas. Quaestiones disputatae. Vol. 4 (De veritate). Turin: Marietti, 1942.

_____. Summa contra gentiles. Rome: Desclée & Co., 1934.

_____. Summa theologica (Deutsche Thomasausgabe). Vol. 13. Heidelberg: F. H. Kerle, 1977.

_____. Summa theologica (Deutsche Thomassausgabe). Vol. 14. Heidelberg: F. H. Kerle, 1955.

_____. Summa theologiae. London: Blackfriars, 1964-66.

_____. Super epistolas S. Pauli lectura. 8th ed. 2 vols. Rome: Marietti, 1953.

Thomas à Kempis. De imitatione Christi. Solisbaci in Bavaria: Seidel, 1837.

Thomson, S. Harrison. "Unnoticed MSS and Works of Wyclif." Journal of Theological Studies 38 (1937):24-36.

Tixeront, Joseph. Histoire des dogmes dans l'antiquité chrétienne. 10th ed. 3 vols. Paris: Lecoffre, 1924.

Todd, John M. Martin Luther. London: Burns & Oates, 1964.

Toinet, Paul. Le problème de la vérité dogmatique. Paris: P. Téqui, 1973.

Torrance, Thomas F. The Doctrine of Grace in the Apostolic Fathers. Edinburgh: Oliver & Boyd, 1948.

Towers, Edward. "Sanctifying Grace." The Theology of the Catholic Church. 6th ed. Vol. 1. Edited by G. D. Smith. New York: Macmillan Co., 1952.

Tresmontant, Claude. *Saint Paul and the Mystery of Christ.* Translated by D. Attwater. New York: Harper Torchbooks, 1957.

Trütsch, Josef. "Facienti quod in se est." *Lexikon für Theologie und Kirche.* 2nd ed. Vol. 3. Freiburg i. Br.: Herder, 1959.

_____. "Glaube - Dogmengeschichtlich. Systematisch." *Lexikon für Theologie und Kirche.* 2nd ed. Vol. 4. Freiburg i. Br.: Herder, 1960.

Tüchle, Hermann. *Geschichte der Kirche.* Vol. 3 (*Reformation und Gegenreformation*). Einsiedeln: Benziger, 1965.

Tyszkiewicz, Stanislaus. "Warum verwerfen die Orthodoxen unsere Verdienstlehre?" *Zeitschrift für katholische Theologie* 41 (1917):400-06.

Vajta, Vilmos. "Sine meritis - Zur kritischen Funktion der Rechtfertigungslehre." *Oecumenica 1968.* Minneapolis: Augsburg Publishing House, 1968.

Vignaux, Paul. *Justification et prédestination au XIVe siècle.* Paris: E. Leroux, 1934.

_____. "Nominalisme - Justification." *Dictionnaire de théologie catholique.* Vol. 11/1. Paris: Letouzey & Ané, 1931.

_____. "Occam et Duns Scot." *Dictionnaire de théologie catholique.* Vol. 11/1. Paris: Letouzey & Ané, 1931.

Vogelsang, Erich. "Luther und die Mystik." *Luther-Jahrbuch 1937.* Amsterdam: J. Benjamins, 1967.

Volk, Hermann. "Aktualismus in der Gnadenlehre." *Lexikon für Theologie und Kirche.* 2nd ed. Vol. 1. Freiburg i. Br.: Herder, 1957.

_____. *Gesammelte Schriften.* 2nd ed. 3 vols. Mainz: Grünewald, 1967-79.

Vorgrimler, Herbert. *Karl Rahner, His Life, Thought and Works.* Translated by E. Quinn. Glen Rock, NJ: Deus Books, 1966.

Vorster, Hans. *Das Freiheitsverständnis bei Thomas von Aquin und Martin Luther.* Göttingen: Vandenhoeck & Ruprecht, 1965.

Wacker, Paulus. *Theologie als ökumenischer Dialog.* Munich: F. Schöningh, 1965.

Watson, Philip S. *The Concept of Grace.* Philadelphia: Muhlenberg Press, 1959.

_____. *Let God be God! An Interpretation of the Theology of Martin Luther*. Philadelphia: Muhlenberg Press, 1947.

_____. "Luther und die Heiligung." *Lutherforschung heute*. Edited by V. Vajta. Berlin: Lutherisches Verlagshaus, 1958.

_____. "Merit." *A Dictionary of Christian Theology*. Edited by A. Richardson. Philadelphia: Westminster Press, 1969.

Weber, Hans Emil, and Wolf, Ernst. *Begegnung*. Munich: A. Lempp, 1941.

Weber, Otto. "Gnade und Rechtfertigung bei Karl Barth." *Theologische Literaturzeitung* 83 (1958):402-08.

Weger, Karl Heinz. *Karl Rahner*. Freiburg i. Br.: Herder, 1978.

Weiss, Karl. "Die Frohbotschaft Jesu über Lohn und Vollkommenheit." *Neutestamentliche Abhandlungen* 12 (1927):3-233.

Weijenborg, Reinoldus. "Miraculum a Martino Luthero confictum explicatne eius Reformationem?" *Antonianum* 31 (1956): 247-300.

Welch, Claude. *Protestant Thought in the 19th Century*. Vol. 1. New Haven and London: Yale University Press, 1972.

Werbick, Jürgen. "Rechtfertigung des Sünders - Rechtfertigung Gottes." *Kerygma und Dogma* 27 (1981):45-57.

Wicks, Jared, ed. *Catholic Scholars Dialogue with Luther*. Chicago: Loyola University Press, 1970.

_____. "Luther." *Dictionnaire de spiritualité*. Vol. 9. Paris: Beauchesne, 1976.

_____. *Man Yearning for Grace*. Washington, D.C.: Corpus Books, 1968.

Wilckens, Ulrich. *Evangelisch - katholischer Kommentar zum Neuen Testament* (Der Brief an die Römer 1 - 5). Vol. 6/1. Einsiedeln: Benziger, 1978.

Wilhelm, Anthony J. *Christ among Us*. New York: Newman Press, 1967.

Wilhelm, Joseph, and Scannell, Thomas B. *A Manual of Catholic Theology*. 3rd ed. 2 vols. London: Kegan, Trench, Trübner, 1908.

Williams, Norman Powell. *The Grace of God*. London: Longmans, Green & Co., 1930.

Wirth, Karl Hermann. Der "Verdienst"-Begriff bei Cyprian. Leipzig: Dörffling & Franke, 1901.

_____. Der "Verdienst"-Begriff bei Tertullian. Leipzig: Dörffling & Franke, 1892.

Witte, Johannes L. "Ist Barths Rechtfertigungslehre grundsätzlich katholisch?" Münchener theologische Zeitschrift 10 (1958): 38-48.

Witzel, Georg. Antwort auff Martin Luthers bekennete artickel. Vol. 18 of Corpus Catholicorum. Edited by H. Volz. Münster/W.: Aschendorff, 1932.

Wolf, Ernst. "Luther." Evangelisches Kirchenlexikon. 2nd ed. Vol. 2. Göttingen: Vandenhoeck & Ruprecht, 1962.

_____. "Martin Luther und die Prinzipien des Protestantismus in katholischer Sicht." Theologische Literaturzeitung 76 (1951):271-76.

_____. Peregrinatio. 2nd ed. Munich: Chr. Kaiser, 1962.

_____. "Die Rechtfertigungslehre als Mitte und Grenze reformatorischer Theologie." Evangelische Theologie 49/50 (1950):298-308.

Würthwein, Ernst. "Μισθός" (Der Vergeltungsgedanke im Alten Testament). Theologisches Wörterbuch zum Neuen Testament. Vol. 4. Stuttgart: Kohlhammer, 1942.

Wyclif, John. Latin Works. London: Trübner & Co., 1883 -.

Zänker, Otto. "Der theologische Ansatz im gegenwärtigen Gespräch mit dem Katholizismus." Zeitschrift für systematische Theologie 18 (1941):107-17.

Zeeden, Ernst Walter. Martin Luther und die Reformation. 2 vols. Freiburg i. Br.: Herder, 1950.

Zerafa, Peter P. "Retribution in the Old Testament." Angelicum 50 (1973):464-94.

Zezschwitz, Gerhard von. Die Katechismen der Waldenser und Böhmischen Brüder. Amsterdam: Editions Rodopi, 1967.

Zöckler, Otto. Kritische Geschichte der Askese. Frankfort/M.: Heyder & Zimmer, 1863.

Zumkeller, Adolar. "Das Ungenügen der menschlichen Werke bei den deutschen Predigern des Spätmittelalters." Zeitschrift für katholische Theologie 81 (1959):265-305.

_____. "Die Augustinertheologen Simon Fidati von Cascia und Hugolin von Orvieto und Martin Luthers Kritik an Aristoteles." Archiv für Reformationsgeschichte 54 (1963):15-37.

www.ingramcontent.com/pod-product-compliance
Lightning Source LLC
Chambersburg PA
CBHW070651300426
44111CB00013B/2371